FOR WEBER

Theory, Culture & Society

Theory, Culture & Society caters for the resurgence of interest in culture within contemporary social science and the humanities. Building on the heritage of classical social theory, the book series examines ways in which this tradition has been reshaped by a new generation of theorists. It will also publish theoretically informed analyses of everyday life, popular culture, and new intellectual movements.

EDITOR: Mike Featherstone, *University of Teesside*

Recent volumes include:

The Cinematic Society
The Voyeur's Gaze
Norman K. Denzin

Decentring Leisure
Rethinking Leisure Theory
Chris Rojek

Global Modernities
Mike Featherstone, Scott Lash and Roland Robertson

The Masque of Femininity
The Presentation of Woman in Everyday Life
Efrat Tseëlon

The Arena of Racism
Michel Wieviorka

Undoing Culture
Globalization, Postmodernism and Identity
Mike Featherstone

The Time of the Tribes
The Decline of Individualism in Mass Society
Michel Maffesoli

Risk, Environment and Modernity
Towards a New Ecology
edited by Scott Lash, Bronislaw Szerszynski and Brian Wynne

FOR WEBER

Essays on the Sociology of Fate

Second edition

BRYAN S. TURNER

SAGE Publications
London • Thousand Oaks • New Delhi

© Bryan S. Turner 1996

First published by Routledge and Kegan Paul 1981
This second edition published by Sage Publications 1996

 SAGE Publications Ltd
6 Bonhill Street
London EC2A 4PU

SAGE Publications Inc
2455 Teller Road
Thousand Oaks, California 91320

SAGE Publications India Pvt Ltd
32, M-Block Market
Greater Kailash – I
New Delhi 110 048

Published in association with *Theory, Culture & Society*,
School of Human Studies, University of Teesside

British Library Cataloguing in Publication data

A catalogue record for this book is
available from the British Library.

ISBN 0 8039 7633 X
ISBN 0 8039 7634 8 (pbk)

Library of Congress catalog record available

Printed in Great Britain by Biddles Ltd, Guildford

Contents

Trevor Ling (1920–1995),
an inspiration as teacher and human being

Acknowledgements

The encouragement and inspiration to write an introduction for the new edition of *For Weber* came from Stephen Barr at Sage Publications, London. For a number of years Chris Rojek has been persuaded that *For Weber* was still a valuable and important guide to the general sociology of Max Weber. This commitment to Weber's sociology has also been sustained by the Editorial Board of the journal *Theory, Culture & Society* who have provided an exciting and encouraging intellectual milieu within which to work. I would also like to thank Georg Stauth for his intellectual encouragement over a number years in which we have shared a common interest in the work of Nietzsche, Weber and Klages. A variety of sociology departments and institutions at Bielefeld, Utrecht, Essex and Deakin have provided both the context and the foil for developing these views about the legacy and importance of Weber. On various occasions my interpretation of Weber has been both encouraged and criticised by Dennis Wrong, Stephen Kalberg, Alan Sica and Dirk Käsler. Creative disagreement with Tony Woodiwiss has helped to shape my approach to postmodernism. For his general encouragement to persist with the project of developing sociological theory as such, I would also like to thank Jeffrey Alexander. Eileen Richardson kindly but critically read and revised the final text. For her assistance in producing this manuscript, I would like to thank Monika Loving.

Bryan S. Turner
Geelong West, Victoria

Introduction: Marx and Nietzsche

For Weber (Turner, 1981) was written as a direct response to theories of social structure which had been primarily influenced by structural Marxism, particularly by the writings of the French Marxist philosopher Louis Althusser. Althusser's influential reading of Karl Marx had been originally published in France in 1965 as *Pour Marx*. The translation of this work appeared in the United Kingdom in 1969 with the title *For Marx*. *For Weber* was intended to be a direct challenge to the influence of structural Marxism by arguing that many of the claims of Althusser were inaccurate when applied to the work of Max Weber, and that there was a structuralist reading of Weber which demonstrated at least some similarities with the work of Marx from a particular vantage point of interpretation.

Marxist critics of mainstream sociology often dismissed the legacy of Weberian sociology as individualistic, subjectivist and unscientific. My study of Weber showed that there was an objective dimension to his sociology which was exhibited in the notion of the unintended consequences of social action, namely consequences which lay outside the consciousness and intention of the social actors involved. The deterministic element in Weber's interpretative sociology was illustrated through a set of historical case studies which showed the fateful or negative consequences of action over which social actors had no significant control, or indeed knowledge. The classical illustration of this fateful view of history was primarily demonstrated in Weber's famous Protestant ethic thesis (Weber, 1965; Lehmann and Roth, 1993). The unanticipated consequence of ascetic religious actions had been the creation of a capitalist culture, the secular outcomes of which often denied or undermined their religious vocations or callings which had given rise to the capitalist spirit in the seventeenth century. Weber's sociology of religion could be read or interpreted as a series of tragic narratives about the negative and unanticipated consequences of actions directed towards personal salvation. This tragic view of Western history was not exclusive to social theory. It was a major theme of literature and art at the end of the nineteenth century. For example, the tragic or fatalistic dimensions of Weber's sociology were in many respects parallel to the narrative structure of the tragic novels of Thomas Mann, particularly in such works as *The Magic Mountain* and *Buddenbrooks* (Marcus, 1987).

Weber's sense of personal tragedy and the fatefulness of Western history were in part the cultural product of the transformations of the academic community in Germany, where there had been a major decline in the status of the independent scholar and intellectual in the late nineteenth century, a transformation which has been captured by Fritz Ringer (1969) in the notion of the decline of the German mandarins. The theme of social tragedy or fate influenced not only the sociology of Weber but also the work of Tönnies, Troeltsch, Simmel and Lukács (Liebersohn, 1988). At a more profound level *Kulturpessimismus* was a reflection of significant changes in the relationship between culture and social class in the educated middle strata of nineteenth-century Germany. This pessimism about culture was reflected in the debate about *Bildung* and personality which shaped the outlook of the late nineteenth-century educated middle classes in Germany. This fatalistic view regarded the growth of civilisation as a direct challenge to traditional culture and thereby to the status of the intellectual as the guardian of high culture (Elias, 1978; Goldman, 1992). The problems of social change, interpersonal ethics, the self and the demise of traditional rural values shaped the narrative content of the *Bildungsroman* in this period, a literary genre which gave special emphasis to the socialisation and training of a cultured individual (Moretti, 1987). In a society where the traditional intellectual was being overtaken and by-passed by the technical specialist within an industrial civilisation, what was the role of intellectuals in such an environment? Weber's bitter complaint about 'hedonists without a heart and experts without a spirit' ('Genußmenschen ohne Hertz und Fach menschen ohne Geist') at the conclusion of *The Protestant Ethic and the Spirit of Capitalism* (Weber, 1965) was an expression of this sense of the decline of the fully educated and comprehensive personality of the traditional intellectual. Weber's critique of the bureaucratisation of intellectual callings was partly inspired by Friedrich Nietzsche's abhorrence of the growing dominance of the state intellectuals within the emergent Prussian bureaucracy. Against these specialists with their calling to serve the state (the new *Berufsmenschentum*) Nietzsche proposed a revolutionary creation, Overman (*Übermensch*). Here again there was an important relationship between the literary treatment of the intellectual in Mann's novels *Death in Venice, The Magic Mountain* and *Doctor Faustus* and Weber's particular concentration on the notion of intellectual vocations in science and politics (Lassman and Velody, 1989). Mann's fiction captured the sense of decadence and futility in the role of the intellectual in the modern world.

For Weber approached sociology from the point of view of an interest in a tragic vision of history which was worked out within the context of his highly technical sociology of social action. This pessimistic view of history was a consequence of his direct and specific engagement with the legacy of the philosophy of Nietzsche, particularly with Nietzsche's concept of resentment (Stauth and Turner, 1988). Various aspects of Nietzsche's philosophy impinged upon Weber's formulation of a sociology of action. For example, there is in Nietzsche the contrast between Apollo, the God of Form and Reason, and Dionysus, the God of Emotion and Sexuality. Weber's analysis of the Protestant ethic thesis can be seen as an account of how the Apollo principle dominated over the emotional life through the formation of vocations in the economic sphere. This conflict between sexuality and civilisation played a general role in Weber's analysis of the civilising functions of religious values (Turner, 1991) and also in his personality as a struggle between family responsibilities and sexual fulfilment (Green, 1974). Weber's personal values were thoroughly ambiguous. He admired the seriousness of the professional calling in science and politics, while also remaining aware of the destructive consequences of this worldly asceticism. Modernity as an expression of world-mastery resulted in a technological destruction of traditional values and lifeworlds; through colonialism, it destroyed dependent societies through slavery, brutality and imperial violence.

Second, the relationship between Weber's concept of charisma and the superman has also been noted in the literature (Eden, 1983). Charismatic power represented the principal challenge to traditional patterns of authority and leadership. Certainly the problem of leadership in a bureaucratic social environment remained a significant issue in Weber's political sociology. Like his colleague and friend Ernst Troeltsch (1931), Weber saw the Protestant sects as a clear illustration of collective charisma in their challenge to organised Christianity. Third, the central importance of power in Weber's sociology as a whole and Weber's interest in German politics in particular (Mayer, 1956; Mommsen, 1984) has often been associated with Nietzsche's concern for the role of the will to power in the shaping of human societies and human culture. Finally, Weber's ambiguous and critical relationship to religion, particularly the ascetic sects of Christianity, was, as a number of commentators have suggested, less influenced by Marx than by Nietzsche's critical attacks on conventional religiosity in the nineteenth century (Ling, 1980; Schroeder, 1992).

These well-known commentaries on the intellectual impact of Nietzsche on Weber may, however, have missed some of the essential features of the legacy of Nietzsche's critical philosophy in Weber's sociology. Nietzsche's philosophy grew out of a cultural critique of late nineteenth-century Germany society within which a new mentality, the mentality of professional specialists, was beginning to dominate cultural debate and ascetic appreciation (Thomas, 1983). These state specialists were in Nietzsche's view closely associated with the dominance of Calvinistic theology and the expansion of the new Prussian state. This dominance of the state specialist was part of a long historical evolution of the relationship between church, state and education in German society. Weber's view of the professionalisation of the scientific vocation was part of this Nietzschean critique of state functionaries. Returning to the Protestant ethic theme, Weber regarded these Calvinistic men of vocations as carriers of an ethic of world-mastery which involved the domination of emotions and affectivity as merely irrational passions which stood in the way of rational action. Their social lives were controlled by a commitment to an ethic of mastery, which subordinated sexuality and emotionality in the interests of self-control. Alongside these Protestant figures, Weber also placed the professional men of calling in science and politics, whose social relations were organised by a commitment to a rational plan in the interests of their personal achievement of public status within the new regime. These religious callings, as we know, drove these men beyond what was actually necessary for the satisfaction of their everyday needs and wants. The personal drive for wealth, power and control was the irrational motivation behind economic rationality. The striving for world-mastery did not lead to a satisfaction with everyday life, however, but rather resulted in a continuing disenchantment with reality which drove out moral significance from everyday existence and rendered life meaningless. Weber argued via his sociology of civilisations that the peculiar danger of the modern world is characterised by expanding rationalisation, which results ultimately in religious and moral disenchantment. He explored various solutions to this dilemma, including, for example, the ethic of responsibility, the development of new forms of communitarian life, the experimentation with new patterns of eroticism, a return to the arms of the Church, and a series of vocations in science and politics. This search for a solution to personal disenchantment and meaninglessness provided the central tensions and ambiguities of Weber's sociological perspective (Stauth, 1994; Stauth and Turner, 1986). Some aspects of the feminist critique of Weber have dwelt on these issues of ethical heroism and world-mastery in Weber's patriarchal view of power and values (Bologh, 1990).

In *Nietzsche's Dance* (Stauth and Turner, 1988), it was argued that the core of Nietzsche's philosophy was an attachment to 'the little things' of everyday life. Nietzsche thought that the values and practices of everyday life, which were centred on reciprocity and emotion, were being transformed by the rationalistic cultures of a technological civilisation driven by industrial needs. For Nietzsche, religion and abstract philosophy were both misapprehensions and distortions of the values of everyday social life. In the terminology of modern critical theory, the lifeworld was being destroyed and rendered inauthentic by the new rationalist culture of the state as the values and morals of the private world were colonized by the rationalistic culture of the public arena. Nietzsche approached this problem of the inauthentication of the lifeworld via a discussion of the demise of Christian authority, or, more generally, religious authority in his famous slogan that 'God is dead'. By this shocking slogan, Nietzsche wanted to indicate that in the modern world it is no longer possible to identify a moral principle that will give a uniform, coherent and unquestioned authority to some general pattern of life or society.

Following Richard Rorty's account of irony, we can say that Nietzsche's vision of the death of God indicates that no 'final vocabulary' is possible and hence we are all exposed to the contingency of our own moral positions. In this ironist view, 'there is no such thing as a "natural" order of justification for beliefs or desires' (Rorty, 1989, p. 83). Weber engaged with this issue through a commentary on the polytheistic character of value conflicts in contemporary society. In short, Nietzsche's so-called 'perspectivism' became a part of Weber's basic epistemology of the social sciences. The 'truths' and empirical findings of sociological research are always the result or product of particular frameworks and methodologies. These partial results are always temporary and contingent. Weber's use of the 'ideal type' was based on the assumption that knowledge is always a biased summary of many possible positions and alternatives.

The Demise of Marxism

In the 1970s the character of sociology, particularly within European universities, was shaped and driven by the historical relationship between Marxism and Weber's sociology. Weber's sociology was seen to be a specific response to the challenge of Marxism and Marxist sociology. For example, Weber's treatment of the conceptual categories of social stratification involving an analysis of status, power and economic categories was often interpreted as a more appropriate interpretation of the social structure of capitalist societies (Aron, 1963) than Marx's dichotomous analysis of class. Weber's notion of social closure as a strategy for the monopolistic control of resources was treated as a fundamental approach to class divisions alongside other divisions in society, and provided a systemic 'bourgeois' critique of Marxist class theory (Parkin, 1979). In other areas, his ontology of human beings provided a radical alternative to Marx's post-Feuerbachian account of the nature of human beings as constituted by social practice (Löwith, 1993). Weber's notion of human beings as creators of meaning through practical action in the world provided an interesting comparison with the varieties of Marxist humanism which have emerged from East European Marxism (Satterwhite, 1992). In addition, Weber's comparative historical sociology (Kalberg, 1994), his macro-sociological theory (Collins, 1986a) and his sociology of power (Roth, 1987) provide contemporary sociology with a systematic and general view of history and society which is deeper, richer and more rigorous than the legacy of Marx's political economy.

Clearly the debate over the intellectual relationship between the social theories of Marx and Weber is controversial and incomplete (Antonio and Glassman, 1985; Weiss, 1986). The unintended consequence of the controversy between Weber and Marx was that it provided a definite and clear flashpoint by which the very nature of sociology could be defined. Sociology was an academic discipline which, through the intellectual interaction with Marxism, produced a distinctive perspective on the structure of industrial capitalist society, generated a clear view of historical development, embraced a sociological approach to ontology and had a philosophy of social science which provided the framework for empirical social research. Weber's social theory provided contemporary sociology with a systematic approach to the construction of social theory (Albrow, 1990), an all-embracing vision of history (Roth and Schluchter, 1979), a distinctive orientation to comparative religious studies (Ling, 1968) and a significant body of political theory (Mommsen, 1989). Finally, Weber's analysis of such notions as value neutrality, value relevance and the fact–value distinction offered sociologists a valuable ethical framework for the conduct of practical research; his account of value neutrality has of course been the topic of much philosophical and political dispute (Runciman, 1972; Wagner and Zipprian, 1994).

The social and intellectual context of the debate over Marx and Weber has of course been radically transformed by two significant social changes in the 1980s. The first has been the political collapse of communism in Eastern Europe and the Soviet Union and the second is the corrosive effect on modernism of the process of postmodernisation. I shall deal with the question of postmodernism towards the end of this introductory chapter; at this stage I am merely concerned to note the collapse of the Marx–Weber debate as a consequence of the institutional catastrophe which hit organised Marxism in the late 1980s. The collapse of organised communism could be taken as some historical validation for Weber's pessimistic view of the 'iron cage' of capitalism, namely that an ethic of socialist solidarity could never triumph over the historical and ineluctable processes of bureaucratisation and rationalisation. The Soviet empire was simply another instance of the processes of rationalisation in everyday life, which overcame the humanistic values of Marxism as a secular ethic of brotherly love. Weber was fascinated by the social struggles in Russia around 1905 and 1906 as the autocratic government of Tsar Nicholas II tried to reach some compromise with the liberal reform movement. He wrote a number of important articles on the provincial and district organisations of local self-government (the *zemstvos*) which were the conduit for demands for civil liberities. He believed that the prospects of significant liberalisation in autocratic Russia were socially limited (Weber, 1995) and his scepticism regarding the possibilities of a socialist transformation of capitalism are well known, but the dramatic collapse of communism in the 1980s was not anticipated in academic circles. However, if we accept Weber's critical attitudes towards centralised socialism, we should not forget his equally ambiguous views of the possibilities of liberal democracy within capitalism. Weber was pessimistic about the possibilities of genuine political participation and believed that the needs of leadership in a contemporary political environment required an authoritarian or plebiscitary form of democracy. Weber's political commentaries on these struggles for democracy are important in illustrating his general approach to historical change, which emphasised the contingent nature of social change as an outcome, typically unintended, of social struggles over resources.

The collapse of organised communism has therefore put an end, for the time being, to the historic debate between Marx and Weber. The demise of Marxism has been associated as a result with new lines of interpretation with regard to the significance of Weber's sociology. As I have indicated, the erosion of Marxism has been associated with a new emphasis on Weber's relationship to Nietzsche and to the romantic critique of capitalism which had developed in Germany. Writers like Stefan George, Ludwig Klages and Alfred Schuler specifically adopted a Nietzschean critique of modern rational culture, rejecting the standardisation of social and cultural reality. Only a new breed or a new creation of men could overcome this cultural debasement. In the contemporary world, the rational intellect threatened to destroy the soul and the body, a theme which was pursued in Ludwig Klages' major work, *Der Geist als Widersacher der Seele* (1929–32), in which the consciousness of human beings appears as the adversary of the soul. Weber admired much of the visionary poetry of George (Bennett, 1954) but rejected his romanticism as inadequate for the tasks of contemporary society. These romantic criticisms of industrial capitalism did, however, exercise a covert and indirect influence on the rise and development of early forms of critical theory in Germany (Stauth and Turner, 1992).

Before the collapse of organised communism, there had been growing disillusionment with and alienation from Marxism as a social movement and with the communist regimes of Eastern Europe. Many leading Marxist theorists of the post-war period who attempted to transform Marxist theory subsequently turned to alternative paradigms such as postmodernism. The intellectuals who were associated with the journal *Socialisme ou Barbarie* in France are typical of this situation. For example, Jean-François Lyotard (1988, p. 63) has complained that behind the façade of the workers' movement 'unions contributed to regulating the exploitation of the labour force; the party served to modulate the alienation of consciousnesses; socialism was a totalitarian regime; and Marxism was no longer anything but a screen of words thrown over real *différends*'. From within sociology, one might argue that the same anxieties about centralised socialism also drove Weber to a clear appreciation of the dangers of Russian socialism.

With the collapse of communism, there has been a theoretical tendency to resurrect the debate about modernisation as an alternative to more traditional contrasts between capitalism and socialism. The view of Weber as a major analyst of capitalism, alongside Marx, Veblen, Schumpeter and Spencer, has given way to an interpretation of Weber as the primary theorist of modernity and modernisation. In the 1960s and 1970s Marxist sociologists condemned modernity and modernisation as false concepts within functionalism, where modernisation typically meant Westernisation. In the 1980s and 1990s there has, however, been a revival of these concepts. Anthony Giddens (1994, pp. 68–9) has recently moved away from an interpretation of Weber as a theorist of capitalism to a theorist of modernity. He asks rhetorically, 'What is Weber's discussion of the Protestant ethic if not an analysis of the obsessional nature of modernity? . . . Weber's work deals quite explicitly with the transition from tradition to modernity.' We might note also that Marx has been restored as an interpreter of modern culture by writers like Marshall Berman in *All That is Solid Melts into Air* (1983). Derek Sayer, in *Capitalism and Modernity* (1990), regards both Marx and Weber as developing a theory of modernity within which capitalism is simply a specific instance. Sociological debate has swung away from the analysis of the structures of capitalism to an interpretation of culture in modernisation and postmodernism. As a result, the concept of culture has superseded much of the original debate about ideology and structure within the sociological canon. Because Weber devoted much of his intellectual endeavour to the analysis of cultural sociology, we may expect that Weberian notions will play a significant part in the contemporary interest in cultural themes.

Reading Weber

The debate between the legacy of Marx and Weber gave rise to a number of more specific, and possibly more interesting, questions about whether it is possible to discover a coherent organising theme or principle in the work of Weber which would integrate his rather diverse collection of publications into a systematic whole. This search for a principle of thematic unity in Weberian sociology is also associated with the dispute regarding the validity of the view of Weber as the founding father of contemporary sociology. The quest for an organising theme in Weber has been complicated by the peculiarities connected with the way his work has actually been published and translated. Weber's academic career was disrupted by severe illness, which, from the winter of 1898, prevented him from systematically conducting research. Various explanations of this crisis have been offered, such as the conflict between the parental values, sexual repression and the failure to achieve a successful political career (Collins, 1986b). Much of Weber's work subsequently, such as the Protestant ethic thesis, was published as separate essays. As a result, much of his work was posthumously published by his wife Marianne. For example, she posthumously published the monumental *Economy and Society* (1968) in an attempt to present Weber's work as a systemic outline of interpretative sociology. His *General Economic History* (1981) was assembled from students' notes relating to his final lectures. Many of his publications, such as *The Agrarian Sociology of Ancient Civilizations* (1976), were in fact collections of articles which had been published separately. Weber's work is clearly large, complex and diverse (Käsler, 1988). The complexity of the publishing history of his legacy has provided an ideal and fertile breeding ground for a variety of interpretations of his work.

Much of the debate has been centred on the notion of rationalisation in Weber's sociology. By rationalisation, Weber referred to a set of interrelated social processes by which the modern world had been systematically transformed. In this perspective, the rise of capitalist society can be taken as simply an illustration of this general pattern of rationalisation. As a social process, rationalisation includes the systematic application of scientific reason to the everyday world and the intellectualisation of routine activities through the application of systematic knowledge to practice. Rationalisation in everyday life was also associated with the disenchantment of reality, that is, the secularisation of values and attitudes. In institutional terms, this process involved the decline of the authority of the Church and the erosion of the status of the clergy. In religious terms, rationalisation involved the development of the intellectual stratum of theologians who produced religious thought as a systematic statement about reality. In legal terms, it involved the decline and erosion of *ad hoc* legal decision-making based upon arbitrary processes and the creation of a deductive legal system following universalistic laws. Within the political sphere, it was associated with the decline and disappearance of traditional norms of legitimacy, such as the dependence upon charismatic leadership. In social terms generally, rationalisation was constituted by the spread of bureaucratic control, the establishment of modern systems of surveillance, the dependence on the nation-state as a controlling agency and the rise of new forms of administration. Rationalisation as a master theme in Weber's sociology has therefore often been compared with the themes of alienation, estrangement and reification in the work of Marx (Löwith, 1993). The rationalisation theme has dominated much contemporary Weberian scholarship (Scaff, 1989; Sica, 1988; Whimster and Lash, 1987). However, the argument that rationalisation is the key to Weber's sociology is most closely associated with the work of Frederich Tenbruck (1975; 1980). It is the argument with Tenbruck's interpretation which has established the contours of recent Weberian scholarship.

Tenbruck's famous essay on 'The Problem of Thematic Unity in the Works of Max Weber' (1980) has two principal dimensions. The first is to question Marianne Weber's description of *Economy and Society* as Weber's principal work (*Hauptwerk*) and the second is to identify and express the underlying anthropological dimension of Weber's sociology, namely his account of humans as 'cultural beings'. For Tenbruck, there is no particular key to the interpretation of *Economy and Society*, precisely because that text is a conglomerate of disparate elements which do not constitute a recognisable major work. By contrast, he draws our attention to the central role of the economic ethic of world religions, namely Weber's interest in the sociology of religion with respect to the rationalisation process. For Tenbruck, Weber's essays on the economic ethic of world religions are the principal consolidation and elaboration of the arguments begun in the essays on the Protestant ethic thesis. The Protestant ethic notion was merely a component therefore of the central analysis of religion and economics which occupied the *Gesammelte Aufsätze zur Religions soziologie* (Weber, 1921). In addition, Tenbruck draws our attention to the special importance of the 'Author's Introduction' (*Vorbemerkung*) to the sociology of religion as a whole which was included by Parsons in his translation of *The Protestant Ethic and the Spirit of Capitalism* (Weber, 1965). Weber also wrote an additional introduction in 1913 which was published in 1915 with the title 'Intermediate Reflections' (*Zwischenbetrachtung*) and was conceived after the 'Author's Introduction' was already in print. The *Zwischenbetrachtung* was translated by Hans Gerth and C. Wright Mills in *From Max Weber* as 'Religious Rejections of the World and their Directions' (Gerth and Mills, 1961, pp. 323–62). Tenbruck's argument is therefore that the analysis of the economic ethic of the world religions dominated Weber's intellectual activities from around 1904 to 1920. Because his publications on religion occupied this creative period of his life, we should regard these texts on religion and economics as his principal work rather than *Economy and Society*.

Tenbruck then argues that the thematic unity of these sociology of religion texts lies in the way in which religious orientations towards the world did or did not lead to an ethic of world-mastery, that is, to processes of rationalisation. In the principal essays of his sociology of religion, that is, in the 'Intermediate Reflections' and the 'Author's Introduction', Weber came to a universalistic and historical conceptualisation of these rationalisation processes. It was these dominant world religious views which generated different patterns of rationalism and rationalisation in the modern world. This development is completely compatible with Weber's interpretative sociology because it was these meaning systems within religion that generated specific world-views that acted as the motivations for action. In particular, it was the problem of theodicy which generated this drive towards world-mastery. This interpretation also falls in line with the idea of fatefulness of world images because it was the irrational quest for salvation which generated a rational solution to being in the world.

This sociological question about religion and salvation also contributed to Weber's implicit anthropology of the rules which govern the practical conduct of life (*Lebensführung*). By 'anthropology', I mean the view of human nature which was the underpinning for Weber's analysis of social action and interaction. In this anthropology of conduct, Weber distinguished between a theodicy of good fortune (*Glück*) and a theodicy of suffering (*Leid*). In coming to terms with fortune and suffering, human beings extend their conception of their personal experience beyond the everyday material world. It is these experiences of fortune and suffering which destroy the rational or purposive categories of pragmatic orientation to reality.

However, it was only within the monotheistic salvational religions that the rationalisation of the issue of theodicy reached its ultimate historical fruition. The development of the concept of a universalistic God who organised reality around a quest for personal salvation developed into an intellectual theodicy of reality as such. In short, it was the legacy of the Judeo-Christian world, which included the notions of ethical prophecy and monotheism, which was crucial to the development of a radical solution to the question of theodicy in forms of intellectualised soteriology. For example, the intellectual rationalism of the Protestant Churches was critical in pushing European civilisation towards a pattern of personal salvation or life regulation.

Tenbruck has provided a radical reinterpretation of Weber's legacy, in particular by raising the problem of 'the world' as a concept in sociology to its proper place (Turner, 1992a). Second, he has demonstrated the importance of the concept of theodicy to Weber's cultural sociology generally, an issue which is explored in chapter 5 of this present study. Third, Tenbruck has identified the anthropological foundations of Weber's sociology. Many of these issues have been taken up and further elaborated by Wilhelm Hennis in his important study *Max Weber: essays in reconstruction* (1988). For Hennis the central question in Weber's sociology is to do with the issues of personality and life orders. Hennis argues that the development of *Menschentum*, rather than rationalism and rationalisation, was the central question of Weber's sociology. He asserts that Weber wanted to understand how certain cultural developments produced a particular type of personality and a particular rational conduct of life (*Lebensführung*), especially in the idea of calling as part of the constitutive question of modern culture. In more precise terms, Weber's sociology is concerned both with the historical origins of life regulation as a form of rational conduct of life in the development of modern vocations in the social world and with the impact of life regulation on personality or mentality. His analysis of the Protestant ascetic organisation of life is therefore simply one dimension of this analysis of *Lebensführung* or the study of the characterological effects of particular kinds of piety. The rationalisation theme to which Weber draws attention in the Protestant ethic thesis was a particular transformation of patterns of discipline and methodology relevant to specific forms of economic life regulation. In this context we can understand the world religions as systems of life regulation producing different personality types and different life orders. Weber's concern with capitalism was not so much to understand its economic structure and functions as to understand how a capitalist civilisation would influence and transform personality, namely what sort of people a capitalist regulation of life would produce. By 'personality' Weber did not have in mind what we would understand within an empirical social psychology, but rather what kind of ontological reality would be produced by different life orders, that is, Weber asks the question from the standpoint of German cultural values. I use the word 'German' here advisedly not only to indicate once again the importance of the legacy of the *Bildungsbürgertum* tradition but also to indicate the 'spiritual' notion of Germany for both Weber and Mann. Quoting from *Reflections of a Non-political Man* (Mann, 1987, p. 36), 'Germany's internal intellectual anitheses are scarcely national; they are almost purely European, opposing one another almost completely without national coloration, without national synthesis. In Germany's soul, Europe's intellectual antitheses are carried to the end.'

Part of the motivation behind the work of Tenbruck, Hennis and Tribe (Tribe, 1989) is to re-establish Weber as a figure in the tradition of classical political philosophy, which was concerned to understand the political order of society as the foundation of ethics and ontology. These issues, particularly as they impinge upon questions of liberalism and democracy, have dominated much of the philosophical debate about the implications of Weber's work in contemporary Germany (Gneuss and Kocka, 1988). The cultural and political context of this debate has often been generated by a critical rejection of American sociology and the American reception of Weber. This critical view of American sociology has been specifically directed against Talcott Parsons's interpretation of Weber as one of the founding fathers of the sociology of action (Robertson and Turner, 1991). Hennis has been fairly explicit in his view of Weber as contributing to a German tradition of political and philosophical inquiry. First of all 'Weber was a German thinker, from the land of "Dr Faustus"' (Hennis, 1988, p. 195). According to Hennis, it is in the novels of Thomas Mann that we are able to understand the intellectual world of Weber. Second, the misunderstanding of the 'Weber thesis' which is so common among followers of Parsons 'no longer happens among German scholars' (Hennis, 1988, p. 26). For Hennis, Weber's central question was about the ethical character of human existence, and therefore sociologists like Gordon Marshall (1982) are mistaken in continuing to debate the origins of capitalism as the central issue of Weber's sociology.

As a critical note, one might reasonably observe that these remarks about sociology outside Germany seem less than generous, for example, to Parsons, since it was Parsons in *The Structure of Social Action* (1949), which was originally published in 1937, who introduced the work of Weber to an American audience, and it was Parsons who was responsible for translating *The Protestant Ethic and the Spirit of Capitalism* (1965) and who drew attention to the importance of the sociology of religion in his introductory essay to Weber's *The Sociology of Religion* (1966). Parsons was, given his own interest in religion and ethics, perfectly aware of the central importance of the concept of theodicy in Weber's historical sociology.

More importantly, one might also question the originality of Tenbruck and Hennis in recent approaches to Weber's anthropology. Much of the recent debate about Weber in fact reproduces the brilliant analysis of Weber by Karl Löwith which first appeared as an article for the *Archiv für Sozialwissenschaft und Sozialpolitik* in 1932. This esssay first appeared in English in 1982 as *Max Weber and Karl Marx* and was recently reprinted as a new edition in 1993 (Turner, 1993).

Löwith's study of Weber and Marx was significant for three

basic reasons. First, Löwith sought to demonstrate that, regardless of the very important differences between Marx and Weber, underlying their sociological perspectives was a common philosophical anthropology. That is, they shared a basic interest in the problem of 'man' in bourgeois capitalism. There was as a result an important convergence in their attitudes towards the destructive features of bourgeois civilisation which Marx developed through the idea of alienation and Weber through the theme of rationalisation. From the perspective of this ontology, both Weber and Marx saw capitalism as a destructive economic system, but one which also opened up new possibilities through the transformation of traditional systems. Weber's sociology was driven by a concern for 'human dignity', but Weber was basically pessimistic about the outcome of capitalism, which was fateful in the sense of producing an iron cage within which human beings were trapped. The unanticipated consequences of action are, for Weber, inevitably unhappy and tragic outcomes. This issue is the topic of chapters 1 and 2 of this volume.

Löwith's interpretation of Weber continues to be important because, second, it was developed out of a philosophical indebtedness to the work of Martin Heidegger. Heidegger's *Being and Time* (1962) first appeared in German in 1927 and involved a critique of metaphysics by concentrating on the facticity of being in the everyday world. Being was always 'being-there' in time and space, but human beings are always in danger of forgetting their place in the everyday world. Human beings are, to some extent, always homeless and live in a condition of existential homelessness (*Heimatlösigkeit*). Heidegger (1977) developed a profound critique of the technological conditions of capitalist society because it creates conditions under which human beings are increasingly alienated from their own embodiment. Löwith, who was a student of Heidegger, was profoundly influenced by Heideggerian existentialism. This Heideggerian focus on being within the everyday world enabled Löwith to come to a profound understanding of Weber's social theory as an anthropological contribution to the understanding of the lifeworld.

The third significant aspect of Löwith's study of Weber and Marx is that by following Heidegger's existentialist critique of metaphysics, he was also able to appreciate the importance of Nietzsche's critique of conventional metaphysics as the background to Heidegger's approach to everyday reality. Nietzsche's rejection of traditional religion as a viable orientation to the lifeworld was the background to Heidegger's critique of metaphysics and, as we have seen, the background to Weber's view of the uncertainty of modern existence. Weber's anxieties about the problem of cultural slavery in the modern bureaucratic machine of capitalism were partly generated by Nietzsche's analysis of the problem of modern existence in terms of the death of God. We should remember that Löwith's social philosophy was grounded in the view that the decisive characteristic of Western culture is to be located in the divorce between the classical view of the world, in which there was no history but merely the harmonious repetition of sameness, and the Christian world-view, in which the advent of Christ created a new teleological framework for reality. History was now meaningful in terms of the revelation of grace through the advent of Christ, the lives of the saints and the creation of the Church leading towards a Second Coming (Löwith, 1966; 1970). In a similar fashion, Weber recognised that the problem of theodicy in Christian theology drove the Protestant Reformers to a new perception of history as catastrophic. These philosophical views about the meaning of history within a Christian framework have been replaced in a secular epoch by the idea that history has no meaning and that we are living in a post-historical period (Niethammer, 1992).

We can detect in the recent interpretation of Weber's sociology a common theme, namely the profoundly ethical character of Weber's social theory and its underpinning in a particular anthropology of personality and life orders. Both Tenbruck and Löwith share this interest in the religious theme within Weber's life and work, particularly the focus on questions relating to theodicy. Hennis (1988, p. 24) is wrong, in my view, to suggest that Löwith, because of the analysis of the relationship of Weber to Marx, was fascinated by the problem of rationality and thereby missed the underlying significance of this question in Weber's sociology. On the contrary, Löwith recognised that the rationalisation theme was a product of the existential question of meaning in Weber's sociological framework.

Weber and Postmodernity

We have noted that in the last twenty years there has been a continuing and growing fascination with the sociological work of

Max Weber. How might we explain this fascination and what is the relevance of Weber's work for contemporary cultural and social problems? A number of sociologists want to claim that, because of some profound transformation of society in recent times, the work of writers like Weber is no longer relevant as a framework for understanding the conditions under which we now live. In particular, Giddens in *The Consequences of Modernity* (1990) and Ulrich Beck in *Risk Society* (1992) have argued that we must go beyond Weberian sociology to grasp the essential features of modern societies. We might say, therefore, that contemporary sociology is confronted with two principal issues, namely whether society has gone through a radical transformation which has altered its very character and whether we need an entirely new theoretical framework to understand these transformations. Both Beck and Giddens are attempting to propose that we do live within an entirely transformed social reality which requires a new theoretical paradigm. Because high modernity in Giddens's terms and risk society in Beck's sociology present us with new conditions, we also need to develop new theories for analysing these societies. This new reality is described in terms of the theory of reflexive modernisation in Beck, Giddens and Lash (1994), which is presented as an alternative to the idea of postmodernisation. In this concluding commentary, I wish to challenge Beck and Giddens, particularly in their interpretation of Weber, and defend the idea of postmodernisation as a real process in contemporary society. Finally, I suggest that Weber's sociology is to some extent compatible with postmodernisation because of his dependence on Nietzsche's perspectivism.

In *The Consequences of Modernity*, Giddens has argued that Weber treated society as the nation-state, had no understanding of the processes of globalisation and failed to address the issue of reflexive modernity as the real focus of sociology. Thus classical Weberian social theory is too unidimensional to offer us a relevant or adequate perspective on our condition. From my point of view, Giddens's position can be questioned by considering Weber's account of personality. Thus Giddens's recent interest in the self in *Modernity and Self-Identity* (1991) and sexuality in *The Transformation of Intimacy* (1992) is not far removed from Weber's focus on personality and life orders. Giddens's argument is that self-reflexivity and in particular the notion of the self as a project is a specific feature of high modernity and the outcome of a process of de-traditionalisation. As we have seen, Weber believed that personality was indeed a project, the outcome of a self-conscious system of discipline and creativity. For Weber, personality was that rational project of the person or self which distinguished human beings from non-human creatures. In his terms personality was not a fact about human beings but something which was achieved by culture through a system of life-long education. He thus elaborated the idea of individuality and personality through a concept of singularity.

This idea of the rational project and the self was part of a German tradition which emphasised the idea of individuality and individual singularity, particularly amongst the cultured middle class (*Bildungsbürgertum*), as a feature of the debate about the relationship between culture and civilisation. Within this tradition personality was the outcome of culture in a struggle against civilisation, against a materialistic culture which was thought to be typical of the Anglo-Saxon world, especially English material-ism. Personality for Weber was thus a calling or vocation whereby a singular individual imposed on him- or herself the disciplines and rationality which were necessary to produce a self as an effect of educational training. This aspect of Weber's sociology has been analysed with considerable insight by Harvey Goldman in *Politics, Death and the Devil* (1992). Weber's principal concern was that personality within this tradition would be undermined by the growth of scientific rationalisation, the growth of the nation-state and the bureaucratic domination of the everyday world. Weber's sociological perspective was concerned to under-stand the cultivation of the self against the constraints of a rational secular order. This focus anticipated at least some of the current debate about reflexivity, the self, emotionality and the collapse of traditional paradigms of the self. Weber's analysis of personality, particularly in his study of Protestant spirituality, influenced a variety of twentieth-century social theorists in their approach to the nature of the modern self. Of particular significance among these was Benjamin Nelson, whose *On the Roads to Modernity* (1981) is a major historical study of the evolution of the idea of conscious in Western cultures, specifically within Weber's historical sociological paradigm. Nelson's task was no less than a history of the self and civilisation.

The point of this commentary is to indicate that Giddens's analysis of the reflexive self is not necessarily an original contribution to sociology since there are a number of well-known traditions in classical sociology by which the self can be approached and understood as a reflexive and rational project of modernity. Consequently there is no automatic justification for abandoning or rejecting traditional sociology as a paradigm.

If it is possible to defend Weber's sociology against Giddens, can we defend Weber against current postmodern theory? In discussing postmodernisation, it is useful to distinguish between postmodernism as a theory of modern society, postmodernisation as a social process and postmodernity as a social condition which is produced by processes of postmodernisation. Postmodern theory plays upon the importance of irony, simulation, self-referential writing styles, randomness and depthless reading of texts. Postmodern theory is fascinated by the artificial and the facile, such as the role of kitsch in popular and youth culture. It seeks to comprehend the importance of simulation in writing and reading techniques. Postmodernism rejects the traditional authority of intellectuals, and mixes and combines both high and low culture. It is in this sense a special form of cultural reflexivity about the complexities of modern popular lifestyles (Turner, 1990). By postmodernity, I am referring to the social condition of modern societies which are experiencing a process of postmodernisation. Social postmodernity involves: cultural differentiation, fragmentation and complexity; the demise of the authority of high culture and elite traditions; the growth of ethnic multiculturalism and cultural diversity as a consequence of the processes of globalisation, particularly tourism and a global labour market; and the prevalence and dominance of certain stylistic devices in culture which use simulation, parody and irony as argumentative styles or rhetoric. This process of postmodernisation produces the subjective experience of the artificial and the constructed nature of social and cultural phenomena. In terms of lifestyle, postmodernisation of the life course involves the disappearance of single career patterns, the emergence of fragmented lifestyles, the erosion of traditional patterns of employment and retirement, and the break-up of traditional household structures into more fragmented and diversified forms. The essential argument of postmodernism has been summarised most neatly by Lyotard (1984), namely that the postmodern condition involves scepticism towards grand narratives. The grand narratives of democracy, liberalism, the nation-state and religion are specific illustrations.

Contemporary societies are characterised by the notion that our commitments are contingent and our beliefs only temporary. Postmodernity means that we cannot continue to 'organize the multitude of events that come to us from the world, both the human and the non-human world, by subsuming them beneath the idea of a universal history of humanity' (Lyotard, 1989, p. 314).

Nietzsche has been one of the most influential philosophers in the development of postmodern theory because it was from Nietzsche's philosophy that the whole problem of perspectivism in the slogan that 'God is dead' was derived. Nietzsche's influence on postmodern philosophy comes to us via Martin Heidegger, and from commentators on Heidegger such as Gianni Vattimo (1988) and Richard Rorty (1989). It should now be fairly obvious that Weber's perspectivism is in many respects highly compatible with the current postmodern mood. Weber was clearly influenced by Nietzsche's analysis of the polytheistic struggle of values in modern society and Weber's philosophy of social sciences was clearly committed to the idea that facts are always observed from a particular perspective and cannot be theory-neutral. Weber was in fact profoundly ambiguous about the nature of rationality and modernity, being specifically conscious of the irrational drive behind the growth of rational values. These issues are taken up in chapter 1 of this volume.

However, it would be a mistake to regard Weber as an ironist in Rorty's terms. I have elsewhere (Turner, 1992b, p. 18) suggested that Weber departed from Nietzsche on at least three grounds. First, while Weber feared and deplored the growth of polytheistic values, Nietzsche celebrated this diversity as a necessary framework for undermining monotheistic values and moralities. For Nietzsche, polytheism was a necessary condition for individuality. Second, Weber's highly rationalistic analysis of the ethic of responsibility would have been rejected by Nietzsche as a form of resentment, namely as Socratism. Finally, Nietzsche rejected the fatalism and nihilism of Schopenhauer, and embraced the idea of the revaluation of values as an escape from the negativity of our period. Obviously, Weber lacked the playfulness and ironic self-reflexivity which we find characteristically in postmodernism (Rojek and Turner, 1993). Weber's tragic view of reality as a fateful order is ultimately incompatible with the sense of ironic parody which pervades postmodern analysis. Weber would have rejected or have been bemused by the argumentative style of postmodern theory. However, his sociological attempt to come to terms with the very ambiguities of modern culture, the uncertainties and conflicts of contemporary political life and the erosion and secularisation of religious traditions provides us with one of the greatest insights into the problematic condition of the twentieth century.

There is another issue which separates Weber's sociology from the moral and aesthetic mood of postmodernism, which is the question of otherness and difference. Modernisation, as Weber recognised, involved standardisation and normalisation; it precluded any sensitivity to and empathy for personal and social difference. Postmodernism follows liberalism in its responsibility towards otherness, but whereas liberalism tolerates individual differences, postmodernism celebrates, fosters and encourages difference. Weber's tough-minded realism with regard to the inevitable domination of rationalisation as a process appears to be far removed from the elevation of concern and care as foundations of postmodern moral orientations. Thus, while Weber's analysis of the 'iron cage' of rational capitalism has a relationship to Foucault's account of panoptic disciplines, Foucault went further to discover that 'our very conceptions of subjectivity are themselves already deeply structured by processes of power. And these processes are inextricably related to the generation of knowledge in the human sciences' (White, 1991, p. 120). The idea that a vocation in science could be a morally adequate response to a secular and pluralistic society would be foreign to postmodern ethics, which turns to concepts such as the sublime rather than reason as an approach to authenticity (Lyotard, 1989).

In Defence of Weber

In this new introduction to *For Weber*, I have noted a number of major changes in the way in which Weber's sociology is received in contemporary social theory. There has been a growing recognition of the importance of Nietzsche for Weber's cultural critique of capitalism, his interest in the growth of discipline and new forms of personality, and in his concern for the relationship between power and knowledge. Second, there has been an increasing concern for Weber's contribution to cultural sociology, in which his analysis of values and meaning is assimilated to an epistemology driven by literary theory. Third, there has been correspondingly a declining interest in Weber's sociology of industrial capitalism, his comparative sociology of industrial societies and his political sociology of the modern state. Fourth, the somewhat ritualistic contrasts between Marx and Weber have been abandoned in favour of comparisons with Foucault or Lyotard. Fifth, and as a consequence of these tendencies, the contemporary interest in Weber centres on the contrast between traditionalism and modernity, and as a consequence there is an emerging debate about Weber's relationship to postmodern social theory and postmodern society. Finally, there has been a debate about Weber's relationship to the classical tradition of sociology, namely to the works of Marx and Durkheim. Writers like Beck, Giddens and Lash have, in their recent work, turned away from any concern overtly with the question of postmodernisation to a focus on reflexive modernisation. In this particular approach to Weber, there has been a concern to undermine the notion that Weber has anything particularly important or interesting to say about the contemporary world, which has been transformed by various processes of globalisation.

In writing this new introduction to *For Weber*, I want to welcome many of these new criticisms in the interpretation of Weber's sociology. In particular the new concern with the ethical dimension of his sociology is an important improvement on previous paradigms for the reception of Weber's contribution. The idea that Weber's sociology was shaped by a number of significant ethical concerns is a welcome development in the analysis of the history of sociology. Clearly Weber's sociology engaged with the problems of a post-Christian reality in which many traditional assumptions about the meaning of life and the significance of the sacred have been challenged by the processes of secularisation, industrialisation and, in Weber's terms, rationalisation. Weber's sociology of religion, while significantly different from Durkheim's contribution to the understanding of the sacred in many respects, nevertheless addressed the problem of the elementary forms of religion in a post-Christian environment. Whereas Durkheim was concerned with the problem of the conditions of social solidarity in a post-religious order, Weber addressed the question of meaning in a world which was disenchanted. As both Löwith and Hennis have noted, Weber was concerned to understand the condition of human beings in an alienated environment where the old certainties of faith had been challenged by secularisation. Löwith's introduction of an existentialist theme via Heidegger's philosophy presented a strikingly original interpretation of the underlying anthropological assumptions of Weber's interpretative sociology.

This recovery of the significance of Nietzsche and ethical issues in Weber has meant that Weberian sociology can engage significantly with questions of secularisation and postmodernisation in contemporary social theory. Weber's perspectivism, his concern for the legacy of Nietzsche, his overwhelming conviction about the provisional nature of social inquiry and his anxiety with respect to the limitations of rationality and reason are all themes which have entered directly into the debate over postmodernism. This evolving paradigm of ethical interpretation has transformed conventional understanding of Weber as the theorist of the fact–value dichotomy. Weber's sociology was ethically engaged with the primary concerns of his time, was sensitive to major theological and moral debates, was driven by a tragic vision of the human condition and was underpinned by a profoundly committed view of the problems of German politics.

While these new developments in Weber interpretations are significant, they nevertheless both exaggerate certain features of Weber's work and understate many important dimensions of his substantive sociology. Against current cultural and ethical interpretations of Weber's sociology, we might start by asking ourselves the question: what are the criteria or conditions which make for the continuity and maintenance of a significant social theory? The successful accumulation of social theory requires an explicit commitment to articulating and developing a set of fundamental concepts and categories by which the nature of the social can be explained. There has to be an overt reflexive commitment to building up theory as an accumulative exercise with the goal of generating a paradigm of some explanatory force. It requires a grounding in a basic research programme of some scope and significance. It depends upon the existence of a public arena within which theoretical concepts and research can engage with contemporary political, or more generally public problems. Finally it prospers within a strong institutional academic environment including the existence of journals and associations by which these theories can be developed and elaborated. In presenting this argument I am suggesting that via the sociology of knowledge we know that a successful social theory needs an institutional climate which can foster and enhance social theory, but we also have a philosophical set of concerns about the coherence, significance and empirical relevance of social theory *per se*.

To some extent Weber's sociology fits rather well within these criteria. For example, although Weber's work was published often posthumously by his wife, he did have access to journals, institutions and associations by which his work could come to public attention, and in recent years there has been significant institutional support for publishing his entire works. By contrast, Georg Simmel was excluded from any significant academic appointment in Germany as a consequence of anti-semitism and his reception into mainstream sociology has been strikingly uneven and slow. Weber's academic status was not held back by anti-semitism or other forms of prejudice or exclusion. However, the essence of this conclusion is that Weber's sociology remains of interest to sociologists precisely because it provides us with an articulate framework of concepts and theories, a project which is grounded in a research agenda, and a sociology which is relevant to and engaged with contemporary political issues.

Recent interpretations of Weber by, in particular, Hennis and Tribe, have understated the richness of Weber's contribution to concept formation in sociology and the diversity of his substantive interests, especially in politics. We have seen that the study of social conditions and certain types of personality and their relevant social orders were indeed a central theme of Weber's ethical and sociological concerns. This focus on life orders does not exhaust the full range of his research interests in substantive sociology. In other words, Weber sought to understand the nature of the times in which we live, namely the conditions and dimensions of modernity. This attempt to understand the nature of modernity involved Weber in a series of interconnected research programmes of which the sociology of religion was certainly dominant. However, in his attempt to understand the conditions under which we live and the problems of a capitalist civilisation, he was particularly concerned to comprehend the legal framework of social existence. Essential to his sociological paradigm was the historical investigation of the juridical foundations of rational life, which is examined in chapter 11 of this volume. Within his sociology of law, Weber engaged in a variety of significant debates, such as the *Critique of Stammler* (1977), which have been neglected in recent discussion. Although Weber was clearly concerned with the economic ethics of the world religions, he pursued a variety of comparative studies in legal history, military organisation, musical systems and economic history (Weber, 1981).

Weber also engaged in wide-ranging debates about economics, economic theory and economic institutions (Weber, 1981; Sica, 1988) but he was also interested in the philosophical and methodological problems of historical economics in his debate with Roscher and Knies (Weber, 1975). It is obvious that recent interpretations of Weber have down-played his substantive interests in law, economics and history but of central importance to Weber was the historical and sociological understanding of the conditions by which liberal politics could operate and within which individuality could flourish and develop. Weber's concern with what we might call 'ethical personality' was thus combined with a profoundly empirical concern with practical day-to-day politics. This concern for the conditions of liberalism underpins his entire political sociology, his comparative study of German, American and British political institutions and his comparative concern with the understanding of authoritarianism (Turner, 1994). The practical orientation of Weber's political sociology was to understand the peculiar problems of German political leadership within an imperial context where the Anglo-Saxon cultures of North America and Great Britain dominated colonial policies and politics. He sought to understand the problem of German leadership against a background of class structures and politics which were dominated by the *Junker* class and which constrained or prohibited more liberal forms of politics. The political failure of the 1848 revolution in Germany, the under-development of socialism and working-class institutions, the legacy of Bismarck's centralised bureaucracy and the dominance of the Prussian state were social conditions which precluded the growth of *laissez-faire* industrial capitalism and the evolution of a liberal middle class capable of exercising significant political leadership. These general social issues lay behind his analysis of the Russian revolutions (Weber, 1995). Weber believed that the promising start of liberalism in Russia in 1905 and 1906 had collapsed by 1917 into a 'pseudo-democracy'. He was concerned to understand the social conditions under which effective political leadership could be achieved in order to secure his particular vision of liberalism against bureaucracy and the state with the ethical objective of sustaining individuality and individualism within a rationalised world.

Weber's version of liberalism was not a cosy middle-class notion of pluralism and free speech. Rather his understanding of politics was based upon an acceptance of the inevitability of political struggle and, where necessary, violence. His concept of politics was driven by an acceptance of Nietzsche which often assumed almost Social Darwinistic characteristics. For example, Weber's concerns about East Germany in terms of Polish migrant settlement was bound up with his commitment to establishing Germany as a dominant political culture and state. The ethical concerns which underlay Weber's interest in individualism were set within the broader context of his acceptance of violence as a method of political action. Here again there is a convergence between Weber and Mann; commenting on democracy in relation to Germany, Mann (1987, p. 36) claimed that 'Whoever would aspire to transform Germany into a middle-class democracy in the Western-Roman sense and spirit would wish to take away from her all that is best and complex, to take away the problematic character that really makes up her nationality.' Similarly in his Freiburg address, Weber had observed that future generations would not thank them if the Germans left no elbow room to grow, that is, did not conquer and protect the eastern provinces of Germany. The German people required an expansionary state.

In Conclusion

In summary, we could say that two central sociological questions lay behind Weber's research programme, namely who owns the means of (physical) violence, particularly military violence, and who controls the means of symbolic violence, especially ecclesiastical or sacred institutions? These two critical questions in Weber's sociology, which derive significantly from both Marx and Nietzsche, are crucial to chapters 4, 5, 7 and 12. Weber's substantive sociology, such as the sociology of law, addressed the problem of how these orders of violence were held together by systems of normative legitimation. The fragmentation of modern cultures presents a significant difficulty for the functioning of these orders of regulation and control. Putting this in rather different terms, we could say that Weber was interested in the interaction between the market (economic institutions), the state (political institutions) and the symbolic order of the Church, and these institutional relations were expressed through a fundamental dichotomy between rationalised bureaucracy and the individual capacity for action on the part of charismatic leaders. Weber was thus overwhelmingly concerned with the ethical dilemmas of leadership and power against a realistic acceptance of the necessity for both violence and legitimacy in any human society. This set of foundational questions concerning politics and religion was also an important feature of Weber's concern with the impact of technology on human societies, particularly military technology, and it was with the military implications of technology, whether in feudal or in capitalist times, that Weber's tragic vision of history found a poignant expression. It seems appropriate therefore to conclude this introductory commentary to the new edition of *For Weber* with a quotation from Weber's essay on 'Russia's Transition to Pseudo-Constitutionalism' from the recently translated collection of essays on *The Russian Revolutions* (Weber, 1995, p. 231).

It is a continuous, unrelenting struggle, with wild deeds of murder and merciless acts of tyranny in such numbers that even these horrors finally become accepted as normal. Modern revolution is like modern warfare, which, robbed of the romantic aura of knightly contest of days gone by, represents itself as a mechanical process caught between the instrumentalized products of the intellectual labour of laboratories and workshops, on the one hand, and the icy power of money, on the other, but at the same time actually is a terrible, unending test of nerve both for the leaders and for the hundreds of thousands of the led.

Contemporary culturalist interpretations of Weber which give prominence to his ethical approach to life orders and personality should not forget his somewhat daemonic vision of human history as an endless series of struggles for dominance, the unintended consequences of which can have fateful consequences for both leaders and led. The modern world with its instrumentalised products of intellectual labour can often create an iron cage of tragic proportions within which the scope for individual action is clearly limited. In his sociological quest to understand the fatefulness of the times in which we live, Weber created a comparative and historical sociology which examined the legal, political and economic conditions of contemporary capitalism. In my study of Weber, I have given special prominence to his comparative religion (Turner, 1974), to his sociology of law in chapter 11 and to his political sociology (Turner, 1992b) in order to bring out the diversity and richness of Weber's sociological project.

References

Albrow, M. (1990), *Max Weber's Construction of Social Theory*, London: Macmillan.

Antonio, R. J., and Glassman, R. M. (eds) (1985), *A Weber–Marx Dialogue*, Lawrence: University Press of Kansas.

Aron, R. (1963), *Eighteen Lectures on Industrial Society*, London: Weidenfeld and Nicolson.

Beck, U. (1992), *Risk Society: towards a new modernity*, London: Sage.

Beck, U., Giddens, A., and Lash, S. (1994), *Reflexive Modernization: politics, tradition and aesthetics in the modern social order*, Oxford: Polity Press.

Bennett, E. K. (1954), *Stefan George*, New Haven: Yale University Press.

Berman, M. (1983), *All That is Solid Melts into Air: the experience of modernity*, London: Verso.

Bologh, R. W. (1990), *Love or Greatness: Max Weber or masculine thinking: a feminist inquiry*, London: Unwin & Hyman.

Collins, R. (1986a), *Weberian Sociological Theory*, Cambridge: Cambridge University Press.

Collins R. (1986b), *Weber, a Skeleton Key*, Beverly Hills: Sage.

Eden, R. (1983), *Political Leadership and Nihilism: the study of Weber and Nietzsche*, Tampa: University of South Florida Press.

Elias, N. (1978), *The Civilising Process: the history of manners*, Oxford: Basil Blackwell.

Gerth, H. H., and Mills, C. W. (1961), *From Max Weber: essays in sociology*, London: Routledge & Kegan Paul.

Giddens, A. (1990), *The Consequences of Modernity*, Oxford: Polity Press.

Giddens, A. (1991), *Modernity and Self-Identity: self and society in the later modern age*, Oxford: Polity Press.

Giddens, A. (1992), *The Transformation of Intimacy: sexuality, love and eroticism in modern society*, Oxford: Polity Press.

Giddens, A. (1994), 'Living in a post-traditional society', in U. Beck, A. Giddens and S. Lash, *Reflexive Modernization: politics, tradition and aesthetics in the modern social order*, Oxford: Polity Press, pp. 56–109.

Gneuss, C., and Kocka, J. (1988), *Max Weber: ein Symposion*, Munich: Deutscher Taschenbuch Verlag.

Goldman, H. (1992), *Politics, Death and the Devil: self and Power in Max Weber and Thomas Mann*, Berkeley: University of California Press.

Green, M. (1974), *The Von Richthofen Sisters: the triumph and tragic modes of love*, New York: Basic Books.

Heidegger, M. (1962), *Being and Time*, Oxford: Basil Blackwell.

Heidegger, M. (1977), *The Question Concerning Technology and Other Essays*, New York: Harper & Row.

Hennis, W. (1988), *Max Weber: essays in reconstruction*, London: Allen & Unwin.

Kalberg, S. (1994), *Max Weber's Comparative Historical Sociology*, Oxford: Polity Press.

Käsler, D. (1988), *Max Weber: an introduction to his life and work*, Oxford: Polity Press.

Klages, L. (1929–32), *Der Geist als Widersacher der Seele*, Bonn: Bouvier Verlag Herbert Grundmann.

Lassman, P., and Velody, I. (1989), *Max Weber's 'Science as a Vocation'*, London: Unwin Hyman.

Lehmann, H., and Roth, G. (eds) (1993), *Weber's Protestant Ethic: origins, evidence and contexts*, Cambridge: Cambridge University Press.

Liebersohn, H. (1988), *Fate and Utopia in German Sociology 1870–1923*, Cambridge, Mass.: MIT Press.

Ling, T. (1968), *A History of Religion East and West*, London: Macmillan.

Ling, T. (1980), *Karl Marx and Religion in Europe and India*, London: Macmillan.

Löwith, K. (1966), *Nature, History and Existentialism and Other Essays*, Evanston, Ill.: North Western University Press.

Löwith, K. (1970), *Meaning in History*, Chicago and London: University of Chicago Press.

Löwith, K. (1993), *Max Weber and Karl Marx*, London: Routledge.

Lyotard, J.-F. (1984), *The Postmodern Condition: a report on knowledge*, Manchester: University of Manchester Press.

Lyotard, J.-F. (1988), *Peregrinations: law, form, event*, New York: Columbia University Press.

Lyotard, J.-F. (1989), 'The sublime and the avant-garde', in A. Benjamin (ed.), *The Lyotard Reader*, Oxford: Basil Blackwell, pp. 196–211.

Mann, T. (1987), *Reflections of a Nonpolitical Man*, New York: Ungar.

Marcus, J. (1987), *George Lukács and Thomas Mann: a study in the sociology of literature*, Amherst: University of Massachusetts Press.

Marshall, G. (1982), *In Search of the Spirit of Capitalism: an essay on Max Weber's Protestant ethic thesis*, London: Hutchinson.

Mayer, J. P. (1956), *Max Weber and German Politics: the study in political sociology* (revised and enlarged edn), London: Faber & Faber.

Mommsen, W. J. (1984), *Max Weber and German Politics 1890–1920*, Chicago: University of Chicago Press.

Mommsen, W. J. (1989), *The Political and Social Theory of Max Weber*, Oxford: Polity Press.

Moretti, F. (1987), *The Way of the World: the Bildungsroman in European culture*, London: Verso.

Nelson, B. (1981), *On the Roads to Modernity: conscience, science and civilizations*, Totowa, N.J.: Rowman & Littlefield.

Niethammer, L. (1992), *Posthistoire: has history come to an end?* London: Verso.

Parkin, F. (1979), *Marxism and Class Theory: a bourgeois critique*, London: Tavistock.

Parsons, T. (1949), *The Structure of Social Action*, Glencoe Ill.: Free Press.

Ringer, F. K. (1969), *The Decline of the German Mandarins: the German academic community of 1890–1933*, Cambridge, Mass.: Harvard University Press.

Robertson, R., and Turner, B. S. (eds) (1991), *Talcott Parsons: theorist of modernity*, London: Sage.

Rojek, C., and Turner, B. S. (1993), *Forget Baudrillard?*, London: Routledge.

Rorty, R. (1989), *Contingency, Irony and Solidarity*, Cambridge: Cambridge University Press.

Roth, G. (1987), *Politische Herrschaft und Persönliche Freiheit*, Frankfurt: Suhrkamp.

Roth, G., and Schluchter, W. (1979), *Max Weber's Vision of History: ethics and methods*, Berkeley: University of California Press.

Runciman, W. G. (1972), *A Critique of Max Weber's Philosophy of Social Science*, Cambridge: Cambridge University Press.

Satterwhite, J. H. (1992), *Varieties of Marxist Humanism: philosophical revision in postwar Eastern Europe*, Pittsburgh and London: University of Pittsburgh Press.

Sayer, D. (1990), *Capitalism and Modernity: an excursus on Marx and Weber*, London: Routledge.

Scaff, L. A. (1989), *Fleeing the Iron Cage: culture, politics and modernity in the thought of Max Weber*, Berkeley: University of California Press.

Schroeder, R. (1992), *Max Weber and the Sociology of Culture*, London: Sage.

Sica, A. (1988), *Weber, Irrationality and Social Order*, Berkeley: University of California Press.

Stauth, G. (1994), 'Kulturkritik und affirmative Kultursoziologie: Friedrich Nietzsche, Max Weber und die Wissenschaft von der menschlichen Kultur', in Wagner and Zipprian (1994), pp. 167–98.

Stauth, G., and Turner, B. S. (1986), 'Nietzsche in Weber oder die Geburt des modernen Genius im professionellen Menschen', *Zeitschrift für Soziologie*, vol. 15, pp. 81–94.

Stauth, G., and Turner, B. S. (1988), *Nietzsche's Dance: resentment, reciprocity and resistance in social life*, Oxford: Basil Blackwell.

Stauth, G., and Turner, B. S. (1992), 'Ludwig Klages (1872–1956) and the origins of critical theory', *Theory, Culture & Society*, vol. 9, pp. 45–63.

Tenbruck, F. (1975), 'Das Werk Max Webers', *Kölner Zeitschrift für Soziologie und Sozialpsychologie*, vol. 27, pp. 663–702.

Tenbruck, F. (1980), 'The problem of thematic unity in the works of Max Weber', *British Journal of Sociology*, vol. 31, no. 3, pp. 316–51.

Thomas, R. H. (1983), *Nietzsche in German Politics and Society 1890–1918*, Manchester: University of Manchester Press.

Tribe, K. (ed.) (1989), *Reading Weber*, London and New York: Routledge.

Troeltsch, E. (1931), *The Social Teaching of the Christian Churches*, London: Allen & Unwin.

Turner, B. S. (1974), *Weber and Islam: a critical study*, London: Routledge & Kegan Paul.

Turner, B. S. (1981), *For Weber: essays on the sociology of fate* (1st edn), London: Routledge & Kegan Paul.

Turner, B. S. (ed.) (1990), *Theories of Modernity and Postmodernity*, London: Sage.

Turner, B. S. (1991), *Religion and Social Theory* (2nd edn), London: Sage.

Turner, B. S. (1992a), 'The concept of the "world" in sociology: a commentary on Roland Robertson's theory of globalisation', *Journal for the Scientific Study of Religion*, vol. 31, no. 3, pp. 296–323.

Turner, B. S. (1992b), *Max Weber: from history to modernity*, London and New York: Routledge.

Turner, B. S. (1993), 'Preface' to K. Löwith, *Max Weber and Karl Marx*, London: Routledge, pp. 1–32.

Turner, B. S. (1994), 'Max Weber on individualism, bureaucracy and despotism: political authoritarianism and contemporary politics', in L. J. Ray and M. Reed (eds), *Organizing Modernity: new Weberian perspectives on work, organization and society*, London: Routledge, pp. 122–40.

Vattimo, G. (1988), *The End of Modernity*, Cambridge: Polity Press.

Wagner, G., and Zipprian, H. (eds) (1994), *Max Webers Wissenschaftslehre: Interpretation und Kritik*, Frankfurt: Suhrkamp.

Weber, M. (1921), *Gesammelte Aufsätze zur Religions soziologie*, Tübingen: J. C. B. Mohr.

Weber, M. (1965), *The Protestant Ethic and the Spirit of Capitalism*, London: Allen & Unwin.

Weber, M. (1966), *The Sociology of Religion*, London: Methuen

Weber, M. (1968), *Economy and Society*, New York: Bedminster Press.

Weber, M. (1975), *Roscher and Knies: the logical problems of historical economics*, New York: Free Press.

Weber, M. (1976), *The Agrarian Sociology of Ancient Civilizations*, London: New Left Books.

Weber, M. (1977), *Critique of Stammler*, New York: Free Press.

Weber, M. (1981), *General Economic History*, New York: Transaction Books.

Weber, M. (1995), *The Russian Revolutions*, Oxford: Polity Press.

Weiss, J. (1986), *Weber and the Marxist World*, London and New York: Routledge & Kegan Paul.

Whimster. S., and Lash, S. (eds) (1987), *Max Weber, Rationality and Modernity*, London: Allen & Unwin.

White, S. K. (1991), *Political Theory and Postmodernism*, Cambridge: Cambridge University Press.

Part one

Marxism

1 Logic and fate in Weber's sociology

With the development of various radical movements in the social sciences in the 1960s and 1970s, Marxists became increasingly insistent on demonstrating the presence of a sharp dividing line between conventional sociology and Marx's theory of society. In mounting a critique of the claims of sociology to a scientific status, Marxists have frequently selected Max Weber's sociology as the principal illustration of the limitations of sociological reasoning or of its irreducible ideological underpinnings. Weber appears to have come to the forefront of this debate because sociologists themselves have claimed that Weber provides the only valid reply to Marx's analyses of socio-economic relationships. Weber's studies of social class, state and religion have been treated from the time of their publication as decisive alternatives to the historical materialism of Marx and Engels. In addition, Weber's neo-Kantian epistemology has often been treated as the most appropriate epistemological foundation for a discipline which wants to be simultaneously value-neutral and value-relevant. Weber's epistemology can thus be approached as the principal alternative to the post-Hegelianism of Marx's dialectical materialism. According to Carl Mayer (1975, p. 719), the 'fundamental problem on this level, which is posed with the confrontation of Marx and Weber, is the problem of Hegel vs. Kant, or Kant vs. Hegel'. Alternatively, other commentators have argued that the fundamental divorce between Weberian sociology and Marxist science is to be found in neither substantive fields of research nor in epistemology, but in the political consequences of Weber's historical pessimism. Since

Weber regarded capitalist technology and relations of production as the 'fate' of our times, he dismissed the notion that socialism could produce an alternative to capitalist rationalisation of the means and conditions of production as purely utopian. By contrast, Marcuse (1968b, p. 214) claimed that Weber's pessimistic sense of 'destiny' merely generalised the 'blindness of a society which reproduces itself behind the back of the individuals, of a society in which the law of domination appears as objective technological law'.

There is, consequently, massive disagreement over Weber's status as a social theorist. On the one hand, Weber provides the 'paradigm of a sociology which is both historical and systematic' (Aron, 1964, p. 67). On the other hand, Weber's sociology is motivated by his commitment to the capitalist system, the German state and blind opposition to revolutionary Marxism. By accepting the 'fate' of capitalist domination, Weber in fact provides a justification for exploitation and imperialism under the guise of a value-free sociology (Lewis, 1975). Although there is fundamental disagreement over the validity and political implications of Weber's sociology (and hence of 'bourgeois sociology' *in toto*), there is also a curious agreement over the characterisation of the content of Weber's epistemology and substantive sociology. Both conventional sociology and Marxism concur that Weberian sociology *is* neo-Kantian. Four aspects of Weber's sociology are typically cited as evidence of Weber's dependence on Kantian philosophy. First, there is Weber's fundamental divorce between factual statements and judgments of value. While science may be useful in the selection and development of appropriate means, it cannot help us in determining what ends are important and valuable. In the last analysis, our empirical knowledge of the world is irrelevant in the field of moral choice. Second, there is the strong nominalism of Weber's approach to such general sociological concepts as 'state', 'status group' or 'corporation'. Weber's *verstehende soziologie* (interpretative sociology) treats all these 'collectivities' as 'solely the resultants and modes of organisation of particular acts of individual persons, since these alone can be treated as agents in a course of subjectively understandable action' (Weber, 1968, vol. 1, p. 13). This nominalist position is closely related to the third aspect of Weber's neo-Kantian epistemology, namely Weber's subjectivism. There are various aspects of Weber's subjectivism. At the most general level, the significance and meaning of reality is not given empirically, but is rather imposed on existence by the action of human will. For example, Weber defines 'culture' as 'a finite segment of the meaningless infinity of the world process, a segment on which human *beings* confer meaning and significance' (Weber, 1949, p. 81). In his typology of social action, Weber distinguishes between behaviour and social action in terms of the subjective meanings which are imposed on action and the subjective meanings which arise from social interaction. Sociology is the science which aims at 'the interpretive understanding of social action in order thereby to arrive at a causal explanation of its course and effects' (Weber, 1947, p. 88). Fourth, the neo-Kantianism of Weber's epistemology is evidenced by Weber's rejection of objective, general, causal laws in sociological explanations. From Weber's viewpoint, the rich empirical complexity of history and social organisation could never be reduced to a set of finite laws. Sociology could properly construct typologies and general classifications, but its explanations of social action would always be expressed in terms of probable outcomes.

Once the description of Weber's sociology as neo-Kantian is accepted, it then becomes possible to formulate a nice opposition between Marx and Weber. Those Marxists who have been strongly influenced by the structuralism of French Marxism, especially Louis Althusser and Etienne Balibar (1970), have argued that while Marx had a clear notion of the central role of objective structural determination, Weber reduces the objective structures of economic and political relations to interpersonal, human subjectivity. One particularly powerful version of this argument occurs in the work of Paul Q. Hirst (1976). In this interpretation, Weber's sociology involves subjective reductionism because all 'social relations are reduced to the plane of inter-subjective relations' (Hirst, 1976, p. 80). Marx's historical materialism, by contrast, presupposes the independence of objective conditions which are not dissolved by a Weberian commitment to the freedom of individual will. This contrast is particularly marked in Marx's arguments about the primacy of productive relations over relations of circulation and consumption. Marx's economic arguments in this area 'are based on a conception of social relations as objective social forms irreducible to the actions and thoughts of human subjects' (Hirst, 1976, p. 103).

In attempting to achieve a demarcation line between Marx and Weber in terms of a contrast between the meaningful social actions of individuals and the independent, deterministic role of objective social structures, the Marxist exegesis has often followed the interpretation of Weber by Talcott Parsons. For example, John Lewis (1975) in presenting a Marxist critique of Weber's subjectivism refers to Parsons's *The Structure of Social Action* as 'the authoritative work' which is 'a first-rate and indispensable exposition'. To some extent, the Marxist and Parsonian interpretation of Weber's sociology intersect because it is central to Parsons's thesis that Weber's neo-Kantianism represents a major break with the rationalism and reductionism of classical positivism, pointing sociology in the direction of a voluntaristic theory of action which gives full weight to the importance of freedom of will in the choice of means and ends to goals. In Parsons's approach to Western sociology, therefore, Weber represents a major turning point in the breakdown of positivism and the emergence of the concept of normatively oriented action. Parsons consequently emphasises the difference between Marx and Weber in terms of the latter's concentration on meaningful action, values, subjectivity and choice. Although Marx and Weber agreed about the task of providing an account of modern capitalism as the *sine qua non* of any valid social theory, Weber provided 'a new anti-Marxian interpretation of it and its genesis' (Parsons, 1949, p. 503).

There has been, of course, considerable criticism of Parsons's contention that not only Weber, but also Durkheim and Pareto, were forced to abandon positivism in its entirety in favour of a voluntaristic theory of action. Parsons has overstated the importance of values in Durkheim and consequently neglected Durkheim's dependence on Saint-Simon rather than Auguste Comte (Gouldner, 1962). In the case of

Weber, Parsons has understated Weber's pivotal interest in domination (Cohen *et al.*, 1975; Butts, 1977). These critical commentaries on Parsons's view of the history of sociological theory are a necessary and important corrective to Parsons's tendency to interpret all sociologists in such a manner that they prefigure Parsons's own interest in integration on the basis of common values. The problem of the Hobbesian basis of social order was not the common concern of classical sociology (Giddens, 1972). At the same time, however, Parsons recognised what he regarded as a Marxian legacy in Weber's pessimistic view of human freedom under capitalist conditions.

The point of Parsons's argument in *The Structure of Social Action* is to show that the rationalist, reductionist positivism of nineteenth-century sociology collapsed under the weight of its own analytical problems as a metatheoretical foundation for sociology as a theory of action. Hence Parsons does not regard Weber as unambiguously voluntaristic in his analysis of social, meaningful action. There is a deterministic feature of Weber's sociology in that, while Weber's position is 'fundamentally a voluntarist theory of action' (Parsons, 1949, p. 683), he did not wish to deny the significance of non-subjective factors (heredity and environmental) as conditions of ultimate values and actions. This recognition of the non-subjective constraints on action is particularly evident in Weber's characterisation of capitalism. Parsons argues that in the 'descriptive aspect of this treatment of capitalism' Weber was 'in close agreement with Marx'. Parsons's statement of the nature of that agreement is particularly interesting. By emphasising the compulsive aspects of the capitalist system, Weber produced

> a thesis concerning the determination of individual action within the system, namely that the course of action is determined in the first instance by the character of the situation in which the individual is placed, in Marxian terminology, by the 'conditions of production'. (Parsons, 1949, p. 510)

The precise location of this thesis of the compulsion of individual action by the capitalist system is ironically in *The Protestant Ethic and the Spirit of Capitalism*, which was first welcomed (by Hans Delbruck, for example) as an anti-Marxist tract. It is worth quoting in full the deterministic element of Weber's position to which Parsons specifically draws our attention:

> The capitalist economy of the present day is an immense cosmos into which the individual is born, and which presents itself to him, at least as an individual, as an unalterable order of things in which he must live. It forces the individual, in so far as he is involved in the system of market relationships, to conform to capitalistic rules of action. The manufacturer who in the long run acts counter to these norms, will just as inevitably be eliminated from the economic scene as the worker who cannot or will not adapt himself to them will be thrown into the street without a job. (Weber, 1965, pp. 54-5)

Both phenomenological commentaries, following Alfred Schutz, and Marxist viewpoints, following Louis Althusser, have persistently understated Weber's deterministic view of capitalist relations and overstated the apparent subjectivism of Weber's methodological essays. In this introductory chapter I would like to consider a number of objections to the type of interpretation of Weber which has been presented by Hindess and Hirst (1975), Hirst (1976) and Hindess and Hirst (1977). In their interpretation of Marx, Hindess and Hirst argue that we must not be seduced by the overt, obvious meaning of Marx's texts. In order to read Marx, we must attempt a symptomatic reading (*lecture symptomale*) which uncovers the deeper problematic which informs the overt meaning. Furthermore, we should not treat the whole corpus of Marx's writing as of equal value since the later scientific texts (such as *Capital*) are separated from the early work by an epistemological break which occurred around 1857. The ideological object of analysis of the early Marx, namely human subjectivity, was replaced by the scientific object of the structure of modes of production. The inconsistency of Hindess and Hirst centres on the fact that when they come to perform a 'reading' of Weber they completely abandon these epistemological principles in favour of taking the overt meaning of Weber's methodological texts for granted. They do not identify different stages and problematics in Weber's sociology. They perform not a symptomatic, but a literal, reading in assuming that Weber's substantive studies, for example, actually embody his stated methodological principles. In fact, Weber's analyses of 'social formations' adhere far more closely to a Marxist structuralism than they do to *verstehen* principles. As Rex (1971) points out, there are at least four separate phases in Weber's development associated with the successive influence of Rickert, Dilthey, positivism and Simmel.

In stressing the subjectivism of Weber, Hirst, in particular, ignores the centrality of the theme of compulsion, fate and irony in human actions. It is odd that a sociologist who is allegedly committed to the centrality of human free will should persistently employ mechanist imagery in describing the interconnection between action, interest and ideas. For Weber, it is not ideas but 'material and ideal interests, directly govern men's conduct. Yet very frequently the "world images" that have been created by "ideas" have, like switchmen, determined the tracks along which action has been pushed by the dynamic of interest' (Weber, 1961, p. 280). These mechanical metaphors follow directly from Weber's abiding interest in historical irony. It is too frequently forgotten that, while Weber is concerned with subjective meaning, he also realised that the effects of human actions are typically the obverse of human intentionality. This aspect of Weber's sociology has been somewhat inadequately conceptualised in functionalist terms as the 'unintended consequences of actions'. Weber 'retains a social determinism by emphasising charisma's routinisation' (Weber, 1961, p. 54) and thus it is through the notion of unintended consequences that Weber is able to show how charismatic loyalties are inevitably transformed into everyday routines under the sway of material interests.

However, the bland Mertonian conception of 'unanticipated

consequences' and 'latent functions' (Merton, 1936; 1957) does not capture the evil ambience of Weber's theory of routinisation. It is not simply that purposive actions have consequences which are not recognised by social actors; the outcome of human actions often work against social actors in such a way as to limit or reduce the scope of their freedom. Weber's sense of fate and evil in human history, his contrast between *virtù* and *fortuna* (Sahay, 1977), results in a reversal of Bernard de Mandeville's optimistic moral philosophy: our private virtues are our public evils so that our personal striving for salvation works itself out in history as the iron cage of capitalist production. Whereas Adam Smith's 'invisible hand' and Wilhelm Wundt's 'heterogony of purposes' had attempted to identify benevolent trends in society, Weber's sense of the fatefulness of our times draws him to detect the underlying malevolence of social reality. The present is disenchanted and the future is a polar night. This aspect of Weber's historical pessimism has been referred to as a 'negative heterogony of purposes' (Stark, 1967). Weber's negativity leads him to assume that meaningful actions become meaningless and that morally impeccable actions become morally flawed. This aspect of Weber's sociology finds its ultimate moral substratum in 'the Calvinistic belief in the fall and total perversion of the human race, a fall and perversion so catastrophic that even men's goodness must in the end generate evil' (Stark, 1967, p. 264).

While Weber appears overtly to adhere to a neo-Kantian view of human freedom within the noumenal reality of moral choices, Weber also adheres to what might be termed a Calvinistic problematic of evil logic. In reading Weber I am not struck *pace* Hindess and Hirst by the subjective freedom of the Weberian actor, but by the innumerable instances in which Weber's account of a particular historical process or an abstract model of social structure depends on the notion of an ineluctable logic of structure. The most frequently cited illustration of a Weberian logic in history is the process of rationalisation. In his classic study of rationalisation as the 'guiding principle' of Weber's whole sociology, Karl Loewith (1970) shows how rationality as a mode of life is a fateful inevitability, expressing itself not only at the level of political bureaucracy and industrial organisation but in sociology *per se*. Sociology is an effect of the process which it sets out to study. A further irony is that rationalisation of means results in the unintelligibility of ends which are no longer given by revelation or prophetic inspiration. For scientist and politician alike, the only honest response to this fate is one of moral resignation. For Loewith, therefore, the ultimate division between Marx and Weber is that Marx's view of human alienation is coupled with a sense of hope, while Weber's notion of rationalisation necessitates an 'unheroic' view of political possibilities.

At one level, therefore, the diversity of interpretations of Weber's sociology appears to result from the fact that Weber's sociology operates as a series of analytical tensions between choice and determinism, subjectivity and objectivity, contingency and logic. For Lukács (1971, 1972) and Marcuse (1968a), these tensions are themselves specific historical manifestations of the 'antinomies of bourgeois thought' which are transcended by Marxist *praxis*. In my view, these polarities are in fact merely different levels of analysis which have to be treated at different planes of sociological theory. To get at this point, we can do no better than quote Weber's statement of what sociology is about, namely:

> The type of social science in which we are interested is an *empirical science* of concrete *reality* (*Wirklichkeitswissenschaft*). Our aim is the understanding of the characteristic uniqueness of the reality in which we move. We wish to understand on the one hand the relationships and cultural significance of individual events in their contemporary manifestations and on the other the causes of their being historically *so* and not *otherwise*. (Weber, 1949, p. 72)

Weber is concerned to demonstrate the logic of social action and social structure by showing, for example, how the logic of capital accumulation works itself out in history regardless of the subjective preferences of individual capitalists and workers or how the logic of prebendalism results in the arbitrary politics of what he calls 'sultanism' regardless of the 'good intentions' of vizierial reform. As we have seen, this logic of history is fateful, even demonic. However, the particular way in which sociological logic works itself out in history is subject to or influenced by the multiplicity of specific, contingent facts and relationships which happen to obtain in given societies and situations. We can express this relationship between sociological logic and historical contingency in two ways. First, for Weber, there often emerges an 'elective affinity' between ideas and material interests which plays a crucial role in influencing the particular direction of historical trends. In the sociology of religion, Weber demonstrates an 'elective affinity' between the Protestant calling and capitalist rationality, or between Muhammad's moral teaching and nomadism, or between the 'practical rationalism' of 'civic strata' and this-worldly asceticism. These contingent features of the life-style of certain social strata facilitated the logic of routinisation in a particular direction. The concept of 'elective affinity' (*Wahlverwandtschaft*) points to the great variety of ironic ways 'in which certain ideas and certain social processes "seek each other out" in history' (Berger, 1963, p. 950).

A second and more precise formulation of this relationship between logic and contingency draws on a distinction between sociological generalisation and historical explanation. Guenther Roth (1975) argues that Weber's historical analysis involves three separate stages. In the configurational stage, Weber constructs a series of typologies or models with a particular historical content as distinct from the universal categories of sociology (such as the categories of social action). At the second level, we find Weber's developmental theories or 'secular' theories of long-term change and development, but these 'secular' theories are neither evolutionary nor predictive. These developmental theories attempt 'the description of the course and explanation of the genesis and consequences of particular historical phenomena' (Roth, 1975, p. 149). At the third stage, Weber turns to situational analysis which tries to explain the particular timing of a historical event as the effect of 'secular' causation and situational contingency. This final level of analysis looks at the way in which certain historical constellations have 'come about not only by virtue of freely willed actions, organisational imperatives, the logic of the system and a plethora of social trends but also because of historical accidents' (Roth, 1975, p. 150).

These two perspectives on the relationship between 'accident' (contingency) and 'logic' (the configurational and developmental) can be brought together by arguing that the particular ways in which the logic of the system and its secular trends work their way out historically is in terms of the elective affinities between developmental processes and contingent events or conditions. It is in these terms that Weber is able to assert both the peculiarities of given conditions for different societies and the presence of certain general societal 'secular' developments. For Weber, therefore, there are no general theories of the transformation of feudalism into capitalism and no general theory of the collapse of capitalism as a historical stage towards socialism, because the situational circumstances of given societies typically preclude any such application of law-like statements. However, certain contingent features of European society—their religious beliefs, legal norms, city organisation, technological development, political apparatus—contributed directly to the developmental rationality of capital accumulation. To express this relationship in another way, there is no necessary relationship between abstractly formulated economic structures and legal/political superstructures, because whether or not a contingently present set of religious (or other) beliefs has an affinity with economic production cannot be stated in advance. The social and economic pre-conditions for capitalist development in feudal England provide an interesting illustration of this issue for both Weber's and Marx's view of capitalist development. According to the general conditions favouring capitalist development in Weber's *General Economic History*, England is a deviant case. Weber acknowledges that England did not possess a gapless, systematic legal superstructure, that English cities did not, as on the continent, develop 'autonomous political ambitions' (Weber, 1958a, p. 182) and that in England the Calvinistic calling was watered down by various strands of emotionalism, Arminianism and quietism in the Methodist, Baptists, and Quaker sects (Weber, 1965, p. 143). The precise manner in which capitalist relations of production developed in England and the development of rationalisation in economic and political structures can only be determined by situational analysis into the conditions which favoured capitalist development despite, rather than because of, the nature of pre-capitalist social features in English society.

Having now provided a sketch of how I propose to interpret Weber's sociology in terms of the analysis of negative heterogony of purposes and in terms of a distinction between sociological logic and historical contingency, it is possible to return to the question of Weber's relationship to Marx. Just as Weber cannot be treated as merely a neo-Kantian sociologist of purposeful action, so, in the decades following the Second International, most writers on Marx have insisted that Marx's historical materialism cannot be reduced to technological determinism, that Marx did not treat the superstructure as simply a reflection of the economic base and that, in various ways, Marx placed human subjectivity and human agency at the centre of his view of history and social organisation. In denying Marx's economism, neo-Marxists came to concentrate on questions of epistemology (especially epistemological issues which derived from the neo-Kantian and neo-Hegelian philosophies of Simmel, Dilthey, Husserl and Croce). The classical focus on substantive questions of economics was partly replaced by a new interest in the superstructure (especially aesthetics and art rather than law and politics). Finally, Marx's optimism in revolutionary struggle gave way to a more 'realistic' but pessimistic assessment of working-class radicalism in late capitalism. These 'thematic innovations' (Anderson, 1976, p. 93) in modern Marxism have had the peculiar consequence of making modern Marxist theory more, rather than less, like Weberian sociology. One of the objectives of this book is to show that attempts to destroy economistic versions of Marxism have often merely repeated Weber's own criticisms of the economism of Social Democratic Party theoreticians. However, it would be wrong to treat modern Marxism as a uniform movement. For example, not all modern interpretations of Marx agree in respect of the apparent subjective humanism of the Paris Manuscripts. If one puts great emphasis on the writings of the early Marx, then Marxism may indeed look rather like a subjectivist sociology in which it would be difficult to distinguish between a neo-Kantian humanism and a neo-Feuerbachian anthropology.

It is precisely in structural Marxism that awareness of this problem has been acute. As we have seen, Marxists who have been influenced by Althusser's formulation of historical materialism (Poulantzas, Hindess and Hirst) have attempted to reject any theory which reduces Marxism to economism or technological determinism or to some form of teleological evolutionism, but their rejection of these interpretations also involved a rejection of the early Marx and Marxist humanism. This position enables structural Marxists to contrast Weber's subjectivism ('the problematic of the subject') with Marx's science of the objective structures of modes of production, while also denying the determinism of technological versions of Marxist materialism. However, this theoretical position, which involves a distinction between the contingency of class struggles at the level of the social formation and the logic of relations of production at the level of modes of production, results in a close analytical parallel between Weber's developmental and situational analysis.

The central problem for Hindess and Hirst is to produce an account of how modes of production change without recourse to an essentialist teleology or to evolutionary determinism. According to this perspective, there is nothing within, for example, the feudal mode of production which results inevitably in its transformation (the non-reproduction of its conditions of existence) or which inevitably propels it towards the capitalist mode of production. The reproduction of the conditions of existence of the mode of production must be sought at the level of the social formation where they are determined by the conjunctural struggle between social classes. Accordingly,

> transition (and non-transition) can only be understood in terms of certain determinate conditions of the class struggle and as a possible outcome of that struggle. 'Transitional conjuncture' refers to a condition of the social for-

mation such that the transformation of the dominant
mode of production is a possible outcome of the class
struggle. (Hindess and Hirst, 1975, p. 278)

In any social formation in which the feudal mode of production
is dominant, the non-reproduction of the conditions of existence of that mode is the contingent outcome of the class
struggle between landlords and peasants over the variant conditions of rent (in kind, money or labour) and over the
landlords' control of the labour process. There is no law which
states as an iron necessity that the class struggle in feudalism
will have a specific and decisive outcome in terms of the transition of the feudal mode. It follows from this argument that
there can be 'no general theory of the transition in the sense of
a specification of the general structure or process that must be
followed in all particular cases of transition from one mode of
production to another' (Hindess and Hirst, 1975, p. 279). In
other words, the developmental logic of modes of production
(such as the law of the tendency of profit to fall in capitalism) is
worked out at the social level in the contingent struggle between social classes which are determined at the level of production.

The criticisms which Hindess and Hirst subsequently
developed against this formulation in *Mode of Production and
Social Formation* reinforced rather than diminished the
Weberian connotations of their view of social transformation.
Their 'auto-critique' came to reject much of the Althusserian
epistemological underpinning of *Pre-Capitalist Modes of Production* such as the distinction between abstract modes of production and concrete social formations. Hindess and Hirst now
want to concentrate on a more complex range of class relations
within given social formations. However, the way in which
they now attempt to describe political and economic practices
has a peculiarly Weberian dimension. For example, the possession of the means of production is now described as a 'capacity'
(Hindess and Hirst, 1977, p. 25), while political practice involves 'the calculation of effect' (Hindess and Hirst, 1977, p.
59). Because politics involve a constant process of calculation
and judgment of effects under political conditions which are

constantly changing as a result of political practice, there can be no *general* knowledge of the political. The political activist has to make calculations in a conjuncture of uncertainty and in this respect the knowledge of the political scientist must be largely irrelevant. If this interpretation of the statement 'there can be no "knowledge" in political practice' (Hindess and Hirst, 1977, p. 59) is correct, then it follows that there can be no general theory of political practice (which is a matter of calculations in a context of uncertainty) in the same way that there can be no general theory of the transition of a social formation (which is the outcome of contingent class struggle). As Weber believed, politics is about the exercise of power in which the outcome is probable not determinate. Despite constant references to 'determinate' relations of production and 'determinate' social class relationships, the effect of their epistemological critique has been to increase the importance of the notion of contingency in political and economic relationships.

Theoretical attempts to refine or to reject the alleged economism and technological reductionism of Marxism in both humanistic and structuralist neo-Marxism have had the peculiar consequence of making modern Marxism more, rather than less, like Weberian sociology. This unwilling merger can be seen in epistemological and theoretical terms, but it also takes place in substantive issues. When neo-Marxists have come to deal with issues where Marx's theory of society was apparently underdeveloped they have often been forced to confront Weber's sociology. This confrontation has been particularly significant in the analysis of the state, legal relationships, religion, agrarian sociology, race relations and bureaucracy. If modern Marxism and Weberian sociology appear to be forced into an unconscious or unwilling partnership, does this mean that much of Weberian sociology (such as Weber's sociology of religion) 'fits without difficulty into the Marxian scheme' (Lichtheim, 1961, p. 385)? The answer to this sort of question depends on whether one believes that neo-Marxism is a radical departure from the historical materialism of Marx and Engels and on whether one argues that Weber was mounting a critique of Marxism rather than of Marx. Both of these questions play a large part in this study especially in the opening chapters. At this point, I shall simply turn to the question of Weber's relationship to Marx which will be greatly elaborated in subsequent sections.

We cannot approach the relationship between Marx and Weber in a unidimensional fashion. My commentary so far has been concerned with the analytical relationship between Marx's determinism and Weber's 'negative heterogony of purposes'. Whereas Weber's sense of the limitations of human freedom is closely bound up with his view of historical fate, Marx more characteristically connected human alienation with specific property relations. It would, however, be possible to develop the argument that Marx also possessed a pessimistic view of human purpose. There is, for example, Marx's famous observation in 'The Eighteenth Brumaire of Louis Bonaparte' that

> Men make their own history, but not of their own free will; not under circumstances they themselves have chosen but under the given and inherited circumstances with which they are directly confronted. The tradition of the dead generations weighs like a nightmare on the minds of the living. (Marx, 1973b, p. 146)

Certain writers on Marx, like Shlomo Avineri (1970) for example, have argued that the ironic passages in Marx's view of history are inherited directly from Hegel's conception of the Cunning of Reason (*List der Vernunft*). There would be an obvious connection in this circumstance between Hegel's notion of historical fate and that of Weber's. Following the publication of James Steuart's *Inquiry Concerning the Principles of Political Economy*, Hegel came to believe that the task of philosophy was not to recapture the values of Greek civilisation in order to halt the regression of history, but to reconcile men to their contemporary fate by grasping the imminent principles of reason in the present. As Hegel poetically expressed this insight, 'To recognise reason as the rose in the cross of the present and thereby to enjoy the present is the rational insight which reconciles us to the actual' (Glockner, 1927–30, vol. 7, p.

35). Hegel's view of reconciliation with fate is, like Marx's, a far more active, hopeful doctrine than Weber's Calvinistic pessimism. These theoretical and philosophical linkages between Marx, Hegel and Weber cannot, however, be properly appreciated without a historical grasp of the relationship between Weber, Marx and Marxism.

Karl Marx died in London in 1883 when Weber was in the process of leaving his law studies at the University of Heidelberg to take up his military service at Strasbourg at the age of nineteen. In Weber's early manhood, specific works by Marx and Engels were not widely read or commented upon, but deterministic and economic interpretations of history were often fashionable among the German intelligentsia and educated bourgeoisie. By the 1880s *The Communist Manifesto*, *A Contribution to the Critique of Political Economy*, *Capital* (volumes I and II), *The Poverty of Philosophy*, *Anti-Dühring* and *The Origin of the Family, Private Property and the State* were all available in Germany. In addition, Weber would have been familiar with Marxist literature through writers like August Bebel, co-founder of the Social Democratic Party and author of *Die Frau and der Sozialismus* (1883). Other avenues for the influence of Marx and Engels on Weber included Werner Sombart (*Sozialismus und soziale Bewegung*, 1896 and *Der modern Kapitalismus*, 1902), Karl Kautsky (*Der Ursprung des Christentums*, 1908) and Levin Goldschmidt, professor of law at Heidelberg and Berlin. The influence of Marx and Marxism on Weber was not significant and continuous (Roth, 1968; Giddens, 1970; Dibble, 1968). As a general perspective on this relationship, Marianne Weber (1975, p. 335) possibly overstated the case:

> Weber expressed great admiration for Karl Marx's brilliant constructions and saw in the inquiry into the economic and technical causes of events an exceedingly fruitful, indeed, a specifically new heuristic principle that directed the quest for knowledge (*Erkenntnistrieb*) into entire areas previously unilluminated. But he not only rejected the elevation of these ideas to a *Weltanschauung*, but was also against material factors being made absolute

and being turned into the *common denominator* of causal explanations.

This commentary from Marianne Weber's biography did, however, reiterate Weber's own judgment of 'the great thinker' and of the problems of converting Marx's heuristic devices into an 'assessment of reality' in Weber's "Objectivity" in Social Science and Social Policy' from the *Archiv für Sozialwissenschaft und Sozialpolitik* in 1904.

The problem with this assessment is that Weber did not possess many of Marx's major works, which were not published until after Weber's death in 1920. The crucial feature of these lucanae in Weber's appreciation of the full extent of Marx's un-published work is that it has been precisely the unpublished material which came to play such a dominant part in the re-evaluation and reinterpretation of Marx's thought. These critical works included the *Economic and Philosophical Manuscripts* (1844), *Theses on Feuerbach* (1845), *The German Ideology* (1846), *Grundrisse* (1857–8) and *Remarks on Wagner* (1880). These texts provided the basis for arguments by Georg Lukács, Karl Korsch, Herbert Marcuse, Alfred Sohn-Rethel and István Mészaros pointing to the fact that iron laws of economic causation as the basis of a cultural superstructure were completely alien to Marx's dialectical thought. These new interpretations of the early *Manuscripts* and *Grundrisse* suggest that the theme of alienation is central to Marx, that Marx's break with Hegel was never absolute, that Marx was committed to a view of human praxis rather than inevitable material causes and consequently that the very idea of material laws is itself the manifestation of a reification in political economy. Weber's criticisms of Marxist materialism, therefore, cannot be criticisms of Marx's authentic theory.

The view that Weber had only a very partial understanding of Marx's complex view of economic relationships has been judicially stated by Mommsen (1959, 1974). In general, Weber never approached Marx's materialist sociology 'in a systematic, let alone in a comprehensive way' (Mommsen, 1974, p. 48) and, to the extent that Weber did directly and specifically confront Marx's theory at first hand, this theoretical appraisal occurred late in Weber's intellectual career in *Economy and Society*. Weber's public lecture on 'Socialism' (in *Gesammelte Aufsätze zur Soziologie und Sozialpolitik*) in 1918 to Austrian officers does provide direct evidence of Weber's attitude to Marx, but it cannot be accepted as a reliable guide, given its politically motivated content and the peculiarity of the circumstances. Weber's sources on Marx's original theoretical development were slight, unrepresentative and largely second-hand. This fact is sufficient warning against the view, originally expressed by Albert Salomon (1934, 1935), that Weber's sociology can only be understood as a life-long debate with Karl Marx. What we must consider instead is Weber's political and theoretical opposition to institutionalised Marxism in the form of the Social Democratic Party in Germany.

With the demise of Bismarck's anti-Socialist legislation, the SDP became from 1890 onwards the largest and electorally the most successful socialist party in Europe operating within a parliamentary framework. The Erfurt Conference of 1891 committed the party to a revolutionary Marxist programme. This Marxist platform was strengthened by Karl Kautsky's editorship of the party's organ, the *Neue Zeit*. The electoral success of the party and the growing prosperity of the still backward German working class resulted in a gap between the revolutionary theory of the SDP leadership and the reformist, parliamentary socialism of its political practice. The goal of a proletarian dictatorship was submerged in the day-to-day championship of working-class demands within parliamentary democracy. There emerged, therefore, an obvious contrast between Kautsky's positivistic view of the inevitability of Marx's economic laws pointing to the inexorable victory of a revolutionary working class and the essentially limited objectives of practical politics (Plamenatz, 1954). By focusing on Marx's materialism as a scientific theory of economic laws providing a description of the 'facts' of the capitalist crisis, Kautsky was forced reluctantly into a position where Marx's moral critique of capitalism was divorced from science to become a largely residual feature of Marx's work. For Kautsky 'there appears occasionally in Marx's scientific work the impact of a moral ideal. But he always and rightly attempted to eliminate it so far as possible' (*Ethik und materialistische Geschichts-auffassung*, p. 141, quoted in Lichtheim, 1961, p. 298). By accepting an implicit distinction between facts and values, Kautsky was forced into a general Weberian problem of the is–ought dichotomy in that one set of moral judgments can have no authority over any other set of moral opinions. Commitment to the Marxist critique of capitalism would thus become simply a matter of idiosyncratic preference.

For German and Austrian Marxists who were also steeped in *Lebensphilosophie* (philosophy of life) and *verstehende Geisteswissenschaft* (social science based on understanding and re-experiencing), Kautsky's positivism and its adjunct in fatalism were totally inadequate philosophical foundations on which to validate Marx's historical materialism. In Germany and Austria, the revisionist critique of Kautsky's orthodox Marxism came to borrow extensively from neo-Kantian philosophy in its attempt to rescue institutionalised Marxism from a positivist epistemology. Eduard Bernstein, who engaged in the theoretical debate of the relationship between Marxism and Darwinistic science, contrasted Kautsky's faith in a cataclysmic class war with what he took to be the facts of Germany in the 1890s, namely the increasing evidence of social order, economic prosperity and political security. Bernstein, however, also had to live through the bitter experience of fighting the reformist faction of the SDP which came to accept the entire programme of German imperialist expansion in 1914–18. Amongst the Austro-Marxists it was Max Adler who emphasised the continuity between the Kantian philosophy of active human consciousness and Marx's philosophy of social consciousness. For Adler, the inner connection between Marxism, sociology and social revolution is also

a connection with classical German philosophy which, likewise, as a philosophy of social consciousness, can only be revolutionary. German classical philosophy always aspired to be a philosophy of action. But it could only achieve this idea; Marxism gave it the scientific knowledge that allowed it to realise this action historically.

(*Der soziologische Sinn der Lehre von Karl Marx*, 1914,
quoted in Bottomore and Goode, 1978, p. 68)

In the perspective of Adler and Karl Renner, Marx's historical
materialism was equated *tout court* with general sociology as
an objective science of society equipped with a neo-Kantian
epistemology, namely a science which occupied the space between natural science and idealist historiography.

Against this background of revisionist criticism of
Kautsky's fatalistic positivism, Weber's criticisms of the
Marxism of the SDP are not isolated and original objections,
but part of the neo-Kantian opposition to an institutionalised
Marxism which assumed that Marx's critique of capitalism
could be assimilated without loss into a natural science model
of social laws. Like the revisionists within Marxism, Weber objected to the conversion of Marx's concept of the laws of
modes of production as a heuristic device into proven laws of
empirical reality. Weber did not follow the neo-Kantian revisionist argument that Marxism represented the historical solution to the riddle of philosophy and action, values and reality.
However, Weber's judgment of the hiatus between revolutionary philosophy and political reformism in the SDP was not
wholly divorced from the revisionist position. Of course,
Weber drew very different conclusions from this hiatus. For
Weber, the German working class was politically immature
and incapable of providing the German state with effective
leadership. Weber was opposed to both the 'socially-minded'
Christian of the Evangelical-Social Congress and to the secular
socialists who believed that the material prosperity and
political emancipation of the working class could be realised
without a strong state. In the years before the First World
War, Weber was convinced that the economic surplus created
by capitalist development could not be secured without imperialist rivalry.

We can now state Weber's theoretical objections to the
Marxism of the SDP in greater detail. While Weber accepted
the heuristic value of historical materialism, he developed five
general criticisms of Marxism (Bendix and Roth, 1971, p. 240,
from Roth 'Das historische Verhältnis der Weberschen

Soziologie zum Marxismus', 1968). These were: (1) a rejection
of all monocausal explanations of history and society in terms
of ultimate causes as unscientific, (2) an assertion that the
same economic base may have different legal and political
superstructures, (3) a denial that socialism was a genuine alternative to the rationality of the market mechanism in
capitalism and therefore that historical materialism and
socialism were necessarily connected, (4) a critique of the
theory of marriage and property as developed by Engels and
Bebel, (5) a critical recognition of the logical incompatibility
between Marxism as a deterministic science and Marxism as
an ethical theory of human agency. The irony of neo-Marxist
recoveries and revisions of the pristine theories of Marx and
Engels is that they have often unwittingly reproduced
Weber's neo-Kantian critique of the Marxism of the SDP.

One of the central problems of Marxism is to reconcile the
centrality of human action and consciousness in Marx's Paris
Manuscripts and *Theses on Feuerbach* with the apparent
economic determinism of *Capital*. There are numerous sub-
sidiary themes which flow from this paradox: humanistic versus scientific Marxism, *Lebensphilosophie* versus natural
science, neo-Kantian epistemology versus positivism. This
paradox is also behind many of the specific debates in modern
Marxism concerning the relative autonomy of law and state
from the economic base and concerning the status of 'social
class' in relation to 'mode of production'. In broad terms, there
are two major solutions to this paradox in Marxism. On the
one hand, the Austro-Marxists, Lukács and the Frankfurt
School stress the continuity between classical German
philosophy (Hegel and Kant) and Marx in order to argue that
Marxism is a critical theory which transcends the
epistemological dilemmas of bourgeois thought (especially
positivistic sociology). On the other hand, Althusserian structuralism emphasises the break between Marx and classical
German philosophy in order to show that Marxism (or more
precisely, historical materialism) is a science of modes of production, but a science which cannot be reduced to a set of simple deterministic laws about the economy. This second option,
as I have attempted to demonstrate, ends by showing that the

effect of the mode of production is contingent on the complex effect of social class conflict on the conditions of existence of the mode of production. While it is more conventional to bring out the analytical relationship between Weber and the first Marxist solution (for example, between Weber and Lukács), there is in fact also a strong connection between Weber and structural Marxism on the grounds that Weber contrasted the logic of ideal type constructions and the fateful contingency of historical situations. On both counts, Max Weber has been an unwanted and largely incognito guest in modern Marxist debates about the real nature of Marx's historical materialism.

While I have been making some introductory observations on the analytical parallels between Weberian sociology and Marxism, I do not want to understate the enormous gulf which separates Weber from Marx and Marxism in political, ideological and ethical grounds. However, even if these asser-tions about the theoretical overlap between Weberian sociology and Marxism should prove to be unwarranted exag-gerations, we would still be left with the paradox of substan-tive overlap between the empirical interests of Weberians and Marxists. In spite of all the methodological and theoretical dif-ferences, 'there exists far-reaching accord in the substantive analysis of the themes identical in both [Marx and Weber]: the structure of what has been called the modern world; its development; and its consequences' (Mayer, 1975, p. 702). This 'far-reaching accord' in substantive characterisation of 'the modern world' is true both in general and in particular. There is an overlap between their view of capitalism as a dynamic and self-destructive system in comparison with the relative stability of feudalism and the stationariness of Oriental societies which is evident in Marx's Asiatic mode of produc-tion and Weber's prebendalism (Turner, 1974). Both Marx and Weber agreed that imperialism was not an accidental but necessary feature of capitalist growth. Their characterisations of the conditions by which classical slavery collapsed have many common features. In more recent debates, Weber's study of the agrarian problem in Germany which was published in the *Verein für Sozialpolitik* in 1892 ('Die Verhältnisse der Landarbeiter im ostelbischen Deutschland') instigated the general debate in the SDP over the agrarian question and stimulated Kautsky's reply in his *Agrarian Question* (Die Agrarfrage, 1899) (Procacci, 1971).

In a similar fashion, developments within the Marxist theory of law have often directly or indirectly returned to analytical problems and substantive issues which lay at the centre of Weber's treatment of law-making and the nature of law in capitalist society. Just as Weber thought that religion in providing rational theodicies of the world had its own inner logic (Kalberg, 1979), so Weber attempted to show that the Western system of law, developing from a common Roman base, possessed its own internal logic which drove the law towards an increasingly gapless system of abstract rules. This autonomous process of legal rationalisation had, as a contingent fact, an 'affinity' with the requirements of the capitalist mode of production for a formal system of dependable law. By raising questions about the form and function of law, developments in Marxism with respect to the relative autonomy of the law from relations of production have often produced theoretical solutions which reflect aspects of Weber's treatment. While E. B. Pashukanis (1978) attempted to demonstrate that the form of law was intimately related to the commodity form in capitalism and therefore the form of law under socialism would be revolutionised, Karl Renner (1949) in 1929 attempted to show that the form of law was always neutral. For Renner, the social functions of law were dictated by historically given specific social class interests, but the form of law, such as the abstract form of a legal contract, could never be reduced to economic interests arising from the economic base. This issue of the relative autonomy of the law continues to play a prominent role in Marxist legal theory.

One reason for the continuing relevance of Weber's sociology for Marxism is that contemporary Marxism has been faced with the issue of whether 'late' capitalism has institutional and productive features which distinguish it sharply from the competitive capitalism of the nineteenth century. The increasing role of the state in production, the internationalisation of ownership and production, the decline of private capital and the emergence of a new middle class were aspects of capitalism to which Austro-Marxism specifically drew attention. In contemporary Marxism the analysis of monopoly capitalism has been the theoretical driving force behind the writing of Nicos Poulantzas, Elmar Altvater, Paul Baran, Paul Sweezy, Ralph Miliband and Ernest Mandel. By focusing on the Bismarckian state in the rise of German capitalism, the role of imperialism in advanced capitalism, the weakness of the German middle class and the rise of a new salariat, Weber's sociology predates many of these contemporary Marxist themes. Of course, the conventional criticism of Weber, in respect to Weber's analysis of social class for example, is that he concentrated on the market and the phenomenal forms of circulation rather than the relations of production which determine these surface institutions of the capitalist mode of production. In this respect, it could be argued that the capitalist mode of production has Marxist causes (the relations of production) and Weberian effects (Protestant religion, status groups, the market mechanism, plebiscitarian democracy). Even on these grounds, one could still claim that Weber provides a masterly, detailed description of the concrete reality of capitalist institutions. However, in my view the value of Weber's sociology goes far beyond this descriptive level on the grounds that Weber's concept of the logic of rationalisation operating independently of the will of agents is directly compatible with Marx's concept of the logic of modes of production.

It has become fashionable (Berger and Luckmann, 1966) to combine the perspectives of Marx and Weber into a theory which attempts to show how social reality is continuously constructed by the social actions of individuals; social reality becomes alienated and reified by the forgetfulness of conscious agents. This book is, by contrast, premised on the assumption that what sociologists and Marxists have in common is a deterministic perspective of social reality whose structure and process has a logic independent of the will and consciousness of individual agents. The operation of this logic is, however, partly shaped and directed by the accidental or contingent features of sets of institutions which happen to be present in given societies. It is not a logical requirement of the capitalist mode of production that capitalists should possess Protestant beliefs. The fact that capitalists did espouse Protestantism rather than Catholicism gave a particular twist to the logic of capital accumulation. In this respect the logic of capital had an affinity with the internal rationalisation of Christian theodicy in its Protestant form. Weber's notion of fate, therefore, places Weberian sociology at the very centre of the sociological enterprise. Sociology's preoccupation with fatefulness can be summarised in the cynical aphorism that, if economics is about scarcity and choice, sociology is about why those choices cannot be realised.

2 Weber and structural Marxism

The term 'sociology' was first employed consciously to designate a new science by Auguste Comte in 1824 in a letter to Valat and became more publicly available in 1838 in the fourth volume of Comte's *Cours de philosophie positive* (The Frankfurt Institute, 1973). While sociology found its origins in the attempt by secular French positivism to give an account of 'moral facts' in industrial society, the constitutive period of modern European sociology has to be located in the 'revolt against positivism' in the 1890s (Hughes, 1959). It is within this historical context that Weber achieved pre-eminence in providing a classical account of the nature, content and objective of sociology as 'a science which attempts the interpretive understanding of social action in order thereby to arrive at a causal explanation of its course and effects' (Weber, 1947, p. 88). Emile Durkheim's account of sociology as the systematic analysis of 'social facts' in *The Rules of Sociological Method* (published in 1895) has not enjoyed the same influence and intellectual currency as Weber's notion of sociology as an interpretative science, despite Durkheim's strategic location in the French university system and his dominance over *L'Année sociologique*. In addition, Weber's metamethodological outline of 'ethical neutrality' and 'value-relevance' has become (however erroneously) the taken-for-granted moral reference of sociologists, especially of sociologists engaged in social survey research in areas of social policy and social administration. In terms of substantive issues, Weber's *The Protestant Ethic and the Spirit of Capitalism* has provided a constant topic for undergraduate sociology essays, thereby providing a virtual *rite de passage* into university sociology courses. Max Weber *is* sociology in a manner which could not be said of Keynes in relation to economics or of Malinowski in relation to anthropology. It is for this reason that Weber has been referred to as 'a Magus: he is that, a living presence to professional sociologists as well as to the sociological laity, and a living authority, unexhausted' (MacRae, 1974, p. 15). A consequence of Weber's role as sociological Magus is that rigorous attacks on sociology as such have often been mounted via an attack on Weber.

Weber's methodology, epistemology and specific elements of his empirical research have, of course, been subjected to lengthy criticism over a long period of time. The early objections of Felix Rachfahl, Lujo Brentano and Werner Sombart to Weber's investigation of the relationship between religion and capitalism were preliminary skirmishes in an intellectual debate over the Protestant ethic which has not yet been adequately settled (Green, 1959). Similarly, critical debates have taken place over other areas of Weber's empirical research with reference to bureaucracy (Merton et al., 1952), social class (Giddens, 1973), Islam (Rodinson, 1974), politics (Stammer, 1971) and so forth. While these criticisms have made serious inroads into the validity of specific aspects of Weber's empirical studies, they do not necessarily challenge the total structure of Weberian sociology. At a much deeper level, one can point to a series of critical analyses of Weber's notion of 'interpretative sociology' (*verstehende Soziologie*) which have far more general damaging implications for Weber's theoretical enterprise.

Weber was not particularly concerned in a systematic fashion with the philosophical basis of 'understanding' and 'explanation'; he consequently borrowed and adopted a variety of concepts from the *Geisteswissenschaft* tradition (human and cultural sciences) in an eclectic fashion in order to develop his own methodological basis for sociological analysis (Burger, 1976). Weber has subsequently been criticised either for not grasping the full philosophical basis of *Verstehen* explanations or for inadequately following his own methodological prescriptions. The phenomenological studies of Alfred Schutz can, for

example, be treated as an attempt to provide adequate philosophical foundations for the human sciences from a Weberian
perspective. The main criticism of Weber is that he 'naively
took for granted the meaningful phenomena of the social world
as a matter of *intersubjective agreement* in precisely the same
way as we all in daily life assume the existence of a lawful external world conforming to the concepts of our understanding'
(Schutz, 1972, p. 9). According to Schutz, Weber's sociology
presupposes the everyday world of intersubjective meaning
without asking the appropriate questions relating to how
social actors make the everyday world understandable
through their 'meaningful lived experience'. In other words,
Weber's *verstehende Soziologie* takes for granted precisely
those features of social reality which it is required to explain.
This viewpoint, that Weber failed to treat *Verstehen* as philosophically problematical, is also presented in Parsons's *The
Structure of Social Action*, in which Parsons follows the
criticisms which had been developed by Alexander von
Schelting in *Max Weber's Wissenschaftslehre* (1934). At a
technical level, Weber's philosophy of social science has been
criticised by W. G. Runciman who argues that Weber was
wrong on three counts, namely 'the difference between
theoretical presuppositions and implicit value-judgments; the
manner in which "idiographic" explanations are to be subsumed
under casual laws; and the relation of explanation to description' (Runciman, 1972, p. 15). The main burden of Runciman's
criticism of 'interpretative understanding' in Weber is that the
identification of the motives, beliefs and practices of a social
group is not merely a preliminary stage in sociological investigation, but a crucial part of sociological explanation. For
example, to identify what will count as a 'religious belief' is not
just a matter of elementary description, but a central and
necessary component of explanation. In a similar fashion,
Peter Winch has challenged 'Weber's implied suggestion that
Verstehen is logically incomplete and needs supplementing by
a different method altogether, namely the collection of
statistics' (Winch, 1958, p. 113). In Winch's perspective, the
problems faced by a sociologist or anthropologist are not
unlike those which confront a philosopher in attempting to

solve a puzzle in language. To understand incest taboos requires the same type of procedure followed by a philosopher in
understanding the use of a word. Understanding involves
describing, translating and grasping the rules of language;
therefore, *Verstehen* is neither incomplete nor a special method
of sociology.

Much of the criticism of Weber's philosophy of social science
from von Schelting (1934) to William Outhwaite (1975) does
not attempt to demolish the whole foundation of 'understanding' as a suitable sociological method. It attempts rather to correct or supplement or refine Weber's unproblematic treatment
of the nature of 'motive' in relation to 'cause', Weber's separation of 'description' and 'explanation' and Weber's attempt to
bridge the gap between nomothetic and idiographic approaches or, more generally, between natural and cultural
sciences. While there are important differences between phenomenological and linguistic philosophers in their criticism of
Weber, there is a general concensus that Weber asked relevant
questions, but that his answers were inadequate or misconceived.
Thus, Schutz, in criticising Weber's philosophical naivety,
admitted that Weber 'had determined conclusively the proper
starting point of the philosophy of the social sciences' (Schutz,
1972, p. xxvii). Similarly, Runciman recognised that not only
does Weber 'advance a number of arguments which are entirely sound: he is also right in the terms in which he asks the questions to which these arguments afford a part of the answer'
(Runciman, 1972, p. 15). The philosophical critique of Weber
does not, therefore, represent an attempt to replace Weber's
verstehende Soziologie so much as an attempt to complete and
purify the philosophical underpinnings of what is regarded as
anti-positivist sociology. These criticisms have, consequently,
to be distinguished sharply from the Marxist opposition to
Weberian sociology which attempts to perform a radical
uprooting of the whole of Weber's analytical and substantive
sociology.

The Marxist criticism of the *geisteswissenschaftliche* tradition with which Weber is typically connected can be summarised
under two headings, namely, criticism of '(a) its contemplative
character, which it shares with historicism in general; and (b)

its idealism, the tendency to collapse history into the history of thought (*Geistesgeschichte*)' (Outhwaite, 1975, p. 56). In this chapter, rather than examining the Marxist critique of Weber's contemplative idealism in general, I shall consider one particular stream of contemporary Marxist criticism to which one can attach the label of 'structuralist Marxism'. As with most labels, there are probably few Marxist writers who would self-consciously define themselves in terms of this category. However, the title does have a certain practical value in delineating a 'school' of Marxists which has a common epistemological outlook and which has been specifically hostile to the notion that Weber's sociology provides a scientific basis for the study of society. The label of 'structuralist Marxism' embraces those theorists who in broad terms derive their epistemology from the French structuralist tradition of Gaston Bachelard, Georges Canguilhem and Louis Althusser. On these epistemological criteria, Weber's sociological categories are rejected because they fail to break with their common-sense, pre-scientific and ideological background; the objects of Weberian sociology are not 'properly' constituted by theoretical practices. Whereas, according to Althusser, Marx discovered a new scientific terrain in the 'mode of production' and Freud broke through pre-scientific categories to uncover a real object of science in the concept of the 'unconscious', there is no 'epistemological break' in Weber; the concepts of 'social actor', 'subjective meaning' or 'rationalisation' are concepts within common-sense discourse. Whereas sociology treats the empirically given social group or social individual as the datum of analysis, the point of structuralist thought is to iden- tify a set of objective, underlying structures which determine human agents as the bearers of structural forces. For example, ideology cannot be treated as a collection of distorted beliefs which are possessed by individuals. For Althusser, ideology is a structure of practices which has the effect of inserting human subjects within their places in society and of securing cohesion between social classes (Althusser, 1971). By contrast, it is held that Weber treats ideology as a problem of human psychology so that theodicy emerges from the need of subjective in- dividual consciousness to make sense of the world. The structuralist critique of Weber's sociology is, therefore, an attack on the whole of Weberianism rather than a random commentary on elements within the Weberian scheme. In so far as Weber has the status of Magus in sociology, the structuralist criticism of Weber's subjectivist idealism is necessarily a criticism of the scientific claims of sociology *per se*.

There are a number of reasons why Weber's sociology has been at the centre of the controversy over the scientificity of sociology and Marxism. As I have shown, Weber's epistemology is held to represent a condensation of the errors of pre-scientific thought. Weber's sociology is located within a 'problematic of the subject' because he attempts to provide sociological explanations in terms of the understanding of the motives of individual social actors rather than an analysis of how political, ideological and economic structures interpellate 'agents' according to determinate processes. There is, however, a far more important reason for the structuralist critique of Weberianism. The theoretical objective of structuralism is to provide a scientific analysis of the laws of motion of modes of production and thus to render intelligible the specific features of given societies (or social formations). To establish the scientific nature of Marx's analysis of the capitalist mode of production, it is necessary to distinguish scientific Marxism from Marxist humanism and thus to demonstrate the crucial difference between the young Marx of the Paris Manuscripts and the later Marx of *Capital*. At the same time, structuralist Marxism has to be distinguished from the reductionism of vulgar Marxism and technological determinism. The problem for structuralism is, therefore, to show that Marxism is a deterministic science, but not a reductionist economism. The elaboration of the concept of 'mode of production', the analysis of the transformation of modes of production and the study of concrete social formations will also contribute to filling out certain gaps in Marx's analysis—such as the nature of the state, the role of law in capitalist production and the nature of the relationship between science, philosophy and ideology. The significance of Weber's sociology for the structuralist interpretation of Marx is precisely that Weber's sociology was founded on a critique of monocausal economist historical explanations. In attempting to provide an alternative to simple economic reductionism, Weber engaged in a series of explorations of the relationship between various structures (especially the economic and political structures) which required an analysis of the place of the state, law and science in capitalist society. The general thrust of my argument is that Weber cannot be adequately treated as a subjectivist sociologist whose analysis is caught within a 'problematic of the subject'. There are important similarities in terms of epistemology and substantive issues between Althusserian Marxism and Weberian sociology which rule out simple, dichotomous contrasts between Marxism and sociology, science and sociology, Marx and Weber. Finally, there are a number of difficulties within Althusserian Marxism which have rendered Althusserian structuralism problematic and uncertain as a coherent interpretation of either Marx or Weber. While I want to argue that there are important similarities in the determinism of Marx and Weber, the implicit structural-functionalism of Althusserianism is to be distinguished from *both* Weber and Marx.

In order to understand the nature of the structuralist critique of Weber in the work of writers like Nicos Poulantzas, it is important to have some basic comprehension of Althusser's epistemological position. Althusser is fundamentally opposed to any distinction between 'theory' and 'facts' which treats external empirical reality in opposition to a knowing subject. Theory is not a collection of propositions which can be arrived at by observation of reality, since reality can never be apprehended without theory. The 'facts' are never theory-neutral. All knowledge is the effect of theoretical practices which take place inside thought itself; scientific practice has no object existing outside its own activity. Knowledge is thus the outcome of theoretical practice on raw materials, but in Althusserian epistemology the 'raw material' is not constituted by the empirically given. Althusser makes an analogy between human labour on the raw material of nature and theoretical work on the raw material of pre-scientific conceptualization. Science emerges from a process of labour based on three generalities. Science takes existing common-sense, intuition and ideological ideas (Generalities I) as raw material which is then transformed by theoretical work (Generalities II) into systematic, elaborate scientific knowledge (Generalities III). Hence new knowledge does not result from the discovery of hitherto unknown facts and knowledge cannot be the product of observation and experimentation. Scientific knowledge is not cumulative, but involves epistemological breaks and ruptures which separate science from its ideological prehistory.

Althusser contrasts this epistemological position with both empiricism and idealism. Whereas empiricism assumes that knowledge is the extraction of an empirical essence from reality, idealism attempts to abstract the essential, real essence from inessential reality. Idealism/empiricism are thus forms of the same problematic which treats science as the outcome of the abstraction of essences from given reality. In Althusser's view, this account of the nature of science provides us with a correct insight into the real relationship between Marx's scientific work in *Capital* and the reality of British capitalism in the nineteenth century. Marx's analysis of the laws of motion of the capitalist mode of production was not arrived at by observation of the empirical reality of capitalist firms in Britain. *Capital* is a theoretical work based on Marx's confrontation with the pre-scientific ideas of Ricardo, Smith, Nassau Senior and the Mills. The statistical tables and empirical references in *Capital* do not offer proof of Marx's theoretical system; at most they are mere illustrations of the theoretical terrain.

This rejection of the idealist/empiricist problematic in epistemology is also closely connected with the anti-humanist stance taken by Althusserian structuralism. The *Theses on Feuerbach* were grounded in the notions of a universal essence of man and of an essence which is the attribute of 'each single individual', but such notions of human essence are characteristic of the idealist problematic. According to Althusser, Marx broke with these pre-scientific notions of human essence in the period 1845 and 1857 by formulating a theory of history based on the radically new concepts of social formation, mode of production and superstructure (Althusser, 1969, p. 35). This new theoretical apparatus was founded on a critique of philosophical humanism and on the recognition of humanism as ideology. The new theory—'a historico-dialectical materialism of *praxis'*—was 'a theory of the different specific levels of human practice (economic practice, political practice, ideological practice, scientific practice) in their characteristic articulations of the unity of human society' (Althusser, 1969, p. 229). Individual human subjects—their wants, nature, history or alienation—cannot be proper objects of science; the proper object of historical materialism as a science are the objective structures which constitute, distribute and interpellate the human subject within the production and reproduction processes.

This perspective on Marxism as the science of the structures and laws of the mode of production is inextricably connected with the structuralist approach to the problem of history and the 'place of the individual in history'. History as a discipline is a major haven for empiricism in its a-theoretical effort to describe how history happened by connecting together historical events in a temporal sequence. The empiricist problematic treats history as merely 'the unexpected, the accidental, the factually unique, arising or falling in the empty continuum of time, for purely contingent reasons' (Althusser and Balibar, 1970, p. 108). In contrast with the empiricist treatment of diachrony, Althusser, discussing passages in *The Poverty of Philosophy* and *Capital*, argues that the different levels of social formations have their own 'histories' which are connected together by a series of complex relationships. The concept of differential temporality of structures is basic to a range of Marxist concepts which point to disjunctures in time and space—'unevenness of development', 'survivals', 'backwardness' and 'underdevelopment'. There is no such thing as 'history in general, but only specific structures of historicity, based in the last resort on the specific structures of the different modes of production' (Althusser and Balibar, 1970, p. 108). The complexity of differential temporalities is not, however, a complexity inscribed in 'historical reality' and it is not an abstraction based on the essential complexity of historical processes. In other words, the theoretical complexity of Marxism is not a reflection of the complexity of reality; it is rather the product of a theoretical practice. Hence, Althusser's analysis of levels of historical time and his conceptualisation of the various structural levels are radically different from those sociological orientations which, having accepted the complexity of the given reality, are committed to notions of casual indeterminacy and multicausality. Althusser wants to produce not a theory of relationships between 'variables' or 'factors' in terms of statistical probabilities, but a deterministic theory of social formations and modes of production. Of course, this deterministic theory is not based on simple or mechanistic determinism, since it incorporates a range of concepts ('overdetermination', 'mediation', 'determinance/dominance') which attempt to theorise the complexity of the articulation between the structures without a direct reduction to the economic base. This epistemology allows Althusserianism, at least in principle, to extricate Marx and Marxism from the charge of simple economic determinism, while also erecting a massive theoretical barrier between Weberian sociology and Marxist science.

For Althusserians, Weber's sociology is subjectivist and embodies the principal errors of the idealist/empiricist epistemology. Weber's empiricist epistemology is clearly illustrated by, for example, the ideal type which is constructed by:

> the one-sided accentuation of one or more points of view
> and by the synthesis of a great many diffuse, discrete,
> more or less present and occasionally absent concrete in-
> dividual phenomena, which are arranged according to
> those onesidedly emphasised viewpoints into a unified
> analytical construct. (Weber, 1949, p. 90)

This methodological statement by Weber is interpreted to mean that an ideal type is constructed via a process of abstracting from and sifting through empirical reality. Such a procedure for the construction of ideal types exemplifies the empiricist problematic because the resulting type is an 'asymptotic adequation to the concrete reality from which it is drawn'. By contrast, Nicos Poulantzas aims to produce:

the concept of a regional instance of a mode of production,
not by an abstraction from the concrete real phenomena
of a social formation, but by the process of theoretical
construction of the concept of this mode of production
and of the articulation of the instances which specify it.
(Poulantzas, 1973a, p. 145)

Ideal type constructions presuppose an 'abstract/real' relationship which structuralism takes as a significant index of the presence of the empiricist problematic of knowledge.

There is, of course, considerable textual evidence to support the Althusserian characterisation of Weberian sociology as humanistic, subjectivist and individualist. At a later stage, I want to suggest that this reading of Weberian text is one-sided and misconceived, but my initial aim is simply to outline the basis of the Althusserian treatment of Weber's epistemological position. For instance, Weber does appear to be committed to a humanist problematic in presenting individual action as the only proper object of sociological inquiry. Weber's definition of sociology in *Economy and Society* would appear to be clear evidence of his concern for the subjective meaning of actions from the perspective of the willing, conscious individual. This individualistic interpretation of action follows from Weber's hostility to 'collectivist' concepts in that Weber overtly sought to establish a radical methodological individualism as the basis of his sociological perspective. In a letter to Robert Liefman in 1920, Weber claimed that:

if I have become a sociologist....it is mainly to exorcise the
spectre of collective conceptions which still lingers among
us. In other words, sociology itself can only proceed from
the actions of one or more separate individuals and must
therefore adopt strictly individualistic methods. (In Mommsen, 1965, p. 25)

Weber's overt commitment to methodological individualism
flows from Weber's personal adherence to a secularised Protestant individualism, from the decisionist ethics which he outlined

in 'Politics as a vocation' and 'Science as a vocation', and from his Nietzschean appreciation of heroism in the moral sphere. This individualistic commitment provides some warrant for the interpretation of Paul Q. Hirst (1975, p.4) that subjectivism, particularly in its neo-Kantian form, finds its ultimate foundation in Christian humanism and in a theology of free will. A similar connection can be made between Talcott Parsons's espousal of the voluntaristic theory of action and his concern with the Christian roots of ultimate value (Parsons, 1934-5). From the Althusserian perspective, Weber's involvement in neo-Kantian individualism is incompatible with the structuralist conception of Marxism as a deterministic science of structures in which 'individuals' appear as the agents or bearers (*'Trager'*) of objective functions.

From the Althusserian conception of scientific work, Weber's conception of the uniqueness, richness and complexity of historical reality and his apparent commitment to 'causal indeterminancy' preclude any rigorous treatment of historical transformations in terms of deterministic, causal models. Structuralist writers typically illustrate Weber's view of the significance of the value commitments of the scholar in the selection of causal factors by reference to *The Protestant Ethic and Spirit of Capitalism*, where Weber declared that his intention was not to substitute a 'one-sided spiritualistic explanation' for an equally 'one-sided materialistic' viewpoint. In Weber's overt methodology, explanation is approached as a form of democratic competition between conflicting approaches by which that theory which is most able to account for the variety and diversity of historical data will be accepted as provisionally valid. Once again the Weberian emphasis on causal indeterminacy, probability and empirical 'richness' contrasts with the structuralist orientation towards causally determinate explanations and with the notion that 'richness' is an effect of theory rather than a necessary feature of empirical reality. There appears to be, therefore, ample evidence for the structuralist claim that Weber's epistemology illustrates the basic characteristics of the idealist/empiricist problematic.

In their application of this epistemological critique, structuralists have attempted to contrast Marx's conceptualisation of capitalism as an objective, determinate structure with Weber's treatment of the rational core of capitalism as an ideal type of economic organisation, the motivations of Protestant entrepreneurs and the ideal type of bureaucratic rationality. For example, Hindess and Hirst (1975, p. 288) point to Weber's analysis of the origins of European capitalism as a conflict between traditonalism as an ethical system and the rational essence of capitalism or the 'spirit of capitalism' as a persistent bourgeois myth of primitive accumulation which had been demolished by Marx in 'The Secret of Primitive Accumulation'. Nicos Poulantzas has also commented on this feature of Weber's treatment of human agents as the real creators of the structures of capitalism which Poulantzas regards as a variety of Hegelian historicism whereby history is the unfolding of an inner essence such as the Idea or, in Weber's case, rationality. In particular:

> the historical problematic is Weber's expressly formulated conception of ideal types as abstract schemes having the possibility of being realized in the historical real concrete....Ideal types of authority and state do not cover structures in the strict sense of the term; in the last analysis they cover only the motives of the 'actors' conduct and behaviour. (Poulantzas, 1973a, p. 147)

Similarly, it is claimed by Poulantzas that Weber's ideal types of capitalism, bureaucracy, church and sect refer to individual behaviour and that all collectivist concepts must be reduced to the social actions of individuals. By contrast, for structuralists the attitudes and behaviour of individual capitalists are not relevant as objects of scientific inquiry since individual norms and behaviour are effects of the operation of objective structures. For Althusser,

> the true 'subjects' (in the sense of constitutive subjects of the process) are therefore not these occupants or functionaries, are not, despite all appearances, the 'obviousnesses' of the 'given' of naive anthropology, 'concrete individuals', 'real men' - but *the definition and*

> *distribution of these places and functions. The true 'subjects' are these definers and distributors: the relations of production.* (Althusser and Balibar, 1970, p. 180)

Weber is criticised consequently for reducing the political structure to a question of subjective legitimacy by reference to traditional, charismatic or rational-legal norms. Similarly, the problem of social classes is converted into the nature of social stratification in terms of individual access to the market and in terms of the differentiation of individuals according to their life-style, ethics and skills. The state is treated as a subject and the autonomy of the state is embodied in "its rationalising will" which operates through the medium of the bureaucracy (Poulantzas, 1975, p. 186).

These structuralist criticisms of Weber have been extended to cover a range of sociologists and Marxists who are treated as representatives of historicism and subjectivism. For instance, Poulantzas argues that Lukács' treatment of class consciousness and, in sociology, the functionalist analysis of system integration are both examples of the conceptualisation of the unity of a social formation as an 'expressive totality' which is derived from Weber and Hegel. The theoretical connection between Lukács, Parsons and Weber

> is that the global structure is, in the last analysis considered as the *product* of a society-subject which in its teleological becoming creates certain social values or ends....For Weber, these social values are the crystallization of social actors' projects and are the elements out of which his ideal types are formed...the theory of class consciousness of Lukács...presupposes an expressive totality, within which there is simply no rule for a dominant factor (as Weber himself correctly saw), yet at the same time it attributes to ideology the role of dominant factor in the social whole. (Poulantzas, 1973a, p. 199)

For Althusser and Poulantzas, by contrast, the social formation is never integrated around a changeless essence; the social formation is conceptualised as an ensemble of contradictory political, economic and ideological structures in which the dominant structure is always determined in the last instance by the economic. The social formation is not a seamless web of integrated structures, but a conjuncture which is periodically ruptured by the mutually reinforced ('overdetermined') contradictions between economics, politics and ideology. Whereas Lukács and Weber treat class-in-itself and status groups as the historical subjects of political and economic struggles, Poulantzas regards social classes as effects of the complex determination of the social formation by the mode of production.

These criticisms of the Marxism of Georg Lukács are developed by Poulantzas to attack the sociological analyses of power and social class by such diverse writers as Ralf Dahrendorf (*Class and Class Conflict in an Industrial Society*), C. Wright Mills (*The Power Elite*), R. Miliband (*The State in Capitalist Society*) and James Burnham (*The Managerial Revolution*). According to Poulantzas, Dahrendorf's dependence on Weberian theory (such as the concentration on relationships of command, the separation of status groups from economically determined class relations, and the notion of 'imperatively co-ordinated associations') produces a number of important epistemological and theoretical errors. Dahrendorf's analysis of 'social groups' and C. Wright Mill's conceptualisation of the 'power elite' are mistaken attempts to solve economistic and historicist definitions of class relations. In Poulantzian terms, social classes are the effects of a complex determination by economic, political and ideological structures and class relations are necessarily at every level also relations of power—'power, however, is only a concept indicating the effect of the ensemble of structures on *the relations of the practices of the various classes in conflict*' (Poulantzas, 1973a, p. 101). The conventional sociological distinctions between 'power elites', 'political classes' and 'dominant groups' derive from Weber's separation of power (political parties), status (status groups) and economy (classes defined by distribution rather than production of surplus) and are associated with the premise that the individuals who constitute such 'groups' are in some sense outside or above class relations. In Poulantzian theory, class fractions, strata and social categories cannot be

conceptualised independently of class relations, since they are
not, as it were, additional to the class structure.

These objections to the conventional sociology of stratification have been most directly illustrated by the debate between
Poulantzas and Miliband over the characterisation of state
power in late capitalism. In attempting to challenge the
pluralist view of power, Miliband has attacked 'bourgeois'
sociology on its own epistemological grounds. One method of
countering the notion of competing and separate elites is to
show that in fact the members of the various sections of the
power bloc (the Church, big business, civil service, local elites
and parliament) are all interconnected by common attitudes,
common training at public schools and intermarriage. Such a
method of criticism is, however, tantamount to employing
Weberian epistemology to undermine Weberian sociology. Instead of approaching social classes and the state as objective
structures, Miliband proceeds as if social classes were reducible
to inter-personal relations; he treats the relations between
social classes and the state as 'reducible to inter-personal relations of "individuals" composing social groups and "individuals" composing the State apparatus' (Poulantzas,
1973b, p. 295). This subjectivist flaw results in a set of false
problems about managerialism, economic ownership and profit
motivation.

There is, therefore, a strong *prima facie* case to be made
against Weber in favour of the structuralist argument that
Weber's sociology treats objective structural relations in
terms of the motives, beliefs and behaviour of individual social
actors. Weber's epistemological commentaries—*The
Methodology of the Social Sciences, Roscher and Knies: the
logical problems of historical economics* and the
methodological observations in *The Protestant Ethic and the
Spirit of Capitalism*—provide *overt* evidence for regarding
Weber's sociology as an extreme form of subjective
methodological individualism. However, the point of a structuralist reading of a text is that the author's overt intention
and the surface meaning of a text are not necessarily the most
appropriate guide for uncovering the covert, implicit problematic which informs and determines the surface meaning of a

literary product. While Althusserian structuralism has attempted to discover the hidden meaning of *Capital*, it has not performed the same type of operation on Weber's sociology. Instead, structuralist criticism of Weber has proceeded by stringing together *ad hoc* observations on Weber's sociology without uncovering the inner 'discourse' of Weberian sociology. The inner meaning of Weber's sociology treats individual intention and purpose as determined by the fateful working out of objective constraints which produces a view of structural determination which is in practice parallel to a structuralist view of necessity.

There is an abundance of biographical and textual evidence to suggest that Weber's own life and the content of his sociology were profoundly influenced by his paradoxical commitment to biblical religion and his conviction that any genuine adherence to religious principles was ruled out by the processes of rationalisation and secularisation in modern society. On the one hand, the sociology of religion provides the key to Weber's sociology as a whole (Wilson, 1976) and, on the other, Weber's overriding sense of the problem of *deus absconditus* which is the root of Weber's 'tragic vision' informs his bleak, pessimistic outlook on capitalism. For example, *The Protestant Ethic and the Spirit of Capitalism* has often been taken to be an anti-materialist thesis demonstrating the autonomy of religious values from economic circumstances. In fact, these two essays provide a cultural history of the *failure* of spiritual values to maintain their own religious authenticity and authority. The 'spirit of capitalism' represented not the triumph of Protestantism over secular practices, but rather the collapse of a genuine religious quest for personal salvation. Weber's attitude to this eventuality is dramatically summarised by a quotation from John Wesley which Weber takes from Robert Southey's *Life of Wesley*. Speculating about the future prospects of English Methodism, Wesley wrote that 'I fear, wherever riches have increased, the essence of religion has decreased in the same proportion. Therefore I do not see how it is possible, in the nature of things, for any revival of true religion to continue long' (Weber, 1965, p. 175). This quotation is an accurate summary of Weber's negative heterogony of purposes, namely that human intentions are subverted in a negative direction by historical processes which exist outside individual human control.

Although the notion of 'ethical neutrality' has been connected with the picture of the emotionally neutral, politically detached observer, Weber was deeply involved at an emotional level in his studies of religious movements. Weber was religiously unmusical ('Ich bin zwar religiös absolut unmusikalisch'), but in 1909 Weber also observed that 'a thorough self-examination has told me that I am neither antireligious *nor irreligious'*. The struggles of the prophets of doom, the ascetic striving of the Protestant virtuoso and the inner longing of the saints had a profound impact on Weber's imagination, but at the same time he felt intellectually cut off from the beliefs which provided the ultimate rationale for these religious quests. As Marianne Weber tells us, this study of world religions 'is connected with the deepest roots of his personality and in an undefinable way bears its stamp' (Weber, 1975, p. 335). The failure of these quests for salvation from an historical perspective 'tugged at his heartstrings' and provided a particular illustration of Weber's more general pessimistic view of history. This aspect of Weber's sociology was further underlined by Marianne Weber's observation that her husband was:

> moved, above all, by the fact that its earthly course an idea always and everywhere operates in opposition to its original meaning and thereby destroys itself. And one also seems to detect some of Weber's own features in the magnificent figures of a heroic Puritanism which he presents. (Weber, 1975, p. 337)

Thus the inspired wrath of the Israelite prophets against the *nabis* and soothsayers became the domesticated doctrine of a parish community; Muhammad's monotheistic vision became the ideology of conquest; Calvin's theodicy became the practical ethic of work, discipline and efficiency.

This pessimistic motif that ideas are inevitably self-destructive was not confined to Weber's specific studies of the world religions. The secularisation of religious ideals provided Weber with a major perspective on the character of modern politics. The problem which lies at the heart of the two lectures given in Munich in 1919—'Science as a vocation' and 'Politics as a vocation'—is that modern science becomes the central criterion by which any rational person approaches reality, but science itself is not a source of ultimate values. Science is merely a routinised procedure for evaluating means for achieving goals. The ultimate ends of human activity therefore take on a random, irrational quality, because science cannot tell us what we *ought* to do. In historical terms, charismatic religious movements have been the principal generators of those absolute values for which people were willing to make great sacrifices. However, religion has been secularised by a process of rationalisation, of which science is the primary example. The critical problem for modern society is that:

> the routines of everyday life challenge religion. Many old gods ascend from their graves; they are disenchanted and hence take the form of impersonal forces. They strive to gain power over our lives and again they resume their eternal struggle with one another. What is hard for modern man, and especially for the younger generation, is to measure up to *workaday* existence. (Weber, 1961, p. 149)

Weber conceptualises the secular world of politics and science as a struggle between competing gods, as a polytheistic realm of conflicting and disenchanted divinities over which human beings have little effective control. This world, from which the scholar and politician are alienated, is determined not by reason but by fate –

> Fate, and certainly not 'science', holds sway over these gods and their struggles. One can only understand what the godhead is for the one order or for the other, or better what godhead is in the one or in the other order. With

this understanding, however, the matter has reached its limit so far as it can be discussed in a lecture-room and by a professor. (Weber, 1961, p. 148)

Because Weber had rejected the teleological assumption that history had any inner meaning and because he was not prepared to make the intellectual sacrifice which was entailed by a return to the wide arms of the Church, he was left with the notion that a 'calling' in the secular world required personal intellectual integrity to face 'the fate of the times'.

These textual and biographical references provide the clue to the inner structure of Weber's sociology. The overt emphasis of Weber's sociology is on the role of the active individual who constructs and creates the meaning of social interaction and on the role of the sociologists who interpret the rational and motivational meanings of social actions. The covert theme of Weber's sociology is that the ultimate origin of the meanings of action is to be found in charismatic, religious movements and that these absolute values dig their own graves with the inevitable logic of fate. The charisma of prophets, saints and other virtuosi provided the dynamic for new values and institutions, but 'Max Weber knew that, once they had come about, social structures were apt to generate their own developmental tendencies; and he devoted a substantial part of his sociological work to exploring them' (Mommsen, 1965, p. 30). These 'developmental tendencies' invariably have a negative, gravedigger quality which undermines the pristine value and significance of charisma. For example, in its struggle with magic, Protestantism laid the foundations for a scientific view of nature as an organised, predictable reality and in turn science laid the foundation for a view of social reality stripped of the mysterious and numinous. Paradoxically science has released a realm of irrational, polytheistic values which are controlled by fate rather than by science. The issue is to turn these indications of a covert problematic into a more systematic statement of the logical organisation of Weber's sociology.

While Althusserian structuralists have not performed a structuralist interpretation of Weber's sociology, Frederic

Jameson in 'The Vanishing Mediator: narrative structure in Max Weber' (1973) has employed the methodology of the French structuralist A.J. Greimas (1966; 1970) to capture the 'plot' in Weber's text. The general aim of Greimas's structuralism is to produce a disciplined method for characterising the meaning of the discourse of a text by locating the elementary units of its isotopy. The isotopy of the text is the set of recurrent, reiterative semantic categories which inform the discourse. Once the random, superflous features of the text have been eliminated, the corpus of the textual message is then broken down into a series of minimal units in terms of the relationships between combinations of 'semes' (capitalist/worker; magic/science; prophet/priest, etc.). The next stage of analysis involves the 'normalisation' of the text by providing a syntaxis or codification of sentences into 'actants' and 'predicates'. Actants are classified in terms of six types of roles—subject, object, sender, receiver, opponent and helper, while predicates are divided into qualifications and functions. These categories provide the basis for the construction of the structural model of the text. In practice, the actantial model is based on a relatively simple model in which a subject desires an object which is also an object of communication between a sender and a receiver. The subject is at the same time located between a helper and an opponent. In diagrammatic form, we have Figure 1.1.

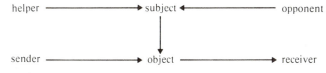

Figure 1.1

A fairy tale has, for example, the typical structure of a subject who desires a princess with the aid of a white magician against the opposition of a villain. The happy dénouement occurs when the king sends his daughter to the triumphant hero. The basic approach of Greimas may also be relevant for the analysis of complex myths and ideology or for any communication which has a narrative structure.

In Jameson's view, there is, as it were, a mythical garment enveloping Weber's scientific work, namely that 'intellectual integrity' brings the ascetic, neutral scholar to record the 'struggle between the gods' in the fate-determined world of politics and science. Historians and sociologists are engaged in the enterprise of telling 'the story of the various "gods" and of their struggles with each other, a story which sometimes, like those told by Nietzsche, involves the mystery of a god's death. What more fitting object, then, for narrative analysis?' (Jameson, 1973, p. 63). Weber's sociology, as Talcott Parsons, Herbert Marcuse and others have frequently observed, is based on a set of formal dichotomies: bureaucracy versus charisma, feudalism versus prebendalism, asceticism versus mysticism, *Realpolitik* versus ethics, priest versus magician. Jameson utilises Greimas's 'semantic rectangle' to generate a set of binary oppositions from Weber's dichotomous models. A term S has its opposite in anti-S and, by extension, we can construct a related opposition between not S and not anti-S as in Figure 1.2.

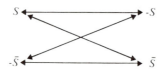

Figure 1.2

This structure provides us with a method of systematically organising the principal 'semes' of the discourse of Weber's sociological narrative. For example, Weber contrasts the power of the magician, which is based on his personal charismatic prestige, employing magical powers to achieve individual gain and the power of the priesthood, which is rooted in a universalistic doctrine and the bureaucratic authority of his role within the Church (see Figure 1.3).

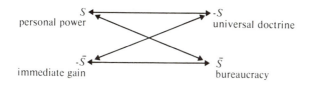

Figure 1.3

In this scheme 'immediate gain' and 'bureaucracy' are not positive explanations, but negative reflexes of the primary distinction between 'personal power' and 'universal doctrine'. We can, furthermore, treat 'magician' as a synthesis of 'personal power' (S) and 'immediate gain' (not anti-S), while 'priest' is the synthesis of 'universal doctrine' (anti-S) and 'bureaucracy' (not S). This combination in turn suggests a final synthesis between S and -S, and -S and S by the terms 'prophet' and 'modern man'. The prophet, in Weber's sociology of religion, breaks the power of the magician and appears as the agent of rationalisation. By working against the importance of personal gain, the prophet prepares the way for bureaucracy which in turn replaces the charismatic authority of prophecy. The outcome of the historical process of rationalisation from its origins in religious prophecy is the emergence of modern, secular man who operates without the benefit of magic or prophetic intervention. The semantic rectangle of Weber's sociology is thus completed as in Figure 1.4.

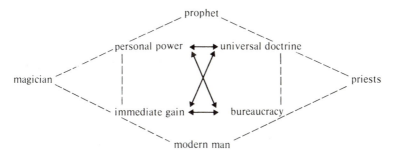

Figure 1.4

The apparently static dichotomies are thereby linked together to form a dynamic narrative of the rise of modern man out of the ashes of religious prophecy and charismatic breakthrough.

The main theme of Jameson's analysis is to show that the recurrent 'plot' of Weber's sociological 'stories' involves an account of the tragic role of the 'vanishing mediator'. Social change is brought about by a set of values and institutions which liquidates existing traditional arrangements and prepares the groundwork for a new social order. In the context of the new social order, however, the revolutionary function of these values and institutions is no longer required and the charismatic mediator vanishes as an effect of its own historical success. As Jameson notes, this story of self-destruction is repeated throughout Weber's sociology in, for example, his analysis of the role of Roman law, Bismarck and the unification of Germany, prophecy and the rise of science. The principal illustration, however, remains Weber's account of the routinisation of the Calvinistic doctrine of the religious calling. By driving religious asceticism into the world so that every Christian in his everyday world became a monk, Calvinism gave a definite stamp to the character of factory discipline, business calculation and capitalist organisation. The result was not only the death of God but the imprisonment of men within the 'iron cage' of capitalist relations of production. The fate of Calvinism resulted in the fact that 'the spirit of religious asceticism...has escaped from the cage. But victorious capitalism, since it rests on mechanical foundations, needs its support no longer (Weber, 1965, pp. 181–2). This narrative 'tugged at his heartstrings' because sociology—at once the narrative medium of routinisation and the effect of routinisation—was silent as to the meaning and significance of these events which the unmusical Weber was forced to watch as a mere bystander.

In reply to the structuralist critique that Weber reduces social phenomena to the free will of the subjective individual, I have attempted to show that in fact Weber's pessimism produces a deterministic sociology in which the intentions of social actors are overtaken by historical fate. An obvious objection to this interpretation of Weber would be that, while

Weber does adhere to a doctrine of negative heterogony of purposes, his sociology is fundamentally individualistic. It is the individual and not the social group, class or social system which is overwhelmed by historical fate; in short, by rejecting any 'collectivist' terminology, Weber treats social relations as the effects of individual wills. My argument is that, although Weber's early statements on epistemology do rule out both collectivist concepts and general laws, his substantive work, especially the studies of world religions in *Archiv für Sozialwissenschaft* after 1915, has a very different character. In his research on the role of the major salvational religions, Weber specifically argued that it was not the religion of the individual that was sociologically important and that it was not even important that the religion was accepted and believed in by individuals. For example, in *The Religion of India* (vol. 11, *Religionssoziologie*), in the discussion of the ethical determinism of the *karma* doctrine, Weber observed that:

it is of no importance that the individual pious Hindu did not always have before his eyes, as a total system, the pathetic presuppositions of the Karma doctrine which transformed the world into a strictly rational and ethically determined cosmos. He remained confined to the cage which only made sense through this ideal system, and the consequences weighed down upon his action. (Weber, 1958b, and quoted in Outhwaite, 1975, p. 54)

The Althusserian conception of ideology as a structure of practices which have effects on the individual and which insert the individual into places in the social structure does not appear to be inherently different from Weber's view of Indian religious culture as an 'ethically determined cosmos' which, regardless of individually held conceptions, has 'consequences' for action. Weber's observation on the effects of Islam is equally clear on this issue:

Industrialisation was not impeded by Islam as the religion of individuals—the Tartars in the Russian Caucasus are often very 'modern' entrepreneurs—but by the religiously determined structure of the Islamic *states*, their officialdom and their jurisprudence. (Weber, 1968, vol. 3, p. 1095)

The course of rationalisation, therefore, is not an effect of the choices and motivations of subjective individuals, but the effect of a common culture which characterises the life of social groups and classes.

This argument, that Weber's sociology is in practice consistently anti-individualistic, can be strengthened by an examination of that classic text—*The Protestant Ethic and the Spirit of Capitalism*—where Weber is conventionally interpreted to be in his most anti-materialist mood. To state my position emphatically, the whole point of this study of Protestantism is to show that capitalism cannot be explained by reference to social psychological, let alone psychological, states of individuals. For example, rational capitalism has nothing to do with the individual drive for gain or with a psychologistically conceived achievement motive. If anything, Weber thought that 'Asiatics' were more inclined to a purely personal quest for gain, whereas boundless 'greed for gain is not in the least identical with capitalism, and is still less in spirit. Capitalism *may* even be identical with restraint, or at least a rational tempering, of this irrational impulse' (Weber, 1965, p. 17). Capitalism requires, for Weber, the rational and systematic restraint from immediate personal consumption by capitalists in order to accumulate surpluses which can be invested in further production of capital. A capitalist enterprise which failed to adhere to this 'law' of accumulation 'would be doomed to extinction'.

For Weber, therefore, the nature of capitalist relations does not emerge from the characteristics of thrifty individuals, but from a set of structures which impose rationality on the behaviour of social actors. Once again, Weber's tragic sense of fate tinges his account of capitalism with a strong sense of pessimism. Weber's description of capitalism resembles both Durkheim's view of 'social facts' as external, objective and constraining and the structuralist conceptualisation of capitalism as a relation which cannot be reduced to interpersonal interactions. Thus, Weber defines the capitalist economy as

> an immense cosmos into which the individual is born, and which presents itself to him, at least as an individual, as an unalterable order of things in which he must live. It forces the individual, in so far as he is involved in the system of market relationships, to conform to capitalistic rules of action. The manufacturer who in the long run acts counter to these norms, will just as inevitably be eliminated from the economic scene as the worker who cannot or will not adapt himself to them will be thrown into the streets without a job. (Weber, 1965, p. 55)

While Marx does not generally discuss capitalism in terms of 'the system of market relations' or refer to relations of production in terms of 'norms' and 'rules of action', there is a common and central theme between these two approaches to capitalism, namely that the labourer is forced to work in order to survive and the capitalist is forced to accumulate in order to stay in business. As Marx tersely observes, capitalism 'presupposes the complete separation of the labourers from all property in the means by which they can realise their labour' (Marx, 1974, vol. 1, p. 668). Similarly, just as Marx often employs Darwinistic analogies to describe the specialisation of labour skills under the capitalist division of labour, so Weber comments that capitalism 'educates and selects the economic subjects' it requires for production according to 'a process of economic survival of the fittest' (Weber, 1965, p. 55).

There are, of course, enormous differences between Weber's sociology and the scientific Marxism of modern structuralism. I have tried to demonstrate that Weber's sociology of fate is riddled with religious metaphors and analogies and that Weber's own existential problem centred on the difficulty of survival in a world where the religious reservoir of absolute values had dried up. The structuralist metatheoretical *Weltanschauung* is entirely different. However, Weber's sociology cannot be characterised as subjectivist, individualist and voluntarist with the result that there are a number of paradoxical parallels between Weberian determinism and structuralist determinism. Furthermore, the idea that the structuralist critique of Weber provides the theoretical vehicle for the demolition of sociology as a whole is questionable on the grounds that the structuralist epistemology is problematic and that structuralist explanations in practice often borrow heavily from sociology and cannot be clearly distinguished from various forms of sociological structuralism, such as structural-functionalism.

The major Marxist schools and theoreticians of Europe after the Second International have been characteristically anti-economist and the Marxist critique of naive materialism has often drawn heavily from philosophical idealism and from neo-Kantian subjectivism. This generalisation applies to Althusserian structuralism as much as to such diverse figures as Max Adler, Georg Lukács, Antonio Gramsci, Theodor Adorno and Herbert Marcuse. Althusser, however, attempts to provide the critique of *both* simple economic materialism and subjective humanism, which sharply distinguishes Althusserian Marxism from, for example, the Frankfurt School, which takes Marx's humanistic view of alienation as an essential element of the radical critique of human exploitation. In order to oppose humanism, Althusser has placed immense emphasis on the scientific status of Marxist theory and this stress on the separation of science and ideology has led some writers (Bernstein, 1979, p. 189) to conclude that Althusser offers a positivistic interpretation of Marx. However, the dominant feature of Althusserianism has essentially idealistic implications. There are a number of aspects to this charge of idealism. In his account of the origins of scientific paradigms, Althusser pays no attention to the social and economic constraints which determine the content and direction of scientific discovery; on the contrary, science emerges as the effect of internal theoretical debates and struggles as a purely autonomous development. Marx, in discovering the new terrain of the science of history, is a Columbus of theory in the same role as Spinoza and Freud. Scientific work requires a *subject* which discovers a new problematic, a new theoretical *object*: 'Marx is such a discovering subject. Marx is comparable to Newton, founding mechanics without ancestors, or Darwin seeking precursors in vain' (Fraser, 1976-7, p. 458). It could be justifiably argued that Althusser reduces the relations of scientific production to the subjective will of individuals in the same way that Weber is accused of reducing the relations of material production to meaningful social interactions. A further feature of this odd parallel between Althusserian epistemology and the alleged epistemological subjectivism of Weberian sociology is that both epistemologies assume that the object of theory is never a pre-given reality. For Weber, the conceptual schema of science—such as ideal types—are not discovered in reality, but are constructed according to the values and theoretical interests of the observer. Thus, there is a remarkable homology between Althusser's insistence on the "constructed" character of the object of scientific knowledge and the neo-Kantians' insistence on the same point (Benton, 1977, p. 185). Of course, Althusserian Marxists claim that Weber constructs his ideal types by sifting through the infinity of empirical reality in order to accentuate certain given elements. However, there is little evidence that Weber actually followed this procedure in constructing, for instance, the ideal type of 'the spirit of capitalism'. Rather, Weber engages in a theoretical debate over the connections between religious culture and capitalist development employing theoretical models and ideas which were already present in historical/ sociological research.

The important difference between Weber and Althusser is that Weber did not in practice employ neo-Kantian, subjectivist epistemology, whereas there is no clear gap between Althusser's statements of intention and execution. It would, in fact, be more accurate to say that Althusser outlines a procedure of Marxist analysis without applying this procedure to the 'concrete-in-thought'. In short, Althusser tells us how to produce knowledge but there are few examples of how the transition from Generalities I to Generalities III is actually realised. One of the few fruitful applications of Althusser's paradigm of Marxist theory is to be found in Poulantzas's studies of late capitalism, dictatorship and the state. Unfortunately, the problems of Poulantzas's analyses of social formations provide further evidence of the unresolved conceptual problems in Althusserian epistemology and theory.

As a conclusion to this study of the structuralist critique of Weber's sociology, I shall present three basic criticisms of the Marxism of Nicos Poulantzas to demonstrate the weakness of structuralism in general as an alternative to Weberian sociology. The first criticism is that while Poulantzas wants to show the existence of a clear separation between scientific Marxism and the ideological practice of conventional sociology, Poulantzas in fact borrows from and is dependent upon sociology, especially Weberian sociology. We find that *Political Power and Social Classes* is riddled with evidence and quotations from American political science, Parsonian sociology and Weber's studies of bureaucracy and the state. Although Poulantzas attempts to criticise sociological analyses of power, the state and social classes, his own theory of the state as an institution which provides cohesion and integration within the social formation is a structural-functionalist conception (Clarke, 1977). Similarly, in *Classes in Contemporary Capitalism* Poulantzas attempts to provide a theory of the new petty bourgeois in terms of three structures (politics, ideology and economics), but he does this by reference to existing sociological categories of socio-economic occupational groups (Abercrombie *et al.*, 1976). In Poulantzas's study of the state and law (1978) there is a very clear dependence on Weber in that the state is defined in terms of the monopoly of force and the law in bourgeois capitalism is seen as a system of abstract, gapless and universal rules.

The second general problem in Poulantzas's structural Marxism is that his theory fails to resolve the basic problems of the base/superstructure metaphor. Poulantzas attempts to overcome the reductionism of vulgar economism by claiming that the political, economic and ideological structures have a relative autonomy so that social classes, for example, are defined by all three structures rather than by the economic alone. The nature and operation of these structures are still, however, defined by the particular character of the mode of production. In Poulantzas's study of capitalism, the ideological and political structures become indistinguishable because Poulantzas adopts Althusser's treatment of the state apparatus which is simultaneously an ideological and political apparatus. These reduce the structures to two, the political/ideological structure and the economy, in which the latter determines the former. Political practices are determined by class relations which are themselves the product of economic contradictions in the mode of production. In practice, the political structure has very little autonomy from economic relations.

Finally, the central role of class struggle between capital and labour in capitalist society is minimised in Poulantzian Marxism. There are a number of reasons why this elimination of class struggle takes place. *Classes in Contemporary Capitalism* and *Fascism and Dictatorship* are both based on the assumption that the working class has been defeated by the failure of working-class political movements, by ideological incorporation and by the success of political control by the capitalist state. The central focus of Poulantzas's work is, therefore, the conflicts between the various fractions of capital—competitive versus monopoly capital, finance versus industrial capital, international versus local capital—within the power bloc where the state plays its cohesive role. In addition, because Poulantzas treats social classes as effects of the mode of production, historical change is treated, not as an outcome of the struggle between classes, but as a consequence of the inner maturation of the mode of production. Poulantzas has not successfully incorporated class struggle into the explanation of modes of production. This failure gives additional support to the view that the Althusserian-Poulantzian model involves a teleological conception of history, regardless of their protests to the contrary, in which history unfolds as a result of the inner logic of the mode rather than as a consequence of the struggle of social classes over the production and distribution of the surplus.

Weber emerges relatively unscathed from the structuralist criticism of Althusser and Poulantzas. Weber has a clear conception of the structural constraints which determine individual behaviour and of the way in which a system of constraints has a 'logic' or 'fate' which overrides individual intention and consciousness. His sociology is not subjectivist and individualistic. At the same time, Weber rejected any attempt to establish general laws of history which stipulated certain inevitable outcomes of developmental tendencies within society. The logic of fate of a social system or process was subject to particular, contingent features of a given historical conjuncture.

3 Weber and the Frankfurt School

Whereas the structuralist perspective in contemporary Marxism resulted in criticisms of Weber's alleged subjectivism and reduction of structural constraints to personal will, the group of Marxists associated with the Institut für Sozialforschung in Frankfurt am Main (the Frankfurt School) has generated a very different opposition to Weber and Weberian sociology. Although certain political and social linkages can be drawn between structuralist and Frankfurt Marxism (Anderson, 1976), there are clear theoretical differences. Althusser wants to extricate Marxism from any associations with a positivist economism, but he wants to underline the scientificity of Marxian analysis of the structures and motions of modes of production. The Frankfurt School also attempts to distinguish Marxist analysis from a natural science model of society, but, rather than emphasising the scientific claims of Marxism, the School has always understood Marxism as a 'critical theory'. The point of this critique is to produce, through a process of self-reflection at the level of the individual and the group, an awareness of and liberation from the socially produced constraints on thought and action. Whereas science is grounded in technical interests which are aimed at the manipulation of the environment, critical theory is founded on an emancipatory interest which requires the liberation of human beings from the contingent constraints of historical societies.

This difference in conception of the nature of Marxism can be illustrated by reference to their distinctive attitudes to Freudian psychoanalysis. The early Frankfurt School treated Marx's analysis of capitalism as the paradigm for critical theory, but they nevertheless recognised the importance of an 'historical materialist psychology' (Slater, 1977) to plug the conceptual gap between economic structures and the psychology of the individual. In orthodox Marxism, the intrusion of any psychological or psychoanalytical theories was regarded as an unwarranted eclecticism. In the Frankfurt School, Freudian psychoanalytic theory has been important in the study of prejudice (Adorno, *et al.*, 1950), the treatment of repression in capitalist society (Marcuse 1969a) and as a model for critical theory itself (Habermas, 1972). In *Knowledge and Human Interests*, Habermas (1972, p. 228) draws attention to the process of self-reflection in emancipatory social science and the process of understanding in hermeneutic psychology. In Freudian therapeutic talk, the analyst attempts to make the meaning of illness intelligible to the analysand by a process of mutual interaction and self-reflection. The therapist does not, therefore, impose a pre-constructed meaning on to the discourse of the patient. Rather, by overcoming the resistance of the neurotic, the analyst encourages self-inspection and biographical analysis. Psychoanalysis has emancipatory, critical interests rather than pragmatic, instrumental concerns and provides a model for the process whereby critical theory encourages intersubjective reflection on the distortions and constraints of industrial society.

The 'eclecticism' of Althusserian Marxism in relation to Freud has taken a very different direction. Like Marx, Freud was less a critical theorist than a scientist who, in breaking with an ideological problematic, discovered the new scientific terrain of the unconscious. The importance of Freud for Habermas is the psychoanalytic *method* of self-reflection and enlightenment; the importance of Freud for Althusser is the *theoretical* stature of psychoanalysis as a science. Thus Althusser criticises those interpretations which approach Freudianism as 'a mere practice' claiming instead that 'psycho-analysis is a science because it is the science of a distinct object, it is also a science with the structure of all sciences: it has a *theory* and a *technique* (method) that make possible the knowledge and transformation of its object in a specific *practice*' (Althusser, 1971, p. 184). However, while Freudian psychoanalysis could be regarded as constitutive of Habermas's view of self-reflexity, in Althusserian Marxism Freud's epistemological breakthrough provides merely an analogy alongside other scientific ruptures. Thus, Althusser borrows a variety of Freudian terms—'overdetermination', 'displacement' and 'condensation'—to express the contradictions of structures, but there is no suggestion that scientific Marxism logically requires supplementation from psychoanalysis or individual psychology. The objects of these sciences are different—the history of the structures of modes of production and the structure of the unconscious as theoretical objects.

This contrast in approaches to Freud reveals a more radical difference, namely their opposed conception of Marx's relationship to classical German philosophy. The aim of structuralist interpretation is to preserve the immaculate separation of Marxian science from political economy, from German philosophy and from sociology (Merquior, 1979, p. 107). The Frankfurt School not only rejects any division of Marx's work into scientific and pre-scientific, it has sought the origins of the Marxian critique in the classical German philosophical tradition of both Hegel and Kant. Instead of theoretical discontinuity, the School embraced the continuity of the critical tradition from Kant's *Critique of Pure Reason* to Marx's *Critique of Political Economy* via Hegel's *Phenomenology of Mind*. As Connerton (1976, p. 15) has pointed out, Habermas's theory of knowledge remains faithful to the central aspect of classical German philosophy in which the development of rational thought and true beliefs cannot be separated from the existence of social and political freedoms. The political conditions for discourse cannot be regarded as accidental to truth claims. Critical theory recognises the fact that 'the truth of statements is based on anticipating the realisation of the good life', whereas pure theory creates the illusion that 'Socratic dialogue is possible everywhere and at any time' (Habermas, 1972, p. 314).

Whereas Althusser has found it difficult to discover a firm location for philosophy in relation to science and politics (Fraser, 1976, pp. 458–60), the philosophical critique of the social conditions of knowledge has been central to the

Frankfurt School's treatment of Marxian dialectical thought as simply *one* version of critical theory in general. This openness to self-reflection in art, in hermeneutics, in Freudianism and in sociology is characteristic of the Frankfurt School which fought against any dogmatic analysis of Marx's texts. While it is true that 'Critical Theory is best approached not as a "branch" of sociology but as a phenomenon of German intellectual history' (Connerton, 1976, p. 15), the openness of critical theory to sociology is important and distinguishes the Frankfurt School from the Althusserian rejection of bourgeois sociology as ideology. The intellectual traffic between Frankfurt Marxism and conventional sociology has been established over a long period.

The Frankfurt School members have consistently raised objections to and criticisms of the standard methodological procedures of empirical sociology (for example, Pollock, 1976). Despite this opposition to quantitative sociology, the School came to produce, during the exile in the United States, a number of empirical investigations which have been regarded as landmarks in the development of sociology. These studies, with the general title of *Studies in Prejudice*, were *The Authoritarian Personality* (Adorno *et al.*, 1950), *Dynamics of Prejudice* (Bettelheim and Janowitz, 1950), *Prophets of Deceit* (Lowenthal and Guterman, 1949), *Anti-Semitism and Emotional Disorder* (Ackerman and Jahoda, 1950), and *Rehearsal for Destruction* (Paul Massing, 1949). Aspects of this research had been anticipated by a collection of essays with the title *Studien über Autorität und Familie* (1936). In methodological terms, these empirical studies are interesting because they employ interviews and questionnaires, psychological typologies and scales, individual psychological variables and hypotheses. When the School returned to Germany in the 1950s, Adorno found himself in the peculiar role of defending empirical research techniques against the opposition of German academics. While Martin Jay (1973) argues that the Frankfurt School never abandoned its critique of mindless empiricism and the cult of quantification, Althusserian Marxists have been particularly critical of this form of electism. Thus Göran Therborn (1977, p. 108) condemns the *Studies in Pre-*

judice on the grounds that 'the stress on individual psychology becomes a complete capitulation to bourgeois social psychology in theory, method and political conclusions'. He goes on to observe that Marcuse's explanation of working-class incorporation depends on the analyses of 'academic American sociology' and that, in his analysis of capitalism, he depends more on writers like William H. Whyte and Vance Packard than on Marxist research.

My argument is that the ambiguous relationship of the Frankfurt School to sociology in general and to empirical methodology in particular is reproduced clearly and crucially in the School's relationship to the sociology of Max Weber. The School and its allies, most notably Jürgen Habermas, have overtly criticised and argued against Weber while covertly accepting and incorporating Weber's analysis of capitalist society. The analyses of the Frankfurt School become *more* rather than less Weberian as their pessimism towards the possibility of revolution on the basis of an autonomous working-class struggle has increased. In other words, the more the School abandons orthodox Marxism, the more Weberian becomes its sociological, intellectual and political character.

The criticisms of Weber which have been developed by the Frankfurt School can be organised under three topics. First, critical theorists accepted the essential features of Weber's account of the process of rationalisation, especially as that process gained momentum under capitalist economic relationships. Like Weber, critical theorists think that late capitalism is characterised by bureaucratisation, by an increasing intervention of science into every detail of everyday life, by the disappearance of every tinge of numinous feeling, by the routinisation of work and play, and finally by a pervasive institutionalisation of 'the iron cage'. They argue, however, that the increasing formal and instrumental rationality of capitalist society was accompanied by massive substantive irrationality. This problem about rationality and rationalisation lay at the heart of the dispute between Marcuse and others at the fifteenth German Sociological Congress at Heidelberg on the centenary of Weber's birth, in 1964 (Stammer, 1971). The Frankfurt School's criticism of Weber's concept of instrumental reason (*Zweckrationalitaet*) is directly related to their existential experience of German capitalism and their sociological fate as a stratum of the German intelligentsia. The original leaders of the School – Friedrich Pollock, Theodor Adorno, Max Horkheimer, Carl Grünberg, Leo Lowenthal and Herbert Marcuse—were from prosperous, bourgeois, Jewish backgrounds. Founded in 1923, the School was eventually forced into exile in the United States from 1934 to 1949 following the Nazi victory of 1933. The total destruction of their cultured, high bourgeois environment was the social context of their rejection of the alleged rationality of capitalist society. Fascism was, therefore, not an accidental consequence of the development of monopoly capitalism, but an aspect of the irreducible irrationality of capitalist economic arrangements and an aspect of the self-destructive feature of instrumental reason.

The second component of Weber's sociology which has been questioned by critical theorists is the relationship between 'world mastery' (asceticism, self-discipline, sexual abstinence and life denial) and capitalist organisation. As with the process of rationalisation, the School accepted the fact that there was an affinity between asceticism and capitalism which Weber had first illustrated in the essays on Protestantism and the spirit of capitalism. To some extent the interest in Weber's treatment of asceticism followed from the search for a materialist psychology to complement Marx's economics. This interest in Weber was particularly important in the work of Horkheimer. In his unpublished essay, 'Vernunft und Selbsterhaltung', of 1942, Horkheimer argued that Protestantism was 'the strongest force in the extension of cold, rational individuality....In the place of work for the sake of salvation appeared work for work's sake, profit for profit's sake; the entire world became simply material' (quoted in Jay, 1973, p. 259). Marcuse's analysis of late capitalism also depends on an amalgamation of Marxism and psychology. Of course, Marcuse turned to a Freudian analysis of instinctual needs and social repression rather than to a Weberian understanding of the meanings of social action. However, Marcuse's commentary on the 'origins' (the ontogenesis and phylogenesis) of civilisation in *Eros and Civilization* bears an odd resemblance not only to Weber's view of the historical role of asceticism, but also to Adam Smith's notion of previous capital accumulation. Re-employing Freud's metapsychology, Marcuse argues that the subordination of the pleasure by the reality principle arises in a situation of socially organised scarcity. Given a situation of scarcity, 'the struggle for existence takes place in a world too poor for the satisfaction of human needs without constant restraint, renunciation, delay...whatever satisfaction is possible necessitates *work*, more or less painful arrangements and undertakings for the procurement of the means for satisfying needs' (Marcuse, 1969a, pp. 44-5). As Weber recognised, with the development of capitalism, the initial economic conditions which required asceticism disappear. However, while Weber thought the religious legitimation of disciplined work would become obsolete, Marcuse believes that sexual repression takes on a new role as a form of surplus-repression.

This observation is not an argument suggesting that either Weber or Marcuse is providing a psychologistic and individualistic explanation of capitalist origins. The point is to draw attention to certain similarities in Freud's view of the incompatibility of instinctual satisfaction and civilisation, Weber's view of the 'natural' resistance of the traditional worker to the capitalist regime, and Marcuse's treatment of sexual repression and political domination in late capitalism. While Weber's study of Protestant teaching on the 'calling' provides the classical statement on religious ideologies of work (Anthony, 1977), Weber also recognised that the worker had to be separated from the means of production by political and legal conditions to force them to work; in part one of *Wirtschaft und Gesellschaft*, Weber produced the sociological conditions which explain the 'natural human aversion to work' (Freud, 1949, p. 34). Because Weber's sociology of capitalist discipline cannot be reduced to a simple psychology of workers, Weber's analysis of capitalist organisation can be directly compared with Marx's political economy of capitalism. It was precisely this comparison that Adorno outlined in *Negative Dialectics* (1973, p. 166):

> The concept of capitalism, for instance, which is so crucial
> in every respect is emphatically set off by Weber from
> such isolated and subjective categories as acquisitiveness
> or the profit motive – in a manner similar to Marx's, by
> the way. In capitalism, says Weber, the oft-cited profit
> motive must take its bearings from the principle of
> lucrativity and from the market chances; it must utilize
> the calculation of capital and interest; organized in the
> form of free labour, with household and business expenses
> separated, capitalism necessitates bookkeeping and a ra-
> tionalistic legal system in line with its pervasive governing
> principle of rationality at large.

There is, therefore, no substantive difference between Weber
and critical theorists over the major *descriptive* features of the
capitalistic organisation of economy and society. What is at
issue is the problem of evaluation.

The Frankfurt School largely accepted Weber's analysis of
rationalisation and asceticism, but they rejected what they
regarded as Weber's characteristic resignation and Stoicism in
the face of what he took to be indubitable 'facts' of capitalism.
Weber holds out no hope of sociology playing an emancipatory
role in a situation of capitalist domination. At best, one
adheres to an ethic of responsibility, sticking to one's post ('doing his damned duty') and facing 'the fate of the times' with
sober realism. Weber treated all other attitudes to the fact of
'disenchantment' as escapist, irresponsible and utopian. It is
interesting to compare Weber's attitude to Freudianism with
that of Marcuse. Whereas the latter looked towards Freudianism as a doctrine of potential liberation, Weber was
typically hostile to a theory which he thought avoided ethical
demands of an absolute kind in favour of psychic 'hygiene'
(Weber, 1978, p. 386). Freudianism reduced the ethical concepts of sacrifice and responsibility to a matter of calculation,
namely what is the cost of repressing my sexual instinct?
While Weber bitterly described capitalism as an 'iron cage', he
did not think any other alternative had a realistic 'chance'—to

use a term which is central to Weber's language. By contrast, 'neither Horkheimer nor Marcuse would capitulate in the face of the rationalised and reified world and be satisfied with the irrationalist implications of individualistic value-judgments. The insistent stress on the concept of objective reason attempted to circumvent that position' (Kilminster, 1979, pp. 233–4). In order to avoid Weber's apparent resignation, it was necessary for critical theory to find a grounding for criticism outside idiosyncratic moral preference. Opposition to capitalism had to grow out of something more than a personal preference for socialism. In other words, it was imperative to overcome the conventional antinomies of fact and value, is and ought.

The third and most crucial topic of criticism by the Frankfurt School against Weber centred on the problem of epistemology. Weber's epistemology and philosophy of science were formulated in the context of a revival of neo-Kantianism, specifically the south-west German neo-Kantian school which included W. Windelband ('Geschichte und Naturwissenschaft') and H. Rickert (*Kulturwissenschaft und Naturwissenschaft*). Weber's contribution to the debate on the role of value-judgments in 'cultural studies' was not a unique or isolated commentary but part of an organised dispute, the *Werturteilsstreit* of 1909–14 (Cahnman, 1964). Weber inherited a philosophical tradition that was expressed pre-eminently in the claim that a statement of fact can never provide the basis for a statement of value. As Weber put this position in 'The meaning of "Ethical Neutrality" ' (1949, p. 23), the discovery of a new fact might result in the readjustment of means to ends, but, 'whether this readjustment *should* take place and what *should* be the practical conclusions to be drawn therefrom is not answerable by empirical science—in fact it can not be answered by any science whatsoever'. As a preliminary statement of Weber's stance, we can say that he wanted to achieve a social science which was value-free (*Wertfreiheit*) and value-relevant (*Wertbeziehung*) (Parsons, 1971). Weber's epistemological position was given explicit and practical expression in the debates of the *Verein für Sozialpolitik*. At the 1909 meeting of the *Verein*, Weber found himself engaged in a debate alongside Sombart against a position being argued by

Eugen Philippovich over the concept of economic productivity. Weber's remarks are interesting because he suggests that absolute values are too important to be treated in a purely technical fashion. Weber claims that:

> to attack in such extremely emphatic terms the jumbling of what ought to be with what exists is not that I underestimate the question of what ought to be. On the contrary, it is because I cannot bear it if problems of world-shaking importance—in a sense the most exalted problems that can move a human heart—are here changed into a technical-economic problem of production and made the subject of a scholarly discussion. (Quoted in Weber, 1975, p. 418)

In Weber's view, the *Verein* which had been founded in 1872 as a movement for social reform should continue to discuss evaluative problems of economic and political reform. Purely technical problems of methodology and issues raised in value-free research should be discussed in a separate professional organisation for the advancement of sociology as a scientific discipline. At the first meeting of the Sociological Society at Frankfurt in 1910, Weber attempted to formulate the aims of the Society in a business report which stated that 'The question shall be asked as to what *is* and why something is exactly the way it is, but there shall be no judgment as to its desirability or undesirability' (quoted in Weber, 1975, p. 422).

Weber's separation of meaning and being on the basis of formal rationality and the argument that our knowledge of reality can never provide us with a statement of duty became the focus of the Frankfurt School's opposition to traditional sociological theory. One objection to Weber is that his formal adherence to rational procedures of argument in fact results in extreme irrationalism. If reasoning about the world and scientific investigation of society can never provide a guide for belief and action, then the value positions we do take must be arbitrary. The meaning we attribute to the world becomes a matter of our personal preference and decision. Social science may provide evidence for the choice of means, but it can never help in the selection of ends. Horkheimer commented specifically on this problem in Weber's subjectivist view of rationality in his *Eclipse of Reason* (1947, p. 6):

> Max Weber, however, adhered so definitely to the subjectivistic trend that he did not conceive of any rationality—not even a 'substantial' one by which man can discriminate one end from another. If our drives, intentions, and finally our ultimate decisions must *a priori* be irrational, substantial reason becomes an agency merely of correlation and is therefore essentially 'functional'....
> Max Weber's pessimism with regard to the possibility of rational insight and action...is itself a stepping-stone in the renunciation of philosophy and science as regards their aspiration of defining man's goal.

As an alternative to Weber's pessimism, the Frankfurt School has advanced a number of separate arguments. Critical theorists reject the equation of instrumental rationality with rationality as such. Rational analysis can and must enter into the debate over ends and values. The second type of objection is bound up with the attempt to show that the validation of truth claims entails a 'discursively achieved consensus' (McCarthy, 1978) which in turn depends on speech situations which are open, unrestrained and complete. In other words, rational discourse cannot be separated from normative issues of freedom and responsibility; discovering what is cannot be separated from maintaining something which is intrinsically desirable, namely human freedom. The third aspect of this critique is to protect the emancipatory interest which informs critical theory from the relativism of sociology of knowledge in the Weber-Mannheim tradition. Habermas (1972) claims that critical theory does not serve the interest of a particular group or social class, since the emancipation it seeks is for the species as a whole. The emancipatory interest cannot be reduced to the interests of a particular group. In so far as the human species is defined by the possession of language, we share a species-interest in freedom of discourse. In this sense the emancipatory interest is transcendental: 'Our first sentence expresses unequivocally the intention of universal and unconstrained consensus. Taken together, autonomy and responsibility constitute the only Idea that we possess *a priori* in the sense of the philosophical tradition' (Habermas, 1972, p. 314). Against the positivist separation of is and ought, Habermas attempts to demonstrate that we possess non-arbitrary, normative and existential interests in open discourse which is central to science and to everyday life.

These three topics—the process of rationalisation, human repression in the form of ascetic discipline and the *Wertureilsstreit*—provide a preliminary sketch of the major criticisms of the Frankfurt School against Weber and Weberian sociology. My account, however, lacks detail and historical depth. Before presenting a limited defence of Weber's sociology, it will be necessary to examine the doctrines of the Frankfurt School in more depth. I shall want to look more closely at (1) the notion of 'disenchantment' in the work of Horkheimer and Adorno; (2) Marcuse's analysis of repression and emancipation in capitalist society; and (3) Habermas's theory of interests and knowledge. Apart from detailed criticisms of their work, my general commentary is that the Frankfurt School's theoretical revision of Marx is based on the assumption of working-class incorporation in capitalist society via a dominant ideology. Not only is the dominant ideology thesis a misconception (Abercrombie *et al.*, 1980), it leads the Frankfurt School into a particularly pessimistic and conservative theory of capitalist society. Weber's pessimistic analysis of the fateful constraints of capitalist rationalisation crept insidiously into the world-view of critical theory which failed to locate a social carrier for its emancipatory doctrine. It is, therefore, necessary to see the Frankfurt School as part of a larger movement in modern Marxism which, in attempting to come to terms with changes in the structure of twentieth-century capitalism, rejected any notion of the inevitability of a revolutionary collapse of capitalist society and hence of any notion that social change could be specified with the precision of laws of nature. The intellectual origins of the School, at least after Horkheimer succeeded Grünberg as director of the Institute in 1930, are very closely connected with Georg Lukács

History and Class Consciousness (1923).

It may appear odd to connect Lukács with the members of the Frankfurt School. On the one hand, Lukács, at least in his later years, contemptuously referred to the Frankfurt School as 'Café Marxism' and 'Grand Hotel *Abgrund* [Abyss]' (Jay, 1973, p. 296). On the other, Lukács' personal submission to the Party and his rejection of *History and Class Consciousness* represented precisely the denial of *theoria* as emancipatory, critical reflection. Despite this mutual criticism, Lukács' attempt to link the criticism of reification in bourgeois society, the teleological role of reason in history and the emergence of a revolutionary class, played a fundamental role in the origins of the Frankfurt School, especially in the development of Adorno's literary and philosophical perspective.

Lukács became a member of Weber's 'Sunday circle' in 1912 which included Georg Simmel; Marianne Weber described the relationship between Lukács and Weber as 'a close friendship'. Certainly Weber expressed considerable interest in Lukács' aesthetics and read *Soul and Form* in 1914. Prior to his friendship with Weber, Lukács had been influenced by neo-Kantian *Geisteswissenschaft* through Simmel's lectures at the University of Berlin (1909–10) and through the lectures of Windelband and Rickert at the University of Heidelberg (1913–14). Although Lukács' social relationship with the Weber circle collapsed as a result of their divergent attitudes to the First World War (Mészáros, 1972), Lukács remained profoundly influenced by his early contact with the neo-Kantian revival. The other principal components of his perspective were the radical syndicalism of the Hungarian student leader Ervin Szabó (1877–1918) from whom Lukács retained a romantic, Jacobinical conception of revolutionary struggles, and finally Lukács inherited Hegelian philosophy of history mediated by the hermeneutics of Wilhelm Dilthey. Lukács, therefore, came to a serious study of Marxist theory in 1918 already full equipped with the traditions of German *Lebensphilosophie*:

the neo-Kantianism of Lask, the neo-Hegelianism of Dilthey, the religious irrationalism of Kierkegaard and the aestheticism of the circle around Gundolf and George;

while his political thinking reflected the influence of Sorel, who was then philosophically an admirer of Bergson. (Lichtheim, 1970, p. 36)

The essays which Lukács wrote on problems in Marxism between 1919 and 1921 and which in their revised form appeared as *History and Class Consciousness* in 1923 reflected this neo-Kantian and Weberian background. We can illustrate this reflection by considering Lukács' epistemology, his concept of reification and his perspective on class consciousness.

While Lukács did not have access to Marx's early work—particularly the Paris Manuscripts of 1844—until he worked at the Marx-Engels-Lenin Institute under the directorship of David Riazanov, in *History and Class Consciousness* he performed the remarkable feat of reconstructing the Hegelian theme of alienation in the young Marx and he was enabled to do this because 'his own experience recapitulated Marx's intellectual development' (MacIntyre, 1971, p. 63). By working his way through the concept of human labour as a sensuous, self-conscious, practical activity via the theme of alienation in Hegel, Lukács retraced Marx's own progress from Hegelian theology through Feuerbachian anthropology to the political economy of labour. Indeed, one of the central arguments of *History and Class Consciousness* reads as a direct translation of the first thesis on Feuerbach:

> The chief defect of all previous materialism (including Feuerbach's) is that the object, actuality, sensuousness is conceived only in the form of the *object or perception (Anschauung)*, but not as *sensuous human activity, practice (Praxis)*, not subjectively. Hence in opposition to materialism the *active* side was developed by idealism. (Marx, 1967, p. 400)

The implication of Lukács' emphasis on dialectic and praxis was that the orthodox Marxism of Engels and Kautsky constituted in fact a return to the 'defect of all previous materialism' because it substituted 'economic laws' for 'sensuous human activity'. For example, in a passage which also illustrates the continuing attraction of anarcho-syndicalism, Lukács argues that 'vulgar Marxist economism' cannot adequately conceptualise the importance of violence in revolutionary struggle. Economism 'bases itself on the "natural laws" of economic development which are to bring about these transitions by their own impetus and without having recourse to a brute force lying "beyond economics" ' (Lukács, 1971, p. 239). By contrast, Lukács tried to demonstrate that orthodox Marxism was not a finite collection of laws of social processes, or a set of fixed dogmas, or a collection of eternally valid empirical observations. The falsification of Marx's 'individual theses' would not cause any real disquiet, since 'orthodoxy refers exclusively to *method*. It is the scientific conviction that dialectical materialism is the road to truth and that its methods can be developed, expanded and deepened only along the lines laid down by its founders' (Lukács, 1971, p. 1).

In writing his critique of economism, Lukács injected into Marxism many of the issues which had been raised by the *Werturteilsstreit*. If the central defining feature of human society is that human beings are active, self-reflexive, conscious agents, then a science model which is relevant for the explanation of external physical objects of nature cannot have unqualified applicability in understanding social relationships. Lukács was hostile both to the notion that dialectical materialism was a sort of natural science of society and that the dialectic could be applied to natural phenomena. Lukács' interpretation of vulgar Marxism had the effect of relativising its claims by showing that the concept of inevitable laws of society was itself an effect of bourgeois ideology and consciousness. For Lukács, 'Historical materialism both can and must be applied to itself' (1971, p. 228) for only in this way would it be possible for Marxism to avoid treating that which was subjectively constituted by social processes as a given, objective reality. For example, 'the growth of the fetish of the pure objectivity of economic relations obscures the fact that they are really relations between men and so transforms them into a second nature which envelops man with its fatalistic laws' (Lukács, 1971, p. 240). To understand Lukács' epistemology, we must, therefore, also consider his attempt to reproduce Marx's analysis of fetishism in *Capital* as a theory of reification.

Any interpretation of Marx—such as the interpretations presented by Lukács and the Frankfurt School—which wants to consider Marx's theory as a unified and homogeneous perspective typically makes a direct connection between the alienation theme of the young Marx and the fetishism of commodities argument in the later Marx. Thus, Avineri (1968), who wants to treat Marx's dialectical materialism as a unified commentary on Hegelianism, observes a distinction in Marx between objectification (*Vergegenständlichung*), alienation (*Entfremdung*), and the reifying (*Verdinglichende*) property of exchange. In the Paris Manuscripts, Marx argued that human beings create their own environment through their own sensuous practical activity and, under certain specified conditions, this objectified world becomes alienated from human beings. In capitalist society, men are alienated (separated) from the means of production, the product of labour, from humanity and from themselves (Marx, 1967, pp-. 287 ff.). In *Capital*, vol. 1, section 4, we find the theory that:

> A commodity is therefore a mysterious thing, simply because in it the social character of men's labour appears to them as an objective character stamped upon the product of that labour; because the relation of the producers to the sum total of their own labour is presented to them as a social relation, existing not between themselves, but between the products of their labour. (Marx, 1974, vol. 1, p. 77)

Lukács elevates this section of *Capital* to the status of the key, 'at this stage in the history of mankind', to all problems, because 'there is no solution that could not be found in the solution to the riddle of the commodity-*structure*' (Lukács, 1971, p. 83). The problem of economism is that it takes the 'phantom objectivity' of appearances as real relationships rather than penetrating the commodity-structure which would disclose the true social processes which lie 'behind' phenomenal reality. In a similar fashion, the philosophical

problems of neo-Kantian philosophy—and hence the epistemological problems of Weber and Simmel—concerning facts and
values, subject and object, will and cause turn out to be
historically determined features of commodity exchange. The
Kantian contrasts between the natural world of causation and
the moral world of choice are intellectualisations of the
characteristic 'antinomies of bourgeois thought' whose origins
are situated in capitalist exchange relationships. These antinomies are generated by the fact that:

> man in capitalist society confronts a reality 'made' by
> himself (as a class) which appears to him to be a natural
> phenomenon alien to himself; he is wholly at the mercy of
> its 'laws', his activity is confined to the exploitation of
> the inexorable fulfilment of certain individual laws for his
> own (egoistic) interests. (Lukács, 1971, p. 135)

Lukács theory is completed by showing the transcendence and
overcoming (*Aufhebung*) of reification and false-consciousness
coincides with the revolutionary overthrow of capitalist society whereby the object of history (the proletariat) also becomes
its subject. The working class thus becomes the embodiment
of valid knowledge of the world.

How does Lukács connect the interest (*Interesse*) of the
working class with unrestrained knowledge (*Erkenntnis*) of
human reality? Lukács produces the notion that became fundamental to Mannheim's ideology/utopia distinction and to
Goldmann's concept of the 'tragic vision', namely that rising
social classes have an interest in social criticism and dominant
classes have an interest in ideology. Bourgeois individualism
was a social criticism of feudal organicism; proletarian
socialism is the principal criticism of, for example, the
bourgeois ideology of equal exchange in the market-place.
With the historical development of the bourgeois class, what

> began as the reactionary feudal criticism of emergent
> capitalism develops increasingly, with the criticism be-
> tween mutually hostile ruling classes into the self-
> criticism of the bourgeoisie and finally turns into its bad

conscience when criticism is progressively concealed and kept secret. (Lukács, 1971, p. 226)

The bourgeoisie is incapable of providing the correct analysis of capitalism. Only the proletariat, which has no interest in the continuity of capitalism, is able with the aid of historical materialism to penetrate the distorted reality of capitalist relations. The proletariat has nothing to lose but its illusions.

The problem is that individual members of the working class may adhere to beliefs that do not correspond to their economic class interest; they may, for instance, support religious, conservative and individualistic beliefs about society. To solve this difficulty, Lukács resorts to a peculiar combination of Weberian ideal types and Lenin's theory of the vanguard party. Thus, 'class consciousness' is not what actual men happen in fact to think; real consciousness is an inference from the thoughts and feelings 'men would have in a particular situation if they were *able* to assess both it and the interests arising from it' (Lukács, 1971, p. 51). Consciousness of the proletariat of capitalism is a rationality which is imputed to a typical position within the total social structure. Thus,

> class consciousness consists in fact of the appropriate and rational reactions 'imputed' (zugerechnet) to a particular typical position in the process of production. This consciousness is, therefore, neither the sum nor the average of what is thought or felt by the single individuals who make up the class. And yet the historically significant actions of the class as a whole are determined in the last resort by this consciousness and not by the thought of the individual. (Lukács, 1971, p. 51)

If the true, rational consciousness of the proletariat is not the sum of the actual consciousness of individual workers, then who is it that performs the crucial task of imputing, assessing and inferring the ideal typical consciousness of this revolutionary class? In Lukács' Marxism, it is in fact the Party which performs this role as mentor of class consciousness. The Party is the final arbiter of reason and truth. The irony of this conclusion to Lukács' study was that, when the Party came to the conclusion that Lukács' analysis of Marxism was incorrect, Lukács was forced by his own logic to accept their verdict.

There are numerous difficulties with Lukács' attempt to resolve the philosophical problems of Kantian philosophy and with the attempt to integrate *Lebensphilosophie* (Jones, 1977; Watnik, 1962). My immediate concern, however, is to bring out the relationships between Weber, Lukács and the Frankfurt School to prepare the way for a more detailed commentary on critical theory. Although Weber and Lukács had been closely associated at Heidelberg, Lukács came to associate Weber with the irrationalism and imperialism of the Romantic movement in German literature and philosophy which culminated in fascism. Weber's sociology was thus characterised as an attack on the theoretical basis of dialectical materialism; it was more importantly an attack on democracy and socialism as processes of bureaucratisation which would stifle freedom and individuality. Weber's emphasis on the critical role of leadership within a bureaucratised, party-dominated democracy produced an inevitable Caesarism. Lukács concluded his criticism of Weber by claiming that it 'can be clearly seen through his case, how the better among the German intellectuals are deprived of all means of making a frontal assault on the generalised irrationalism which constituted fascism' (Lukács, 1972, p. 398). Weber's resignation in the face of bureaucratic irrationality bears a close resemblance to the stoicism of Thomas Mann, whom Lukács treated as the epitome of the bourgeois artist in an age of revolutionary change who stands outside the flow of history (Lukács, 1964). Given Lukács' painful awareness of the interconnection between idealism and political irrationalism, it is a poignant irony that Lukács appears in *The Magic Mountain* disguised as Naphta whom Lukács in his *Essays on Thomas Mann* (1964) described as 'the spokesman of the reactionary Fascist, anti-democratic *Weltanschauung*'. In a similar fashion, Marianne Weber (1975, p. 466) recognised that Lukács was one of the 'young philosophers' who 'were moved by eschatological hopes of a new emissary of the transcendent God, and they saw the basis of salvation in a socialist social order created by brotherhood'.

Regardless of Lukács' attempt to distance himself from German classical philosophy in general and from Weber in particular, his version of Marxism was deeply imbued with the tragic vision of *Lebensphilosophie*. First, as Gareth Stedman Jones (1977) has documented, Lukács inherited the romantic opposition between science and nature. In opposition to the view of industrialism as a potentially liberating force in human society, the romantic attitude saw industrialisation as a process which, in destroying the harmony of the traditional order, subordinated men to the machine. The idea that traditional, affectual and organic relationships (*Gemeinschaft*) were fundamentally contrasted with rational, utilitarian, egoistic relationships (*Gesellschaft*) arose out of this pessimistic view of the effects of science and came to dominate the thought not only of Tönnies, but also of Weber, Simmel and Troeltsch (Freund, 1979). Lukács' *History and Class Consciousness* represents the translation of this romantic, anti-scientific ethos into Marxism. In Lukács' analyses 'there is no suggestion of the liberating effects of industrialisation and scientific discovery, let alone of Marx's belief that the theory of historical materialism was itself a real and responsible science' (Jones, 1977, p. 34). Marx and Engels had no romantic illusions about the harmony of feudal society which in fact depended on the exploitation of peasant labour; they also recognised that *industrial* capitalism was a necessary precondition for the development of socialism. A future classless society would not present a return to *Gemeinschaft* cosiness. In Lukács, however, this historical process

is given no material content. There is absolutely no vision of an advanced industrial *socialism*. The proletariat merely dominates that social totality to which it had always ascriptively aspired, and from which commodity fetishism and reification had hitherto separated it. (Jones, 1977, pp. 36-7)

Lukács' epistemological attack on the positivism of Kautsky and Engels cannot, therefore, be separated from his romantic protest against science as a social institution and against industrialism based on scientific rationality. His epistemological criticisms of 'laws' of society depended on the neo-Kantian conceptualisation of the relationship between natural and cultural sciences; his social criticism of capitalist industrialism depended on the peculiar marriage of Lukácsian 'reification' and Weberian 'rationalisation'.

The second aspect of Lukács' dependence on *Lebensphilosophie* is found in the sense of fate which inspires his analysis of the process of reification. It is this concept which directly links Lukács to the world-view of Weber and Simmel. As we have seen, one of the most bitter and pessimistic statements against capitalist routinisation occurs in Weber's 'Author's Introduction' to *The Protestant Ethic and Spirit of Capitalism*, which was in fact originally the introduction to the posthumously published *Gesammelte Aufsätze zur Religionssoziologie* of 1920 (Nelson, 1974). The message of that 'Author's Introduction' is that the very processes which liberated human beings from magic and superstition come eventually to bind human beings to a new form of slavery in bureaucratic, rational capitalism. There is a similar theme in Simmel's sense of tragedy whereby the creative content of human endeavour continuously takes on the rigidity of its external forms. Simmel was deeply affected by the idea of estrangement in life whereby, 'the vibrating, restless life of the creative soul, which develops toward the infinite contrasts with its fixed and ideally unchanging product and its uncanny feedback effect, which arrests and indeed rigidifies this liveliness' (1968, p. 31). Simmel thus reaffirms the Weberian theme that men are enslaved by what, from a normative standpoint, often appears to be the most exalted of cultural products. Lukács' notion of the reification of consciousness bears a striking similarity to the underlying pessimism of Weber's 'rationalisation' and Simmel's 'externalisation'. Thus, in capitalist society the division of labour and the commodity-structure have the effect of converting human products into external phenomena which men experience as alien objects. We come thereby to experience the products of human sensuous activity as if they were part of an external and hostile reality. We experience this humanly constructed world as if it were an 'iron cage'.

Unlike Weber, the young Lukács also thought that there was a very decisive route out of the realm of necessity to the realm of freedom. The intellectual had a clear choice. He could either adopt the stance of Mann by realistically observing the course of history as an outsider or he could espouse the cause of proletarian revolution. Erstwhile merely contemplative philosophy would at last realise itself in praxis. Unfortunately, Lukács' combination of reason and revolution will not do the job intended for it as a route out of cultural pessimism. There are four major problems with Lukács' theoretical position. First, his argument is irreducibly teleological in that history has a definite end, namely a society in which fetishism, the division of labour and ideology will have no place. Hence, this future classless society will have no requirement for a critical theory. It follows that historical materialism will have no relevance in social analysis under socialist conditions, but this appears to contradict Lukács' commitment to historical materialism as a method which can be applied to any object. The idea that a future socialist society would have its own contradictions and at least some contradictions inherited from the previous capitalist society does not arise in this version of historical development. The revolution in capitalist society must, therefore, take on a total, apocalyptic character liquidating all existing capitalist contradictions.

The second difficulty with Lukács' theory is that, against economism, he correctly emphasised the crucial role of class struggle and violence. He claimed that any Marxist theory which concentrated on the inevitability of the laws of society could not adequately conceptualise the importance of revolutionary violence in the transition to socialism. However, any theory which takes class struggle to be the motor of structural change in society must at the same time treat history as a fortuitous, contingent development. If class struggle is the principal historical agent, it would be difficult to imagine a clear transition to socialism, because the class structure will be empirically complex; various social classes, such as the peasantry, may well survive the transition to socialism without any immediate change in their relationship to the land. Lukács' problem is that he wants to treat society as a site of contingent class struggle and history as determined by teleological necessity. You can't have your historical cake and eat it.

The third problem is that Lukács produces an elitist theory of knowledge. The aim of *History and Class Consciousness* was to show that the struggle of the working class for the end of capitalist exploitation also coincides with the struggle of reason against fetishism and irrationality. It is obvious, however, that individual members of the working class do not necessarily embody or anticipate this process. True class consciousness has to be interpreted and inferred by a separate body, namely Party intellectuals. This interpretation of class consciousness is inconsistent with the source in Marx from which Lukács draws inspiration. The third thesis on Feuerbach criticises materialist theories of knowledge which divide society into two separate groups; one group is determined by circumstance and does not possess knowledge of its situation, while another superior group is not determined and has possession of correct knowledge. Bourgeois intellectuals like Lukács find themselves in the peculiar situation of being falsely conscious in terms of their material interests in capitalist society, but at the same time being in possession of correct knowledge of society and of its future development (Abercrombie, 1980). The problem is that one cannot make any straightforward equation between true knowledge and ascending classes.

The final difficulty is that Lukács has to operate with a particularly powerful version of the dominant ideology thesis (Abercrombie *et al.*, 1980). If the existence of capitalist relations of production is in fact contrary to the real interests of the working class, then it is important to explain the apparent acceptance by this class of capitalist exploitation. The principal answer of *History and Class Consciousness* is that the working class is penetrated by a dominant ideology so that workers come to accept capitalism as an inevitable fate, as a 'natural' order. Lukács, however, provides no account of how that ideology is transmitted; there is no apparatus of ideological incorporation, since fetishism merely emanates from commodities. Whereas Marx had argued that in early capitalism the economic structure was itself sufficient to discipline labour, Lukács places the superstructural control of workers at the centre of his picture. Furthermore, his superstructure does not contain a powerful state and legal apparatus for the purpose of enforcing class rule. It is true, of course, that, on renouncing *History and Class Consciousness*, Lukács did develop a very clear notion of the significance of the State. For example, in his study (1924) of the cohesion of Lenin's thought, there was an explicit recognition of the fact that class relations are maintained, not be fetishised consciousness, but by force (Lukács, 1970). However, with the attack on the Blum Theses, Lukács was forced to withdraw from political action and political analysis into the study of aesthetics and the philosophical problems of ontology. Indeed, despite rejections of German philosophical romanticism, Lukács was forced, through an acceptance of Stalinism, into the resigned outlook of *Lebensphilosophie*, namely 'stoical acceptance of the established powers of the external, political world, combined with an internal, aesthetic contempt for them' (Jones, 1977, p. 56).

This outline of the issues raised by Lukács' rejection of economism provides a necessary basis for the study of the Frankfurt School because the difficulties which are present in his analysis of consciousness are also present in critical theory. In its search for a revolutionary group capable of receiving a critical theory of society, the Frankfurt School has also been troubled with the problems of elitism, teleology and pessimism. Lukács' employment of classical German philosophy as a critique of positivism and empiricism anticipated the future development of Frankfurt critical theory. The implication of this observation is not that critical theory was merely a pale replica of the theoretical advances which Lukács had made in the 1920s. As Buck-Morss (1977, p. 29) points out, it was particularly difficult for the Frankfurt School to commit itself to a belief in an imminent revolution led by a class-conscious proletariat because the political development of fascism in Germany and Stalinism in Russia ruled out any such commitment. On a range of other issues—such as Lukács' conservative taste for the bourgeois novel—there were more important differences between the early Frankfurt School and Lukács. Nevertheless, there are major connecting themes, not least of which is the idea that instrumental rationality paradoxically liberates men from magic and religion only to enslave them in a new form of domination. One obvious, if superficial, illustration of this continuity can be gained from the very titles of their publications—*The Destruction of Reason* (Lukács, 1974), *Eclipse of Reason* (Horkheimer, 1947) and *Dialectic of Enlightenment* (Adorno and Horkheimer, 1973).

The most suitable starting point for illustrating this continuity between Lukács and the Frankfurt School is Horkheimer's essay 'Traditional and critical theory' (1976), which first appeared in the *Zeitschrift für Sozialforschung* in 1942. The point of the essay was to show the limitations for both empirical and theoretical sociology resulting from imitation of 'the lead of the natural sciences with their great successes'. Systematisation, quantification and verification in natural science were theoretical results which flowed from the application of science to pragmatic goals:

> The manipulation of physical nature and of specific
> economic and social mechanisms demand alike the amass-
> ing of a body of knowledge such as is supplied in an
> ordered set of hypotheses. The technological advances of
> the bourgeois period are inseparably linked to this func-
> tion of the pursuit of science. (Horkheimer, 1976, p. 211)

The reified categories of scientific understanding of society are thus directly linked to the development of a particular kind of society and economic organisation. Traditional theory reproduces in its abstract categories the alienation and reification of capitalist society in which the objects of human labour are constantly separated from their real producers. While reason encourages individual awareness and social collaboration, the products of human labour 'are alienated from them, and the whole process with its waste of work-power and human life, and with its wars and all its senseless wretchedness, seems to be an unchangeable force of nature, a fate beyond man's control' (Horkheimer, 1976, pp. 216–17). This social alienation is reflected in theoretical work itself, where knowledge and action, facts and values, activity and passivity are separated in a professional division of labour protecting the 'savant' from the tensions experienced by the critical theorist. The autonomy of the bourgeois academic to pursue 'pure' research is in fact an illusion which masks the acceptance of limitations imposed on science by social arrangements. By contrast, critical theory recognises that knowledge can never be separated from the form of society in which that knowledge is constituted 'but coincides with the struggle for certain real ways of life' (Horkheimer, 1976, p. 223). Critical theory aims at the rational reorganisation of society and its approach to knowledge is very different from conventional sociology of knowledge in the Mannheim tradition, since critical theory has a distinctively normative goal. The aim of critical theory 'is man's emancipation from slavery' (Horkheimer, 1976, p. 224).

There are obvious Lukácsian aspects to this criticism of traditional theory. Those social sciences, which attempt to ape the success of the natural sciences, have, in fact, reproduced the fetishism of bourgeois society by treating humanly constituted phenomena as 'natural objects'. Whereas traditional theory takes society as it is for granted, critical theory anticipates the transcendence of existing arrangements by connecting itself with the struggle for freedom. In addition, there is, especially in the *Dialectic of Enlightenment*, an anti-industrial theme that instrumental reason is leading to a general destruction of 'the good life'. The *Dialectic of Enlightenment* contains the Weberian-Lukácsian thesis that the rationalised and reified world of human products takes on a thing-like life of its own and dominates the subjects who produced the reified world, but this study of enlightenment is far bleaker and pessimistic than *History and Class Consciousness*. In the Preface to the Amsterdam edition of 1947, there appears to be little hope of a revolutionary working class rising to embody the analysis of critical theory since Adorno and Horkheimer (1973, pp. ix-x) refer pessimistically to 'the residues of freedom' and 'tendencies toward true humanism, even if these seem powerless in regard to the main course of history'. The Weberian pessimism concerning the outcome of purposive rationality is present in every aspect of their critical treatment of 'enlightment' which they define by reference to the disenchantment (*Entzauberung*) of the world. Enlightenment destroys pre-scientific methods and results in the domination of nature by men, but the irony of the control of nature by enlightenment is that it produces a civilisation in which men are increasingly dominated by totalitarian states, technology and the division of labour.

To illustrate their theme, Adorno and Horkheimer take the *Odyssey* 'as one of the earliest representative testimonies of Western bourgeois civilization' (1973, p. xvi) as part of their attack on the myths of bourgeois rationality—the golden age of ancient Greece and the progressive nature of eighteenth-century Enlightenment. The central episode of the journey of Odysseus to which Adorno and Horkheimer call attention concerns the encounter with the Sirens. This story above all illustrates Odysseus' own asceticism, energy and fortitude in his single-minded endeavour to achieve his goal and underlines the moral that personal ecstasy is 'a promise of happiness which threatened civilization at every moment' (Adorno and Horkheimer, 1973, p. 33). Odysseus' response to the promise of the Sirens is typical of a society based on patriarchal power, property and the values of systematic discipline. Confronted by the temptation of the Sirens, the sailors have their ears plugged with wax so they can row hard without diversion, while Odysseus is bound to the mast. Adorno and Horkheimer use this myth to illustrate the characteristic requirements of 'the spirit of capitalism'. With their ears stopped with wax, 'The laborers must be fresh and concentrated as they look ahead, and must ignore whatever lies to one side. They must doggedly sublimate in additional effort the drive that impels to diversion. And so they become practical' (Adorno and Horkheimer, 1973, p. 34). Odysseus listens, but his response is impotent and passive; the greater the temptation, the tighter become his bonds. This response is parallel to that of the burgher class which, with every growth in their wealth and power is forced to restrain and discipline any inclination to consume. Thus, whereas Marx and Engels saw the history of human society as the history of class struggle, Adorno and Horkheimer define the 'history of civilization' as 'the history of renunciation' (Adorno and Horkheimer, 1973, p. 55). Every advance in productive capacity with technical improvements and an increase in the division of labour carries with it the promise of greater social wealth, but, in fact, this potential gives way to greater domination and to increased psychological repression.

There are good reasons for believing that this account of the effects of bourgeois rationality and disenchantment is another version of the transition from *Gemeinschaft* to *Gesellschaft* which also exercised the imagination of Tönnies, Simmel and Weber. It is essentially a high bourgeois, anti-scientific critique of industrialisation. This accusation has been specifically denied by Buck-Morss (1977, p. 61), who argues that the book is a 'critical negation' of the myth of progress as the cornerstone of the bourgeois conception of reason. Adorno and Horkheimer, it is claimed, argued against bourgeois rationality 'for the sake of the Enlightenment'. This defence of the radical quality of the Adorno and Horkheimer critique of bourgeois instrumental rationality is not easily maintained. A number of writers (Therborn, 1977; Jay, 1973; Anderson, 1976) have commented on the gradual drift of the Frankfurt School away from Marxism, away from commitment to working-class politics and away from any political engagement at all. The crucial difficulty lay in identifying the social class for whom critical theory would be a real consciousness. Whereas Lukács had identified the proletariat as the subject-object of history, Horkheimer, in 'Traditional and critical theory', had argued that the industrial working class was not the exclusive vehicle of reason. Adorno went one stage further in denying that any group could be the carrier of critical reason. The progressive trend would be embodied within creative individuals. For example, while *Minima Moralia* was written under 'conditions enforcing contemplation' (Adorno, 1974, p. 18), it nevertheless expresses Adorno's withdrawal from politics into individual experience. Adorno's 'fate' gives adequate expression to Weber's contention that in an age of bureaucracy charismatic creativity would have to withdraw into the private, secluded world. The Frankfurt School thus failed to solve the problem that lay at the heart of Mannheimian sociology of knowledge.

If the working class was no longer the existential basis for correct knowledge, then what grounds were there for believing that critical theory could transcend the contemporary limitations of enlightenment rationality (Jay, 1974, p. 82)? While the Frankfurt School began with a refusal to accept Weber's resignation in the face of process of rationalisation and disenchantment, Adorno and Horkheimer ended either with withdrawal into the individual critical consciousness or with open acceptance of existing late capitalist arrangements (Anderson, 1976, p. 34).

While Herbert Marcuse has been defended against similar charges on the grounds of having an 'exemplary' political record (Therborn, 1977, p. 110), in my view Marcuse's *theoretical* position cannot be easily and nicely separated from that of Horkheimer and Adorno. Marcuse's entire analysis of capitalist society is premised on the defeat and submission of the Western working class. While Lukács, in *History and Class Consciousness*, did not develop a theory of the apparatus by which ideologies are transmitted, in *One-Dimensional Man*, Marcuse develops an elaborate account of the apparatus by which the working class are incorporated. In late capitalism, mechanisation, improvement in managerial domination, increases in the technical division of labour and the creation of a permanent defence economy produces an increase in wealth. Although massive inequalities in income continue, capitalism is able to satisfy the basic needs of the majority of the population. At the same time, the advertising industry can create a range of 'artificial wants' which also contribute to the incorporation of the industrial white working class. Colonialism, welfare and warfare provide the material means by which key sections of the population are bought off, leaving a lumpenproletariat of 'the outsiders and the poor, the unemployed and the unemployable, the persecuted coloured races, the inmates of prisons and mental institutions' (Marcuse, 1964, p. 56).

Late capitalism possesses powerful processes by which protest and opposition are contained and administered. In addition to the economic basis of incorporation through affluence and consumption, there is a large measure of political incorporation through superficial democratisation of political institutions and enfranchisement of the population. Late capitalism is able to tolerate a relatively extensive element of deviance and opposition which is neutralised in the process of democratic debate in political parties and assemblies. The democratic process provides for the discussion of grievances and for legal change. Deviance is repressively tolerated in so far as it does not question the basis of the system as a whole. Capitalist society is thus relatively stable and,

> capitalist mass-democracy is perhaps to a higher degree self-perpetuating than any other form of government or society; and the more so the more it rests, not on terror and scarcity but on efficiency and wealth, and on the majority will of the underlying and administered population. (Marcuse, 1969b, p. 70)

While Marcuse's critique of bourgeois democracy often reads like Alexis de Tocqueville's *Democracy in America* in which there was an equally clear vision of the repressive effects of democratic majorities combined with an unlimited drive for individual prosperity, Marcuse conjoins the institutional mechanisms of incorporation with psychological mechanisms of repression.

The history of civilisation is a history involving a transition from immediate to delayed satisfaction, from pleasure to pain, from play to work, from receptiveness to productiveness, and from the absence of repression to security (Marcuse, 1969a, p. 30). The argument which Marcuse takes from Freud is that self-repression is the prerequisite for the existence of any society. In order to operate in social groups, the individual is required to sacrifice his egocentric, libidinal interests to maintain the collective interests of the group. Within the family, the oedipal drives of the sons towards the mother must be inhibited in order to protect the patriarchal control of property and the reproduction of a stable society. For Freud, the achievement of individual happiness is incompatible with the requirements of civilisation. Marcuse, however, modifies Freud's pessimistic view of society by arguing that, although repression of sexual pleasure may have been important for the *origins* of organised society, in late capitalism scarcity is no longer a key feature of social existence. Therefore, repression has become 'surplus-repression' which is aimed at the maintenance of specific and alterable social arrangements. Sexual liberation is an area where the general revolt against capitalist domination can be initiated.

The white urban working class of industrial society has been successfully incorporated into an administered capitalist system. Its incorporation is explained by the existence of a powerful ideological apparatus which subordinates the working class at the political, social and psychological level. The possibility for radical change is, therefore, to be found in a variety of social groups which permanently or temporarily fall outside the control of this apparatus—the populations of underdeveloped societies, black populations in urban ghettos, the unemployed and students. Critical theory vacillates between recognition of the fact that the majority of the population accepts the legitimacy of capitalism and the expectation that capitalism periodically runs into deep economic and political crises which provide opportunities for protest (Marcuse, 1964, p. 13). The conclusion of *One-Dimensional Man* suggests, however, that containment is a permanent feature of capitalism and that periodic disruption is not likely to provide the occasion for fundamental revolutionary change. The irrationality of capitalism is painfully obvious—waste, war, exploitation, dehumanisation—and dialectical theory is perfectly able to transcend these facts by pointing to alternative possibilities. In order to realise these possibilities political practice must respond to theory, but 'at present, the practice gives no such response' (Marcuse, 1964, p. 198). Similarly, in *An Essay on Liberation*, Marcuse (1969b) recognises the possibility of a 'revolt' by the ghetto minorities and of 'rebellion' by the youth and their intelligentsia, but he does not envisage any possibility of revolution in late capitalism.

Marcuse, therefore, recapitulates many of the arguments and issues which have dominated neo-Marxism since the publication of *History and Class Consciousness* in 1923. There is the central paradox that those processes which offer hope of human liberation, especially from the dark powers of religion and magic, in fact create new and more vigorous forces of human domination and alienation. In Marcuse, the creation of new forms of wealth through mechanisation and the growth of Western democracy do not bring in a new age of freedom and plenty, but, in the contrary, they result in political domination, repression and misery. However, while Lukács had a messianic vision of working-class revolutions throughout Western capitalism, Marcuse has a definitely limited expectation of revolt and rebellion by marginal groups and lumpen-proletariats. Given these limitations on the possibility of revolution and given Marcuse's obvious dependence on the notions of rationalisation and ascetic repression, Marcuse's objections to Weber's apparent resignation to the fate of capitalist disenchantment of reality were not exactly warranted. There are, however, more fundamental difficulties with Marcuse's revision of Marx and Engels.

We can consider some of these difficulties by looking at Marcuse's reception of Freudian psychoanalysis. Marcuse breaks with Freud and Weber over a crucial issue, because Marcuse believes that it is possible to be both happy and rational. By contrast, Weber argued that once we have bitten from the tree of knowledge, we have forsaken any possibility of happiness and contentment in this world—or the next. For Freud, we can virtuously tie ourselves to the mast but we cannot also expect to be happy. The same separation of virtue, happiness and reason in society was also true of the philosophical tradition from Kant. It is, in short, the tragic vision of the world; it is Weber's 'fate' (MacIntyre, 1971, p. 85). Marcuse thinks that it is possible to transcend these limitations and separations, but only just. He gets into difficulty, however, in providing some account of the contents of that happiness. At one level, he thinks that sexual permissiveness constitutes a real protest against the sexual asceticism which late capitalism has inherited from its Protestant origins. There is, however, very little hint in *Eros and Civilization* of the specific content of a 'non-repressive libidinous culture' and hence of what we would actually do with our liberated sexuality (MacIntyre, 1970, p. 47). At another level, Marcuse recognises that modern capitalist societies are typically characterised by a relatively wide tolerance of sexual deviance and by encouragement of public sexuality by comparison with early capitalist societies. Sexual therapy, particularly in the United States, is widely promoted and sought after. Marcuse's argument appears to work both ways regardless of the facts (Morgan, 1975, p. 177). If we deny our sexuality in capitalism, we are repressed; if we give endless expression to our sexuality, our permissiveness is further illustration of 'repressive desublimation'.

The possibility of liberation is, however, a limited one, partly because Marcuse paints a picture of capitalism in which the repressive/ideological apparatus is so powerful and all-pervasive that it is difficult to imagine how *any* oppositional belief and activity is possible. Dissent seems to occur only on the margins of capitalist society, leaving the core institutions relatively unscathed. It is interesting, therefore, to draw a comparison between Talcott Parsons's *The Social System* and Marcuse's *One-Dimensional Man*. Their evaluation of capitalist society are polar opposites. Parsons believes that highly differentiated, industrial systems have solved most of the major problems of adaptation, integration and continuity. Marcuse, as we have seen, condemns modern capitalism as highly irrational and dysfunctional. Both writers are agreed, however, on the massive stability of late capitalism and they also agree on the social processes by which this stability is achieved. First, there is a powerful common culture ('ideology') which binds individuals together. Second, there is a process of socialisation ('psychological repression') which insures that people are psychologically rewarded for social conformity. Third, the social system is legitimised through a differentiated political system so that consensus is more important than force. Both Parsons and Marcuse converge on an 'end of ideology thesis' in that they feel that open conflict is no longer a major feature of the relationships between classes in modern society (Abercrombie *et al.*, 1980). The emphasis on the role of the superstructure in explaining the incorporation of the working class is a typical feature of neo-Marxist explanations. By contrast, Weber correctly noted that common values are not available in capitalism because the great source of absolute ethics (charisma) had dried up and because late capitalism was held together by force, by bureaucratic centralisation and by repressive law.

If Marcuse's critical theory represents a major shift away from Marx and Engels, then this theoretical process of making Marxist analysis come to terms with the transition from early to late capitalism has been carried even further and more systematically in the critical theory of Jürgen Habermas. Of course, a shift away from Marx's historical materialism is not in itself important to my argument. The main point to be established is that a shift away from Marx has the consequence of drawing Habermas towards a Weberian sociology. For example, one aspect of Habermas's argument is that, while Marx's analysis may have been highly relevant for the analysis of early capitalism, the theory requires major modifications to deal with the new structures of late capitalism. It is characteristic of late capitalism that the state intervenes directly in, and becomes constitutive of, the economic base of society so that the state enjoys a substantial autonomy from the economic process. There have also been fundamental changes in the nature of 'social classes'. There has been a general rise in the standard of living and the existence of a welfare state means that we can no longer literally believe that labour is forced to work on pain of starvation. The problems of consciousness and emancipation can no longer be stated in directly economic terms. These structural changes have important consequences for Marx's crisis theory and especially for Marx's labour theory of value. Government intervention in the public sector provides a system of mass education and heightens the general productivity of labour; these interventions lower the cost of constant capital and increase surplus value. In addition, wage levels are not set by simple market mechanisms in terms of the cost of labour reproduction; they are now politically calculated by a class compromise which is determined by labour organisations, employers and government. These changes in capitalism cannot be adequately conceptualised in terms of theoretical categories which have relevance to the early stages of capitalist development; it is necessary to develop entirely new theoretical strategies for which Habermas has provided preliminary guidelines in *Legitimation Crisis* (1976a) and *Zur Rekonstruktion des Historischen Materialismus* (1976).

These reformulations of Marx's analysis of capitalism are, however, only prolegomena to major recasting of the deeper theoretical structures of historical materialism as a whole. Perhaps the most important change in this area concerns Habermas's restatement of the whole 'base and superstructure' metaphor. Marx's concept of 'labour', despite his early interest in 'sensuous activity' and his emphasis on the social organisation of labour, tended to be mechanistic and instrumentalist. By taking material production and reproduction as the basic model for that which is constitutive of human behaviour as such, Marx developed an idea of 'labour' which was far too narrow and which had the consequence of the 'reduction of *praxis* to *techne*' (McCarthy, 1978, p. 17). Combining the various contributions of hermeneutics, symbolic interactionism and role theory, Habermas attempts to conceptualise society along the two major and autonomous axes of 'labour' and 'interaction'. The latter is defined as '*communicative action*, symbolic interaction...governed by binding *consensual norms*, which define reciprocal expectations about behaviour and which must be understood and recognized by at least two acting subjects' (Habermas, 1971, p. 92). Interaction or work refers to the processes of social labour by which humans produce their conditions of existence and the reproduction of those conditions. Human activity, therefore, involves two fundamentally different action systems—symbolic action and rational-purposive (instrumental) action—which have different norms and skills. Individuals shape and determine their world by language and labour.

Just as the symbolic world cannot be reduced to that of purposive-rational action, so the disciplines which are concerned with the explanation of those worlds cannot be reduced to some master discipline. The systems of purposive-rationality are based on a technical interest in the manipulation and control of the environment; the disciplines associated with the technical interest are 'analytical-empirical'. The systems of symbolic action are based on a practical interest which is aimed at achieving understanding and normative consensus in interactive situations or communities; the disciplines or knowledge associated with the practical interest are 'historical-hermeneutic'. Habermas is, of course, perfectly aware of the problems of an idealistic characterisation of human societies. He specifically recognises that human language and labour are set within natural and social constraints. Furthermore, human interaction and discourse are constantly distorted by inequalities of power which arise in the course of social evolution. An interpretative sociology which did not take into account the objective constraints of domination could not provide an adequate sociology of human societies. The objective framework of society is constituted by language, labour and domination.

The aim of critical theory is to identify those constraints in society which are contingent and whose liquidation would produce an enlargement of human freedom in a rational society. Thus, 'Critical theory aims to restore to men an awareness of their position as active, yet historically limited subjects' (Scott, 1978, p. 4). The 'critically oriented sciences' are grounded in their own set of interests. Whereas the 'systematic sciences of social action' (economics, sociology and political science) have the aim of producing knowledge of regularities in social action, critical science

> is concerned with going beyond this goal to determine when theoretical statements grasp invariant regularities of social action as such and when they express ideologically frozen relations of dependence than can in principle be transformed. (Habermas, 1972a, p. 310)

A critique takes into account the fact that statements of invariant regularities in human life sets off a train of reflective thought in the subjects about whom those statements of invariance are made. Critical theory does not, therefore, replace either analytical-empirical or historical-hermeneutic perspectives. Knowledge of genuine uniformities, regularities and invariance is crucial; conventional sociology has an important task to fulfil in providing such information. Habermas, however, goes much further than this in recognising that contemporary sociology in Germany has in fact come very close to fulfilling the role of a critical theory because sociology has 'assisted the self-reflection of social groups in given historical situations' (Habermas, 1976b, p. 221).

These reflections on the nature of the interests which direct knowledge have raised the problem of the relationship of criticism to positivism. While the Frankfurt School recognised the affinity between the use of the term 'critique' in theological criticism, Kant's philosophical critique and Marx's ideological critique, they also recognised that both Marx and Freud thought they were establishing a positivist science of society akin to the natural sciences of the physical world. Although Engels exaggerated the parallel between Marx's view of social evolution and Darwin's theory of natural evolution, Marx did appreciate the *Origin of Species* and had intended to dedicate volume 2 of *Capital* to Darwin (McLellan, 1973, p. 424). This provides an anecdotal indication of the positivistic tendency in Marx's conception of a science of modes of production. In replacing Hegel's idealistic and Kant's individualistic treatment of the history of human self-realisation with a history of class struggle, Marx produced a one-sided focus on instrumental actions and instrumental rationality. Habermas believes that this fact is the principal clue to Marx's ambiguous conceptualisation of the relationship between 'critique' and 'historical materialism' (Habermas, 1972, p. 46). A similar problem is encountered in the psychoanalytical theories of Freud, who consistently treated psychology as a natural science. From his training in medicine and neuropsychology, Freud imported a physicalistic language into psychoanalysis, but an 'energy distribution model only creates the semblance that psychoanalytic statements are about measurable transformations of energy' (Habermas, 1972a, p. 253). Freud's clinical observations from therapeutic sessions are not comparable to scientific observations from controlled experiments in natural science since the crucial and distinctive element of therapeutic talk is not control but intersubjectivity. In order to extract and to recover the emancipatory critique which is partly hidden in the mechanistic and positivistic language of Marx and Freud, Habermas has attempted to show that critical theory is, at least at one level, a form of linguistic analysis which exposes the distortions which are present in different forms of communication (Habermas, 1972). Marx's critique of political economy and Freud's psychoanalysis (when correctly interpreted) are thus specific examples of a more general project of critical theory whose aim is to expose the constraints inhibiting full, open, reflective communication. The goals of critical theory are also the goals of substantive rationality, namely the creation of the good society.

Habermas's approach to the sociology of Max Weber is not essentially different from that of other members of the Frankfurt School. There is no need to repeat the basic criticisms of Weber which have been made by Adorno, Horkheimer and Marcuse. Fundamentally, Habermas cannot accept what he takes to be Weber's equation of instrumental rationality with rationality as such. Because Habermas believes that the rational evaluation of ends is a proper task for critical theory, he cannot accept Weber's apparent resignation before the ruthless irrationality of bureaucratic capitalism. On the other hand, as McCarthy (1978, p. 140) points out, there is a fundamental parallel between the epistemological task confronted by Weber and that confronted by Habermas. In *Zur Logik der Sozialwissenschaften* (1970), Habermas treats the principal epistemological problem of social science in terms of bringing the natural sciences and the humanities 'under one roof' so that neither causal analysis nor interpretative understanding have an exclusive, privileged position. The problem facing Weber in the original *Methodenstreit* was of the same order. Weber's epistemological arguments have, therefore, provided Habermas with an important starting point for his own philosophical analysis. Closely related to this common issue is the whole problem of rationalisation and disenchantment in Weber which has been important, not only for Habermas, but the 'central preoccupation' (McCarthy, 1978, p. 18) of neo-Marxism since the early 1920s.

As with other members of the Frankfurt School, the success of their critique of Max Weber depends partly on the analytical security of their own alternative. Although Habermas has made enormous contributions to the development of critical theory, his theoretical position has to come to terms with serious difficulties and objections. Habermas's philosophy is less infected by the *'Kulturpessimismus'* (Merquior, 1979, p. 110) than is the case for Adorno, Horkheimer and Benjamin, but there are nevertheless definite limits on his optimism. Like Marcuse, Habermas cannot categorically identify those individuals or social groups which could be the *effective* carriers of critical theory. Indeed, Habermas believes that the emancipatory interest cannot be associated with or reduced to the specific interests of an identifiable group, but this has only resulted in a great vagueness as to the character of the transcendental nature of the emancipatory interest. By claiming that the emancipatory interest cannot be reduced to an 'empirical status' by an anthropological interpretation, Habermas in fact removes the emancipatory interest from close rational scrutiny (Brand, 1977, p. 12). Habermas's obvious reluctance to identify the urban working class as the bearers and recipients of critical theory is connected by Therborn (1977, p. 136) with Habermas's contemplative and individualistic treatment of theory separated from politics. Another aspect of the limitations on Habermas's optimism lies in the fact that he does not think that the crises of contemporary capitalism point necessarily to its demise. Capitalism is subject to four *'possible* crisis tendencies' (Habermas, 1976a, p. 45) of economy, administration, legitimation and motivation. There is no logical reason for these possibilities to produce a real crisis. Indeed, since Habermas conceptualises the social system as a cybernetic system, one might expect capitalism to produce an endless series of adjustments and adaptations to these tendential crises without fundamental reorganisation and restructuring. For Habermas, adjustments to crises tend to produce further crises-laden solutions, but the evolution of capitalism might be along the lines of Parsonian differentiation rather than Marxian collapse. Certainly the whole messianic image of apocalyptic self-destruction in *History and Class Consciousness* has disappeared in *Legitimation Crisis*. In short, Habermas's critical theory is not entirely free from the 'consistent pessimism' (Anderson, 1976, p. 93) which has typified so much of neo-Marxism and which was the hall-mark of Weberian sociology:

One obvious defence of Habermas would be that, since he is concerned with the conditions for the emancipation of the whole human species rather than a segment of it, he cannot possibly identify reason with the interests of a specific group. Nevertheless, it is important that an undistorted speech situation could be realised in an actual human community; the possibility of real communication must be more than a utopia. Habermas, it seems to me, underestimates the irreducible nature of constraint (regularity, invariance and limitation) in human society which would remain after criticism had removed merely contingent constraint. In short, Weber's pessimism and his belief in 'fate' are justified, because inequality, domination and force appear to be permanent features of all known, empirical societies. Habermas could be defended either by arguing that it is not the place of critical theory to dictate for someone else what their future freedom should look like or by arguing that critical theory should attempt to anticipate and promote extensions of freedom of discourse. In his discussion of non-distorted communication, Habermas does provide one major illustration of self-reflective discourse, namely psychoanalysis. This is a dubious illustration of open intersubjectivity of free communication. As Bernstein (1979, p. 222) points out, it can be claimed that analysis is effective not for the reasons suggested by Habermas, but as the result of 'a complex pattern of negative and positive reinforcement'. If we knew how the patient was conditioned in this process, we could perfect the conditioning without recourse to existing analytic practices.

There are, however, far more serious objections to Habermas's use of the psychoanalytic interview as an indicator of self-knowledge emerging from therapeutic talk. It is possible to argue the opposite case, that Freudian analysis is a good illustration of distorted communication in which distorted knowledge arises from the presence of domination. There are important status inequalities between analyst and analysand in terms of skill, training, knowledge, self-control and often social status. The analyst presents an image of friendship and trust, but he must also distrust the verbal offerings of the patient whose resistance must be broken. The analyst belongs to a professional body; there is no professional collectivity of the sick. The analysand pays a fee both as a mark of respect for the analyst and as an indication of commitment to recover. The fee is also an indication of the underlying impersonality of the analyst behind the overtly personal contact (Rieff, 1973, p. 87). Psychoanalysis along with other medical institutions can be regarded as part of the apparatus of social control of late capitalism (Zola, 1972). As a form of social control, psychoanalytic therapy can also be regarded as a secularised version of the sacrament of penance which in mediaeval Catholicism had similar social functions of maintaining public order through the manipulation of private conscience (Turner, 1977b). These comments on some recent criticisms of psychoanalysis are not meant to provide a powerful challenge to Habermas's use of Freudian therapy as a model of communication. It is an indication of Habermas's tendency to underestimate the irreducibility of constraints which operate both in labour and symbolic interaction. For example, much of the recent research into the role of questions in everyday language point to the fact that, when challenged by a question, it is very difficult to maintain silence. Questions constrain us into answers. This feature of questions is of crucial significance in police investigations and it illustrates the problematic nature of voluntary behaviour in connection with the presentation of evidence in legal proceedings (Hepworth and Turner, 1974). The constraints from which we can be liberated by critical theory are probably far less than the Frankfurt School imagines.

Is it possible, however, to provide a more substantial defence of Weber against the objections of critical theory other than noting that critical theory is not entirely satisfactory as a coherent analysis of society? It should be acknowledged at the outset that the Frankfurt School's interpretation of Weber is far more accurate than the analysis of Weber presented by various members of the Althusserian-structuralist tradition in Marxism. The key to Weber's sociology is not his epistemological distinctions or his subjectivist definition of social action. On the contrary, the key, as critical theory correctly perceives, is Weber's analysis of the ineluctable processes of rationalisation, routinisation and secularisation. For Weber, it is the fate of modern man to be overwhelmed by these forces, to which he can only respond with stoical resignation. Furthermore, Weber thinks that this fate is particularly ironic since it has been conjured up by rationality. History could be seen only as a contingent process. Nevertheless, it is possible to detect a sinister affinity between interests and structures which resulted in 'the iron cage' of disenchanted capitalism—'The logic of history would be the logic of the elective affinities' (Howe, 1978, p. 368). Weber's analysis of the unintended consequences of instrumental rationality and ascetic discipline in history does not appear to be far removed from Horkheimer's *Eclipse of Reason* or from the analysis of the Odyssey myth in *Dialectic of Enlightenment*. Indeed, both Weber's metasociology and the Frankfurt School's metaphilosophy are neatly summarised in an aphorism from Nietzsche's *The Genealogy of Morals*—'All great things perish by their own agency, by an act of self-cancellation' (*Selbstaufhebung*). The term '*Aufhebung*' is itself loaded with paradox since it means 'abolition' and 'cancellation' as well as 'transcendence' and 'preservation'. There is a dialectical cancellation of form, but also a preservation of content. The Frankfurt School could be said to have cancelled the form of Weber's sociology while preserving its contents. The first defence of Weber is then the argument that there is a major continuity between Weber and critical theorists which is mediated by such writers as Simmel and Lukács.

The second defence can be understood by examining the Frankfurt School's interpretation of Freud's relationship to his social context. While I have concentrated on the positive use which Marcuse and Habermas have made of Freudian psychoanalysis, Freud was severely criticised by Erich Fromm in a series of essays which were collectively published under the title *The Crisis of Psychoanalysis*. Fromm criticised Freud's theory of instincts, the Oedipus complex and the psychoanalytic model of man not so much because they were incorrect, but because their scope of application was severely limited to a particular family structure of a particular social class at a particular conjuncture of capitalism. According to Fromm (1973, p. 47), Freud's *homo sexualis* was simply a 'variant of the classic *homo economicus*' so that Freudianism provided the psychology of bourgeois political economy. Fromm argued that Freudianism also provided a defence of the role of force and threat in bourgeois society because Freudianism was in fact a legitimisation of parental power. By reinterpreting the case of Little Hans, Fromm (19734, p. 101) claimed that Freud's treatment of the child's incestuous desires 'is, up to a point, a defence of the parents, who are thus absolved of their incestuous fantasies and the actions that are known to occur'.

The psychoanalytic theory of Freud was subsequently defended by Horkheimer in a letter to Leo Lowenthal after Fromm's break with the Institute. Horkheimer, while denying the general argument that Freudianism was simply a reflection of the neuroses of the Viennese bourgeoisie, defended Freud on the grounds that 'The greater a work, the more it is rooted in the concrete historical situation' (quoted in Jay, 1973, p. 102). Freud's death instinct had no universal biological basis, but it was nevertheless a profound insight into the malaise of modern man. Similarly, Freud's psychology of the individual gave rise to the concept of the libido which was outside social institutions of control and which was to be preferred to Fromm's attempt to psychologise society and culture. A similar rejection of 'neo-Freudian revisionism' was developed by Adorno (1967–8) and by Marcuse (1969a). Adorno wanted to preserve Freud's instinctualism because it reinforced the idea of a fundamental contradiction between human happiness and the social order. Marcuse praised psychoanalysis as a 'radically critical theory' which 'demonstrated that constraint, repression, and renunciation are the stuff from which the "free personality" is made' (1969a, p. 190).

As we have seen, Marcuse rejected Weber's analysis of capitalism because Weber wrongly treated the contingent constraints of capitalism as insurmountable regularities. While Weber approached rationalisation as a 'fate' equivalent to 'gravity' in natural science, Marcuse (1968b, p. 214) argued

that 'society is not "nature". Who decrees the fate? Industrialization is a phase in the development of men's
capacities and needs, a phase in their struggle with nature and
with themselves'. Weber's sense of hopelessness in the face of
capitalist routinisation, his 'spiteful fight' against socialism
and his bleak conception of a political calling could be easily
traced back to Weber's academic role, his failure to achieve a
powerful political role, his personal neuroses and his origins in
the liberal wing of the burgher class. There is an analogy between Freud's narrow view of the intransigence of human instinctual needs in relation to his class location and Weber's
narrow view of the intransigence of capitalist structures in
relation to his class position. Horkheimer's dictum—'The
greater the work, the more it is rooted in the concrete historical
situation'—would appear to apply equally to Freud and Weber.
Weber's insight into the concrete reality of German class
structure, capitalist development and scientific culture in
terms of his own value-interests was precisely the greatness of
his sociology. The lasting importance of Weber's sociology is
to be located in its limitations.

It is necessary to assert, in addition, that the importance of
Weber's sociology transcends those concrete, historical limitations. I take it that a major aspect of the analyses of Marx,
Freud and Weber is to show that there are certain structures
which exist independently of human will and often of human
consciousness. These structures in the economic, biological,
political and other dimensions of social life may be variously
described as 'independent social relations', 'social facts',
'unintended consequences', 'libidinous structures' or 'fate'.
The important lesson of positivist sociology has been to
demonstrate the intransigence and facticity of social structures which cannot be undermined either by revolutionary
political struggle or by the critique of fetishised consciousness.
There are, in any case, difficulties involved in the use of Marx's
concept of 'fetishism' to criticise Durkheimian 'social facts' or
Weberian 'fate' as merely descriptions of the illusionary forms
of capitalism. Marx is usually interpreted as claiming that in
capitalism real relationships are obscured by a fantastic ex-
terior by which social relations appear as things. However,

Marx (1974, vol. 1, p. 78) in fact notes that the relations between the labour of various producers appears to them, not as social relations between individuals who labour 'but as what *they really are*, material relations between persons and social relations between things' (my emphasis). This observation could be interpreted as claiming, not that fetishised relations are an illusion in capitalism, but that in capitalism social structures really are objective structures with thing-like properties. From this perspective, the growing pessimism of the Frankfurt School, or at least their very qualified view of the possibilities of change in capitalist society, was not a function of their increasing age, a defect of their epistemology or their incorporation within an academic bourgeois environment. Their pessimism, like that of Weber, was a perfectly justified sociological appraisal of, on the one hand, the intransigence of constraints (economic, political and cultural) in social life generally and, on the other hand, of the adaptability of capitalist organisation to periodic crises in particular. That we enter into social relationships which are 'independent of our will' and that we make history 'but not as we please' are not conditions peculiar to capitalist production; they are unalterable facts of the very texture of everyday relationships in all human societies. To give expression to this unalterability was one of the great achievements of Weber's sociology of fate.

Part two

Religion

4 Religious stratification

In that exemplar of sociological wit, *The Theory of the Leisure Class*, Thorstein Veblen (1925) developed the theory that all dominant classes whose wealth resides in the ownership of productive property must be seen to be idle and unproductive. Their patterns of consumption must serve to illustrate their massive separation from the profane world of money and production. This isolation from profane wealth must also include their servants whose livery overtly symbolises their separation from usefully productive work. The same principles of idleness and conspicuous consumption also extend into the next world. The divinity must be in possession of idle servants and enjoy 'a peculiarly serene and leisurely habit of life' (Veblen, 1925, p. 93). Refinement, both sacred and profane, must be separated from mundane activities and the vulgarities of mere wealth. Max Weber implicitly developed a similar theory of the relationship between religious and secular stratification—this time without the humour. In Weberian sociology, we can discover the notion that all religious virtuosity must be developed in isolation from the work-place and from domestic chores.

Weber's sociology as a whole and his sociology of religion in particular are characteristically ambiguous in relation to Marxist materialism. This theoretical and political ambiguity can be clearly illustrated by applying Weber's analysis of religious stratification and the economic basis of charisma to a wide variety of religious groups. Weber's studies of religion have been viewed as a series of refutations, if not of Marx's own analysis of religion, then at least of the more vulgar reductions of religious phenomena to class interest by Engels, Kautsky and Bernstein. From a Parsonian perspective, Weber's comparative studies of Protestantism, Confucianism, Hinduism and Islam appear to demonstrate the independent role of religious beliefs in shaping the economic organisation of society. However, it can also be shown (Turner, 1977a and 1977b) that Weber's analyses are not only compatible with those of Marx, but that Weber's 'vision of history' is fundamentally deterministic and pessimistic. His sociological perspective is grounded in the doctrine of the inevitable fatefulness of historical processes in which human intentionality is always undermined and denied by its social consequences. Illustrations of these historical self-cancellations (*Selbstaufhebung*) in Weber's sociology are plentiful. Muhammad's inspired monotheistic and salvational prophecies were transformed by their very success 'into a national Arabic warrior religion' (Weber, 1966, p. 262) with a distinctly feudal character. The spiritual *jihad* for salvation was translated into a feudal movement for 'world domination and social prestige' (Weber, 1966, p. 148). All charismatic breakthrough are inevitably undermined by the material interests of disciples and later reconstituted under the process of social routinisation. While charismatic authority demands pure devotion, followers are motivated by mundane interests and everyday problems. Furthermore, priests have an important role to play in diluting charisma before it can be served up as a mass religion. Thus, the teachings of Jesus 'contained passages of an ethical substance which first had to be explained away by priestly interpretation (and thus in part turned into their exact opposite) before they were suitable for the purposes of a mass church in general and a priestly organization in particular' (Weber, 1958b, p. 26). Within a broader framework, Weber argues that precisely those features of Western history which promised to liberate men from the magic garden of enchantment produced the 'iron cage' of capitalist society. The anti-magical asceticism of the Protestant sects and secular instrumental rationality destroyed themselves in the disenchanted nightmare which Weber regarded as 'an unalterable order of things'.

Weber's pessimistic view of history is coupled with a

deterministic analysis of social relations in which economic interests and political power occupy the dominant part. It is not surprising, therefore, that the metaphor of machinery is central to his sociological discourse. Weber's social world is littered with 'cages', 'cogs', 'switchmen' and 'tracks'. Weber wants to avoid reductionism and materialism, but his analysis of human society drives him inevitably to a recognition of the centrality of economic and political interests. This ambiguity between his epistemology and his *Weltanschauung* is preeminently to be discovered in his study of charisma, virtuoso religion and routinisation. The origins and distribution of charisma in society are apparently not determined by economic relations, but material interests of the carriers and disciples of charisma shape and determine the outcome of charismatic movements. Pure loyalty is intended to be the contraceptive device which protects charisma from debasement, but we find that at every level of Weber's analysis economic interests continuously penetrate the inner mechanism of charismatic relationships. The point of this commentary is not, however, to give the 'dry bones' of the debate between Weber and Marx yet another rattle, but to show that a discussion of Weber's concept of virtuoso religion provides an insight into the economic processes of sanctification in a variety of religious contexts. However, to demonstrate the relevance of Weber's virtuoso model is also to show that the *sanctum sanctorum* cannot be secured against the profane effects of economic requirements.

Although Weber's general treatment of the charisma/ bureaucracy distinction has been widely discussed, his more specific contrast between virtuoso and mass interests has not been systematically explored (Roth and Schluchter, 1979) in relation to religious phenomena. Weber nowhere offered any sustained elaboration of virtuoso and mass religious styles, despite the centrality of this distinction to his view of Hinayana Buddhism, 'the god-suffused *bhakti* piety' of the Hindu cults and the importance of saints in Catholicism and Islam. Because Weber provides no sustained analysis of religious stratification, this dichotomy has to be picked rather carefully out of his text and to provide this exegesis it will be necessary to quote from Weber's sociology of religion at some length.

Weber observes that religion is a 'quality' which is unequally distributed through human society. As an 'empirical fact',

> men are *differently qualified* in a religious way....The sacred values that have been most cherished, the ecstatic and visionary capacities of shamans, sorcerers, ascetics and pneumatics of all sorts, could not be obtained by everyone. The possession of such facilities is a 'charisma' which, to be sure, might be awakened in some but not in all. (Weber, 1961, p. 287)

Since these religious gifts of 'commodities' are in demand but, in the nature of the case, in short supply, there develops in all religions various forms of spiritual inequality and stratification of grace. Thus, 'all intensive religiosity has a tendency towards a sort of status stratification in accordance with differences in the charismatic qualifications' (Weber, 1961, p. 287). Weber goes on to characterise these skills or qualifications of the adept by making an analogy between musical and religious ability. Heroic or virtuoso religiosity is contrasted with mass religiosity. The mass of the population are those who are religiously unmusical rather than those who stand at the bottom of the secular hierarchy.

Weber treats the 'drive for salvation' as one of the crucial dimensions of all world religions. Whether or not this religious drive was directed towards salvation in terms of inner-worldly asceticism or other-worldly mysticism had major consequences for civilisation as a whole. All religions which place an emphasis on rebirth and spiritual renewal will create a religious 'aristocracy' since people are unequally attuned to religious impulses. Weber argues that it must be recognised that:

> not everyone possesses the charisma that makes possible the continuous maintenance in everyday life the distinctive religious mood which assures the lasting certainty of grace. Therefore, rebirth seemed to be accessible only to

an aristocracy of those possessing religious
qualifications....In Islam there were the dervishes and
among the dervishes the particular virtuosi were the
authentic Sufis. (Weber, 1966, pp. 162-3)

Despite the very strong commitment to egalitarianism in
religious matters in both Christianity and Islam, the unequal
distribution of charisma produces an aristocratic hierarchy of
virtuosi. These spiritual elites have been historically under
pressure from the religious mass to water down, to simplify
and to minimise the moral and ritualistic requirements of
'authentic' charisma. There are, therefore, two aspects to
Weber's model of virtuoso/mass religiosity. First, there is the
stratification of populations into layers of charismatic ability.
Second, there is the tendency for virtuoso requirements to be
reduced to match the mundane limitations of the everyday life
of followers, supporters and disciples.

Weber's analysis of virtuoso religion directs us to the question of the economic support which is necessary for the cultivation and maintenance of a religiously musical elite. Since,
especially in the case of other-worldly asceticism and
mysticism, the virtuoso had to be free from employment in the
economy and liberated from the mundane requirements of food
and shelter, the virtuosi had to rely on the charity of their lay
sympathisers. There developed, therefore, a set of reciprocal
economic relations between the virtuosi, the inner circle of
devotees and the outer circle of laity. In exchange for these
mundane gifts, the laity received the charismatic blessings of
the virtuosi. Weber notes that

As the peasant was to the landlord, so the layman was to
the Buddhist and Jainist bhikshu: ultimately, mere
sources of tribute. Such tribute allowed the virtuosos to
live entirely for religious salvation without themselves
performing profane work, which always would endanger
their salvation. (Weber, 1961, p. 289)

Weber's model of the stratification of charismatic gifts has,
therefore, to make the assumption that there is such a

phenomenon as a religious 'talent' with the same sort of logical status as athletic, mathematical or musical talents. The idea is that certain individuals are better equipped to receive and to develop spiritual talents than the inept mass of the population. To some extent this analogy raises a 'nature/nurture' debate inside religion as to the exact manner in which certain individuals 'are better equipped'. From a sociological perspective, it is important to argue that the distribution of charisma and religiously talented persons is as much determined by the social structure as the distribution of 'military talent' among Highland Scots is determined by the clan system, the political role of the chiefs and the absence of alternative employment. Given the economically fragile base of virtuoso religion, there are good grounds for suspecting that virtuosity will become associated with certain privileged status groups. Since heroic religiosity requires freedom from economic want, the cultivation of this type of religiosity will be made easier for privileged social groups.

For the disprivileged, the transition from mass to virtuoso status, or from the outer circle of followers to the inner circle of adepts, is made problematic by their very involvement in the world. This is especially true where the novice is heavily encumbered with work, familial and kinship responsibilities. The transition from a privileged social position to a privileged religious one is not only far easier but far more 'natural'. The humble occupational origins of Jesus and Paul are not necessarily an obvious refutation of my argument that an economically employed virtuoso is a contradiction in terms, since both men abandoned carpentry and tent-making in favour of lay contributions. In the case of other religious leaders, Gautama and Muhammad could draw upon existing wealth to finance the initial stages of their meditation and religious development. In particular, Muhammad's spiritual development would have been impossible without the economic support of his wife Khadijah. Additional support for the claim that religious and social status are closely connected can be taken from the fact that in Christianity the 'official' saints of the Church have been predominantly over-recruited from dominant, privileged classes (George and George,

1953-5). However, it is not just the upper class that moves naturally into adept or virtuoso religious roles, for the same logic of availability applies also to such groups as widows, the young, the retired or any group which is socially marginal. Wherever there is no pressing, day-to-day requirement for direct employment in the labour market, leisure may be available for cultivating religious talent and joining in the supererogatory demands which are characteristic of virtuoso religious styles. Obeyesekere (1968) has made an analysis of the stratification of Buddhism to show how elderly villagers, particularly widows, become *upasaka*. This religious stratification occurs because widows are more able to fulfil virtuoso precepts than are villagers employed in demanding economic roles. Another example can be taken from Judaism, in which ideally men should give themselves 'night and day' to the study of the Torah. This ideal can only be achieved by an elite which enjoys the benefits of intellect and financial support. Financial offerings from the mass support the long study of the elite and, as a result, the traditional Jewish community was divided into scholars and workers. This contrast can be directly connected with the religious opposition between spirit (the world of learning and devotion) and matter (the profane sphere of ignorance and work). The contrast is encapsulated in the Talmudic dictum 'an uneducated man cannot be devout' and in the mystical image of the Jews as a vine on which the scholars are grapes and the people, leaves (Meijers, 1979). Thus, while there is no necessary link between religious and social elites, there are good grounds for believing that there is a strong probability for such secular and religious linkage. In order for any heroic religiosity to appeal to the mass and to become a religiosity fostered by the mass, certain transformations of the pristine elitism of the virtuoso requirements must take place. Weber's virtuoso/mass dichotomy is, therefore, not a static ideal-type construct, but a dynamic model of the continuous reconstitution of elitist religiosity into popular forms.

These transformations are, however, not to be conceived in a uniform or simple fashion. The supply of charisma cannot be readily controlled and the demand for religious services is itself often specialised and differentiated. The production and consumption of charismatic phenomena take place in a religiously competitive situation where the source of supply may well be elastic. In short, the language of conventional Samuelsonian economics provides an appropriate framework for elaborating Weber's analysis of popular and elitist religiosity. Charisma is a 'commodity' which is exchanged for money, services and other commodities. The charisma at the centre of religious activity moves outwards bringing healing, comfort and teaching to the laity. The gifts at the outer lay circle are transferred inwards bringing the material conditions for charismatic reproduction. Given Weber's pessimism about the survival of truly heroic religion before a mass audience, virtuosity is always compelled to make concessions to popular needs. Thus,

> With the exception of Judaism and Protestantism, all religions and religious ethics have had to reintroduce cults of saints, heroes or functional gods in order to accommodate themselves to the needs of the masses...Islam and Catholicism were compelled to accept local, functional and occupational gods as saints, the veneration of which constituted the real religion of the masses in everyday life. (Weber, 1966, pp. 103–4)

Over-production of religious commodities in response to market demands produces inevitable devaluation of quality. However, it could be suggested, as a qualification to Weber's argument, that there would be considerable charismatic specialisation and differentiation of religious gifts in response to existing social differentiation in the religious market. There may be 'up-market' and 'down-market' religious products which are consumed by various groups within the status hierarchy of the market-place. Spiritually demanding, rigorous and theologically sophisticated charisma may satisfy the consumption wants of the social elite while remaining outside the 'income range' of the socially and religiously disprivileged. In order to illustrate this model of charisma and religious stratification, I shall consider the cases of Wesleyan Methodism and Islamic Sufism.

Many historians have drawn attention to the deism of the aristocracy and the intellectual elite which formed part of the background of the Wesleyan movement and the evangelical revival. By an analysis of 'Nature', rationalists hoped to derive laws for society which would be as self-evident as those of physics and mathematics. These rationalist assumptions had a radical impact on theology: the angry God of the Old Testament was replaced by the benign Mechanic of Nature and reason removed the necessity for revelation. There was a general tendency to tone down traditional doctrines of sin and damnation, thus mitigating the need for salvation. The Church of England was itself invaded by deism and pelagianism. Lecky (1883, Vol. 2, p. 545), writing of the Anglican pulpit, noted that:

> the moral essays which were the prevailing fashion,
> however well suited they might be to cultivate the moral
> taste, or to supply rational motives for virtue, rarely
> awoke any strong emotions of hope, fear or love, and were
> utterly incapable of transforming the character and ar-
> resting and reclaiming the thoroughly depraved.

It was this intellectualised moralism which the evangelicals ought to replace by a soteriological religion of conviction and emotion.

Wesleyanism was a clear example of a religious movement that contained within itself much that would appeal to the disinherited by emphasising emotion and personal experience rather than formal, cognitive orthodoxy. Wesley argued that:

> The traditional evidences of Christianity stand, as it were,
> a great way off; and, therefore, although it speaks, loud
> and clear, yet it makes a less lively impression....Whereas
> the inward evidence is intimately present to all persons,
> at all times and in all places....What reasonable assurance
> can you have of things whereof you have no personal ex-
> perience? (Telford, 1931, vol. 2, p. 384)

The emphasis in Wesleyanism was not on orthodoxy or so

much on conventional morality, but on holiness. Wesley summed up this position by a clever analogy:

> Our main doctrines which include all the rest are three—that of repentance, of Faith and Holiness. The first of these we account, as it were, the porch of religion; the next, the door; the third, religion itself. (Telford, 1931, vol. 2, pp. 267–8)

While Wesleyanism reacted to eighteenth-century society in common with evangelicals generally, Wesleyanism differed from these in many important respects.

It is well known that Wesley's notion of holiness was deeply influenced by the Catholic mystics and Wesley himself made specific reference to the influence of Thomas à Kempis, Francois de Sales and Fénelon. The mystical elements of early Wesleyanism were even more emphasised in the hymns of Charles Wesley (Lofthouse, 1965). Wesley, according to Jean Orcibal, was most open to a mystical religiosity before 1738 and after 1765. In the intervening years, Wesley turned against mysticism, partly because he could not agree with Moravian 'quietism' which rejected the ordinances of religion. Wesley was also deeply concerned by the antinomian trends which Wesleyanism had sparked off among many of its followers and which he associated with 'stillness' and mysticism. Regardless of these changing orientations, the point to stress at this stage is simply that Wesley's view of sanctification was heavily influenced by mysticism. In so far as Wesleyanism had an ascetic component, it was other-wordly rather than this-wordly. The major theme of Wesleyanism was not world-mastery, but the development of a spiritual path or technique which would facilitate the achievement of holiness. It was holiness which the early Wesleyan virtuosi sought and, while Wesley accepted that complete sanctification was a gift of grace dependent on faith, there was a marked ritualism in the Wesleyan method. Wesleyanism may, therefore, be described as a virtuosity of devotionalism.

It was because of their 'practical spirituality' that Wesleyans earnt the titles 'Methodists', 'Holy Club', 'Sacramentarians' and 'Supererogation men'. The Oxford

method included daily observations of the offices, mortifica-
tion, fasting and penance. Holy Club spirituality was summed
up in Wesley's treatment of instituted and prudential means of
grace. The former were:

prayer (private, family, public)
searching the scriptures (by reading, meditating, hearing)
The Lord's Supper
fasting
Christian Conference (George, 1963)

Wesleyan additions to the practice of ordinary lay Anglicans
marked Wesleyans off as a virtuoso group of devotional
adepts. The stratification of more or less proficient religious
adherents of the Wesleyan path to holiness was, however,
most clearly illustrated by the prudential means of grace.

Wesleyanism grew up in an age in which religious societies
were experiencing a considerable boom. Wesleyanism borrowed
much from these societies, in particular from the Moravians.
The Wesleyan societies differed from these in that few
societies could have been governed with such meticulous
scrutiny. Kissack (1964, p. 83) has observed that, 'Since
holiness was the overriding doctrinal objective, Church Order
must have as its mainspring a corresponding principle. This
was "watchfulness".' Organisational watchfulness may be
seen as a series of expanding circles of control. Adepts
migrated between these circles according to whether or not
Wesley and his assistants thought promotion or demotion was
warranted. To some extent the outer circles, who were more involved in the demands of mundane living than the inner
circles, tended to finance the spiritual life of those adepts who
were closer to the pivot of Wesleyan virtuosity.

At the centre stood those who had received remission of sins
and who had testified to their sanctity by consistent Christian
living. These were termed the select societies. Those whom
Wesley regarded as having remission of sins but whose
spiritual life was yet indeterminate were united into Bands.
The third circle, the united Societies, were described as
'awakened persons' and the fourth circle were 'those who have
made shipwreck of the faith'. This outer circle met 'apart as
penitents' (Baker, 1965).

This organisation of outer and inner circles was somewhat modified by the introduction of the class system. In February 1742, Wesley divided the Bristol Society into classes for raising a penny a week from each member to pay off the debt on the New Room. This system of fund-raising soon spread throughout the societies and in time the class both changed its function and to some extent ousted the band meetings. Through the class leaders, Wesley gained even greater control over lay Wesleyans. The purpose of the class was to encourage discipline, fellowship and devotion. However, Wesley continued to insist that without the bands Wesleyanism would decline spiritually and, while the system of holy circles lost much of its precise definition, as late as 1789 one still finds references to Select Societies and Penitents' meetings.

Much of Wesleyan fund-raising was necessitated by the growth of preaching houses. Money came from the donations of sympathisers and wealthy members, ticket and class money plus the shilling per member at the visitation. Apart from the debt from building new chapels, a proportion of the funds was earmarked for travelling preachers. Because of the nature of their strenuous and mobile life, Wesley urged the preachers to remain single men. In addition, single men were less of a drain on limited finances. While in circuit, preachers 'lived off the land', often by lodging with Wesleyan supporters. Preachers were originally instructed not to accept money, since Wesley thought that his critics would claim that Wesleyans grew affluent by being holy. This instruction proved impracticable and in 1752 Conference allocated £12 for English preachers as a clothing allowance and an additional £10 for married preachers. The result was that circuits attempted to avoid married itinerants because of the additional costs. Many preachers found the grant inadequate and were forced to take up some part-time employment. The problem came to a head in 1768 and Conference declared that an itinerant preacher must not be employed since 'he receives his allowance for this very end that he may not need to do anything else' (Baker, 1965). Preachers, especially the married ones, who still followed a trade, were often removed from the select group of itinerant preachers to the lower grade of local preachers. The financing of preachers was more than a measure to achieve good preaching: it was also a means of preserving the holy life of preachers free from mundane wants and influences.

Wesleyanism was a virtuoso movement of adepts systematically following a path of holiness. Hierarchies of religious qualifications were quite explicit in Wesleyanism. In terms of theology, Wesley differentiated the 'Sons of God' from the 'servants of God'. Sonship involved union with God manifested in holy living; the servants were those persons in whom the spiritual life was merely aroused. In organisational terms, Wesleyanism consisted of circles of greater and lesser sanctification. The circles were determined by spiritual growth or, at least, holiness determined by Wesley. The distribution of holiness was markedly influenced by social standing. Many of the original adepts were free from toil either because of support or because of their Anglican livings, or both. At a lower level barbers, shopkeepers and tradesmen, while involved in mundane pursuits, were to some extent free from the burdens of full-time manual employment, since self-employment gave them control over their work situation. In general, the system of holiness was dependent on the contributions of the outer circles of Wesleyan followers. There was, however, an abiding conflict between the full demands of the Wesleyan ethic of methodical pursuit of holiness and the demands resulting from involvement in the world. This conflict, along with many others, was an early crack in the Wesleyan holy wall through which mass religiosity began to flow.

The accommodation to mass religiosity was greatly facilitated by the incongruity between heroic devotionalism and Wesley's commitment to Arminianism. Of course, evangelical Wesleyanism would not necessarily have undermined the original virtuoso style had the movement insisted on strict criteria of entrance, a more precise definition of orthodoxy, and had the rate of recruitment not been so rapid. At first, deviant recruits or 'disorderly walkers' were rooted out by the class system, but during the nineteenth century this system collapsed and internal control became lax. In the absence of an enduring discipline, Arminianism pulled Wesleyanism towards mass religiosity: the dilemma of the movement was that heroic religiosity could not be completely accepted by the mass who were unavoidably committed to work, community and family. In order to pinpoint this mutation of religious style, it is interesting to examine the different appeal certain aspects of original Wesleyanism had for two social groups, namely the disprivileged of both town and country and the growing number of artisans, tradespeople and small businessmen.

The image of Methodism as a straight-laced nonconformist denomination resulted from the impact of artisan needs and life-styles on the Methodist societies. If Wesleyanism had a strong other-worldly ascetic and even mystical element, it also had the beginnings of an inner-wordly ascetic ethic. Wesley himself had, of course, turned away from his early interest in mysticism after his return from Georgia. Wesleyans were expelled from the societies for, among other things, gossiping, swearing, unfair practice, gambling and for wearing large bonnets. There was an affinity between the ascetic components of Wesleyanism and the life-styles of the *nouveau riche*. Wesleyan ascetic norms were already implicit in the routines and virtues which successful businessmen practised in their day-to-day lives. Such groups were able to work on Wesleyan asceticism, bending it more and more to the rationalism of their secular employments. While Wesleyan asceticism had an appeal for businessmen and artisans by clothing their matter-of-fact occupational routines with a religious meaning, Wesleyan other-worldly asceticism and devotionalism had far less affinity with their needs. Lawson (1965, p. 207), has observed that:

> Busy shopkeepers approved of that part of Methodist discipline which in the name of God bade them 'scorn delights and live laborious days'. They had room for the regular Sunday Service and dutiful family prayers.
> However, the more ascetic and ecclesiastical discipline of the 'morning preaching', the Friday Fast and having one's heart searched to the bottom at the penitential Band was less congenial.

At the local level, these social groups had an impact on

nineteenth-century Methodism out of proportion to their actual numbers. Their wealth and position on committees meant that their style of religiosity could not be successfully opposed.

The other side of early nineteenth-century Methodism was its emotional appeal to the disprivileged urban and rural labourer. Methodist emotionalism emerged as the result of a combination of its doctrines with the needs of the working class. While Wesleyanism was Arminian, it came frequently, as Wesley observed, 'to the very edge of Calvinism', but whereas the certainty of salvation was indicated by worldly success in later Calvinism, it was indicated in Methodism by an emotional conversion experience. Conversion in Methodism became a key event in what Wesley termed the 'way to Heaven'. While Methodist artisans tended to develop an almost Calvinistic interpretation of work as a 'calling', in popular Methodism paroxysm, glossolalia and other conversion phenomena were taken as signs of divine selection. Emotionalism was both an inner certainty and an outward demonstration of the achievement of a higher religious status. While Wesleyan leaders came to recognise the incipient antinomian consequences of their doctrine of sanctification, they were often powerless to prevent these reinterpretations of their doctrines.

The external pressures contributing to emotional conversion were present in the disruptions and deprivations brought about by rapid industrialisation. Methodism provided a relief from hardships in its joyous hymns, its love-feasts and in its fellowship, while the camp-meetings of the Primitive Methodists were perfect occasions for emotional release. Hobsbawm (1959, p. 131) has drawn attention to the social consequences of Methodist preaching:

> Visions of splendour, of judgment and of hellfire for the evil men filled those who needed support to bear the burden of their suffering, and the emotional orgies of hellfire preaching, revivals and similar occasions brought diversion to their lives.

It was in this way that, as Thompson (1963) has argued,

Methodism came to serve simultaneously as a religion of the poor and of the rich. For the poor, it compensated for earthly misery; for the rich, Methodism provided a legitimation of their earthly success and a work-ethic capable of injecting discipline into their employees. But Methodism's very success in appealing to these social strata resulted in a transformation of devotional virtuosity into two distinguishable types of mass religious style. Both types were deviations from Wesley's elitist path of sanctification.

The history of Sufism has often been written in terms of an undimensional transition from elitist asceticism to popular religiosity. As Kritzeck (1973, pp. 153–4) brusquely comments, Sufism started out as a protest against Islamic worldliness on the part of 'high-minded ascetics' but, under the influence of 'mediocre students' and the popular lodges, it came to have 'nothing to do with the original spiritual ideals. That was the point at which they started to take drugs, pierce their flesh and whirl.' The word 'Sufism' was derived from 'suf', the undyed wool worn by Christian ascetics of the East. The woollen garment was later replaced by a patched frock which the sheikh gave to his novice. Sufis referred to themselves as 'the folk' (*al-qawm*), 'the poor' (*al-fuqara*) or *darvish*. However, the original woollen garment was indicative of their asceticism and the Sufi movement was founded on 'aversion to the false splendor of the world, abstinence from the pleasure, property and position to which the great mass aspires and retirement from the world into solitude for divine worship' (Ibn Khaldun, 1958, vol. 3, p. 76).

Given this ascetic and elitist withdrawal, many Orientalists treat the progress of Sufism as one of perpetual decline in the direction of popular religion. The popular success of Sufism as a social movement exposed Islam to the influence of indigenous beliefs and practises, heterodox attitudes and local customs (Gibb and Bowen, 1957; Gibb, 1969; Rice, 1964). These popular Sufi saints became dependent on the alms of the laity and in return they had to demonstrate their magical and miraculous capacities. The hierarchical order of the saints came to depend on lay evaluations of their miraculous powers. Thus, 'the purity of the saint's life or doctrine is of secondary importance; if he can work miracles, that is enough, he is a saint and therefore to be feared and one whose protection is to be sought. A saint without miracles is no saint at all' (Trimingham, 1965, p. 128). According to this type of perspective, whereas heroic Sufism was founded on the assumption that the goal of the religious path was extremely difficult to achieve and required strenuous training and demanding commitment, in popular Sufism saintship was achieved by recognition in fire-eating, snake-charming, divination and wizardry. The other important change was that the saint's *baraka* became almost entirely a matter of inheritance: the pure charisma of achievement was thus transformed into lineage charisma. Furthermore, popular Sufism came to include not only adherence to living saints, but the cult of dead saints and their tombs. From these horizontal saints in their tombs there appeared to be an endless flow of charismatic power.

There are a number of problems with this type of interpretation of Sufism and a particular difficulty connected with the distinction between popular and official Islam. It is always difficult to make judgments about the purity of original Sufi asceticism without also raising traditional issues in Orientalism as to the 'authenticity' of Islamic spirituality as such and its dependence on Christian and other religious sources (Massignon, 1922). The view of writers like Trimingham (1971, p. 26) that 'Sufism provided a philosophy of election which was diluted and adapted to the needs of the masses by the orders' clearly supports Weber's fatalistic history of self-cancellation, but it is not entirely adequate as a sociological analysis. Rather than treating Sufism as a 'decline' from or 'corruption' of pure Islam, popular religion is more properly regarded as a form of 'practised Islam' (Waardenburg, 1978) and the relationship between scholarly religion and its popular manifestations as an interaction between social groups interpreting their practices by reference to common formulae. Popular religion is not in historical terms simply a vulgarisation of the Islamic mysticism of Ibn Al-Arabi and al-Ghazzali. Intellectualised mysticism and popular religion have always stood side-by-side, oriented to different clientele with different social and religious interests. This is not to ignore the fact that the general sociological status of popular religion has been fundamentally transformed by the process of the rise of decolonisation, puritan reformism and the formulation of nationalist ideology (Brown, 1972). Returning to the analogy of economic and religious commodities, it is more accurate to regard popular and official religion as a form of differentiation and specialisation of religious services in connection with different lay markets than to treat 'mass religiosity' as the contaminated progeny of pure religious consciousness.

As Weber (1966, p. 101) notes, the disprivileged mass of the population, especially the peasantry, is rarely oriented towards an impersonal, rational theodicy. From the point of view of the religious elite, the rural peasantry were traditionally regarded as heathen (*paganus*) who obstinately clung to magical practices as a medium for manipulating local gods. Within this social context, charismatic authority is significantly exposed to mundane interests and needs of followers. 'Folk religion' is historically very closely bound up with 'folk medicine' because one of the primary interests of the mass is the acquisition of remedies and cures in a social context where alternative forms of medical treatment are not available. Much of the contemporary discussion of Sufi brotherhoods has focused on their political functions (Geertz, 1968; Gellner, 1972; Wolf, 1971). It is equally important, however, to concentrate on what might be broadly referred to as the 'medical' or therapeutic component of exchanges between saints and their followers in order to illustrate the specialisation of religion around the life-styles and interests of various classes. In their traditional rural setting, it is difficult to distinguish the sheikhs from other practitioners of religio-magical healing within the folk system of spirit-possession and its treatment. Within the shantytown context, the religious 'clubs' have the effect of integrating urbanised peasantry into a network of primary social relationships.

In general etymological and sociological terms there is, in any case, a close interconnection between social membership, therapy and religion. To save the soul and to salve the body are verbs which have their roots in the Latin *salvare*. The mediaeval summa and penitentials expressed the view that sin was a conflict of the body and soul which could be resolved through the healing ministry of the sacrament of penance and through the grace monopolised by ecclesiastical institutions. In this respect, confession can be regarded as a ritual of inclusion whereby the restoration of the individual to group membership involves a simultaneous healing of the body (Turner, 1977b). While in Islamic cultures a comparable sacrament of penance was not fully institutionalised (Gilsenan, 1973), it is possible to identify similar mind/body conceptions in popular belief and ritual (Kennedy, 1967, p. 193). The notion of *baraka* also embodies the meaning of plenitude and wellbeing in the symbolic form of bread.

While the social significance of *baraka* may depend on its systematically distorted meanings (Gellner, 1970), there is also a popular lay consensus concerning its alleged therapeutic effects. Among the Hamadsha, Crapanzano (1973) demonstrates that *baraka* is regarded as the force which lies behind the cure of sickness, especially illness brought about by spirit-possession. However, the therapeutic effect of *baraka* cannot be analysed in isolation from the cathartic results of participation in the collective rituals of ecstatic dance (the *hadra*) and pilgrimage (*musem*). Participation in these collective rituals draws the individual into a network of supportive social relationships—

> The ailing individual is not isolated and ignored, but becomes a patient who is the concern of the whole group. The group consists of family friends, and neighbours as well as the Hamadsha, not only offers the patient sympathy, encouragement, and the hope of cure, but also mobilizes itself to cure the patient of his troubles.
> (Crapanzano, 1973, p. 215)

These Durkheimian rituals reorganise the social relationships which are in part the cause of the patient's stressful condition. Employing a Freudian psychoanalytic view of spirit-possession and their hysterical sequels, Crapanzano goes on to argue that these 'socially generated tensions' are effects of the psychological contradictions of masculine identity in a society which is structured in terms of the subordination of women to men and the domination of men over boys. While masculine identity is defined in terms of sexual prowess, control of women and political dominance, sons are forced by social custom to be subservient, dependent and obedient in relation to their fathers. The social role of young males is, therefore, parallel to the social role of women in general. The social and psychological problem is consequently that of how mature male identities can emerge out of these dependent 'feminine' roles. The symptomatology of spirit-possession and attacks by *jinn* include tremors, convulsions, mutism and paralysis. The symptomatology is symbolic of the underlying contradictions in the sexual division of labour and the social allocation of sexual identity. Being struck by *jinn* on the face is both the cause of paralysis and an indication of the crisis of male identity. The treatment of these afflictions involves an intensification of group membership (such as becoming an active participant in the Hamadsha) and involvement in particular rituals which are directed at the discovery of the appropriate musical formulae (*rih*) which will pacify the offending *jinn*.

If treatment and sickness are sociologically connected by the intensification of rituals of social interaction and renewal of social membership, then long-term incumbency of a 'sick role' may be regarded as a form of social deviance (Parsons, 1951). In the Islamic Middle East, Morsy (1978) argues that illness behaviour may be a method of legitimising behaviour which deviates from traditional norms. In the Egyptian Nile Delta, the *ma'zur* or *ma'zura* (possessed male or female) may give off a wide variety of symptoms of a medical character, but the social manifestations have a common theme, namely the breaking of social customs. A woman who suffers from *'uzr* may turn down the offer of marriage to a particular man selected by her father, oppose her husband's desire to take a second wife or decline to nurse a child. The social importance of *'uzr* is that it provides an acceptable socio-medical label for deviant activities and at the same time provides some legitimation and institutionalisation for the behaviour. Thus, 'the very term *'uzr* (excuse) provides the illness with a social definition. It offers the *ma'zur* (excused) a temporary dispensation from the requirements of social canons' (Morsy, 1978, p. 603). The onset of *'uzr* is intimately connected to conflicts within the domestic setting and to the exercise of power by men and elders such as a forced contract of marriage or the threat of divorce. Those afflicted by *'uzr* are able to retain a marginal status within the community and to avoid the process of social exclusion and punishment traditionally associated with serious forms of deviance. The occupation of the social role of the *ma'zur* may, however, be brought to an end by involvement in a number of collective, therapeutic rituals. The ambiguities and conflicts of female status have been aggravated by the development of migrant labour conditions which denude these isolated villages of their male inhabitants. The saint cults and the *zar* ceremonies are both concerned with the 'return of husbands, marriage of children, material goods, cures and the like' (Kennedy, 1967, p. 189) in a social context where alternative welfare and medical institutions are not available. The *zar* works 'to untie' depressions, ennui and isolation by involving these women in socially supportive rituals and communal practices.

In human groups, the incidence of sickness and its appropriate therapy are not randomly distributed through the population, but are 'allocated' to individuals by channels which are determined by social and economic criteria of class membership, occupation and gender. The social distribution of sickness and disease in industrial society also has parallels in pre-industrial and developing societies. Contemporary research by medical sociologists in modern Britain has, for example, shown that standardised mortality rates and rates of perinatal deaths are significantly correlated with social class. A number of mental and physical illnesses are also clearly influenced by sexual identity. The connection between depression and the domestic situation of working-class women is a case in point (Brown, 1976). Furthermore, differences in the treatment of mental illness by social class position in industrial societies have been systematically documented (Dohrenwend and Dohrenwend, 1969; Hollingshead and Redlich, 1958). While sickness in North Africa obviously has a very different cultural ambiance from the social organisation

of sickness in European societies, it is still possible to conceptualise illness and its treatment on a comparative basis in relation to the class and sexual characteristics of individuals. In
the absence of a medical system dominated by a centralised
professional monopoly of medical care, the various virtuoso
religious groups, lodges and orders retain important social
functions in treating the religio-medical needs of their lay
clientele. In exchange for *baraka* and therapeutic practices of
dance music and pilgrimage, the virtuosi are financed out of
alms, gifts and services. These charitable gifts contribute to
the separation of the saints from places in productive labour,
domestic chores and maintains their isolation from everyday
routines. Through these exchange relations, the stratification
of *baraka* replicates the hierarchical organisation of the
population by social class.

We can characterise the religious styles and organisation of
North African Islam by reference to two contrasted syn-
dromes. In the towns, immediate access to the Qur'an is
associated with egalitarianism, a minimal role for saintly intervention, the scholarship and puritanism of the *'ulama* and
an absence of colourful emotionalism and elaborate ritual practices in worship. In the rural areas, there is a non-literate,
ritualistic and ecstatic religiosity. There is also the presence of
religious hierarchy, mystical states and the mediation of
saints. There is also, therefore, a contrast between the north-
ern and southern shores of the Mediterranean basin. In the
Roman Catholic context, saints are defined by bureaucratic
means as the paragons of true faith, orthodox practice and are
consequently proper objects of lay devotion. The process of
canonisation of saints is protracted and ensures that all saints
are simultaneously orthodox and dead. Saintly grace cannot be
inherited through the male descendants of official saints,
although their charisma may be encapsulated in their relics
and tombs. By contrast the saints of Islam are not
bureaucratically controlled by an ecclesiastical institution, not
regarded as orthodox, not necessarily deceased and their
charisma may be transmitted by contagion and inheritance
(Turner, 1974). Where urbanised Sufi lodges develop,
mysticism is an alternative to the *'ulama*-dominated religious

styles whereas in the rural hinterland it is a substitute for legalistic practice (Gellner, 1968). Within this broad framework there is the interstitial growth of Sufi lodges which minister to the needs of shantytown inhabitants by developing specialised, competitive religious frameworks. The competition over clientele develops in part from the fact that there is an over-production of religious personnel in relation to local requirements. Because Sufi saints could never adopt a policy of official celibacy and because their *baraka* could be inherited, the number of eligible saints tends to be in excess of existing social roles. These surplus descendants of virile saints could either become dormant experts awaiting future employment or they could become geographically mobile, moving from the countryside to the cities and *bidonvilles*. Innovation in social practices is characteristically associated with competitive social situations where surplus social actors create the need for new markets and audiences. The competitive religious market is no exception to this sociological rule where the migrant saint,

> in order to obtain new converts and to win members from the existing lodges, improved his competitive position by developing his own special technique which won new supporters and distinguished one lodge from another. The saint sold both himself and his commodity on the urban market and, as in other types of salesmanship, he developed a certain personal panache: the more unusual the commodity, the more likely it was to attract a new audience. (Mulkay and Turner, 1971, p. 50)

Where these saints are successful in identifying an audience or in creating a new order, these religious 'clubs' offer mutual support and psychological satisfaction for their followers in an urban location where most traditional forms of social interaction have declined or collapsed.

This distinction between rural and urban forms of Islam offers a sociological context within which to discuss the religious style of the urban *zawiya* operating within an established town and the religiosity of the informal loosely structured teams which perform in the *bidonville*. Whereas the new urban *zawiyas* are organised for the support of the saint, the shanty-town teams, providing public ceremonies such as the *hadra*, are more explicitly involved with illness and the treatment of spirit-possession. Whereas the litanies and rituals of the urban *zawiyas* are modest and sober, the *bidonville* celebration of the *hadra* tends to be exuberant, intense and dramatic. The involvement of these devotees (*muhibbin*) of the Hamadsha teams provide them with wider social involvement and enables the urbanised peasantry of the shantytowns to enlarge their circle of social contacts. Membership of these religious 'clubs' has the consequence of integrating the rootless poor into primary groups in an urban environment which is often anomic and uncertain. The 'underclass' of the *bidonville* (Worsley, 1972) experiences a psychological discharge in the head-slashing rituals of the Hamadsha teams. The sociological connection between social deprivation and religious involvement can, however, be more precisely expressed in terms of class membership because,

> the concern for ritual differences seems to symbolize the differences between madina and bidonville inhabitants which the bidonville dweller senses. He prefers the bidon-ville teams because their devotees are very much in the same position as himself....The foqra, who consider themselves city people, have never been anxious to develop a large following of bidonville muhibbin despite the obvious increase in income these devotees would bring. (Crapanzano, 1973, p. 127)

Differences in religiosity can, therefore, be associated with the contrast in rural and urban experiences, the deprivation of shantytown conditions and the emotional problems associated with the power relationships of domestic life. The religious rituals are simultaneously symbolic of social differentiation and therapeutic responses to personal crises which are the products of these structural conditions. There is, in addition, an important economic component to this religious structuration. In terms of Weber's virtuoso typology, the supererogatory demands of an elitist religious programme are incompatible with the routines and requirements of mundane existence. The religious demands of the 'elite' brotherhoods and *zawiyas* are incompatible with the requirements of secular employment and domestic work. Religious affiliation and involvement correlate directly with the life-cycle, sexual status and socio-economic class position. In this context, the theoretical parallel between Weber's virtuoso–mass typology and Troeltsch's church–sect distinction is clearly detected. The middle class and the middle aged are over-represented in established churches and denominations. However, institutionalised Christianity does have an impact on the working class through the medium of sectarian emotionalism and convertionist enthusiasm (Niebuhr, 1929). Similarly, throughout Islam the audience for the therapeutic aspects of the saints cults and other popular religious movements is predominantly drawn from women and disprivileged groups in general who are troubled by mundane problems of marriage, childbirth, health and employment (Geijbels, 1978). For women, their choice of saint is often restricted by the limitations placed on their geographical mobility away from the home and village. Access to alternative systems of treatment may also be circumstantial. Women will also select those orders and lodges which will easily fit into the everyday routines of domestic work.

> [In] the Jilaliy order, for example, certain devotions and prayers need not be said exactly at the proper hour nor with undivided attention. Instead a Jilaliyya can gear her schedule more closely to household demands....These feelings serve to explain why most women carefully avoid membership in the Tijaniyya even into old age. (Dwyer, 1978, p. 593)

While the *Tijaniyya* order is not the most rigidly ascetic and demanding of Sufi orders, it has been closely connected with the rich and the politically dominant sectors of the community (Abun-Nasr, 1965, pp. 47–57). However, the litanies of the order have to be performed twice every day and they make a particularly demanding inroad into the routine chores of peasant women and on the work pattern of ordinary men. Thus, the hired wage-earner, 'at harvest time or the vegetable seller in the market cannot easily leave his work to perform the exacting Tijaniy devotions. Workers of this sort require greater flexibility. The Jilaliy, ben Nasriy and Derqawiy orders more readily meet these needs' (Dwyer, 1978, p. 596). Other Islamic orders, such as the *Demerdashiya Khalwayiya*, also provide examples of social and religious elitism which works against the involvement of women and the economically underprivileged (Trimingham, 1971; Gilsenan, 1973). In the African context, the Mourides of Senegal have occupied a key social position in the distribution of property in land (O'Brien, 1971). Thus, we can conclude that in order to satisfy the more exacting regime of their orders or to change their membership to one of the more rigorous orders, both men and women may be required to wait until their old age allows some release from domestic involvements and other forms of employment.

All spiritual elitism demands some form of withdrawal from mundane demands especially those related to employment. Freedom from regular employment not only offers the means for creating and adhering to supererogatory religious requirements, it is also more consistent and in keeping with sacred duties. In order to preserve that freedom, the virtuoso needs some system of financial support. This economic aid can be provided by some form of patronage, as when one class pays a group of religious specialists to pray on its behalf (Rosenwein and Little, 1974). It is more usual for the virtuosi to be maintained as an unproductive class from lay payments, fees and gifts. In the case of mystical experts, this produces a paradoxical situation where the religious flight from sinful reality is financed by the very continuity of that profane world. It is interesting to note the similarity of Weber's charisma/rationality distinction and Durkheim's dichotomous model of the sacred and profane world. Complete involvement in profane activities precludes strenuous adherence to sacred requirements so that men

are exhorted to withdraw themselves completely from the

profane world, in order to lead an exclusively religious life. Hence comes the monasticism which is artificially organised outside of and apart from the natural environment in which ordinary man leads the life of the world, in a different one, closed to the first and nearly its contrary. (Durkheim, 1961, p. 55)

Weber catches this religious paradox with his characteristic perspicacity:

The contemplative mystic lives on whatever gifts the world may present to him, and he would be unable to stay alive if the world were not constantly engaged in that very labor which the mystic brands as sinful and leading to alienation from god. (Weber, 1966, p. 172)

The Buddhist monk conceives agriculture to be a religiously valueless occupation yet it is precisely agricultural offerings which support the Buddhist virtuosi. In official Islam the development of contemplative mysticism and rejection of the profane world has been less prominent than in mystical Christian groups and Buddhism. That Islamic saints marry and form charismatic lineages is one index of this contrast. There is, nevertheless, an obvious pattern of exchange in which the gifts of adepts and devotees pays for the saintly services of saints to lay followers.

The saint/devotee relationship is both an exchange relationship and ideally a means of economic redistribution. Gifts from the lay population and *muhibbin* are transferred to the saint and/or his descendants (*wulad siyyid*) via the group of the adepts (*foqra*) and the leader of the saint's lineage group (the *mizwar*). This economic surplus is then redistributed through the *wulad siyyid* to poor pilgrims and the sick. In exchange, both the poor and the general laity receive the blessings of the saint's charisma. Charity is the activity of individuals who themselves are in principle without self-interest. In practice, both the *mizwar* and *hadra* team members were in a position to accumulate considerable wealth. One important social test for the presence of valid *baraka* is economic wealth. It is, therefore, crucial that saints and their offspring should be wealthy and, therefore, the charitable redistribution of gifts from pilgrims to the poor laity must leave behind a substantial remainder. It is through economic accumulation that the maxim 'a poor *agurram* is a no-good *agurram*' (Gellner, 1970, p. 143) is validated. Team members extorted money and gifts from *muhibbin* and the general laity by veiled threats of sickness and loss of employment resulting from the displeasure of *jnun*. By this means, team members make a living from enactment of the *hadra*. In addition, 'the mizwars were able to maintain their economically advantageous position without losing, at any rate outside their descent group, the image of pious and charitable men endowed with great baraka of their own' (Crapanzano, 1973, p. 123). The *baraka*-infested men of North Africa follow the pattern of the mystics of European Christianity and the Buddhist monks of Asia because, as Weber observes, their withdrawal from and disesteem for the world of labour and reproduction are financed by followers who are themselves completely immersed in profane duties. Like university teachers, saints are unproductive workers who are supported out of social revenue, charity and systems of patronage.

In the Judeo-Christian world, Christ's charisma flowed fully in his spittle at the pool of Siloam and his blood at Calvary (Vermes, 1973). Since the early Church was not a kinship system through which this grace could be stored, the theologians developed a doctrine of the Church as a treasury of merit which could be unlocked by the keys of the episcopacy. Against this fiduciary issue of grace, the laity offered their penance and their tithes. As the system of penance was institutionalised in the thirteenth century, there appeared to develop an imbalance between the penitential demands and the capacity of the laity to pay up. Indulgences were created as a form of spiritual mortgage, mitigating the burdensome nature of these penitential payments. The selection of the term 'treasury' by Cardinal Hugh St. Cher in 1230 is suggestive of the exactness and calculative mentality with which the ecclesiastical authorities sought to quantify the circulation of charisma in the world. In Islam, by contrast, the Prophet's *baraka* is distributed through kinship ties—or at least through a group of men who *claim* charismatic descent. *Baraka* is thus inherited by saints and their children (*wulad siyyid*). *Baraka*, however, is also contagious and can be obtained by contact with a saint or his tomb. In Morocco, for example, the existence of both personal and institutionalised charisma creates an inflationary movement where grace can be mobilised without an adequate spiritual reserve. In studying the legends of the Hamadsha, Crapanzano (1973, p. 53) notes that one resolution between these androgynous and contagious criteria is a feminisation of the saint who is thereby transformed from a personal to an institutionalised holy man. These legends seek an ideological answer to the problem that institutionalised charisma can only be obtained by contagion. The treasury doctrine in Christianity and the hereditary principle in North African Islam both have the consequence of placing some institutional brake on the social distribution of a religious commodity which commands a very high exchange value among the ordinary people.

The theoretical development of an economic language of saintship raises some obvious difficulties, especially in connection with the argument that saintliness and work are not readily conjoined. Obviously, dead virtuosi have long abandoned their secular positions in this world for more ghostly callings in the next. Among contemporary saints, Sheik Ahmad as-Alawi the cobbler and Salama ibn Hassan Salama the government employee do present clear difficulties for my argument. In point of fact, Sheikh Ahmad turns out to be no serious exception to the thesis being presented (Lings, 1961) While the Sheikh was apparently engaged in economic activities, most of the business became the direct responsibility of his friend and partner as the Sheikh began to attract a large following of lay adepts. The more he was pulled into his religious role, the more he was drawn out of his business calling and away from his secular duties. At a later stage, the financial support from his business was supplemented by the gifts and services which flowed from his expanding circle of devotees. Salama, the founding Sheikh of the Hamidiya Shadhiliya, also perhaps provides a case against this economic model of religious stratification.

Born into a poor quarter of Cairo in 1867, Salama rose quickly from his position as a junior clerk to head of a department in the office of the state domains (Gilsenan, 1973). He enjoyed the reputation as a reliable, sober and effective employee. An important part of his religious teaching was that the members of the brotherhood should not avoid the responsibilities of work just as he had not abandoned his official duties and his worldly responsibilities. Indeed Salama 'encouraged the brothers to work, and the most hateful thing to him was the idle man who would not go out and seek for his daily bread, but rather lived as a burden on other people' (Gilsenan, 1973, p. 18). That the Sheikh continued to work while also directing the *tariqa* was a clear indication to his supporters of the importance of securing an occupation in society. Gilsenan (1973, p. 139) points out that, while this did not involve a Weberian ethic of asceticism forcing the individual into a worldly calling, it did provide a serious appraisal of the importance of work as a form of personal restraint and control.

The case of Sheikh Salama is a striking illustration of the transformation of the saintly role and the importance of the religious brotherhoods in secular twentieth-century society. Given the changing connections between the state and society, between the puritan intellectuals and the Sufi holy men, both Sheikh Ahmad and Sheikh Salama were forced to maintain a careful balance between the enthusiasm of their urban working-class followers and the damaging criticisms of *'ulama* and government against popular religion. The ethic of restraint, discipline and work is the outcome of changed social circumstances. Sheikh Ahmad rejected his early virtuosity in fire-eating, snake charming and the other quasi-magical practises of the Isawi *tariqa* so that he could foster a more spiritual set of techniques. In response to orthodox criticism he claimed in *A Mirror to Show up Errors* that dance and use of the rosary were correct orthodox practice of classical Sunni Islam. In support of these claims for the orthodoxy of the Hamidiya Shadhiliya, there were severe limitations placed on outbursts of emotion and on frenzied activities during communal services. Hostility against the *dhikr* and *hadra* of the various Sufi orders by government officials has led to various methods for controlling and restraining members. A number of rules of the Hamidiya Shadhiliya outlaw the employment of certain instruments at the *hadra* and ban the eating of glass, fire and cactus. The puritanical work-ethic of Salama and the general moderation of the order is, therefore, not evidence against the argument that saints do not labour, but rather evidence about fundamental changes in the nature of sanctity in Islamic societies and in the social functions of lodges and orders.

Within a context of secularisation and urbanisation in Christendom, the number of candidates who successfully meet the Church's regulations concerning translation, beatification and sanctification will decline. In short, the religious and social circumstances that produced the need for saints in Christianity have largely evaporated (Mecklin, 1955). In Islamic societies, a similar process is taking place, albeit for very different social reasons. In rural areas, saints are much less important as mediators between tribes than in former times. In the towns and *bidonvilles*, the arrival of new forms of secular medicine, political allegiance and association will also restrict the social functions and social role of the Sufi. The cathartic role of the *zar* may in similar fashion be replaced by secular or Western therapy, while the older generation of men and women who persist with folk medicine and the advice of the *zar* practitioners may come to be ridiculed by their children (Fakhouri, 1968, p. 56). Social circumstances therefore appeared to be arranged against the creation of new saints. The dead saints

> might continue to play a vital part in popular religion both in the mass pilgrimage and the private prayer. Secure in posthumous reverence they maintained their individual reputations for blessing and help. But the situational possibilities for new sainthood to be claimed or acclaimed by large numbers of Egyptians grew ever more restricted. (Gilsenan, 1973, p. 46)

Without adequate audiences and hence unable to win alms and support, there may be increasing economic and social pressure on men who claim personal charisma to continue within their secular callings. In the urban areas, there may well develop in popular Islam the 'worker-saint', whose expertise is largely self-financed. Whether the 'worker-saint' experiences the same religious fate as the 'worker-priest' of Christianity remains to be seen. These comments on secularisation should not be regarded as criticism of saintship disguised behind a neutral sociological vocabulary. In *Capital* Marx took the position that the individual capitalist could not be morally blamed for exploiting labour since all capitalists had to obey the laws of accumulation on pain of extinction. The same can be claimed in respect of saints. Unless they accumulate secular wealth they can neither redistribute property nor their sacred blessing. Like good capitalists, saints who fail to obey Marx's observation (Accumulate! accumulate! That is Moses and all the prophets!) are obliged to abandon the market-place.

At a more theoretical level, the obvious criticism of my thesis is that the connection between the holy man and his supporters does indeed require exchanges, but these are symbolic rather than economic in character. By extension, my discussion of religious stratification has imposed concepts of economic structures which may have application within a capitalist mode of production but which have little or no relevance within agrarian, tribal, segmented, stateless communities. Furthermore, it could be objected that the argument concentrated illegitimately on the curative aspects of these relations of exchange with the intention of giving them a spurious concreteness, that is, the therapy through the medium of *baraka* is exchanged for a direct payment. To answer these objections fully would involve a long digression through Levi-Strauss's analysis of *'l'efficacité symbolique'* to Goux's conceptualisation of multiple exchange systems (D'Amico, 1978). There is a tough-minded anti-Winchian response to these *verstende* criticisms that we should not be too anxious about imposing on our own theoretical categories on unwilling subjects, but in the case of virtuoso religion the idea of economic (or, at least, material) exchange is already embedded in the manner in which adepts and followers *themselves* interpret charismatic exchanges. It has already been argued that, whatever else is involved in the notion of *baraka*, religious grace is bound up with ideas about prosperity and physical well-being. In addition, followers of Sufi saints often admit that the exchange of alms for *baraka* is not only material but unequal. Sinhalese peasants are known to describe mendicant Buddhist monks somewhat disparagingly as 'rice-eaters', while the *bidonville* Hamadsha are often called 'exploiters'. If anything, this economic model of religion may in fact underestimate the economic functions of Sufi lodges at the macro level by limiting our analysis to micro-economic transactions. The Sanusiya lodges, for example, were not only centres of charismatic influence, but major locations of secular commerce, education and politics (Evans-Pritchard, 1949).

The central point of this argument has been that all extraordinary religious excellence requires economic support even where that source of financial aid is systematically despised by religious doctrine. Weber argues that, while charismatic stratification does not necessarily parallel secular inequalities, virtuoso criteria are easily undermined by mass religious interests because of the 'booty' mentality of followers. In this analysis of Islamic Sufism and Christian holiness, the aim has been to extend and reinforce Weber's virtuoso/mass typology in relation to an exchange theory of saintship organised around the notion that the virtuosi require the mass to finance their religious elitism. A number of variations on the issue of combining and separating religious and occupational tasks has been institutionalised in religious history from the monastic communities of Christendom to the lineage systems of Islam. Perhaps the final solution to these contradictions is a form of subterranean and covert spirituality practised by the followers of the revived Malamatiyyah who,

> finding it necessary to pursue their sanctity through the very humiliation of not being able to display their unworldliness before the world, joined together in a regular tradition of concealed piety, which people should practise even while appearing worldly and without any Sufism at all. (Hodgson, 1974, vol. 2, p. 457)

Such a strategy seems to involve, however, the preservation of a religious role at the cost of any distinctive content. This strategy perhaps provides a sociological example which is relevant to the vulgar adage that if you can't beat them, join them.

5 Theodicy, the career of a concept

While sociology emerged out of theoretical debates in political economy, 'social physics', eugenics and 'moral statistics', sociology also stands in an interesting and historically important relation to theology. Today the theoretical traffic between the two disciplines is somewhat one-way, given the dependence of death-of-God theology on a quasi-sociology of modern consciousness. In classical sociology, the relationship between the secularisation of theology and the emergence of modern sociology was far more dynamic, although unregistered in modern histories of sociology. The sociology of religion itself, of course, is very much the intellectual heir to the perspectives of Strauss, Feuerbach and Troeltsch (Mackintosh, 1964) and a theological perspective is still present in the school of Gabriel Le Bras under the title '*sociologie religieuse*'. In contemporary sociology, as I shall illustrate later, some of the basic conceptual apparatus of Peter Berger and Thomas Luckmann is characterised by theological assumptions. At a more general level, I have attempted to show in this study of Weber that his metatheoretical conception of human fate is infused by a puritan pessimism and Weber thereby represents an interesting contrast to the Catholic optimism of a writer like Luigi Sturzo (Timasheff, 1962). Given the religious or clerical or rabbinical background of so many 'founding fathers' of sociology in Europe and America (Hinkle and Hinkle, 1954), it is perhaps hardly surprising that there should be biographical linkages between sociology and theology. One indication of this relationship is that, for Durkheim, Simmel and Parsons, the social has its roots in religious phenomena (Nisbet, 1967, p.

142

262). A more specific index of this intellectual connection would be to examine the terminological baggage which became part of the sociology of religion – church–sect typology, the sacred, vocation, nomos or inner-worldly asceticism – from theology. In this chapter, I shall examine the historical relationship between theology and sociology by tracing the careers of three concepts with strong theological connotations, namely 'alienation', 'charisma' and 'theodicy'. My argument is that, while these concepts now have in sociology a neutral and technical meaning, they still carry with them a theological and existential significance. These are concepts which, as it were, resisted their sociological fate.

My principal concern is with 'theodicy' which, starting as a theological response to sceptical rationalism, became part of a sociological analysis of ideology via Weber's analysis of Judaism as the culture of a 'pariah group'. My commentary on 'alienation' and charisma' merely sets the stage for this more detailed analysis of theological justification of the presence of evil in the world. The observations on 'alienation' and 'charisma' will consequently be presented in a summary and introductory fashion. While studies of alienation (Aptheker, 1965; Mészáros, 1970; Ollman, 1971; Schacht, 1971) and charisma (Shils, 1965; Berger, 1963; Lipp, 1977; Piepe, 1971) are legion, the employment on the concept of theodicy to designate a particular class ideology has crept into sociology hardly without detection (Berger, 1969a; Obeyesekere, 1968). This neglect provides an additional reason for concentrating on the intellectual history of theodicy.

The manner in which 'alienation' became part of everyday sociological discourse at the cost of its critical content is by now notorious. In Christianity, human alienation was part of the Calvinistic conception of man's original separation and estrangement from God in the evil world. As a concept, it entered sociology through the secular theology of Hegel and the Young Hegelians under the auspices of the early Marx. Hegel transformed the theological problem of alienation into an historical question by examining the emergence of human consciousness through the analogy of the master-slave relationship. Human estrangement was to be overcome through the dialectical development of consciousness and the criticism of the social limitations on human self-realisation. Hegelianism was thus an ambiguous defence of the historical role of Christianity in human society, since philosophy replaced theology as the main avenue to knowledge of God (MacIntyre, 1967). It was the paradoxically atheistic implications of Hegel's philosophy of religion that provided the impetus to the Young Hegelian transformation of the concept of alienation into social criticism. In David Strauss's *Life of Jesus* we find the argument that the attributes which the Church ascribes to Christ as the God-Man actually belong to the human race as a whole, while Ludwig Feuerbach, in *The Essence of Christianity*, completed the process by converting Hegelianism into an anthropology of man. The attributes of God were idealised attributes of man arising from the anthropological conditions of the human species. Marx's originally enthusiastic support for Feuerbach's doctrine—all philosophers had to pass through 'the brook of fire'—was later qualified in the *Theses on Feuerbach* by the recognition that Feuerbach's solution to human alienation was largely idealistic and contemplative. Religious illusions could only be finally overcome by radically changing the social structures which gave rise to alienation. The anthropology of alienation was gradually replaced by political economy as Marx came to specify the conditions of alienation in terms of the separation of workers from the conditions and objects of labour.

In Marxism, whether or not the concept of alienation remained central and crucial to a critique of society has become a major issue in the debate over the young and the late Marx. For Althusserians, the disappearance of the concept of alienation represents part of Marx's epistemological break with pre-scientific modes of thought. Other Marxists, in particular the Frankfurt School, argue that the concept is an essential element to an epistemological critique of the separation of values and facts in positivistic thought. Political alienation stands in the way of open communication and therefore inhibits the very processes of critical thought. In sociology, the concept is either rendered as a description of the psychological state of workers in modern factory conditions (Blauner, 1964) or it appears as the biological essence of the human species in their separation from a socially constructed reality (Berger and Luckmann, 1966). The career of the concept of alienation (Feuer, 1963) is thus problematic. The rediscovery of alienation by George Lukács and its refurbishing by Berger represent a return of its contemplative and theological sources, since the concept now refers not to the specific conditions of production within a given mode of production, but to a general and essential condition of the human species. In Lukács' Marxism, the concept became part of a romantic critique of industrialisation as such in which science itself became part of a reified consciousness expressing man's alienation from self and society; his conception of history was a form of 'secular eschatology' (Bell, 1965, p. 365). In a similar fashion, Berger's sociology turns 'alienation' into a permanent condition of human biology rather than a particular manifestation of particular processes of production. While Berger and Luckmann (1966, p. 225) avoid the use of the term 'alienation' on the grounds that it is terminologically confused, they in practice equate 'reification' (*Verdinglichung*) with 'alienation' (*Entfremdung*). Thus, men inhabit a world which is humanly constructed and which is experienced as an objective and external reality. This externalisation of the constructed social world 'is very probably grounded in the biological construction of man' (Berger, 1969a, p. 4). The concept of alienation has passed from Feuerbachian anthropology to biology as an account of the human essence outside social space and time.

It is difficult to see how, indeed, the concept of alienation could, without loss of serious content, be used independently of some romantic, idealist or theological connotation. In order to use the term at all, we are also obliged to spell out some account of a situation not characterised by alienation. Attempts to define the de-alienated society typically present some version of *Gemeinschaft* relations in which there is very low division of labour, absence of property and absence of ideological mystification. It is difficult to conceive of a society which is both industrialised and not alienated (McLellan, 1969), and the more general implication is that use-values have to be treated in an a-historical, anthropologically static framework. The de-alienated society becomes a sociological Garden of Eden before man's descent into property. The major alternative to this position involves reducing 'alienation' to a description of workers' opposition to modern conditions of production in which case the concept loses typically its critical and political significance. 'Alienation', like 'anomie', cannot be easily incorporated within a neutral, technical terminology because these concepts draw their sociological vitality from a theology of man (Horton, 1964; Lukes, 1967).

The concept of 'charisma' represents a well-known case of theoretical debasement in sociological literature. The term appears in New Testament theology to describe the great variety of divine gifts bestowed upon the faithful so that a number of charismatic signs were interpreted as an indication of supernatural favour. In the nineteenth century, Rudolf Sohm used the term to describe the transformation of the primitive community of followers of Jesus into the institutionalised church of Rome. In sociology, Weber takes up the term in *Economy and Society* to treat charismatic authority not as a specific feature of early Christianity, but as a general category of authority. Weber's examples of charismatic leadership include the berserk, the shaman, the prophet and other ecstatic leaders who break with existing forms of traditional leadership. For Weber, however, charisma is not an intrinsic property of the individual, but involves the attribution of authority by disciples and followers. The possession of charisma is tested by followers and depends on pure devotion and loyalty to the claims of a charismatic leader. Thus, charismatic authority as a concept was developed as a contrast to traditional and legal-rational discipline and control. Weber follows Sohm, however, in directing attention to the instability of charismatic authority, which is typically routinised into 'charisma of office' following the death of the original leader. Charismatic leadership is most likely to emerge in periods of social crisis and disruption when socially dislocated groups turn towards 'extraordinary' leaders.

In Weber's sociology, the concept of charisma cannot be divorced from an analysis of the social environment and discipleship in which it is located, and the transformation of charisma is part of Weber's more general interest in the question of unintended consequences of action. Weber thinks that charismatic leadership is uncommon in modern politics which is dominated by party machines, electoral bureaucracy and state organisations. In Germany, the legacy of Bismarck had produced a docile middle class and a civil service of efficient 'yes-men' without a sense of national purpose. Weber's attitude towards charisma is thus ambiguous. On the one hand, traditional and charismatic authority have been largely replaced by party politics which depends on bureaucracy and legal-rational rules. On the other hand, he felt that the crisis in German society leading up to the First World War demanded a new vision backed up by personal charisma. While it is often said that Weber's theory of charisma is not a Great Man theory of history, Weber does retain a residual commitment to the ideal of the power of extraordinary personality in situations of political crisis.

After Weber, the term 'charisma' passed into the common usage of all political journalists when it means little more than leadership as such. Any leader who is successfully manufactured by the party machine is now dutifully regarded as charismatic. The term has thus been stripped not only of its theological, but also its sociological content. In the modern world, the charismatic leader is now shorn of ecstatic and divine attributes. It nevertheless remains a problematic term, since even Weber wanted to draw a distinction between 'pure' and 'impure' charisma. The charismatic prophet is somebody who defies public and popular demands in order to impose his own, unique charismatic message on the situation. This distinction raises the problem of whether charismatic authority can be simply the product of recognition by followers or whether charisma requires something in addition to popular support and recognition. Unlike tradition and legal-rational authority, charisma cannot be wholly reduced to the conditions which produce it.

Concepts like 'anomie', 'alienation' and 'charisma' are, therefore, products of the interchange between theology, humanistic philosophy and sociology. Regardless of the attempts to neutralise the meaning of these terms by the conventional methodology of American positivism, they retain a residual theological significance in that all three concepts indicate man's essential homelessness within the social world. The same can be said for the concept of theodicy. The problem of theodicy—the problem of justifying the presence of physical pain and moral sin—is an inevitable by-product of any human culture which incorporates strong beliefs in beneficent monotheism. If a wise and just God exists, why is there evil in the world? Weber (1966) identifies three 'pure types' of religious solutions to the problem of evil. In the first, the inequities of this world are compensated by eschatological beliefs which point to a future kingdom when the poor and weak will replace the powerful as the true followers of a righteous God. While these millenarian beliefs often gave rise to politically radical movements, the failure of the kingdom to materialise often led to passive, other-worldly aspirations. The second solution is dualism, of which Zoroastrianism and Manicheism are the primary examples. In this conception, an all-powerful god of light is confronted by powers of darkness arising from the wickedness of men or demons. Human history is witness to the prolonged struggle of light to dissipate the power of these dark forces in a final eschatological victory. The third, and in Weber's view the most complete, solution to the problem of theodicy is represented by the doctrine of *karma*, that is, the belief in the transmigration of souls. Moral or immoral actions in this world are compensated by rewards and punishment in future lives, just as suffering in this life is the effect of previous wrong-doing. Responsibility for sin is thus placed firmly on the shoulders of the individual who 'forges his own destiny exclusively' (Weber, 1966, p. 145).

The problem of theodicy is central to Weber's sociology of religion since the contradiction between an ethical God and the presence of evil lies behind the development of distinctive salvational pathways of world-flight and world-mastery. It is this contradiction which presents Weber with his principal contrast between the puritan solution to evil in the drive for world-mastery and the mystical solution of resignation and withdrawal. It is the horror of sin which drives religious man towards actions which may have socially radical or socially conservative consequences. At the cultural level, the crucial differences between East and West may be traced back to fundamental differences in the human response to pain and finitude. At this level, we find a major difference between Marx and Weber, since Weber intends to demonstrate the systematic effects of the solution of the problem of theodicy on economic, political and social developments in world history. However, as I shall demonstrate shortly, when Weber goes on to formulate the relationships between theodicies and class privileges, he comes very close to treating theodicy as the ideological expression of class interest.

As with the concept of charisma, Weber did not coin the term 'theodicy'. He adopts the term for his own purpose from existing debates in so-called 'natural theology', where it had been a central theological issue for some two centuries. The problem of evil is critical for any theistic theology since it raises not only the question of divine justice, but also the issue of human freedom and responsibility. If a just God cannot be the author of evil, then he cannot be omnipotent. If man is the author of evil, then God can be good but not all-powerful. Like Kant, Weber implies that, however satisfying in psychological terms, a rational theodicy can never by purely intellectually satisfying because it tends to place some limitations on divine power or divine justice. The orthodox rational theodicies of intellectuals are typically supplemented by magical practices and beliefs. The problem of theodicy also, therefore, leads into Weber's major distinction between mass religiosity and virtuoso elitism. While I am primarily concerned to show the analytical importance of the concept of theodicy in Weber's general sociology, the problem of evil is a necessary feature of Weber's metasociological world-view. Weber did not believe that it was possible to construct a total, optimistic metaphysical system in response to human finitude and did not believe, in particular, that there was a way out of the iron cage of modern society. Because he 'stressed the tragic aspects of life and the unavoidable emphasis on power' (Honigsheim, 1968, p. 20), Weber held all doctrines of human progress in permanent contempt. For Weber, the world is evil, but the demons of this world are sociological not theological.

The term 'theodicy' is first systematically used to mean a plea 'in the cause of God' demonstrating divine justice by Gottfried Leibniz in an essay entitled 'Essais de Théodicée sur la bonté de Dieu, la liberté de l'homme, et l'origine du mal' in 1710 as a memorial to Queen Sophie Charlotte of Prussia. While the eighteenth-century debate about evil was probably initiated by William King's *The Origin of Evil* in 1702, it was Leibniz's *Theodicy* which came to be regarded as the main reply to Cartesian rationalism and to Pierre Bayle's view of the restricted role of reason as a justification for religious faith (Barber, 1955). In the discussion of 'Manichéens' in the *Dictionnaire historique et critique* (1695–7), Bayle had argued that reason supported dualism because, in our everyday experience, we do perceive a constant struggle between the forces of good and evil. There is no rational objection to Manichean dualism. The only Christian defence lies in revelation which discloses the intervention of a just and powerful god. The task of Leibniz's *Theodicy* was to demonstrate the rationality and morality of the universe without resource to dualism and without separating faith and reason. Leibniz attempted to reconcile Christianity as a revealed religion with rational philosophy by demonstrating the goodness of God as the creative author of the universe which is 'the best of all possible worlds' and completely intelligible to a rational man. The world is not arbitrary, but the most complete realisation of God's creative will.

Leibniz's analysis of the universe as the best possible creation rests on the notions of possibility and compossibility. Before the universe was created, God conceived of a range of possible worlds, but, since He is a perfect being, He created the best possible world. The best possible universe is the fullest and most complete realisation of His will consistent with the compossibility of phenomena. Individual concepts are compossible if they are capable of joint realisation. Reality is a full, gapless and compossible expression of divine will. Every substance in the universe is a mirror of all other substances which are unified by mutual accommodation. While Leibniz wants to claim that the universe is the fullest realisation of the principle of perfection, he also wants to avoid the necessitarianism of Spinoza's metaphysics, which would imply that God is compelled by logic to act in this way, and Leibniz attempts to solve this problem by an emphasis on contingency. He draws an analogy between the infinite comparison of problems in the mathematical calculus of variations and God's selection of that possible world which contains the maximum perfection. Thus, the principle of perfection 'furnishes the mechanism of God's decision among the infinite, mutually exclusive systems of compossibles' (Rescher, 1979, p. 40). Whereas Spinoza's God is compelled to act in a particular way, the God of Leibniz's best of all possible worlds is only committed by 'infallibly inclining' reasons. The results of this theory is to extend the traditional arguments about the existence of God, in particular the ontological argument of St Anselm, to emphasise arguments from the 'order of things'.

On the basis of theistic arguments, Leibniz proposes two answers to the problem of why, in the best of all possible worlds, we find evil. First, the presence of evil (metaphysical, physical and moral) is admitted by Leibniz who recognizes that, in a world based on infinite plenitude, God has 'been induced to permit evil'. Second, Leibniz denies that evil predominates over good and asserts that evil is not real and positive, but merely a limitation of finite human beings. Thus, 'God is the cause of all perfections, and consequently of all realities, when they are regarded as purely positive. But limitations or privations result from the original imperfections of creatures which restricts their receptivity' (Leibniz, 1951, p. 384). Third, evil often results in morally valuable situations and therefore the greatest good would not be possible without the presence of evil. Imperfections and privations are often

> a means to an end, that is, to prevent greater evils or to obtain greater good. The penalty serves also for amendment and example. Evil often serves to make us savour good the more; sometimes too it contributes to a greater perfection in him who suffers it, as the seed that one sows is subject to a kind of corruption before it can germinate: this is a beautiful similitude, which Jesus Christ himself used. (Leibniz, 1951, p. 137)

In the best of all possible worlds, evil can play a role in moral and religious instruction and development, thereby pointing to God's perfect creation rather than to the imperfections of the universe.

Leibniz's essay on theodicy occupies a controversial place within his philosophy as a whole. While Leibniz was concerned with the problem of a philosophical justification of evil, his essay has been criticised as a disguised social justification for the inequalities in human society. In his preface to the second edition of *Critical Exposition of the Philosophy of Leibniz* in 1937 and in the *History of Western Philosophy* of 1945, Bertrand Russell argues that Leibniz had two distinct philosophies, one of which was radical and private, and the other optimistically conservative and popular. Russell argues that Leibniz's popular doctrines are 'logically possible, but not very convincing' (1945, p. 613). In reply to Leibniz, the Manichean sceptic might equally argue that we live in the worst possible world. His doctrine of plenitude, however, was acceptable as a useful social theory which legitimated the inequalities of the political *status quo*. The notion of the 'best of all possible worlds' 'apparently satisfied the Queen of Prussia. Her serfs continued to suffer the evil, while she continued to enjoy the good, and it was comforting to be assured by a great philosopher that this was just and right' (Russell, 1945, p. 613). As Leibniz's unpublished works have become more widely available, it has been claimed against Russell that Leibniz did not have a secret philosophy which contradicted his popular stance (Curley, 1972). However, Russell's position would still hold in that, regardless of Leibniz's own intentions about publishing or withholding his more radical views, the essay on theodicy had the effect of legitimating the social position of the privileged classes. However, we have to modify this observation by recognising that the *Théodicée* did not enjoy the extensive popularity that Russell's criticism might imply. While the essay was welcomed by Jesuits, Christians of very diverse opinions and by royalty such as King Stanislas I of Poland, 'there is little evidence that the book achieved any widespread popularity' in France (Barber, 1955, p. 91).

While the impact of *Théodicée* may have been fairly specific, the debate with Leibnizianism became a very general aspect of eighteenth-century intellectual culture. Voltaire was familiar both with the *Théodicée* and with Pope's *Essay on Man* and formulated his own response to the principle of perfection via Newtonian natural laws. Voltaire wanted to steer a course between Pascal's tragic vision of man and Leibniz's optimistic metaphysics by arguing that, while contemporary society was clearly imperfect, life could be improved by reform and by reason. The Lisbon earthquake of 1755 in which some twenty thousand people died had put paid to Leibnizian confidence in the 'order of things', but Voltaire in *Candide* had indicated that the human evils of vice, need and boredom could be contained by improvements in human institutions and social manners. However, Voltaire was not a bland utilitarian: evil is real and overwhelming, and all existing theodicies are unsatisfactory as intellectual responses to evil. Yet, optimism about the present does not include the possibility of radical improvement in the human condition. Against optimistic philosophies, Voltaire described the brute facts of life and society with the literary weapons of satire and irony. Unlike *Théodicée, Candide* was an immediate and massive popular success.

In the eighteenth century, Leibniz's views of theodicy were disseminated through the philosophy of C. Wolff, especially in *Theologia Naturalis* (1739-1741). It was through Wolfian rationalism that both Voltaire and Kant formed their early impressions of Leibnizian natural theology. Kant was thus originally a follower of Leibnizian theodicy and, in *An Attempt at Some Considerations on Optimism* (1759), Kant adopted the arguments of 'sufficient causation' and plenitude arguing that the universe is subject to 'benevolent necessity'. However, Kant's early adherence to Leibnizian principles was undermined by exposure to Newton's conception of casuality and by Kant's appreciation of the centrality of the 'dignity of human nature' in Rousseau's *Emile*. Leibniz's unified world of monads gave way to Kant's distinction between the mechanical (phenomenal) world of nature organised by Newtonian physics and the moral (noumenal) world of man as the realm of practical reason. Kant was, therefore, far more concerned than Leibniz with the issues of human freedom, choice and moral responsibility. The concept of an all powerful God threatened to reduce men to mere slaves in a system of cosmic teleology. As with many other eighteenth-century philosophers, Kant feared that a deterministic theodicy would create Oriental fatalism. However, the centrality of human volition also brought with it the ever present possibility of sin and evil which made a rational, optimistic theodicy unacceptable and morally damaging.

Kant does not want to underestimate the importance of reason, but he does want to recognise its limitations in respect of the problem of evil. The proper location of human response to suffering is not in science, but in faith. In his essay 'On the failure of all attempted philosophical theodicies' (1791), Kant argues that all existing theodicies are inadequate, but 'we are capable at least of a negative wisdom. We can understand the necessary limits of our reflections on the subjects which are beyond our reach' (Kant, 1791, p. 290). Kant encourages us to accept the wisdom and honesty of Job who did not question God's intentions or offer spurious theodicies for which there were no rational or honest grounds. Any attempt to explain evil away is mere rationalisation and consequently rational theodicies are themselves sinful deceptions. The honest man of faith trusts in God and confronts evil in the world with sincerity and honesty. Kant rejects the extreme pessimism of Pascal and the optimism of Leibniz to find a middle ground which recognised the limitations of human reason but also the moral value of human dignity. To paraphrase Kant with a mistranslation of Wittgenstein, whereof we cannot speak, we must be honest.

While these eighteenth-century theodicies were formulated in very different ways, they shared a number of important themes in common. They were predominantly the product of Protestant thinkers working with puritanical views of man, sin and God. There was little social dimension to their conception of theodicy and hence they were attempting to come to terms with the problem of the individual, equipped with reason and emotion, in relation to a natural world which is paradoxically divinely created and painful. There was little conception of the fact that thought itself is a social and historical process.

Despite the emphasis on natural teleology, on human biology and, in Kant's case, human anthropology, the debate about evil was conducted without any sociological awareness of the social roots of reason. It was this recognition of the history of consciousness in society which Hegel brought to the traditional individualistic conception of the problem of evil. If Hegel injected into theodicy the sense of history in terms of the positive and negative development of consciousness in the master-slave analogy, then it was Nietzsche who demonstrated that the analysis of moral systems could not be achieved without a psychology and sociology of group conflicts.

Hegel saw that the possibility of self-realisation and self-consciousness is limited by the social forms in which thought takes place. In Christianity, this conflict between possibility and actuality is symbolised by the fallen world of men and the perfect world of divine creation. For the early Hegel, the problem was to recover the ideal of community, citizenship and public religion which was essential to Greek society and which has been lost in Christianity with its emphasis on personal salvation. With the loss of communal life in classical society, doctrinal Christianity had become an expression of human estrangement following from the separation of public and private life. Human alienation found its counterpart in the theology of a supreme, perfect and transcendent God. Traditional Christianity could not resolve the tension between the sacred world of divine transcendence and the profane world of human emotion and reason. All efforts at negating this world through Christian stoicism, asceticism and faith in the next world result in the 'Unhappy Consciousness' which paradoxically re-affirms the reality of present alienation. The reconciliation of men with the world involves the reconciliation of public and private life in a new community. In his later philosophy, Hegel places less emphasis on the recovery of Greek communalism and perceives reconciliation as imminent within the historical process itself. The dialectic between human consciousness and reality is progressive as each new level of self-consciousness transcends existing contradictions which are then formulated at a new level of awareness. For Hegel, therefore, the solution to the problem of theodicy is not to be found in thinking the infinite in finite concepts, but in comprehending theodicy as part of the structure of history and society: 'To recognize reason as the rose in the cross of the present and thereby to enjoy the present, this is the rational insight which reconciles us to the actual' (Glockner, 1927–30, vol. 7, p. 35). In Hegel's later work, the role of philosophy in relation to human alienation is to elucidate the development of self-consciousness in relation to nature and society as a process which constantly transcends its biological and social limitations.

Traditional dogmatism failed to provide an adequate solution to the problems of metaphysics because, in dealing with mutually exclusive either-or categories, it failed to realise that metaphysical questions can only be approached as totalities. While Kant's discussion of the 'Antinomies of Pure Reason' had anticipated Hegel's conception of the importance of totality, Kant's conclusions were insufficiently radical (Soll, 1969). The absence of a dialectic in dogmatic theology had given rise to a one-sided conception of the absolute and perfect nature of God without a corresponding negation. Nature is the self-objectification and self-alienation of God at different moments of the historical process of the Absolute. The process of human development is thus linked with the process of divine development in the historical unfolding of human society. It is in this idea that we can trace both the radical and the conservative aspects of Hegel's theodicy. The 'rose in the cross of the present' reconciles us to actuality rather than advocating the restoration of communal life as a solution to human estrangement. The role of philosophy is neither to restore the past nor to actualise the future. Because 'philosophy is the exploration of the rational, it is for that very reason the apprehension of the present and the actual, not the erection of a beyond' (Knox, 1942, p. 10). The left Hegelians interpreted Hegel as meaning that the present is always a transitional stage in the realisation of human freedom. The right Hegelians saw the present as the climax of the historical process of the Spirit and as the synthesis of historical development. These contradictory interpretations of Hegel's philosophy were probably inevitable in the case of a philosopher who was himself torn by sympathy for the French Revolution and loyalty to the absolutist Duke of Württemberg, by commitment to classical and Christian culture (Harris, 1972, Reardon, 1977; Walsh, 1969).

The ambiguities of Hegel's theodicy can be illustrated by an account of Nietzsche's view of the justificatory role of Christian morality. In *The Genealogy of Morals*, Nietzsche treats theodicy from the perspective of what might be called the psychological point of view of dominant and subordinate social groups. The historical origins of conventional Christian morality are to be found in the hatred of the Jews against powerful outsiders. Our notions of virtue and goodness are in fact the product of resentment by the dispossessed against powerful aristocracies. It is in the eschatological beliefs of Jews that Nietzsche attempts to locate the origin of morality in the revolt of slaves against their masters—

> It was the Jews who, in opposition to the aristocratic equation (good=beautiful=happy=loved by the gods), dared with a terrifying logic to suggest the contrary equation, and indeed to maintain with the teeth of the most profound hatred (the hatred of weakness) this contrary equation, namely 'the wretched are alone the good; the poor, the weak, the lowly, are alone the good'. (Nietzsche, 1910, p. 30)

What we conventionally regard as moral evil is in fact merely an account of the world from the point of view of the powerless. There is, in this sense, not one problem of theodicy, but two. Aristocratic conceptions of virtue and evil are totally incompatible with slave moralities. While Nietzsche does not explicitly state his argument in these terms, in practice he implies that the theodicy of the poor acts simultaneously as a critique of power and as a compensation for their powerlessness. The notion of 'happiness' consequently has a very different content for the noble than for the slave. For the Greek nobility, happiness is simply part of their natural, positive and energetic response to the world, but among slaves and vulgar men 'happiness appears essentially as a narcotic, a deadening, a quietude, a peace, a "Sabbath", an enervation of the mind and relaxation of the limbs—in short, a purely passive phenomenon' (Nietzsche, 1910, pp. 36–37). What conventional Christian morality treats as sinful and evil is, thus, simply the world 'distorted by the venomous eye of resentfulness' and thereby merely a partial view of the moral world. While Nietzsche rejects Hegel's metaphysics, he incorporates the kernel of Hegel's historical perspective and consequently relativises Christian claims to ultimate truth by showing Christianity to be a system of anti-values in a particular historical moment (Stern, 1978).

The background to Weber's sociological analysis of theodicy is constituted by very diverse currents in German philosophy and theology. Weber responds critically both to Marx's view of religious compensation as 'the opium' of the people and to Nietzsche's treatment of Judaism as the historical root of all life-denying slave moralities. Weber recognises that the moral honesty of a scholar is to be judged in terms of his 'posture toward Nietzsche and Marx' (Mitzman, 1970, p. 182). As we shall see, Nietzsche's concept of resentment is largely taken over in Weber's discussion of theodicy except that Weber believes that this factor operates only in very special social circumstances. In particular, Buddhism represents 'the most radical antithesis to every type of *ressentiment* morality' (Weber, 1966, p. 116). While Weber is clearly influenced by Nietzsche's views (Fleischmann, 1964), Weber is far more sympathetic towards the Kantian position. Weber accepts the Kantian dichotomy of reason and emotion, and treats man as faced in the noumenal world by the choice between the ethics of responsibility and absolute ends. However, Weber's view of evil in the world takes a far more pessimistic direction than Kant's philosophy and, therefore, Weber is opposed to both Leibnizian and Hegelian doctrines which, in their different ways, represent an optimistic response to the present. Weber found Nietzsche's philosophy attractive because of Nietzsche's hostility to naive theories of social progress which were incompatible with his profoundly tragic conception of man in society.

Weber's sociology of theodicy is worked out at two levels. In the first, Weber offers in *Ancient Judaism* a specific and detailed analysis of the problem of evil in Old Testament culture where he is concerned with the sociological importance of revenge and resentment. In the second, Weber provides a more general discussion of the role of theodicy in monotheistic culture in *The Sociology of Religion*. My general argument is that, in both studies, Weber's sociology provides a parallel to a Nietzschian reduction of morality to class psychology. These two studies of theodicy in turn link up with the problem of the sociology of outgroups, ritual uncleanness and pariah status which is fundamental, not only to Weber's sociology of religion, but to his analysis of social groups and social closure.

Weber's study of *Ancient Judaism* is made up of a number of related themes. In part, it is a study of the social role of prophecy and prophetic discipleship in which Weber emphasises, against Karl Kautsky's *Foundations of Christianity*, the social isolation of Jewish prophets from the proletarian instincts of the masses. In this aspect of his study, Weber employs the prophet as a particular illustration of his more general concern with charismatic authority. This study of Judaism is also part of his analysis of the role of anti-magical systems of belief which provide the context of Weber's analysis of rationality in the rise of capitalist relations of production. It is also an illustration of Weber's interest in the political impact of various forms of radical millenarian theodicy as the ideology of a pariah group. Weber's account of Judaic theodicy starts with the central aspect of Yahwe as the war leader of a tribal confederacy with which He is connected by obligations following a sacred covenant. This God of the Ark of the Covenant was a jealous God, demanding loyalty and rejection of all competing gods, and as a god of war, required political allegiance rather than personal, ethical commitments. Yahwe was not simply a local God or God of the land, but a partner in a legally binding social obligation. Yahwe, however, did not belong exclusively to Israel, but was at liberty to form contracts with other tribes and was consequently not dependent simply on the support and sacrifices of Jewish tribes. This religious contract provided the context for the struggles between the prophets of the traditional Yahwistic obligations and the ecstatic, magical cults in periods of political collapse and conflict. The pure prophetic message ruled out any form of dualist theodicy since

> Yahwe also sent all evil. In Israel, all evil was punishment or ordainment of the powerful god. Therefore, the development of magical defense against demons was confronted with that of the purely ethical Torah and with the confession of sins as genuine means of control in the hands of the Levitical priests. (Weber, 1952, p. 222)

While the Jewish masses sought compensation in magic and supernatural saviours, the war prophets and Torah prophets sought to impose the high ethical demands of a passionate God on the course of political events. Yahwe was not a God with whom one sought mystical union, but a God of tribal contract who intervened in the political history of Israel. Judaic prophecy, therefore, encouraged a purely ethical rather than ritualistic relationship between the community and Yahwe. The effect of this ethical covenant with a passionate God was to provide an extaordinary coherence of a tribal confederacy based on 'religious fraternization'. From the point of view of group solidarity, ritual circumcision was part of the ascetic ritualism of a war confederacy led by war prophets.

With the decline of the peasant militia and the rise of monarchy, an important relationship developed between the intellectuals, the Torah teachers or Levites, and the demilitarised peasantry. The intellectuals produced a literary, written response to the new situation created by the monarchy in which they proclaimed the traditional values of the contract between Yahwe and the rural peasantry. These intellectuals were not ethical innovators, but merely stated a conventional view of the Yahwistic contract. The prophets 'neither announced a new conception of God, nor new means of grace, nor even new commandments. At least, they had no intention of doing so. It is presupposed that God is known to all and that "He hath shewd thee, O man what is good" ' (Weber, 1952, p. 300). The prophets emphasised the consistency of God's obligations in the face of social changes resulting from the creation of a monarchy. They pointed to the catastrophic misfortunes which awaited Israel, should the confederacy deviate from its original contract with Yahwe.

The crucial historical test of the covenant between Yahwe and Israel came in the period of exile with the end of Yahwism as a state religion and the diaspora of believers. In the period of exile, Judaism developed a profound conception of in-group and out-group morality based on economic and ritualistic exclusiveness. In this context, there developed the theodicy of Deutero-Isaiah which represents 'an apotheosis of sufferance, misery, poverty, humiliations and ugliness which in its consistency is not even second to New Testament prophecy' (Weber, 1952, p. 369). In response to present misery, exilic prophecy held out the promise of better things in the future. Whereas the pre-exilic beliefs contained no equation of misery with religious elevation, in post-exilic times the 'plebeian virtue of humility was increasingly made the exclusive value' (Weber, 1952, p. 370). The ignominious subjugation of Israel was henceforth interpreted as part of Yahwe's holy plan in which Israel itself became the instrument of atonement and in which Israel was transformed into a 'chosen people'. The blameless suffering of God's chosen people became part of a universalistic soteriological design, the Judaic theodicy of misfortune anticipates the ethic of humility encapsulated in the Christological doctrines of the Sermon on the Mount. Guiltless martyrdom and humble acceptance of suffering became the central themes of a theodicy of misfortune geared to a soteriological climax.

The social consequences of this doctrine of theodicy were very considerable. Israel was transformed from a political association into a religious community whose pariah status was confirmed by the activities of a righteous God. The doctrine of meekness reinforced the practices of circumcision, ritual purity and economic separation to produce a pariah group which was justified by God's historical mission (Shmueli, 1960). This religious orientation to suffering was sociologically dependent on the specific role of the prophets and in turn these 'giants cast their shadows through the millennia into the present, since this holy book of the Jews became a holy book of the Christians too, and since in the entire interpretation of the mission of the Nazarene was primarily determined by the old promises of Israel' (Weber, 1952, p. 334). This transformation of the Israelite community from a political organisation to a religious community was a crucial sociological condition of its survival in post-exilic times.

Weber's study of the confederacy of Israel in *Ancient Judaism* has given rise to considerable controversy. Some commentators believe that Weber's analysis has weathered the test of subsequent biblical criticism (Peterson, 1979). Weber has, however, been criticised for exaggerating the rationality of pure Yahwism and ignoring the use of magical practices by the prophets (Schiper, 1959). For Weber, the Jews were 'the most superb historical example' of pariah-status and he has subsequently been criticised for employing diverse and inconsistent criteria—ethnic segregation, ritual separation, endogamy, economic specialisation and precarious legal status—in his definition of pariah groups (Sigrist, 1971). These criticisms, in part, relate to the vexed question of the role of 'ideal types' in Weber's sociology and these objections to Weber to some extent miss the great sociological value of Weber's theory of the social dynamics of in-group and out-group relationships and what Weber called 'pariah-ethics'. Of particular interest is Weber's attempt in *Ancient Judaism* and *Economy and Society* to give a more neutral and sociologically precise content to Nietzsche's concept of 'resentment'. While Marxists have been concerned with the problem of revolutionary consciousness in relation to the development of class positions, Weber directs attention to the parallel question of 'dignity' in 'positively privileged status groups' and to the sense of 'providential mission' in 'negatively privileged status groups'. Such status groups have very different conceptions of value and time. Whereas positively privileged groups inflate their present dignity by reference to a glorious past, the moral value of negatively privileged groups:

> refers to a future lying beyond the present, whether it is of this life or of another. In other words, it must be nurtured by the belief in a providential 'mission' and by a

belief in a specific honor before God. The 'chosen people's' dignity is nurtured by a belief either that in the beyond 'the last will be the first', or that in this life a Messiah will appear.... This simple state of affairs, and not the 'resentment' which is so strongly emphasized in Nietzsche's much admired construction in the *Genealogy of Morals*, is the source of the religiosity cultivated by pariah status groups. (Weber, 1961, p. 190)

The evil which is experienced in this world by pariah groups is a sign of their historic mission and a promise of their coming restoration to positive dignity. Weber's formulation of the problem of time perspectives in different social groups within a social hierarchy of privilege anticipated later studies of utopian world-views (Mannheim, 1966) and millenarianism (Thrupp, 1962).

Although Weber provides a number of critical observations on Nietzsche, in *The Sociology of Religion* he does appear to adhere fairly closely to the idea that monotheistic religions tend to produce two clearly identified theodicies, namely a theodicy of compensation for the disprivileged and a theodicy of legitimation for the privileged. Having recognised the irrelevance of Nietzsche's notion of resentment in the case of Hinduism and Buddhism where suffering is dealt with on an individual basis, Weber appears to give very specific support to Nietzsche's analysis of the role of revenge in Old Testament sources. Resentment is an important feature of any religious ethic which treats the unequal allocation of resources in this world as the consequence of injustice and sinfulness of privileged social groups. The Psalms are specifically dominated by the feeling of resentment and revenge. In fact 'the majority of the Psalms are quite obviously replete with the moralistic legitimation and satisfaction of an open and hardly concealed need for vengeance on the part of a pariah people' (Weber, 1966, p. 111). The Psalmists looked forward to a time when the God of wrath would show compassion on the sufferings of His righteous people and crush their enemies. Alongside this collective theodicy, there also developed an individual theodicy of personal fate which found its model in the

Book of Job and which was produced by the Jewish upper classes. This individualistic theodicy involved, not a collective vengeance against an outside enemy, but rather a personal submission to the absolute will of Yahwe. While the history of the Jews provides Weber with his principal illustration of a theodicy of revenge, he argues that, as a general rule, a theodicy 'of disprivilege, in some form, is a component of every salvation religion which draws its adherents primarily from the disprivileged classes' (Weber, 1966, p. 113). Although the New Testament is also significantly influenced by these themes of future compensation, the indifference of the Gospels to this world meant that wealth as such was not an inevitable obstacle to eventual salvation. Contrary to Kautsky's view of the importance of 'class hatred' in the Gospel of St Luke, Weber asserts that the doctrine of Jesus was not motivated by 'proletarian instincts'.

Thus, Weber tries to place some theoretical limitations on the importance of resentment as an explanation of the content of religious systems. However, if we combine Weber's treatment of the general problem of theodicy with his analysis of the religious styles of different social groups, we can see that Weber, in practice, follows Nietzsche's distinction between different conceptions of 'goodness' very closely. Those social groups which are privileged in this world expect terrestrial principles of social stratification to be reproduced in the next world. The theodicy of the privileged confirms their status in the present and the future because, in religions 'under the influence of the ruling classes', this-worldly and other-worldly status differences are divinely guaranteed. From the point of view of socially dominant groups, it is an affront to their sense of personal worth and social dignity to admit either that their social status is in any sense illegitimate or that they are personally sinful. The incompatibility of the notion of sin with social privilege is particularly marked in the case of feudal nobility and warrior groups. This is because the life-style of 'a warrior has very little affinity with the notion of a beneficent providence, or with the systematic ethical demands of a transcendental god' (Weber, 1966, p. 85). Thus, all Leibnizian theodicies of happiness perfectly suit the class interests and status requirements of dominant classes; all theodicies of disprivilege offer compensation to pariah groups or subordinate classes by the promise of coming revenge (Stark, 1964).

Weber provides himself with an escape from any simple reductionist argument, however, by placing great sociological emphasis on the autonomous role of religious intellectuals in their articulation of religious themes. Hence, Weber is impressed by the social isolation of the prophets. Unlike priests, the prophet has a personal calling and is not a religious teacher since the prophet declares his calling through 'vital, emotional preaching'. As an illustration of charismatic authority, Weber has to note that, while prophets do not have regular congregational support, they do need the validation of an audience of disciples and followers. It is very unusual for a prophetic leader to succeed 'in establishing his authority without charismatic authentication, which in practice meant magic' (Weber, 1966, p. 47). However, in the case of the Old Testament prophets, Weber wants to argue that they were socially isolated individuals struggling with their highly personal conception of the relationship of Yahwe to the confederacy. Weber makes the contradictory claim that the prophets were the 'intellectual leaders of the opposition against kingship' and that, as prophets of doom, they were socially isolated and failed to achieve any following (Weber, 1952, p. 109). Whereas the 'false prophets' of happiness were employed by the court, the prophets of doom were isolated men crying in the wilderness against the evils of the day. Contemporary scholarship (Peterson, 1979) supports Weber's view of the social isolation of the prophets, but this leaves the contradiction between the 'pure' charisma of the prophet and its authentication unresolved.

My argument is that Weber's admiration for the isolated prophet of doom preaching against the evil of the present is part of Weber's personal theodicy as distinct from his sociology of theodicy. Marianne Weber clearly recognised the parallel between Weber's own political isolation and his scholarly interest in the charismatic isolation of the Old Testament prophets. As Weber read passages from his manuscript on the Jewish prophets, it was clear that he was 'particularly moved by the figure of Jeremiah, the prophet of doom, and

Weber's analysis of him, like his analysis of the Puritans, betrays great inner involvement. When he read excerpts from his manuscript to Marianne in the evening, she saw his own fate expressed in many passages' (Weber, 1975, pp. 593-4). It was precisely the isolation of Jeremiah and the fact that his charisma, unlike the Christian prophets, was not validated by a mass following that appealed to Weber, who, according to Jaspers (1953), was a wartime prophet without disciples. Weber recognised the public yearning in Germany for political prophecy, but also realised that it was their destiny to live in a godless era. In the speech on 'Science as a vocation', Weber warns his listeners not to yearn or tarry as Jews calling out, as in Isaiah, 'Watchman, what of the night?', but to confront the 'demands of the day'.

The problem of theodicy is not, therefore, merely a technical problem in Weber's sociology of religion, but a major component of his metasociological and personal outlook on society, which is dominated by the demon of godless rationality. Weber is too pessimistic to believe that this sociological evil is merely a transitory state of affairs anticipating a happy future. Weber does not accept that any collectivist solution à la Hegel and Marx is possible. He responds instead to the 'demands of the day' in Kantian terms by stressing the importance of 'the ethic responsibility' by which the moral individual honestly selects his vocation. This existential choice cannot be guided by a religious tradition or by science which is indifferent to human ends. In the absence of gods or knowledge, men have to choose in the dark, at best trusting to their fate.

In contemporary sociology, the problem of theodicy in the sociology of religion has been developed principally by Peter L. Berger in *The Social Reality of Religion* (1969a). The essentials of Berger's sociology are that, unlike other animals, *homo sapiens* enters the world in an 'unfinished' condition without personality, language and culture. The instinctual structure of mankind is not highly specialised or specifically directed in relation to the environment. Through language, symbols, gestures and labour, man has to fashion his own environment and, in this sense, Berger refers to society as a socially constructed reality. The world is not given, but the product of endless, on-going human actions of construction, definition and interpretation. This situation means that the human world of culture is inherently unstable, shifting and precarious. The legitimate, taken-for-granted cultural environment or 'nomos' is thus constantly threatened by chaos and 'anomie'. The individual experiences the humanly constructed world as an objective reality handed down from generation to generation by the processes of socialisation and internalisation. The apparatus of cultural transmission and the process of socialisation can never guarantee in advance that the nomos will be fully and adequately acquired and accepted by new generations. Furthermore, the plausibility of the nomic reality can only be sustained by mutual agreement and by, as it were, a collective conversation. Confidence in the normality of the world depends on public agreement and collective loyalty. The nomos is thus constantly challenged by the possibility of disagreement, deviance and outright opposition.

According to this interpretation of the roots of social order, religion is historically the principal institution in 'world-maintenance'. Religion confronts the ever-present threat of chaos with a sacred canopy which shelters man from disorder by providing massive legitimation for traditional practices and common sense reality. From this sociological perspective, 'evil' is simply a general term for all those events, processes or situations—illness, death, insanity, change, disorder, violence—which threaten to de-legitimise the normative order and plunge men back into a state of nature. In Berger's sociology, therefore, the problem of theodicy is a specific instance of the general need to make the world meaningful and legitimate. The need for a theodicy is located in the biology of the species, in the psychological importance of stability and predictability, and finally in the social requirement of order and consensus.

Within the context of this general discussion of social construction, Berger recognises, following Weber, that the specific nature of these religious theodicies may vary considerably between societies and between social groups. At the level of the individual, theodicy helps the individual social actor to come to terms with the problems of their own existence and experience. A plausible theodicy enables the individual 'to integrate the anomic experiences of his biography into the socially established nomos' (Berger, 1969a, p. 58). Of course, a theodicy does not remove pain or bring about social justice, but it does offer the promise of an interpretation of finitude which consoles and reconciles the individual to his fate. Thus, it 'is not happiness that theodicy primarily provides, but meaning' (Berger, 1969a, p. 58). Theodicies provide us with a meaningful interpretation of the pain, anguish and death which disrupt our orderly social routines. At a social level, collective theodicies provide explanations of existing social inequality, unequal power and economic injustice. These common, shared theodicies may legitimate the social order, but Berger recognises that, in any given society, there may well be two alternative theodicies, a theodicy of suffering for the poor and a theodicy of happiness for the rich. By offering compensation to the poor, theodicy may stabilise the political order by transferring the demand for social justice into a future world. Theodicy may, therefore, have either revolutionary or conservative implications. Berger follows Weber in identifying three major types of religious theodicy, namely transmigration of souls in the *karma-samsara* system, the messianic-millenarian theodicies of the religions of the Book, and the dualistic theodicies of pre-Islamic Iran.

Given Berger's sense of the all-pervasiveness of legitimating theodicies, the potential of a radical theodicy of resentment for social change must be severly limited. Any political overthrow of the existing order by an out-group, pariah caste or disprivileged class must be quickly followed by frantic efforts to repair or replace the normative order. Death and chaos are constant features of all human society by definition and, therefore, the need for theodicy is a permanent aspect of all social relationships. It is true, of course, that in modern society, where a pluralisation of life-worlds has taken place, the task of making theodicies plausible is particularly difficult. While in many respects *The Social Reality of Religion* suggests that some form of theodicy is an anthropological necessity, the book also has a critical content by suggesting that religion is merely a Feuerbachian projection of man's homelessness.

Berger himself subsequently recognised that the book could be 'read like a treatise on atheism' (1969b). In his *A Rumor of Angels*, Berger sets out to correct this interpretation by providing an examination of how the anthropological condition of man constantly points to or demands a transcendence of immediate reality and everyday life. As a parallel to the traditional theological arguments for the existence of God, Berger promises a set of arguments for human transcendence. These arguments are the arguments from ordering, hope, damnation and humour. To illustrate Berger's socio-theology, it will be sufficient to take the case of the argument from damnation, which is most closely related to the traditional problem of theodicy. Berger argues that there are certain crimes which go beyond our common-sense notion of what is morally permissible and which cannot be adequately incorporated within the routine process of secular laws. Nazi crimes against the Jews appear to be outside the bounds of enormity and existing legal responses to these crimes appear to incorporate our sense of human condemnation in a totally inadequate fashion. We want to call these offences against humanity not simply crimes but actions which are 'monstrously evil' (Berger, 1969b, p. 82). In the face of monstrous evil in the world, the relativising framework of science simply cannot encapsulate our feeling that the agents of evil deserve absolute damnation. There is built into our humanity the transcendent categories of damnation and vindication which go beyond the secular apparatus of law. These transcendent features of human anthropology are signs of a fundamental reality which cannot be encapsulated within the relativising framework of modern sociology.

There are a number of objections to Berger's analysis of theology, all of which centre on Berger's theoretically illegitimate conflation of the problem of order and the problem of meaning (Light, 1969). It is perfectly possible to experience social reality as a structured, ordered and routine reality without finding that reality either meaningful or legitimate. The inmates of total institutions and concentration camps find the social order perfectly organised, stable and determinate without conferring any necessary legitimacy or meaning on these social relationships. Alternatively, revolutionary groups may find the conflicts, contradictions and instability of capitalist society perfectly intelligible as the effects of an inherently exploitative system, but they do not ascribe meaning and legitimacy to the social system. In short, social order and social meaning are distinct and separate issues which need not coincide. Berger argues that we need order and meaning because of the paramount threat of chaos, but the concept of 'chaos' has little sociological content and is not treated as a serious possibility since a society without a nomic order, however minimal, is conceptually ruled out. Berger's social theodicy turns out to be a powerfully conservative argument in favour of accepting the *status quo*, not as 'the best of all possible worlds', but as preferable to the unknown terrors of a de-legitimised and precarious society verging on an unspecified chaos. Berger's attempt to incorporate Weber's sociology of religion into a normative sociology of knowledge has the effect of demolishing Weber's central interest in power. The exercise of force and the threat of violence are crucial dimensions of all societies. Whatever else Weber has to say about religion, his analysis of theodicy cannot be separated from his analysis of the power relations between in-groups and out-groups. For Weber, theodicy may be a fundamental part of man's response to evil, but theodicy is also a dimension of the politics of exclusion and social closure.

Although I want to criticise Berger's attempt to show that the need for a meaningful order is an anthropological and biological necessity, Berger's sociology of knowledge has served the useful function of demonstrating the sociological importance of the traditional problem of theodicy. Any sociology which comes up against pain and death, accident and misfortune, inequality and injustice in social life must necessarily find itself confronted with the problem of theodicy. It is not without interest that the concept of theodicy often plays a part in medical sociology. In his study of encephalitis lethargica, Oliver Sacks (1976) was driven back to the philosophy of Leibniz as a framework within which to criticise a purely mechanistic and a-social analysis of the nature and consequences of Parkinsonism. Similarly, Margaret Voysey's research (1975) into the processes by which parents come to terms with their handicapped children makes specific use of the concept of theodicy. However, physical and emotional suffering are not the only or primary issues which raise in sociology the traditional questions of theodicy. In the last analysis, the central question is how sociology will come to terms with the problem of justice within the framework of value-neutrality. While the term 'theodicy' is not regularly and routinely employed by modern sociologists, the problem of social theodicy is present in any sociology which attempts to raise the question of the origins and causes of inequality among men (Dahrendorf, 1968).

In part, the question of whether terms like 'justice', 'exploitation' and 'power' can be properly employed by sociologists is a problem of methodology. In political science, for example, there has been an attempt to extricate the scientific analysis of political behaviour from the traditional concerns of political philosophy on the grounds that terms like 'justice' are inextricably subjective, evaluate and biased (Taylor, 1967). The analysis of voting behaviour, political parties and political movements has, thus, replaced what are regarded as the evaluative, normative interests of political philosophy. In sociology, the problem of justice has similarly been replaced by the more technical questions of socio-economic classification, income distribution and social mobility. At the same time, there is considerable dissatisfaction with the current state of value-neutral social science and its empirical methodology. For example, Charles Taylor in 'Interpretation and the sciences of man' (1971) presents a powerful hermeneutic attack on the empiricist tradition in contemporary political science.

The mainstream of empiricist political science attempts to reconstruct political reality in terms of 'brute data alone' which are behaviour (voting, negotiating, protesting) and individual beliefs (political opinions, preferences, attitudes). Such an approach excludes consideration of the sharing of shared values which is constitutive of the political reality as the proper object of inquiry. Conventional empiricism 'excludes, for instance, an attempt to understand our civilization, in which negotiation plays such a central part both in fact and in justificatory theory, by probing the self-definitions of agent, other and social relatedness which it embodies' (Taylor, 1971, p. 32). This failure to take the intersubjectivity of meaning seriously creates particular difficulties in the area of comparative political analysis where the categories of Western political science are artificially and illegitimately applied to non-Western political systems. In dealing with such questions as 'legitimacy', empirical political science fails to acknowledge the shared meanings surrounding legitimacy which cannot be reduced to brute data. By ruling out the intersubjective significance of legitimacy, what comes 'into scientific consideration is thus not the legitimacy of a polity but the opinions or feelings of its member individuals concerning its legitimacy' (Taylor, 1971, p. 36). Under the cover of 'value-neutrality', political science avoids posing the problem of the legitimacy or justice of the societies which it studies by merely recruiting the opinions of individuals as to its legitimacy or justice. In this way, legitimacy always appears in quotation marks. One criticism of Weber has been that, while Weber defines sociology as an interpretative science, he too avoids the moral issue by thinking that any form of compliance or acceptance of power gives it legitimate authority. Such a stance, it can be contended, involves a value-judgment by giving a tacit sociological approval to regimes which are illegitimate and unjust. The problem with the hermeneutical approach, however, is that, while its objections to empirical science are often valid, it often fails to demonstrate in practice its ability to provide a rigorous alternative to an empiricist methodology. Because its programme often appears to be greater than its achievements, an empiricist might claim that it does not deliver the goods.

It is interesting to compare the programme of hermeneutic social science with those studies of power and legitimacy which share Taylor's objections to 'value-neutral' social science without sharing his epistemology. In other words, it is still important to ask whether it is possible to have an empiricist and critical social science. Can we be empirical and evaluative? Two recent studies—*Power, a radical view* (Lukes, 1974) and *Reflections on the Causes of Human Misery and upon Certain Proposals to Eliminate Them* (Moore, 1970)—advance the argument that social science can properly and empirically address the problems of power, exploitation and justice. For Lukes, there are a range of 'essentially contested' concepts in the social sciences which are necessarily evaluative and radical, but which nevertheless are applicable in empirical research. He rejects the view of functionalists in political science that the concept of power is contaminated by its 'ineradicably evaluative' character and proposes a three-dimensional analysis of power which embodies social criticism without abandoning the question of empirical verification. Behavioural definitions of the exercise of power and influence are rejected on the grounds that they are too individualistic and ignore the issue of structural restraints on decision-making processes. They fail to recognise that non-decision-making may be an exercise of power through the organisation of topics which appear on the political agenda. By conducting analysis at the level of subjective preferences, behaviourism does not attempt to analyse those real interests which may not be articulated in the subjective awareness of the actors themselves. For Lukes, it is necessary to examine those counter-factual situations where actors may have chosen or behaved differently had they been fully aware of their real interests in a given political context. Human interests and needs may be important products of a system of exploitation and domination and so a radical view of power must involve an evaluation of underlying real interests. Matthew Crenson's *The Un-Politics of Air Pollution: a study of non-decisionmaking in the Cities* (1971) fulfils Lukes's criteria of research which is evaluative and empirical. Counter-factually, human beings would prefer not to be poisoned by air pollution, but, despite these real interests in fresh air, city politics are such that the movement for clean air is frustrated by political structures which enable non-decision-making to operate.

In his study of *The Causes of Human Misery*, Moore argues that there are certain subjects—authority, justice and human purpose—which are essentially moral issues and that it is 'impossible therefore to avoid taking some kind of amoral position, not only in writing about politics but also in *not* writing about them and going about the ordinary business of life, as scholar, shoemaker, mechanic or plumber' (Moore, 1970, p. 3). Like Lukes, Moore argues that the task of providing a scientifically rigorous and empirically testable analysis of 'essentially contested' and evaluative concepts is not ruled out *a priori*. To avoid these emotive terms is to cripple social science by excluding from scientific analysis 'some of the most significant social facts in nearly all human societies' (Moore, 1970, p. 53). One example is the reluctance of behavioural science to admit the term 'exploitation' into their vocabulary. As an empirical definition of exploitation, Moore suggests that 'we can say that exploitation forms part of an exchange of goods and services when (1) the goods and services exchanged are quite obviously not of equivalent value, and (2) one party of the exchange uses a substantial degree of coercion' (Moore, 1970, p. 53). Moore openly admits that there will be huge 'grey areas' separating just exchange of services and open exploitation and that, in addition, there will be many technical difficulties in providing some measurement of what we mean by 'equivalent exchange' or 'coercion'. However, these methodological questions do not render the question of exploitation meaningless in principle. To admit otherwise would be to take the pessimistic view that all societies, by definition, are exclusively grounded in force and fraud. In defence of his view, Moore quotes Joan Robinson's *Freedom and Necessity* with approval to the effect that no consistent pessimist would ever write down their pessimism since there would be no point in expressing it.

While these contemporary discussions of whether it is possible for sociology to be simultaneously normative and scientific are direct responses to certain epistemological issues in social science, they are also part of the historical discussion of theodicy. The problem for theologians was that if you believe in a just and powerful God, then you have to come to terms, either by critique or by justification, with the presence of evil in human relations. The problem of theodicy forces you either to believe that we live in the 'best of all possible worlds' or that the world is improvable by human action or by the logic of history. Most sociologists, by contrast, are not theists, but they are still left with the issue of what is the role of sociology in relation to the 'evils' (or 'social problems', 'deviance' and 'malfunctioning') of society. Those who adhere to value-neutrality argue that, however wicked the world may be from a moral perspective, it is no business of mine *qua* social scientist. Those who criticise this position argue that we cannot ignore the moral question of evil without emasculating the vocation of sociology. Interestingly, both sides of this debate appeal to the philosophy of science of Max Weber as a warrant for either neutrality or passion. The oddity of Weber is that he provides a reasoned argument for separating facts from values, while also providing a passionate critique of the capitalist system.

The place of values in Weber's philosophy of science is a particularly vexed area of debate. There is some general agreement that, while Weber thought that it was impossible for sociology to proceed without presuppositions, sociologists had no privileged position to preach values on the basis of empirical research. There is also some agreement that value-neutrality is not equivalent to 'moral indifference' (Gouldner, 1973, p. 6). It is also the case that Weber's views on value-neutrality have to be seen in the historical context of German universities where Weber attempted to create a certain intellectual freedom for sociology to follow its own interests free from state interference (Wrong, 1977, p. 244). It has even been claimed that the real meaning of value-neutrality is that it forces us to confront values seriously and honestly (Dawe, 1971). It is important, therefore, to connect the doctrine of ethical neutrality with Weber's view that the modern world is no longer an enchanted garden. There are no certain absolute values, no prophets to interpret God's will, no charismatic leaders to resolve our crisis and no noumenal world into which we can flee. Like Kant, Weber recognises that in this situation our only policy is one of intellectual honesty. We have to live with uncertainty and conflict, recognising the limitations and the great strength of sociology as a secular calling. It is for this reason that writers like Wolfgang Schluchter have sought Weber's methodological position not in the overtly philosophy of science discussion in Weber's *Roscher and Knies: the logical problems of historical economics*, but in 'science as a vocation' and 'politics as a vocation'. The ethic of responsibility has, therefore, to be seen alongside the doctrine of value-neutrality which permits the sociologist to work with intellectual integrity in a world of conflicting values. Weber's insistence on 'a value-free empirical science aims, in the first instance, at making *possible* practical empirical research under the conditions of an antagonistic universe of values, but it is also meant to *make* such research *desirable*' (Schluchter, 1979, p. 79). Weber's twin notions of neutrality and responsibility must consequently also be linked with the problem of theodicy. As we have seen, the question of theodicy is specific to a monotheistic religious culture where there arises a contradiction between divine goodness and evil. Since Weber argues that the disenchanted garden is now populated by conflicting gods, the classical theistic theodicy no longer obtains in its original starkness. While there may be a social theodicy relating to human inequality, there is no longer, for the sociologist, a specifically theistic problem. We have to apply the principle of responsibility without the comforts of a Leibnizian theodicy. I think, therefore, that, while we might agree that Weber is not morally indifferent, his principle of responsibility is passive rather than active. Since the alternative to capitalism is likely to be a society which is still based on rational science, bureaucratic organisation and industrial production, there is no enchanted world round the corner. Hence, Weber responds to the dilemma of knowledge and action with an attitude of stoic resignation rather than with active engagement. This resignation is nowhere better summarised than in the 'Author's Introduction' where Weber says that:

> It is true that the path of human destiny cannot but appal him who surveys a section of it. But he will do well to keep his small personal commentaries to himself, as one does at the sight of the sea or of majestic mountains, unless he knows himself to be called and gifted to give them expression in artistic or prophetic form. (Weber, 1965, p. 29)

The problem with ethical neutrality and the ethic of responsibility in a world of conflicting values is that they rule out artistic and prophetic utterance. One is appalled, but resigned.

6 Weber on medicine and religion

The influence of Max Weber's sociological perspective has been felt in every area of sociological analysis from the study of Jewish prophets to industrial relations, from the sociology of law to the study of string instruments. The relevance of Weber's sociology in the sociology of medicine and health has, however, been largely neglected in contemporary sociology. In a recent bibliography of the secondary literature on Weber by Seyfarth and Schmidt (1977), an examination of over two thousand citations on Weberian sociology demonstrates the existence of this peculiar gap in modern sociology. The two principal exceptions to this generalisation involve the employment of Weberian models to analyse the institutionalisation of the medical profession (Berlant, 1975; Ritzer, 1975) in the United States. While the sociology of medicine has been heavily sponsored and funded by government agencies, medical sociology has not been traditionally regarded as central to classical sociology. Yet the issues raised by illness behaviour are in fact crucial for sociological theory. Thus, in the chapter on 'Religious stratification', the sociological connections between religion, health and social membership were illustrated by, among other things, the etymological relationship between 'to save' and 'to salve'. In other areas of sociology, Parsons (1951) drew attention to the 'sick role' as an important illustration of his general views on role expectations and the professions. Subsequent sociological approaches have developed important areas of research which outline the parallels between deviance, labels and illness (Zola, 1972). In recent years, a number of Marxist texts have appeared which concentrate on the class

177

basis of health and on the political economy of health in relation to the reproduction of the labour force in capitalist society
(Navarro, 1977). There does, therefore, appear to be an area in
contemporary sociology where specifically Weberian themes
and concepts could be applied and developed to provide a new
set of sociological perspectives. In this chapter, I employ
Weber's metatheoretical focus on social fate as a framework
for examining the paradoxical relationship between religious
beliefs and the institutionalisation of medical care with special
reference to the secularisation of nursing and the specialisation of the modern hospital.

My main argument in this study of Weber is that, while his
sociology is normally couched in the language of social actions
and actors' intentions, the actual content of his arguments
relates to the question of historical paradox, namely the
fatefulness of human intentionality. Weber concerns himself
constantly with the theme that in history social movements
are transformed by various processes of institutionalisation into
social structures which deny or contradict pristine motives
and intentions of the founders of these movements. At the
level of social actions, Weber's sociology analyses the unanticipated consequences of values and beliefs. Yet the notion of
'unanticipated consequences' does not adequately capture
Weber's metaphysical pathos. Even sociological theories do
not permit human actors to anticipate their fate. At the level
of social structures, Weber concerns himself with the logic of
situations which operate against the grain of human will. The
history of all hitherto existing societies is the history of human
failure. The central illustration of this pessimism in Weber's
cultural sociology is presented in *The Protestant Ethic and the
Spirit of Capitalism*. In Calvinistic theology, God's cosmic
scheme for the human race and for individuals cannot, in the
last analysis, be apprehended. Furthermore, this God cannot
be influenced by magic, by sacramental manipulation or by
other forms of merit-taking. The faithful are consequently not
able to resolve their salvational quest by routine or magical
manipulation of religious institutions. In response to this
religious *Angst*, Calvinism developed two forms of pastoral advice for the faithful. Anxiety about one's status within this

predestined world was itself evidence of lack of faith and trust in God. Anxiety could be contained by serving God in the world through a 'calling'. It was through this process of pastoral interpretation and counselling that religiously motivated men found a vocation in this world which had the effect of providing a dynamic system of rational motivation and an ethic of world-mastery. Secular capitalism had its motivational origins in specifically irrational feelings and beliefs about salvation. The religious drive for meaning found its historical denial in the cog-like precision of economic calculation. While the 'Author's Preface' provides a very different perspective on the question of capitalist origins, the central issue of the two essays on Protestantism and the spirit of capitalism is the fateful transformation of a religious into a secular culture. This theory of capitalism also provides us with some idea as to Weber's view of secular vocations and professionalisation.

In his historical sociology, Weber attempts to provide a linkage between the ascetic drive towards conduct and the vocational component of professions. The religious 'calling' becomes the model of subsequent service professions. Thus, the decisive 'and uniform goal of this asceticism was the disciplining and methodical organization of conduct. Its typical representative was the "man of a vocation" or "professional" (*Berufmensch*), and its unique result was the rational organization of social relationships' (Weber, 1968, vol. 1, p. 556). While ascetic ideals and the religious ethic may have historically provided part of the core of professional standards, the continuing maintenance of the privileges of a professional stratum require purely market practices to enhance the scarcity of professional services. Protection of the monopolistic position of professional groups within the market requires a system of restricted entrance into the profession by various forms of social closure, the elimination of external and internal competition, and by the monopolisation of services by legal privileges (Berlant, 1975, pp. 51–5). Weber's discussion of forms of social closure in *Economy and Society* thus provides a parallel to this discussion of the effects of Protestantism in *The Protestant Ethic and the Spirit of Capitalism* in one important respect. Protestantism carried the asceticism of 'monastic cells into everyday life' and 'did its part in building the tremendous cosmos of the modern economic order' (Weber, 1965, p. 181). However, once the economic system of capitalism had been established, it acquired a logic of its own which was mechanical and technical. Capitalism no longer required the moral prop of Calvinistic asceticism. The same argument can be applied to the professions. Although their origins may be traced back to religious models of ethical conduct, their continuing existence and their day-to-day practices rest on technical claims to competence backed up by the monopolisation of services, legal privileges and power resources which enable the profession to impose its definitions of service on its clientele (Johnson, 1972).

Although Weber's ideas on social closure have been applied to the medical profession (Berlant, 1975) in particular and to professionalism (Parkin, 1979) in general, Weber's view of the transformation of religious ethics into autonomous secular practices does have a special relevance to the development of nursing as a secular vocation. The notion that modern nursing grew out of a specifically religious vocation towards the sick has been a common assumption within the sociology of the professions. For example,

> until recently the only nursing worthy of the name was inspired by religious or at least philanthropic motives. Nurses were 'called' to a life devoted to the alleviation of suffering, and when the 'call' was not given or not heard, the task was left undone or was abandoned to persons to whom the honourable title of nurse was not appropriate. (Carr-Saunders and Wilson, 1933, p. 117)

The argument which I develop here is that the effects of the reform of nursing in the nineteenth century, especially by Florence Nightingale, resulted in nursing as an occupation which was subsequently shaped, not by religious motives, but by professional strategies in the market-place. Specifically, Florence Nightingale took the character of the religious nun as the model for reforming the reputation and status of the nurse;

the consequence of taking the asceticism of the 'monastic cells into everyday life' was to create a secular calling for middle-class women which did not require any religious legitimation. In presenting this historical argument, I am not succumbing to the conventional picture of 'The Lady with the Lamp' or to the mythology of Florence Nightingale as an anti-political vehicle of pure charity (Whittaker and Olesen, 1978). The argument is that the historical roots of the role of nurse are to be located in the religious orders for the care of the sick and in the domestic servant. The reform of nursing under the aegis of Florence Nightingale involved the employment of the role of the nun to reform the characterology of the domestic servant. The result was that the nurse-nun was driven out of the 'monastery' into the 'hospital'. The secularisation and professionalisation of nursing involves the substitution of a quasi-religious character and set of ethics by predominantly market interests of social closure and occupational power.

In order to understand the modern history of nursing, we have to possess a history of the hospital. The emergence of a specialised role for nursing the sick is bound up with the separation of the family from the hospital when the domestic care of kinfolk is replaced by outside services. We cannot understand the specialisation of nursing independently of the specialisation of institutions for the care of the sick. Furthermore, the secularisation of the medieval spital provides the larger framework within which we can approach the question of the secularisation of nursing. Weber's concepts of asceticism and bureaucratisation apply equally to both the historical development of the bureaucratic hospital and the emergence of nursing as a secular and technical occupation.

We can conveniently divide the historical development of the hospital into three broad phases—the period of religious foundations (335–1550), the age of charity hospitals (1719–1913), and the rise of the modern hospital (1913–48). The period of religious patronage of spitals opens with the decree of Constantine to close all pagan temples which had offered some form of care for the sick and closes with the dissolution of monasteries in the sixteenth century in England. The term 'hospital' derives from the Latin *'hospites* or 'guests' indicating that the medieval spital or hospice or '*hospitium*' was essentially a way-station offering hospitality to pilgrims who had fallen ill during pilgrimages. In England, the establishment of spitals developed rapidly after the Norman conquest when there was an upsurge in the number of pilgrims crossing the channel on religious missions. These early spitals for pilgrims were entirely unspecialised institutions catering to the needs of the sick, the poor, the infirm and the old. In addition to spitals, there existed a variety of similar institutions – almshouses, bedehouses and Maison Dieu—providing services for the sick. Between 1066 and 1550 about seven hundred spitals were established in Britain, but most of these institutions were relatively small-scale with less than twenty inmates (Cartwright, 1977).

In general terms, spitals were open to pilgrims regardless of the nature of their illness, their age and social status. We do, however, find some evidence of institutional specialisation around the care of leprosy, venereal disease and lunacy. Some leprosaria or lazar-houses were founded as early as the twelfth century, but they were greatly expanded in the thirteenth century when many old almshouses were converted into places for lepers. The importance of specialised leprosaria declined in the middle of the fourteenth century when famine and the Black Death killed off the majority of lepers who were prone to infection. Syphilis quickly replaced leprosy as the major crippling illness of the English population and existing lazar-houses were converted to 'lock hospitals' for victims of venereal disease. In medieval theories of disease, it was often the case, however, that no distinction was made between syphilis and leprosy. The main example of provision for lunatics is provided by the hospital of St Mary of Bethlehem in London which was founded in 1247.

While the majority of patients in spitals were short-term inmates, those entering lazar-houses were life-long inmates. The rules regulating the life of lepers were particularly severe. The rules relating to the control of lepers did, however, vary according to social class. A leper from a privileged social background could obtain permission to live outside the leprosarium or to build a separate home on the land of the leprosarium. In certain French leprosaria, there were separate dwelling places for nobles, ladies and common people (Brody, 1974). Ecclesiastical laws controlling leprosy prevented lepers inheriting property and forced them to live as beggars. Inside the lazar-houses, there were austere rules regarding drunkenness, foul language and sexual relationships. Inmates had to swear on oath to obey the rules of the house. Because lepers were inmates for life, one method of maintaining peace and order was that new patients had to be accepted by all existing inmates. In short, the lazar-house had many of the attributes of a 'total institution' (Goffman, 1961) and the regulations of such leprosaria were often models of monastic procedures for achieving social control over inmates. For example at the asylum of Illeford, leper inmates were forced to accept the monastic vows of poverty, obedience and chastity. In this period, the principal aim of all spitals, almhouses and lock-hospitals was the spirtual care of the inmates rather than a medical cure; they also served to isolate the sick from the rest of the population.

Medieval spitals were financed by episcopal provision, through the guild system, royal patronage or through taxation on the local population. In Shrewsbury, for example, local lepers took corn from sacks in the market-place. The medieval hospital and its system of economic support collapsed in the sixteenth century as the result of political and social factors. The dissolution of smaller religious houses in 1536 removed many existing hospices which were traditionally situated at the gates of monastic and other religious institutions. The revenues from these religious houses did not, as intended, contribute to the reform of medieval spitals, and this process of closure to support royal revenues was completed by further Acts in 1545 and 1547. As sheep-farming began to replace traditional agriculture, there was a sharp increase in rural vagrancy in the fifteenth and sixteenth centuries and many spitals were occupied by unemployed labourers. It was believed that the spital had become a centre for crime and banditry, and that they were controlled by 'lusty rogues' and 'stubborn knaves'. The reputation of religious spitals was finally undermined by various abuses of patronage.

The medieval system of spitals was, therefore, dominated by religious bodies and religious concerns. Patrons often established spitals as acts of penance in response to their own sins and God's mercy, or they were specifically established to cater to the needs of pilgrims. The moral regime of lock-houses and lazar-houses was analagous to the moral order of the monastic cell. The unspecialised services which they provided were designed to care for the patient rather than to cure. The hospitals which developed as charitable institutions in the eighteenth century were founded on different principles and by a different class of people. Charity hospitals were founded by the new bourgeois class and rich merchants inspired by middle-class philanthropy and the social doctrines of John Locke and Jeremy Bentham. These hospitals were unsupported by state and church but sustained by individual benefactors, often with the aid of unpaid medical staff. Charity hospitals first appeared in London, but between 1719 and 1798 nearly every county in England could boast about its voluntary 'infirmary'. Although these hospitals no longer had specifically religious origins, the rules for inmates continued to be puritanical in proscribing smoking, gambling, drinking and swearing. These hospitals were also selective in respect of the patients who could be admitted. Most hospitals refused to care for patients with infectious diseases, incurables, lunatics and patients who lived outside the immediate area.

One of the most significant developments in the nineteenth century was the specialisation of hospitals for the treatment of different types of illness. There were, of course, examples of specialised voluntary hospitals in the eighteenth century—such as the Rotunda Hospital of 1745 as a lying-in hospital—but the real movement towards specialisation came much later (Evans and Howard, 1930). Between 1802 and 1863, numerous hospitals were established for the treatment of diseases of the throat, eyes and chest along with hospitals specialising in cancer, smallpox or the care of children. This was also the period in which asylums for the institutional incarceration of lunatics were constructed on a wave of utilitarian optimism and enthusiasm. Asylums were built to control and discipline unruly passions which interfered with the exercise of the individual rational will. The asylum inmate was to be cured by physical restraint and public surveillance in the same way that the inhabitant of the Benthamite panopticon was to be controlled by public opinion. The number of asylums in England grew rapidly from nine in 1827 to 66 in 1890. It has been estimated that this increase implied that the ratio of lunatics to sane persons had increased from one in seven thousand to one in eight hundred between 1810 and 1829 (Jones, 1955). Throughout the century, there was an accumulation of evidence pointing to the failure of asylums as centres for curing lunacy. The highest recovery for admissions to lunatic asylums was 42 per cent, recorded in 1885, and the lowest was 37 per cent in 1873. Asylums failed to validate the utilitarian optimism with which they had been built and they had, in fact, operated as mere dumping grounds for social wrecks (Scull, 1977). It was under these circumstances, where the asylums were seen to be ineffective and economically burdensome, that the movement for the abolition of restraint of lunatics and the psychiatric theories of Philippe Pinel gained ground. However, the continuing low status of lunatic patients in the medical world into the twentieth century was also reflected in the status of asylum attendants in their struggle for professional recognition (Adams, 1969).

The age of the charity hospital and the county asylum was brought to an end by the impact of reformist opinion which demonstrated that the rapidly growing population of lunatics was not compatible with the view that asylums could cure lunacy. It was also the case that the economic burden of maintaining and replacing asylums was no longer acceptable to middle-class rate-payers (Scull, 1977; Skultans, 1979). The voluntary hospital service could not provide adequate medical care for Britain's rapidly increasing urban population and the inadequacies of voluntary hospitals and amateur nursing care were made glaringly obvious by the advent of modern, mass warfare. The Crimean War (1854-6), the Boer War (1899-1902) and the two World Wars demonstrated two crucial medical facts. First, as recruits were taken into the army from the civilian male population, it became evident that the majority of young men suffered from serious and widespread disorders—TB, poor eyesight, respiratory diseases, syphilis, low weight and low height. Britain, regarded as a great nation with extensive colonial possessions, was unable to muster a large army of healthy males at short notice. These wars also demonstrated the total inadequacy of medical provision, care and administration for the British army. As Florence Nightingale and her committees clearly showed, more British soldiers died from exposure on the heights of Sebastopol and in the medical centre at Scutari than on the battlefield. Even in peace-time, the mortality rate of soldiers living in barracks was higher than the civilian rate. These nineteenth-century military disasters and the subsequent public criticism initiated a period of reform of medical care within the British army and the establishment of the Nightingale School of Nursing in 1860.

While wartime conditions created the major impulse towards medical reform, the increasing misery of the social conditions of the urban working class also prompted middle-class reformers to legislate for improvements in sanitation. A series of outbreaks of infectious diseases among the poor also threatened the health of the rich. The Public Health Act (the Chadwick Act) of 1848 was partly motivated by fear of the spread of cholera in London. The Act increased the power of local authorities to clean the streets, improve drainage and sanitation, and collect refuse. An adequate public health system was also seen as an economy for tax payers. When workers fell ill, their dependent families were forced into workhouses which had to be supported by tax-payers' money. The Poor Law Amendment Act of 1834 reduced the cost of Poor Law administration and, by making the internal regime of the workhouse as punitive as possible, attempted to reduce the number of people seeking Poor Law assistance. The doctrines of *laissez-faire* and the notion that the poor had only themselves to blame conflicted with the need for an efficient army and a healthy work-force. Imperialism depended on 'national efficiency' and the complete 'failure of the treatment of tuberculosis, the very poor diet and health standards revealed by education authorities' surveys and the shocking standard of physique found among army recruits made no economic or military sense' (Widgery, 1979, p. 15). The principals of Social Darwinism and Spencerian evolution were ultimately negated by the intervention of the state in response to the economic and military requirements of competitive capitalism.

The reforms of Lloyd George's liberal government—the Unemployed Workman Act (1905), Old Age Pensions Act (1908) and National Insurance Act (1913)—went a long way in replacing the *laissez-faire* voluntarism of the age of charity with a system of obligatory, national administration of social security and medical provision. These liberal reforms did not, however, produce a systematic, rational scheme for medical care. There was a perplexing variety of medical provision and types of service which produced overlap and muddle. The relationship between public and voluntary hospitals was not properly co-ordinated, so that two hospitals in the same area might be providing specialised units. There was also felt to be grave shortages of doctors and nurses in poor areas and over-provision in the more wealthy regions of the United Kingdom (Watkin, 1978). While definite steps were taken to reform the hospital system in the 1930s and 1940s, it was warfare which once more paradoxically came to the aid of the sick. In the years immediately preceding the outbreak of the Second World War, it was widely assumed that the existing muddle of public and voluntary provision of hospital beds would be totally unable to cope with the casualties following mass aerial bombardment of civilian populations. The Emergency Medical Services were set up to co-ordinate medical administration and to increase the availability of hospital beds. These new measures were not fully tested until the evacuation of the British army from France in 1940, the Battle of Britain and the arrival of flying bombs in 1944 (Dainton, 1961). The immediate background to the National Health Act of 1946 was, therefore, the devastating impact of modern warfare and the necessity for an efficient labour force. The motivating principal of national health was the assumption that there was a backlog of ill-health in the nation which could be removed by injection of public expenditure on a national basis.

The point of this historical sketch has been to establish that the history of the modern hospital can be seen as a movement from unspecialised, *ad hoc* religious foundations to specialised, bureaucratic institutions dominated by professional bodies of trained experts. The next stage of my argument is to show that the emergence of modern nursing is a parallel movement in which the vocation of the nurse-nun emerges in the professionalism of the medical technician. The historical origins of the modern nurse are to be found in medieval Catholic religious orders whose religious vocation lay in the care of the sick and in the lay nurse or domestic who performed household duties in the context of the hospital ward. Nursing orders appeared in twelfth and thirteenth centuries with the Crusades. Among the Third Order of St Francis, men and women of the order, living outside the religious community, concerned themselves with the needs of the sick and the poor. The Augustinians also were involved in hospital work, taking charge of the Hotel Dieu in the twelfth century. In a later period, the continental nursing orders such as the Sisters of Charity became well-known throughout Europe. In these orders religious interests cannot be easily separated from physical care of the sick because their work also included the saving of souls and the celebration of last rites. While religious orders provided one model of the nursing role, the other historical 'antecedents of the nursing profession were domestic servants. Indeed at the beginning of the nineteenth century, nursing amounted to little more than a specialized form of charring. Such was the background of the women employed as nurses in the voluntary hospitals' (Abel-Smith, 1960, p. 4). Nurses who were employed in charity hospitals or in Poor Law Infirmaries had a very low, stigmatised reputation for prostitution, dishonesty and drunken behaviour. In literature, Charles Dickens in *Martin Chuzzlewit* provides the caricature of the secular nurse in the person of Sairey Gamp.

In charity hospitals and workhouses, the nurses were often recruited from among the patients and wages were either very low or nonexistent. In these circumstances, there was a strong motivation and ample opportunity for petty pilfering. Prostitution and moonlighting were equally obvious sources for supplementing their pay. As part of their treatment, patients were often allowed a pint of porter and a glass of gin per day, which meant that nurses also had free access to alcohol. Furthermore, in return for unpleasant chores, such as laying out the dead, nurses were rewarded with gin. The low status of these nurses was partly a reflection of the low status of their patients. Those nurses who worked directly with patients were largely drawn from working-class domestics, while the sisters in charge of nurses were more likely to be middle-class widows. Matrons who controlled wards tended to be recruited from a higher social class since their duties were primarily administrative and secretarial. It is against this occupational background that we have to understand Florence Nightingale's particular concern with the character of the nurse as the central feature of the reform of nursing and the creation of a female occupation suitable for ladies of respectable, middle-class origin.

Florence Nightingale (1820–1910) was a typical product of her social class and historical period. Born into a rich and politically influential family, her childhood and adolescence was passed in a routine of enforced leisure which precluded rich women from the serious concerns of social and political life. Florence, however, was a sensitive and intellectual child who found this role within the leisure class deeply frustrating. A respectable marriage was the only legitimate way out of the boredom of adolescence, but Florence felt called to a more rewarding occupation outside the triviality of this domesticated, female world. Her refusal to comply with parental expectations resulted in a permanent conflict in the home. Her time

> at home was hateful; impossible that God should have bestowed the gift of time on His female creatures to be used as Fanny [Nightingale] wished her to use it, sitting nicely dressed in the morning-room doing worsted work, having a little rest, going for a little drive, doing the flowers, practising quadrilles. (Woodham-Smith, 1950, p. 35)

Florence and her sister were subject to the nervous syndrome of fainting, tears and depression common to females of her class. Her escape from this leisurely existence was not via matrimony, but through a vocation in nursing. On 7 February 1837, Florence felt called by God to his service, but at this stage she had no specific interest in nursing as a secular vocation. It was not until seven years later, after some casual involvement in philanthropic work among the poor, that she formed a clear idea that her specific calling was to work in hospitals for the sick.

Florence Nightingale's vocation for nursing had its origins, therefore, in a specifically religious calling, but it was also shaped by her early experience of institutionalised nursing during her visit to the Kaiserwerth institute for Lutheran deaconesses. Florence did not receive any training at Kaiserwerth and she later described the hygiene of the institute as 'horrible'. What impressed her was not the quality of care, but the character of the nurses. Towards the end of her life she wrote that 'never have I met with a higher tone, a purer devotion than there' (Woodham-Smith, 1950, p. 91). Throughout her life, the question of training for nurses in the technical aspects of healing was always secondary to the issue of the reform of character, especially the sexual character of the nurse. Apart from her own moral views on sexual ethics, 'expediency alone demanded that the new nurse should not only be, but should be proved to be, as chaste as the members of any religious order' (Abel-Smith, 1960, p. 22). It was only through character reform that Nightingale could open the ranks of secular nursing to the daughters of the middle class. Her rules controlling the behaviour of nurses who served at Scutari during the Crimean campaign were consequently clear and strict. Any evidence that nurses had been misbehaving with the troops resulted in instant dismissal. Young women were not accepted for service and Nightingale looked for elderly widows as her principal recruits. Their uniforms were not to be decorated with coloured ribbons and nurses were not allowed outside the hospital without an escort.

While Florence Nightingale thus brought to nursing a moral and religious vision of the chaste nurse, the relationship between her nurses and those of the religious orders was in fact very complicated. She thought that the task of the modern nurse was to assist doctors in achieving a medical cure of alleviation of physical suffering, not the cure of souls of sick soldiers. She complained bitterly about the ministration of spiritual help to soldier, in the absence of physical care, offered by the religious orders in the Crimea. She observed that many of the nuns were 'fit more for heaven than a hospital, they flit about like angels without hands among the patients and soothe their souls while they leave their bodies dirty and neglected' (Woodham-Smith, 1950, p. 145). Her attitude towards religious orders of nurses was also coloured by her experience of inter-denominational rivalries between the groups of religious nurses which were sent to the Crimea. Nightingale was attacked in the British press as an 'Anglican Papist' on the grounds that in recruiting her nurses she had deliberately turned down Protestant, evangelical applicants. There were good political reasons for stressing the central importance of physical rather than spiritual care. Her attitude towards religious 'ladies' who wanted to arrange flowers in the wards rather than care for the sick tends, however, to understate her very real debt to the example set by religious orders of nursing. Her *Notes on Hospitals* (1859) make it clear that her own system of reform owed a great deal to the work of Sister Mary Jones and the Sisterhood of St John the Evangelist which provided nurses at King's College Hospital and Charing Cross. Nightingale and Sister Mary worked together in establishing the importance of the District Nurse and in the training of midwives. By the end of the nineteenth century, however, the religious nurses had lost ground to the trained nurses who were by now emerging from the new schools for nursing, but a religious content remained an important element within the vocational ethics of nursing.

Florence Nightingale's attitude towards the question of moral and technical training was the principal feature of her objections to the registration of nurses in the battle for state recognition of professional qualifications for nursing. Over the registration issue which had split the Hospitals' Association committee and resulted in a separate British Nurses' Association of 1887, Nightingale took the position that character could not be developed by technical training and could not be measured by examination. For Nightingale, nursing was primarily a calling, not a profession based on credentials. The movement for registration came from educated, middle-class nurses, who wanted a register as a method of controlling entrance and enforcing technical standards which would enhance the social status of nursing and create a career pattern inside the occupation. The qualified and militant nurses in the BNA regarded training not primarily as a method of disciplining the moral character, but as an apprenticeship producing technical and intellectual qualifications. A period of three year's training and a registration fee would be the first step towards professional status. The militants were opposed on the grounds that restricted entry would exclude girls of humble origins and limit the supply of nurses in a period when there was already a shortage. The BNA formed a pressure group to work for state registration and, as a preliminary measure, formed their own voluntary register in 1889. They were successful in recruiting a daughter of Queen Victoria as their patron, but their attempts to secure registration by Act of Parliament were unsuccessful and they had to content themselves in the short run with a Charter.

An important precedent for the registration of nurses was provided by the Midwives Act of 1902 which excluded unqualified midwives from attendance of women in childbirth and created the Central Midwives Board to control entry into the occupation. The Midwives Institute had been founded in 1881 to raise the status of midwives and to petition Parliament for recognition. As with nursing in general, the issue of registration for midwives was complicated by the difficulty of separating the functions of doctors and female midwifery. Although the Royal College of Physicians, for example, recognised the importance of training and registration for midwives, it took two decades for a Bill to pass successfully through Parliament. Furthermore, the Midwives Act of 1902 was not entirely satisfactory since, in contrast to similar measures,

> concerned with the recognition of professions, midwifery legislation was not designed to protect legitimate practi-

tioners from the competition of unqualified rivals. The Midwives Institute itself represented only a fraction of the existing practitioners and never allowed the interests of its members to influence what it regarded as its public duty. (Walker, 1954, p. 336)

It was, despite its weakness, an important legal step in the organisation of female labour within modern medicine.

Each year between 1904 and 1914 a registration bill for nurses came before Parliament, but no Act was passed because Parliament was itself divided by sectional interests within the medical profession and nursing bodies. Once again it was war that settled the issue and resolved the legal tangle. The influx of unqualified nurses into hospital work during the First World War united the profession behind the need for registration and the bravery of nurses at the front won the open admiration of the War Office (White, 1978). The Act of 1919, under the sponsorship of the Minister of Health, recognised a training period of three years as the basis of registration and set up a council to approve training schools for nurses. The Nurses' Registration Act meant that 'With its military heritage showing in its language, its religious tradition conveyed in its sentiment and its humble ancestry revealed in its uniform, the profession had come of age' (Abel-Smith, 1960, p. 99).

In becoming a profession, nursing had begun to experience a definite shift away from its vocational ethos towards a new self-conception which emphasised professional and technical criteria of occupational excellence. The achievement of registration implies an important transformation of the character of nursing as an occupation since,

at the beginning of the century nursing was one of the few 'lady-like' vocations, there are now many such vocations some of which offer greater attractions. In consequence recruitment has come to be from a rather different stratum of society, and entrance is less often than formerly the result of a 'call' inspired by religious motives. (Carr-Saunders and Wilson, 1933, p. 121)

The vocational view of nursing focused on self-sacrifice, service and submission to the authority of male doctors. The professional ideology of nursing, by contrast, recognises, in the language of the Briggs Committee, that nursing is not 'ancillary to medicine, but complementary to it'. The new language of professionalism makes a claim for greater equality between doctor and nurse, stressing the skill and technical competence of the latter (Williams, 1978). The schools of nursing that have developed on university campuses reject the Nightingale imagery of the loyal bedside domestic by stressing the intellectual and technical character of the contemporary nurse. There is thus a conflict between the public image of the nurse as a 'mother surrogate' and the professional image of the nurse as a technical specialist (Denton, 1978). Within a Weberian framework, we can see that the original religious content of the role of nurse has been replaced by technical criteria which are fitting to the status of nurse as a professional occupation. The traditional 'calling' to nursing as a religious activity which is exercised in the world has been translated into credentialism.

The professional and class strategy of social closure which Berlant (1975) and Parkin (1979) develop out of Weber's analysis of power and professionalism applies equally to the occupational strategies of nursing. The battle for registration in nursing involved a social closure of the profession to domestic and untrained nurses. It represented an attempt to control recruitment to the occupational group and a monopolisation of the supply of nursing skills. By restricting entrance to the occupation, registration had the effect of increasing occupational loyalty to nursing and reinforcing group membership and individual identification. In particular, the experiences of the First World War had the effect of limiting internal and external competition within nursing by uniting the various sectional groups within the occupation. The result of these different processes was to increase the market scarcity of nursing skills and to raise the economic cost of their provision. The irony was that Nightingale's vocationalism was being translated into occupational credentialism while the Nightingale myth was achieving a dominant place in official and lay images of the nature of nursing as a social role.

The Nightingale myth has, however, been radically challenged in recent years by both professional historians and radical feminists. Historians have criticised the popular notion that Florence Nightingale actually created nursing *de novo*; clearly a wide range of social changes, institutions and personalities contributed to the nineteenth-century development of nursing. Schools for nursing existed before Nightingale went to the Crimea; religious orders, such as the Protestant Sisters of Charity inspired by Elizabeth Fry, cannot be ignored. In stressing the importance of Florence Nightingale in this analysis of the secularisation of nursing vocations, it is not intended to suggest that nursing was the single-handed creation of this mythical heroine. My argument is that Nightingale contributed a specifically religious dimension to the occupational ethos of nursing which had the effect of making nursing a respectable occupation for a particular class of women. While historical scrutiny points to the myth of Nightingale as the authoress of modern nursing, the feminist critique concentrates on how Nightingale's moral reforms contributed to the social and professional subordination of women in the bureaucratic sructure of the modern hospital.

Nightingale regarded nursing as the 'natural function' of women, and if she drew much of the ethics of nursing from religious vocations, then she equally saw nursing as a form of 'mothering'. Nursing was to be the female occupation *par excellence*. The hierarchy between male doctors and female nurses perfectly matched a division in nature between male and female skills. She wrote that the art of nursing care

> is performed usually by women, under scientific heads—physicians and surgeons. Nursing is putting us in the best possible conditions for nature to restore or to preserve health. The physician or surgeon prescribes these conditions—the nurse carries them out (Nightingale, 'training of nurses and nursing the sick poor', 1882 and quoted in Gamarnikow, 1978, p. 105)

This 'over-determination' of sexual differences by theoretical/practical, mental/manual divisions was partly a reflection of the specific problems of organising nurses in the Crimean campaign. The 'ladies' who volunteered for service had no conception, according to Nightingale, of the importance of discipline, duties and orders. She wanted to make it perfectly plain that following the instructions of doctors was in the patients' interest. She also recognised the fact that military doctors initially regarded civilian nurses as well-intentioned, bungling amateurs who were interfering in areas where they were entirely incompetent. In order to win the support of military and medical authorities, Nightingale had to guarantee the subordination of nurses to medical control. Her attitude towards women's rights was equally tactical. She thought that women could achieve greater results off the political stage rather than on it. These tactical considerations were, however, overlaid by a deep distrust of women whom she regarded as weak and unreliable—'women crave for being loved, not for loving' (Woodham-Smith, 1950, p. 386).

Nightingale's definition of nursing as a female occupation subordinate to the male occupation of doctors perfectly suited her conception of nursing as a religious and maternal 'calling' for middle-class spinsters. As Gamarnikow (1978) points out, asymmetrical relations between doctor, nurse and patient faithfully reflect the relations between father, mother and child. The idea that nursing is akin to mothering was a perfectly acceptable doctrine from the point of view of the medical profession, which was itself engaged in a fierce struggle to achieve a monopoly over medical services. In America, doctors were concerned to establish legal and economic prohibition of 'irregulars', suppression of the popular health movement and restrictions on the practice of female midwives. The results of social closure in the professions of doctor and nurse produced paradoxical results because,

> while some women were professionalizing women's domestic roles, others were 'domesticizing' professional roles, like nursing, teaching and, later, social work. For the woman who chose to express her feminine drives outside of the home, these occupations were presented as sim-

ple extensions of women's 'natural' domestic role.
(Ehrenreich and English, 1973, pp. 56–7)

I would add that the subordinate religious role of women also slotted 'naturally' into these social and occupational divisions.

While in radical and academic circles the whole mythology of the Lady with the Lamp has been drawn into question, the popular imagery of Nightingale as an altruistic, humanitarian servant of the public still plays an important role in the occupational choices of idealistic recruits to the profession. The student nurse is typically motivated by 'instrumental activism' in the sense that they perceive nursing as a practical activity, which, employing technical skills, results in successful medical outcomes. This instrumental activism is fused with 'a somewhat amorphous, though nonetheless deeply felt, Christian-humanitarian conviction of love, care and a desire to help others' (Davis, 1975, p. 120). The professional socialisation of nurses into a 'realistic' conception of their occupational role brings about important changes in this instrumental humanism. Nursing activities are shown to be broader and more intellectually demanding than the simple model of caring initially suggests. The 'innocence' of the humanistic motivation is replaced by an awareness of the theoretical knowledge which lies behind knowing how to perform. Professional socialisation thus plays a major part not only in conveying technical and theoretical knowledge, but in producing an occupational character which matches the new status of nursing as the end product of occupational closure.

Although the analogy between mother and nurse or nun and nurse may be relevant to the question of establishing nursing as a respectable vocation, the analogy is totally unsuited to the problem of converting nursing into a technical, skilled occupation for both sexes. The contemporary issues of reorganising nursing as a skilled profession are inevitably joined with the question of 'defeminisation'. If the reduction of the status of certain occupations, such as clerical work, is associated with 'feminisation', then conversely the professionalisation of nursing may involve rapid recruitment of men to previously female roles, such as midwifery. While the role of male nurse may involve a status contradiction (Segal, 1962), the attempt to remove the connection between nursing and mothering must open the profession to male recruits on an increasing scale. In addition, the emphasis on credentials and professional training in theoretical rather than practical knowledge must undermine the Nightingale conception of nursing as a 'natural' activity of women. However, to change the sexual structure of the occupation without a change in the sexual division of labour in society as a whole has the effect of creating a male elite in an occupation which is still predominantly female. While male nurses have been a regular feature of mental hospitals and psychiatric wards, they are now beginning to be a common feature of the nursing staff of general hospitals. Although the male nurse is in a numerical minority, he enjoys far greater prospects of rapid promotion within nursing than his female counterpart. In Britain in the 1970s, men represented about 11 per cent of all nurses, but occupied one-third of all posts in the two highest grades in all hospitals; only one woman was a Chief Nursing Officer (Brown and Stones, 1973). Unionisation and bureaucratisation of previously low-status female occupations may work against the more general political interests of women (Hacker, 1953).

While the sexual character of nursing as an activity which is as natural as mothering has been challenged by the arrival of the male nurse, the personal intimacy between patient and nurse is changing in a corresponding manner. The bureaucratisation of the modern hospital, the increasing technical and social division of labour between nurses and the existence of hierarchical structures of communication have the effect of depersonalising interactions between nurses and patients, and these new arrangements act as a defensive mechanism in emotionally charged relationships (Menzies, 1960). The practice of 'stripping' patients of personal belongings and individual identity is another feature of the routine management of inmates in bureaucratically organised hospitals (Watkin, 1978) which complements the translation of vocational mothering into a technical task. This emotionally charged language of bureaucratisation and depersonalisation is deliberately employed here to bring out the parallel between Weber's vision of the translation of the Calvinistic calling into the calculative behaviour of rational capitalism and the translation of Nightingale's vocational ethic of nursing into credentialism. In nursing, religious calling has also been smothered by the necessity of strategies of social closure in the market place. In this way the history of modern medicine provides us with a case study of Weber's vision of fate.

It is ironic that, while in his intellectual activity Weber makes no specific reference to the sociology of the hospital and nursing, Weber was himself for a short period a hospital administrator. After the outbreak of the First World War, Weber accepted a post with the *Reservelazarettkommission* and assumed direct responsibility for the organisation of nine military hospitals. In this capacity, Weber was faced with administrative inefficiency, inadequate supplies of basic materials and official procrastination. Weber submerged himself in the practical details of organising wards, kitchens, staff and supplies. He was also hampered by pointless bureaucratic inquiries, requests and unnecessary interference. It was characteristic of Weber to respond to this situation by imposing his own authority and sense of organisation on the existing administrative chaos. Marianne Weber, however, also emphasises Weber's deep sense of care and admiration towards the ordinary German soldier. She writes glowingly that the military

hospital now was a world that obeyed its own laws. Everyone who was washed ashore in a mutilated condition by the waves of fate became a new gift and a precious treasure worth saving from destruction with the utmost effort of all healthy forces. Every person who had recently been mercilessly sacrificed to the common good was here reinstated into his right to live. (Weber, 1975, p. 521)

It is tempting to draw a comparison between Florence Nightingale's heroic efforts at Scutari, not only to create a new sense of professional responsibility, but to eliminate the social stigma attached to the common British soldier, and Max Weber's struggle with bureaucratic incompetence at Heidelburg. Such personal heroism becomes the stuff of occupational ideologies.

Part three

Development

7 Feudalism and prebendalism

In volume three of *Economy and Society*, Weber draws our attention to three crucial problems in the sociological analysis of any social system. The first question relates to the nature of ownership of land. In feudalism, property in land is based on a system of inheritance of rights which is transmitted through legitimate male heirs backed up by various forms of law. The most important collection of feudal laws, the *Libri Feudorum*, spelt out the rights of descent, conveyance and forfeiture. These property rights were held in return for certain services, especially military ones, to landlords in a system of hierarchical power relationships. In prebendalism, property rights are concentrated in the state or a royal family which allocates land in return for military service, but the institution of individual inheritance is absent or exists alongside the depersonalised property of the state bureaucracy. In practice, Weber employs a variety of concepts to describe this major dichotomy. The term 'prebend' is occasionally used interchangeably with 'benefice'. A right of benefice (*beneficium*) was a non-inheritable grant of land and its enserfed population to provide the needs of an individual who had assumed ecclesiastical and government duties. While in principle the fief is inherited and the benefice or prebend is not, the dividing line between these is fluid. There are many examples between the tenth and thirteenth centuries in Europe where the principle of inheritance is conjoined with the rights of the *beneficium* to produce a *de facto* system of inherited feudal property (Fourquin, 1976). While Weber recognises a variety of forms of property in land, his main concern is to draw a distinction between decentralised personal rights in feudalism and centralised impersonal rights in prebendalism.

The second major question for Weber is the nature of the ownership of the means of physical violence or, to put this question in terms of contemporary jargon, the possession of the apparatus of repression. Weber distinguishes between three situations. The state may raise and supply mercenary armies out of revenue and thereby separate the general population from ownership of the means of violence. This institutionalisation of violence is characteristic of late capitalism and of prebendal empires. Depersonalised ownership of violence by the state is contrasted with situations where the ecnomically dominant class is either itself militarised or employs professional warriors (knights) to protect its own domains and property. Finally, there are civilian militias which are mobilised on an *ad hoc* basis for the protection of the local populace and, in this case, the militia is neither professional nor mercenary. The relationship between these situations is fluid empirically. In the Ottoman empire, the slave army of the state only gradually replaced the feudal cavalry of the landed aristocracy. Historically in Europe, feudal military relations grew out of the original *Gefolgschaft* ('fellowship') which was 'a personal bond of mutual loyalty and affection between a warrior chief and his hand-picked revenue of close associates' (Poggi, 1978, p. 19). The urban militias which developed later were a system of defence for individuals who separately were powerless. The militia was the military dimension of a social contract of powerless but equal individuals who were mobilised against professional men of war in defence of their urban property.

Weber's third question concerns the relationship between land rights and military power, between relations of production and relations of violence. Clearly, Weber believes that property ownership and control of violence are empirically closely related. In feudalism, militarised landlords, united by oaths of mutual responsibility, were organised to protect themselves and their property against external invasion and internal rebellions and uprisings. Alternatively, their propertied wealth enabled them to employ professional warriors in their service. However, whereas Marxism typically conceptualises the relations of violence as ultimately under the control of the dominant class, Weber believes that there can be a degree of separation between economic and military power. It is interesting that, in his definition of feudalism in *The Agrarian Sociology of Ancient Civilizations*. Weber not only combines property ownership with military power, he suggests that the issue of military organisation is the determining factor. In Weber's agrarian sociology the term 'feudalism' covers all those social institutions 'whose basis is a ruling class which is dedicated to war or royal service and is supported by privileged land holdings, rents or the labour services of a dependent, unarmed population' (Weber, 1976, p. 38). However, the variations within feudalism are to be explained by reference to 'variations in the manner in which the warrior class was organised and economically supported' (Weber, 1976, p. 38). In prebendalism, the state army acts as a line of defence against the localised power of feudal cavalries. The relationship between the dominant class and the apparatus of violence may also be a contingent problem relating to the degree of coherence between the various strata or fractions of the class which controls the means of production. Just as Marxists refer to the 'relative autonomy of the state' in situations where the dominant class is internally divided, so, following Weber, we can conceive of varying degrees of separation between property rights and the means of force. The manner in which power over land and power over military institutions are conjoined is, for Weber, bound up with the centralising and decentralising processes of feudal and prebendal societies.

Feudalism and prebendalism have parallel, but different, contradictory social structures and their own characteristic ideologies of power and responsibility. Both feudalism and prebendalism are subject to 'centrifugal tendencies' (Critchley, 1978), but the precise manner in which these tendencies work themselves out vary according to the contrasted economic and military structures of societies based predominantly on either the *feuduom* or the *beneficium*. The characteristic crisis of feudal Europe has been called 'feudal anarchy'. Thus,

The development of progressively greater autonomy on
the part of fiefholders generated increasing numbers of

jurisdictional rivalries and boundary disputes, which were difficult to settle by appeals to the increasingly nominal rights of higher lords and suzerains....The growth of feudalism led, in most parts of Western Europe, to a drastic erosion of the landed patrimony of territorial rulers, who granted fiefs to tie to themselves men who in turn replicated the process downward toward pettier vassals. (Poggi, 1978, p. 31)

The growing autonomy of lesser vassals resulted in local centres of power where feudal immunity from overlords could be secured, if necessary by force of arms. This dislocation of hierarchical power was reflected in two conflicting theories of medieval kingship. As landlords, feudal kings attempted to assert their superiority over other feudal landlords by appealing to a theory of divine kingship. In this descending principle, kings were responsible directly to God rather than to a community of equal landlords. Against these absolutists claims, feudal landlords claimed that the king was simply one amongst equals whose responsibilities lay not with God, but with his fellow landlords. Kings thus employed a theocratic principle to limit their contractual obligations as landlords, while, particularly in feudal England, barons appealed to customary law (*leges Anglorum* and *lex terrae*) to enforce feudal contracts against a sacral conception of royal immunity (Ullman, 1965). In Islam there were similar ideological practices related to the political struggle between an imperial centre and feudal peripheries (Zeitlin, 1960). Caliphs who were leaders of conquering armies consistently appropriated new titles with religious and often messianic implications which attempted to appease the religious sensibilities of their subject populations. In this respect Shi'ism represents an important political peculiarity; it was originally an oppositional movement whose major doctrines are consequently problematic as the basis for legitimising the political *status quo*. According to the doctrine of the imamate, the imam can only be designated by God as a chosen person in possession of complete religious knowledge (Jafri, 1979). The traditional doctrines of Shi'ism cannot, therefore, be routinely mobilised in the service of legitimating the state or cabinets which emerge from plebiscitary democracy. Alliances between the religious leadership and the radical nationalists has been a peculiar feature of Iran from the Tobacco Uprising to the Ayatollah Khomeini (Keddie, 1966).

Similar problems of religious legitimation in the context of political struggles between patrimonial centres and autonomous local sources of power have been analysed in the case of Bhuddist societies. The traditional polity of Thailand oscillated between periods when local lords gained power and undermined the authority and religious legitimacy of kingship. The formation of new dynasties and renewed prosperity involved the exercise of physical violence which was incompatible with Buddhist doctrine. The typical history of Thai dynasties involved a period of violence when new royal households were formed, to be followed by a period in which the king acquired religious merit through purifying monastic institutions and encouraging religion. The kingly roles of world conqueror, righteous ruler and world renouncer were thus merely different dimensions of religio-political phenomenon (Tambiah, 1976). The mythic history of kingship from conquest to renunciation parallels the political conflicts of Thailand's 'galactic polity'. The patrimonial centre is surrounded by satellites which, while replicas of the royal palace, enjoy increasing degrees of autonomy according to their distance from the king. The weakness of the system lay in the fact that there were no clearly enforceable rules of succession so that the death of the righteous ruler was invariably followed by rebellion and millenarian opposition. The endless search for religious credentials for cosmic legitimacy was the counterpart of massive political insecurity. Weber's prebendal/feudal typology can be further extended to analysis of another illustration of the 'galactic polity', namely Iran, in which in recent decades we have witnessed the attempt to impose a modern state on to a traditional cycle of prebendal and feudal rulership (Sheikholeslami, 1978).

One of the persistent errors of many standard approaches to Iranian history is the presupposition that Iranian society can be characterised by the dominance of one mode of production.

Thus, sociological analysis has searched for an adequate account of the Iranian social structure in terms of a 'tributary mode of production' (Amin, 1978) or an 'hydraulic economy' (Wittfogel, 1957) or an 'Asiatic mode' (Marx and Engels, 1972) or 'a semi-feudal mode' (G.O.P.F., 1976). A more adequate approach involves studying Iranian society as constituted by a number of overlapping modes of production. I want to suggest in particular that Iranian history is the effect of the oscillation at the macro level between prebendalism and feudalism in which the feudal mode of production is dominant and at the village level by the survival of the *boneh* system. Second, we need to notice that the pattern of land ownership in Iran has always been mixed and cannot be reduced to a single, uniform pattern. Third, the argument for the dominance of the feudal mode allows us to perceive the similarities between Iran and other forms of feudalism—both Oriental and Occidental. There is consequently no Iranian 'essence' which permits an Orientalist differentiation between Western democratic and Oriental despotic history.

While I have been critical of Weber's general history of Oriental societies in another chapter, Weber's concept of 'prebendalism' does have a specific validity in the analysis of certain imperial structures. For example, unlike the notion of 'Asiatic' modes of production, Weber's concept of 'prebendalism' does have a specific validity in the analysis of certain imperial structures. For example, unlike the notion of 'Asiatic' modes of production, Weber's 'prebendalism' has no necessary geographical connotations. As we have seen, 'prebend' was originally an ecclesiastical term signifying the stipend drawn from land granted to a canon from a cathedral estate. Weber uses this term to mean 'allowances in kind' or 'rights of use of land in return for services' where these allowances or rights are not granted on hereditary principles. The point of the prebend is that it provided a patrimonial ruler greater control in principle over his military subordinates because, unlike feudal land rights, it provided merely conditional rights of ownership. From the patrimonial ruler's point of view, prebendalism could be secured most adequately in a situation of territorial expansion when neighbouring states were weak. In a period of imperial contraction, however, when patrimonial monarchies were experiencing fiscal crises and general difficulties of taxation, there was political and economic pressure to convert prebendal holdings into feudal land rights. Prebendalism was consequently inherently unstable. All pre-capitalist social formations have strong tendencies of decentralisation and disintegration. The feudalisation of patrimonial empires, thus, represents a powerful disintegration of prebendal control of previously subordinate officials, chiefs or nobility.

In Weber's view the collapse of prebendal empires represented a diminution of the money economy as tax revenues were replaced by payments in kind. One illustration of this argument concerned the transformation of Seljuq and Mamluk slave troops into feudal landlords:

> the feudalization of the economy was facilitated when the Seljuk troops and Mamelukes were assigned the tax yield of land and subjects; eventually land was transferred to them as service holdings, and they became landowners. The extraordinary legal insecurity of the taxpaying population vis-à-vis the arbitrariness of the troops to whom their tax capacity was mortgaged could paralyze commerce and hence the money economy; indeed since the period of the Seljuks (ca. 1050–1150) the oriental market economy declined or stagnated. (Weber, 1968, vol. 3, p. 1016)

Weber argues that the development of patrimonial domination away from prebendalism towards feudalism strengthened traditional attitudes towards economic relations, restricted rational calculation of leases, limited the money market and directed the use of money towards consumption. Where the patrimonial state encouraged trade monopolies, these openings for profit were often left to nobles or administrative staff. Similarly, the organisation of tax-farming, provision of armies and state administration created opportunities for capitalistic development but this was often 'diverted in the direction of political orientation' (Weber, 1966, p. 355). Weber's standpoint on the traditional limitations on capitalism in patrimonial empires does not necessarily reproduce the full gamut of Orientalist assumptions. Weber does not want to treat the existence of prebends or benefices as a peculiarity of asiatic societies, does not treat prebendalism as inherently static (indeed it has a built in tendency towards change as a result of its own contradictions) and, finally, he does not have to treat prebendal states as powerful and efficient since they are subject to powerful decentralising, feudal tendencies. Weber's distinction between the 'feu' and 'prebend' can also provide a theoretical framework for the analysis of the Iranian social structure which can be conceived in terms of a cyclical movement between centralisation and decentralisation, between prebendalism and feudalism and between peripheral nomadism and prebendal centralism.

The political history of traditional Iran can be conceptualised as a cyclical process between conditional and unconditional forms of landownership. Each invasion of nomadic or steppe people into Iran claimed the land of Iran as state land (*divani*). With subsequent settlement, this state land was then redistributed as a conditional land right in return for economic and military services and these conditional or prebendal rights were referred to as *egta* holdings and the owner of such land were *megtas*. During times of imperial expansion, that is with the emergence of a new dynasty, *divani* counted for the largest proportion of land under cultivation. These *megtas* who successfully over time were able to claim unconditional rights of land in turn became separate minor rulers or kings in their own right and consequently converted *egta* into *divani*. The new dynasty would then redistribute *divani* as *egta* property. At the macro level, therefore, Iranian history takes the form of a cyclical process between *divani*, *egta* and *mulk* (unconditional rights to land).

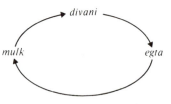

Figure 7.1

Iranian social structure thereby presents a further illustration of the centralising and decentralising processes which are common to pre-capitalist societies. This process provides us with a preliminary scheme of types of land and taxation in classical Iran. The sources of revenue for the state included a land tax on privately owned land, a poll tax on non-Muslims, *zakat* (alms), a tax on surface mines, customs duty, real estate tax and royalties on minting coins. The variety of sources of taxation parallels the variety of types of land ownership. These were state land (*divani*), private domains of the royal family (*khassa*), religious land (*waqf*), conditional ownership (*egta*) and lands which were held unconditionally (*mulk*). By a cyclical process, under the Umayyad and Seljuk rulers, the prebendal rights had been gradually converted into hereditary rights conditional on military service while under the Mongol control of the Il-Khans ('subject khan') in the thirteenth and fourteenth centuries the hereditary *egta* and unconditional *mulk* had greatly expanded at the cost of state land resulting in a concentration of land in the hands of feudal lords. From this period also the peasants were bound to the land and where the landlord exploited his own land slaves were used since the peasantry did not provide *corvée*. The general features of Iranian 'feudalism' can be best summarised by a lengthy quotation from I.P. Petrushevsky:

> The most typical features of specifically Iranian feudalism antedating the [Mongol] conquest survived it also. Such were the outstanding importance of irrigation; the coexistence of settled agriculture and nomadic and semi-nomadic cattle-breeding; the absence of demesne and *corvée* in the villages; the combination of large-scale feudal landownership with small-scale peasant tenants; the predominance of product rent (money and labour rent had only secondary importance); the growth of the military fief system; the close connexion between the big merchants and the caravan trade and a group of feudal lords, and even their coalescence; the absence of self-governing towns, so typical of western Europe in the Middle Ages; and the widespread use of slave labour in the crafts and agriculture (irrigation and market gardening) alongside

the exploitation of the labour of dependent peasants.
(Petrushevsky, 1968, p. 514)

Although Petrushevsky made a distinction between
nomadic cattle-breeding and settled agriculture, it could be
argued that we need a stronger distinction between a
nomadic/pastoral mode of production and a feudal mode in
which the latter was dominant. The political balance of forces
in Iran between the centralising state and the local autonomy
of tribal chiefs was a reflection of the balance between these
two modes of production. The strength of the state under
feudal conditions can be measured by its success in subor-
dinating the local or provincial khans and their tribal power
base. The symbiosis between tribal pastoralism and settled
agrarianism has been, of course, a traditional theme of Middle
East analysis from Ibn Khaldun's theory of tribal elite circulation to Frederik Barth's study of the sedentarisation of the
Basseri (Barth, 1961). In Iran, the periodic penetration of
nomadism into settled society in the form of invasion and conquest had catastrophic and long-term consequences. The
Mongol conquest in the thirteenth century was of particular
significance, resulting in depopulation, decline of agriculture, a
decline in urban life and a loss of trade.

While at the macro level the notions of conditional and unconditional property helps us to comprehend the oscillations
between prebendal rights which cannot be inherited and feudal
rights which can, at the village level there develop a distinctive
pattern of peasant production which cannot be easily summarised under such terms of 'prebendalism' and 'feudalism'.
Iranian peasant villages were organised in terms of communal
production known as *boneh*. Iranian villages were organised into
a number of *boneh* groups, the individuals of which had rights
of cultivation (*nasaq*). Each *boneh* had access to village land
which was graded according to its fertility and hence according to the availability of water. The head of the *boneh* (*sarboneh*) was in charge of the land and labour process, but did
not enjoy any juridical rights of ownership. The peasant
(*ra'iat*) was the owner of rights of cultivation (*nasaq*) which
usually applied to a non-specific piece of land (*mosha*). This

boneh system did not strictly correspond to peasant communal production because the local landlord intervened in production through his agent via the *sarboneh*. In addition, landlords had ultimate control over the distribution of *nasaq* rights of cultivation. This sytem of *boneh* production remained intact regardless of macro-changes from *divani*, *egta* and *mulk*. At the village level, therefore, we find a form of production which is self-sufficient and resistant to political changes of dynasty. Iranian history in consequence brings together Marx's theme in the Asiatic mode of production relating to the historically stationary quality of village production and Weber's theme of feudal-prebendal swings at the level of imperial political structures.

We have established that, contrary to the traditional Orientalist account of Asiatic societies, private property in land which was unconditional and secure did develop in Iran with a corresponding distinction between landlord and peasant classes. It is true that state lands were far more common in Iranian feudalism than was the case in European feudal societies. There was a general coincidence between taxes and rents. Petrushevsky (1968, p. 515) comments that one 'peculiarity of State ownership of land was that the State itself exploited its tenants—the village communes (*Jamā'at-i dīh*)—by means of finance officials ('*ummāl*)...rent and tax coincide, and the rents or taxes (the land-tax, etc.) paid in cash and kind to the State by the tenants, were then redistributed amongst the military caste as wages, pensions, subsidies, gifts, etc.' Thus, while Petrushevsky demonstrates that precapitalist Iranian society was feudal, he wants to preserve some notion that Iranian feudalism was nevertheless distinctive in terms of the presence of state land, the tax/rent couple, the absence of autonomous cities and the use of slave labour in agriculture. In short, his argument involves a theory of the dominant social role of a centralised state.

Petrushevsky's view of the position of the state in thirteenth- and fourteenth-century Iran has been replicated by Marshall Hodgson's study of the state in the Safavi empire (1503–1722). Hodgson describes the Safavi absolutist state in terms of the 'military patronage state'. In Safavi times,

Hodgson claims that the central bureaucracy was able to gain effective control over local, peripheral regions through its civilian and military apparatus. The absolutist Shahs of this period were able to concentrate wealth at the imperial centre, reduce the autonomy of the *'ulamā*, to bring the guilds under state supervision and to extend the influence of the state machine throughout civil society. The outcome was that 'the empire was yielding to classical dangers of agrarian absolutism' which made it 'vulnerable to internal paralysis' (Hodgson, 1974, vol. 3, pp. 56-7).

One problem with Weber's contrast between the state in European feudalism and the patrimonial rulership of Asian societies, between Hodgson's view of 'the military patronage state' and European political structures is that such ideal typical contrasts tend to suppress the issue of the absolutist state in Europe and the relationship between political absolutism and the rise of capitalism. In order to make this contrast, we need a more sophisticated analysis of the development of the state in Europe. In the thirteenth century a new political pattern emerged in Europe which gave increased autonomy to towns and strengthened their enjoyment of feudal immunity from the king. These urban franchises were defended by enlarged civil militia, fortifications and city walls. The new corporate identity of the towns was the legal expression of an increased urban division of labour in production and commercial relations which gave the urban burghers a greater sense of economic identity and coherence. The new independence of the towns was matched by the development of other assemblies to represent the interests of universities, clergy, lawyers and political groups. The growth of the system of '*Ständestaat*' is conventionally contrasted with the absence of legally autonomous assemblies, parliaments and towns in Asiatic society, but such a contrast ignores the fact that the '*Ständestaat*' system was greatly weakened by the emergence of the absolutists state in the seventeenth and eighteenth centuries.

The struggle between urban burghers, feudal landlords and monarchs had rather different outcomes in different societies. In France, the estates were successfully weakened by a dynasty which managed to build up an effective state apparatus around the centralised power of the monarchy. In England, by contrast, Parliament achieved a decisive limitation of monarchical power in a series of political struggles which spanned the seventeenth century, culminating in the constitutional settlement of 1688. In Germany,

> centralization was carried out at comparatively low levels by territorial rulers who successfully opposed attempts by higher-level forces to make the Empire itself a state. In most parts of Germany, the failure of high level centralization meant that the establishment of strong political-administrative structures was retarded at all levels. The main exception was Prussia. (Poggi, 1978, pp. 58–9)

Although there are regional variations in the development of absolutism, there are a number of important common factors. The restrictions on the power of assemblies *vis-à-vis* the bureaucratic state did not represent an outright defeat of urban assemblies by either the monarchy or the traditional feudal class. On the contrary, the expansion of centralised power was a necessary condition for the growth of the urban economy. Protection of the internal economy of the town became less important than the territorial expansion of a uniform economy under the political protection of the state. The absolutist state provided greater uniformity and reliability for economic expansion than was possible under a system of autonomous, local, town-based productive systems. This affinity of interests between the urban burghers and centralised monarchies corresponded to a decline in the economic and political power of the system of military fiefs which had been the core of European feudalism in the period between the eighth and twelfth centuries. The growth of urban commerce and the influx of bullion decreased the value of land rent which was the main buttress of feudal power. In England, the nobility was demilitarised by the time of the Tudors and commercial groups bought their way into the aristocracy. In France, at a later stage, the richer elements within the burgher class were able to purchase offices which had been traditionally held by the nobility giving rise to the distinction between *noblesse de robe* and *noblesse d'épée*.

The precise relationship between the absolutist state and the rise of capitalism is, of course, a controversial issue. Poggi (1978) regards the centralisation of political power in the seventeenth century as a necessary condition for capitalist development. By contrast, Anderson (1974) treats the absolutist state as a response by a politically threatened feudal class to defend itself against the urban merchantile class and against the peasantry which had achieved considerable commutation of dues. However, Anderson also recognises that, in attempting to recharge the apparatus of feudal domination, the absolutist state performed important functions for nascent capitalism in providing a new infrastructure of national taxation, codified law, a permanent bureaucracy and a unified market. My argument is that, whatever view one takes about absolutism, some degree of state intervention was crucial for capitalism and this intervention was particularly important on the continent after the capitalist mode had become dominant in England. In other words, the establishment of English capitalism precluded a policy of *laissez-faire* economics in so-called 'late developers' in Europe. In Germany, Italy, France and Russia where the urban bourgeoisie was weak and underdeveloped, the state became the major agency for capitalist development by encouraging and providing investment, by creating a politically unified nation and economic market, by protecting new industries from foreign competition and by developing new systems of communication and education (Gerschenkron, 1962). It has, for example, been frequently suggested that the slow economic development of Middle East and Asian societies can be connected with the fact that these societies lack an independent class of entrepreneurs or that these societies, in the absence of a middle class, will be forced to depend on the military as a modernising elite (Alexander, 1960; Halpern, 1962; Meyer, 1959; Perlmutter, 1977). However, the same type of argument would fit the case of European capitalism equally well. European capitalism developed through a variety of agencies such as an alliance between agrarian capitalists and politically subordinate bourgeois industrial class (England), through the investment of banks (Italy), through state control (Germany). The idea that capitalism depends on primitive accumulation brought about by an ascetically motivated class of politically autonomous bourgeois is simply a sociological myth which found early expression in Adam Smith's notion of 'previousness'.

The contrast between the system of *Ständestaat* in Europe and the powerful, centralised bureaucracies of Asiatic society as an explanation for the absence of independent capitalism in Asia is fundamentally misconceived. There are two aspects to this criticism. The first is that it is not possible to ask questions about the failure of spontaneous capitalism in non-European societies by taking the latter as a privileged model of how capitalism develops. Following the arguments of Frank, Barratt Brown, Baran and Hobsbawm, the underdevelopment of capitalism in Asia and South America is precisely the historical effect of capitalism development in Europe. If there is such a thing as a *general* set of conditions for capitalism, then they would not apply in Asia because of the 'contaminating' effect of colonialism and neo-colonialism. It is in any case difficult to spell out a general theory of capitalist development because the experience of capitalism in Europe took very divergent forms. One only has to think, for example, of the great differences in class formations in the societies that underwent capitalist development in the eighteenth and nineteenth centuries. If there is one common feature, it appears to be the presence of a powerful political agency, namely the centralised state, which played a crucial role in creating the institutional framework for economic development along capitalist lines. The main contrast between Asian—in this case, Iran—and European societies is not the presence of an all-pervasive state in Asia as opposed to the innovative European bourgeoisie, but exactly the opposite. It was the weakness of the Iranian state apparatus and the subordination of the Iranian state to Russian and British economic interests which inhibited economic changes. Because the Iranian state could not supersede the powerful decentralising forces present in Iranian feudalism and pastoral nomadism, the Iranian state was not equipped to integrate the divergent class interests of merchants, bourgeois, clergy, tribal chiefs and feudal landlords which constituted the various sectors of the dominant class. Anticipating subsequent aspects of this argument, Iran was a feudal society whose potential for independent capitalist and commercial development was externally stunted by the effects of European imperial interests in the nineteenth century and internally limited by the village economy and nomadic pastoralism. While Iran in the twentieth century has undergone a process of capitalist development of agriculture and industry under the aegis of a centralised state, these developments have taken place in the context of political and economic constraints which have been set by the global requirements of capitalism.

The effects of European colonialism on Iran in large measure replicate the pattern of underdevelopment which was experienced by North Africa, Egypt and greater Syria. Petty commodity production and small scale industry collapsed under the effect of imported finished goods from Europe which had the advantage of concession arrangements. With the development of mono-crop exports, an unfavourable balance of payments situation resulted in heavy dependence on imported agricultural commodities. The fiscal crisis of the post-colonial state reinforced the degree of dependence on foreign governments. The capitalist development of certain sections of the economy produced a variety of internal social contradictions within the society and the state responded by introducing a series of political and social reforms under external pressures which were designed to forestall revolutionary tendencies within peripheral economies. These processes in Iran can be dated from the emergence of concessionary treaties with Russia and Britain following the Iranian-Russian War (1828), the Herat expedition (1855) and the Anglo-Iranian War (1856).

These unfavourable economic relations with Russia and Britain had a number of dramatic consequences. The Iranian manufactories which had grown during the Safavid period were destroyed, European manufactured goods superseded local Iranian commodities and the export of raw materials replaced the export of manufactured goods. In the nineteenth century, industrial centres in Isfahan, Kashan, Tabriz, Yazd, Kirman and Mashhad all declined (Ashraf, 1970). The principal exports from Iran became opium, tobacco, cotton, almonds and rice, and through a policy of dumping and low customs duties, the British textile industry undermined indigenous production. External economic constraints often prevented Iranian producers from achieving an economic surplus from agricultural exports. For example, the price of wheat fell from one and a half dollars a bushel in 1871 to twenty-three cents a bushel in 1894 on world markets. Although the export of wheat from Bushire expanded eight times between 1869 and 1894, the value of the wheat exported remained virtually constant (McDaniel, 1971). In the same period, agricultural production was hit by a series of natural disasters. The staple silk industry was crippled by a low rainfall between 1869 and 1872; the spread of silkworm disease in the 1860s reduced silk production in Gilan from 20,000 bales of silk per annum to less than 6,000 bales by the 1870s. In a situation of reduced foreign exchange earnings and a depreciating currency, Iranian landlords responded by increasing peasant rents which had the consequence of stimulating the process whereby land was progressively concentrated in fewer hands. While landlords were unable to realise fully the value of agricultural production, the independent Iranian bourgeois was also restricted by nineteenth-century social and economic conditions. According to Ashraf (1970) the limitations on the Iranian bourgeoisie included the penetration of foreign capitalist interests which favoured the European bourgeoisie, the decline of indigenous industry, the failure of Persian money dealers and traders to establish an autonomous local and national banking system, the preference of Iranian merchants to invest in land rather than industrial production. These circumstances contributed to the process whereby

many prosperous Persian traders were converted into the agents of Russian and British commercial firms and lost their independence. The predominance of the two colonial banks over the Persian money market, the apathy of the Asiatic rulers toward the local bourgeois elements in a

situation of decentralized patrimonialism, and the intervention of the two powers to protect the interests of their
traders and investors, forced Persian traders to work with
the foreign firms to survive. (Ashraf, 1970, pp. 326–7)

If the economic history of nineteenth-century Iran was
parallel to the economic subordination taking place in other
dependent societies in Asia and Africa, then the political
history of Iran was similarly a replica of other anti-colonial
struggles throughout the Islamic world. Reactionary regimes
and their compradorial elites were challenged by an alliance of
intellectuals, *'ulamā* and dispossessed merchants which, in the
name of restoring pristine, unadulterated Islam, sought to in-
troduce some element of modernisation and liberalisation. A
return to Islam became the principal method of simultaneously rejecting Western political control and democracy. In
response to Western hegemony, Muslim intellectuals
discovered that the true meaning of *ijma* was democratic,
public opinion, that *jihad* had to be read as the positive effort
of economic man, that *maslaha* was in fact Benthamite
'utility', that *taqlid* (imitation) was inimical to Islam and that
'the gate of *ijtihād*' (independent reasoning) had to be re-
opened. The only significant alternative to the employment of
Islam as an anti-colonial ideology was the rediscovery of a pre-
Islamic national culture demonstrating the wealth of a golden
past in contrast with contemporary decline. Iran, like Egypt,
espoused both forms of anti-colonial ideology.

The political events which marked the Iranian struggle
against external, colonial domination need not be documented
in all their complex detail (Upton, 1960). It is possible to examine the modern history of Iran in terms of five crises (Halliday, 1979). The first crisis concerns two related episodes,
namely the Tobacco Uprising (1890–2) and the Constitutional
Revolution (1905–11). Nasiruddin Shah (1848–96) was embarked
upon a number of social reforms (such as improvements in
printing and distribution of newspapers) which remained
somewhat superficial and which were achieved at the cost of
extending concessionary arrangements to both Britain and
Russia. In 1889, de Reuter was given the right to organise the

Imperial Bank of Persia which was to be a commercial bank with limited privileges for the issue of notes. In the following year, a British company was awarded a tobacco monopoly over the export and internal trade in tobacco. This monopoly had very general implications for all social classes in Persia: tobacco growers would find themselves increasingly under foreign control, small traders would be forced out of the market and smokers would purchase their supplies from the hands of infidels who were ritually impure. In this situation, Jamaluddin Afghani, the Muslim reformer, persuaded the chief *mujtahid* to declare that to smoke tobacco under conditions of foreign monopoly was against religion. This religious ban on tobacco resulted in its virtual disappearance as a commodity and in the dismantlement of the concessionary arrangement. The importance of Afghani's intervention was that it helped to cement the alliance between the intellectuals, the tradesmen and the Shi'i 'ulamā against the Shah whose economic policies were mortgaging Iran to foreign companies. The rift between the merchants and 'ulamā and the Shah was further deepened in the first decade of the twentieth century when a number of clergy and merchants sought refuge (bast) from the Shah at the Abdul'azim shrine outside Tehran in 1905. This event was followed by a series of sympathetic *basts* in Tabriz, Rasht, Isfahan and Shiraz. The *bastis*, mainly merchants and guildsmen, called for a constitution, a national assembly, a code of law and regular courts to be a check on royal finances and administration. Following the provisions of the Belgium constitution, the opposition called for the establishment of a national assembly (Majles) elected on the basis of a limited franchise. The Majles sought to restrict the Shah's power by curbing royal expenditure, directing taxes to the treasury rather than to the Shah's personal needs and by establishing a national bank. These early attempts at constitutional reform were thwarted by resistence from the Shah, tribal leaders and the Russians, but they were also swamped by the social turmoil resulting from foreign invasion during the First World War.

The second period of crisis concerned the attempts by the Pahlavi Shahs in the period before the Second World War to

establish an autonomous state apparatus which would encourage industrialisation, secure independence from colonial
powers and suppress opposition in the countryside. The reign
of Reza Shah (1925-41) has been compared with that of
Ataturk's in Turkey. Reza Shah attempted to base his power
on a modernised army by, for example, introducing conscription in 1925. Like Ataturk, Reza Shah pursued a policy of
secularisation by limiting the power of the *'ulamā* (in such
areas as education and public festivals), by proscribing the veil
for women and by laws designed to change traditional dress.
The new regime also attempted to develop railways, industry
and production by a policy of tariff protection. The new regime
also represented a growth of centralised state power at the
cost of the decentralising force of tribal groups through a process of conscription, disarmament and sedentarisation. At the
same time, there was an extension of government system of
monopolies. One great weakness of Reza Shah's economic
strategy was its neglect of agriculture and irrigation which
placed a severe restriction on the capacity of the government
to raise internal revenues. However, in Halliday's view the
'state he created provided the context for the later capitalist
development of Iran but it was incapable itself of initiating the
major changes required in this direction' (Halliday, 1979, pp.
24-5). The programme for state-directed industrial change was
terminated by the third major crisis of the twentieth century,
namely the invasion of Iran in 1941 by Russian and British
troops. After the collapse of Kurdistan and Azerbaijan as
autonomous republics under Russian sponsorship, the Pahlavi
regime re-asserted its control over the whole country which
was left with a wartime legacy of high inflation and food shortages.

The fourth major crisis involved the attempt by Dr Muhammad Musaddeq's government (1951-3) to nationalise the Iranian oil industry and to achieve some control over supply and
refinery. With the exile of Reza Shah and his replacement by
his son Muhammad Reza, the government passed into the control of the Majles. In this period, the national assembly was
not dominated by conservative businessmen and landlords
who opposed the movement towards political liberalisation of

reform of agriculture. The Majles was, however, willing to support Musaddeq's policy of preventing oil concessions going to the Soviet Union and in 1951 they supported the decision to nationalise the British-held oil field. Musaddeq also enjoyed the support of the *'ulamā* which sought to re-establish its social postion following the fall of the secularizing Reza Shah regime. Despite this popular internal support, Musaddeq's strategy of oil nationalisation as the basis for national independence was quickly terminated by a combination of internal and external forces. The British oil company was able to enforce a successful blockade of Iranian oil on the world market, while production and refining of oil was affected by the loss of Western technicians. Musaddeq failed to gain the support of the new Eisenhower administration which assumed that Musaddeq was too closely associated with the Tudeh Party or that the Musaddeq government would not be able to control the spread of communist influence. With the loss of oil revenue, it was difficult to retain the loyalty of the bourgeois elements within the national assembly. Musaddeq also lost popular support because he was forced to exercise much tighter control over the population by the extension of martial law, prohibitions on strikes and labour unrest, suspension of the senate and elections for the Majles. A combination of forces loyal to the Shah (the army, nationalist merchants and bourgeoisie with CIA backing) was able to stage a *coup* against Musaddeq and to drive the Tudeh Party underground. With the incarceration of Musaddeq, the Pahlavi state under Muhammad Reza emerged even stronger than its position before oil nationalisation (Wilber, 1958).

The fifth crisis covers the period from the early 1950s to the fall of the Shah in the late 1970s. The White Revolution of land reform (1960–72) was largely in response to pressure from the Kennedy administration which recognised that land reform was one strategy in securing the continuing loyalty to pro-Western underdeveloped or peripheral regions. Thus, the G.O.P.F. argues that 'the political and cultural superstructure of feudalism could no longer meet the economic needs of imperialism. Nor was it in its political interests to preserve such an archaic system : feudalism was a decrepit system which had outlived its usefulness, and it was dangerous to support it' (G.O.P.F., 1976, p.5). The White Revolution marked a rapid advance of capitalist development in agriculture and industry. The state's control over industrialisation was aided by a rise in oil revenues from around 1971. The process of capitalist industrial development was accompanied by a decisive advance of political dictatorship, a growth of repressive institutions, and a curbing of minority rights and regional autonomy.

The point of this description of recent Iranian political history is not to provide a chronology of the dilemmas of the Iranian elite, but to draw some sociological lessons about the political economy of capitalist development in peripheral, feudal societies. For example, it would be a mistake to assume that the Pahlavi state is simply a modern reproduction of the 'military patronage state' of Safavid times or, more generally, the survival of oriental despotism. Halliday correctly stresses the profound *discontinuity* between the state in feudal Iran and the Pahlavi state under conditions of dependent capitalist development. Thus, the Pahlavi Shahs of the twentieth century

> have ruled in a manner quite distinct from that of those who went before them, and the social classes associated with the regime today are quite different from those associated with the monarchy in the nineteenth century.... Moreover, whereas the monarchy had very little power over the rest of the country a century ago, it now commands a unified and highly centralized country.... [The modern Iranian state] controls the whole of its national territory, whereas the other's writ did not run outside the main cities. It promotes economic development, whereas the other neglected it. It has a large standing army, whereas the other had virtually no armed force at all. It has to be a considerable extent transformed socio-economic relations in the Iranian countryside, whereas the other left the countryside alone. (Halliday, 1979, pp. 29–30)

In other words, the dissolution of feudal relations of production required the intervention of a relatively autonomous, centralised state which orchestrated the transformation of feudal landlords into agrarian capitalists and which created an intermediate service class between workers and capitalists.

The history of capitalism is often written as if merchants were the principal corrosive agent of feudal production. In the case of Iran, writers like Ashraf have suggested that there were three major obstacles to capitalist development. These were the existence of tribal power in the countryside and frequent tribal invasions, the dependence of economic initiative on the state and colonial penetration which undermined the traditional artisan and bourgeoisie, creating a dependent bourgeoisie. These circumstances meant that merchants and traders acted in a traditional manner so that 'the non-rational practice of hoarding by treasury and money dealers, the disposition towards luxurious living and resulting corruption set strict limits to the development of rational economic activities (Ashraf, 1970, p. 321). This interpretation ignores the fact that merchants operating in the sphere of circulation have not historically contributed to the development of productive relations and that merchants play a largely conservative role in economic change. In this respect, Marx's view of merchants as a class has been confirmed by more recent historical analyses. Merchant capital was not used in an innovative fashion in agricultural or industrial production and the intervention of merchants did not become historically decisive until the process of feudal dissolution was well under way (Hilton, 1976). The origins of English capitalism are to be found in the class struggle between landlord and peasant over the economic surplus, the collapse of feudal serfdom after 1348 when bubonic plague wiped out half the English population, the crisis of land revenue and the eventual separation of the peasantry from the means of production and their transformation into agrarian wage-labourers. The secret of primitive accumulation for Marx was not Smithian previousness, but the draconian separation of the peasant from the land by political and economic coercion. What, however, is the secret of accumulation for peripheral capitalism, for late developers, for nascent capitalism without external colonies or for young socialist societies? The answer must be, as Evgeni Preobrazhensky recognised in the *New Economics*, the endogenous production of a surplus under the primary control of the state. The importance of the Pahlavi state has been precisely its ability to organise social forces towards the dissolution of feudal relationships in the countryside and the deployment of oil revenues for industrialisation. The Pahlavi State terminated the traditional cyclical relationship between feudalism and prebendalism. In this respect, however, Iran is not essentially different from any other society undergoing capitalist development, since capitalist development in Italy, Germany and Russia also required massive state intervention. The lesson to be drawn from this is that, while the conditions for capitalism in Europe and the Middle East did differ in some respects,

> certain common factors, and certain specific factors, make investment in industry as little attractive in that region (The Middle East) as it was in the Europe of three centuries ago. Hence the important role of the state both in Europe in the age of mercantilism and in Turkey, Iran, Egypt and Japan at the start of their industrialization. (Rodinson, 1974, p. 142)

The problem of state-directed accumulation in peripheral, dependent capitalist societies is that, as we have seen in the period from the Tobacco Uprising to the fall of the Pahlavi Shahs, the economic role of the state is severely circumscribed by the exegencies of external, global structuring of the capitalist world economy, and by a constellation of internal problems of class conflict and economic unbalance.

In theory, the existence of substantial oil revenues should allow oil-exporting countries in the Third World to industrialise rapidly without massive increases in direct or indirect taxation and without running into crippling problems of inflation. As the second largest oil-producer with annual revenues averaging 20 billion US dollars between 1975-7, Iran has been thought to possess the greatest potential for development in the Middle East. Economic and social development on the basis of oil revenues does, however, take a peculiar form. Oil-production does not necessarily stimulate widespread economic effects, since it employs a very small section of the labour force and many skilled manual and white-collar workers will be drawn into the economy from outside the host society. Oil-production does not necessarily lead to manufacturing development since, in a society like Iran, most of the oil will go directly for export. Oil provides the state with an income which can be regarded as a form of rent (Halliday, 1979, p. 139), and hence we may use the term 'rentier state' (Mahdavy, 1970). What becomes crucial in this situation is the social and political context of the ruling class in directing investment into manufacture or into consumption, waste and unproductive outlay of the oil surplus, on the one hand, and the state's ability to operate in a global context to shape world market demand for raw materials, on the other.

It would be difficult to deny that Iran has experienced a period of industrialisation via state-financed factories in sugar, cement, textiles and matches. Production workers have increased from 23 per cent in 1957 to 29 per cent in 1972. Heavy industry has been developed in chemicals and fertilisers by the Shahpur Chemical Company, the Iran Fertiliser Company and the Aryamehr iron and steel plant. There has also been a significant increase of the construction industry and major improvements in transport. However, despite the obvious signs of industrialisation and urbanisation, economic growth and investment has fallen far below the economic plans of the Iranian government and below the expectation of foreign economic assessment. A series of economic explanations have been offered to account for this under-performance. These economic and technical explanations often include references to inadequate long-term economic management, shortages of appropriate skilled labour, failure to protect the informal sector of the economy, bottle-necks in supply, inflation in the costs of imported capital goods and the determined effect of monopolistic markets on the workshop economy (Wilson, 1979).

Perhaps a more adequate explanation can be found in the notion of the rentier state as a post-colonial state apparatus

(Alavi, 1972). The post-colonial state inherits an overdeveloped bureaucratic-military apparatus which is required to maintain artificial territorial boundaries and to manage a power bloc constituted by landlords, small indigenous capitalist class and compradorial bourgeoisie. Recruitment to the bureaucracy creates a client class of petty bourgeois elements which form the governing, as opposed to the ruling, class, while oil revenues are directed to the unproductive class of bureaucrats and military personnel. As with other rentier states, Iran has experienced a rapid development of the service sector from 32 per cent of GNP in 1959–60 to 39 per cent in 1974–5, while industry amounts to only 16 per cent. Military expenditure in 1974 accounted for 32 per cent of the state's budget and 31 per cent of planned expenditure in the 1973–8 plan, or 9 per cent of GNP. Thus, the state employs around ten per cent of the economically active population. The Pahlavi state appears to have developed along classic post-colonial lines in accentuating the combined and uneven development of the social formation. The most important aspect of this uneven development is illustrated by the fate of the agricultural sector. Some measure of the problem can be obtained from the fact that, while the population of thirty-four million is increasing by approximately 3 per cent per annum and food consumption is increasing by 10 per cent per annum, domestic crop production is rising by a mere 2 per cent per annum. The consequence of these relationships is that Iran has switched from being a food-exporting economy to a net importer. In order to understand this transition, it is important to examine the land reform programme of the 1960s (Lambton, 1969).

As we have seen, prior to land reform the land tenure system of Iran was a mixture of public and private feudal land. To be more precise, we can distinguish between state land, royal land and villages, religious (*waqf*) property and collective, tribal property. The majority of villages (around 72 per cent) were owned by landlords, whereas royal villages represented around 2 per cent, public domain and tribal property were both less than 4 per cent. Property was in fact more concentrated than these figures suggest, since thirty-seven families owned 1,900 villages. Where Reza Shah had in the 1920s acquired some

2,100 villages, peasant proprietors owned a mere 5 per cent of the land they cultivated. Since the majority of landlords lived in the large cities, the village contained a number of distinct social groups—the local agents of absentee landlords, *boneh* leaders, peasants and landless labourers. Peasants were bound to landlords by share-cropping and tenancy arrangements. Tenancy contracts which were arranged on a short-term basis were paid in money or crops. Share-cropping contracts which were regulated by local custom were based on five factors of cultivating the land, namely water, land, seeds, oxen and labour. Peasants who possessed four factors of production would receive four-fifths of the crop, those with only two factors would receive two-fifths of the crop and so on. The most common situation was that the landlord possessed three factors (land, water and seed) so that the peasant share of the crop was determined by the input of oxen and labour. The peasant share was further reduced by payments to the village headman, field watcher, religious officials, blacksmith and others. Peasants were also subject to additional levies and personal service involving unpaid, compulsory work for the landlord. Below the peasants were the landless labourers who did not possess cultivation rights (*nassaq* or *wasagh*) and who were hired by peasants to perform seasonal work such as weeding and threshing. These labourers who constituted between thirty and forty percent of the village population provided a pool of cheap labour for landlords. These labourers could be used to discipline peasants because landlords could transfer *nassaq* rights from unruly peasants to previously landless workers.

Prior to the Musaddeq period and White Revolution, the land tenure system was predominantly feudal in character. Peasants were subordinated by the fact that, although they had customary rights to land, the landlords owned the land, controlled the production process by their control of irrigation and exercised political control through their local agents. Exchange was in terms of barter and the use of money was limited. Production by peasants was for subsistence rather than for commodity exchange on the market. In this context, the land reforms of the Shah were designed for a number of political objectives: to reduce the potential for agrarian unrest, to weaken the power of the large landlords in order to provide the state with a wider social base in the villages, and to diminish the political power of tribal chiefs. The economic objectives of the land reforms were to increase the purchasing power of the peasantry in order to expand the home market for industrial goods and to increase agricultural productivity to provide further labour for capitalist industry. To achieve these goals it was necessary to redistribute land and extend long-term credit through a system of rural co-operatives.

The first stage of land reform (1961) sought to break-up large-scale ownership of land and attempted to reduce land ownership to the equivalent of one village (Shesh-Dang). The feudal landlords responded to this situation by redistributing their villages among their wives, children and relatives. Furthermore, since the landlords were able to select which village lands they intended to sell to the government, they were able to retain top quality agricultural land for their own use. Certain clauses of the law exempted the sale of orchards, grazing land, suburban villages and mechanised farms and these clauses provided the loop-hole for the redefinition of remote villages as 'suburban' or barren land as 'orchards'. As a result of these responses to the land reform law, the landlords remained the major economic power in society, despite the redistribution of land to peasants through the rural co-operative and the consequent liquidation of large estates. At the village level, the co-operatives became the vehicle for the introduction of a variety of manufactured goods (such as washing powder and vegetable oil) as well as commodities (tea and sugar). However, the co-operatives have to borrow money to pay instalments on the land and to purchase commodities and because 'the societies want their money back at a certain date, the farmers often have to borrow from money-lenders and shop-keepers in the village, or even perhaps in the town, at a much higher rate of interest in order to pay back the loans' (G.O.P.F., 1976, p. 38). The effect of this situation has been an expansion of money relationships into the village, an extension of the social role of money-lenders and an increase in peasant indebtedness.

In a situation of growing political conflict from landlords and religious leaders, the second stage of land reform (1962) took a conservative direction by normalising the existing situation by attempting to remove the share-cropping system. The new land reform measures provided land owners who had been exempted under the initial legislation with a choice of five methods of settlement: to rent their lands to peasants; to sell their lands to peasants; to share their land; to form joint-stock agricultural units; to buy peasants cultivation rights and farm the land with wage labourers. The first of these options—to rent land—proved to be the most popular so that over a million peasants were involved in this scheme. These arrangements worked to the disadvantage of peasants who found that their new rents were more exploitative than traditional feudal duties and land which was acquired by peasants was often too small or too infertile to support their families.

In the third stage of land reform (1968) the five settlement options were reduced to two, namely the sale or distribution of rented lands (in proportion to share-cropping) and the sale or distribution of lands under the joint-stock arrangements. In this stage, attempts were also made to bring religious endowments within the land reform policy and to facilitate appropriate arrangements for the sale of orchards which were jointly owned by farmers and landlords. The object of this final stage was simply to complete the process of eradicating feudal land ownership and to finalise the transformation of the agrarian class structure. The general effects of all three stages have been summarised by the G.O.P.F. (1976) research report (*Land Reform and its Direct Effects in Iran*) under six headings: the expansion of mechanisation and agricultural investment; a growth in the class of small landlords (farmer-owners); a rapid increase of landless wage-labourers; the growth of money relationships and of a bureaucratic financial bourgeoisie; an extension of orchards and finally a growth of class consciousness among villagers. This conversion of feudal agrarian production in capitalist agriculture perfectly illustrates my argument that primitive capitalist accumulation in dependent, peripheral societies is achieved through an extension of state activity but at the cost of distributing revenues to client classes in the service sector, on the one hand, and to fractions of the capitalist class, on the other.

Iran cannot be classified under the general rubric of Oriental despotisms or as a society dominated by the Asiatic mode of production. Orientalism operated with the assumption that Asiatic and Middle East societies were precluded from capitalist development by the absence of autonomous cities, independent guilds and merchants, rational law and *Ständestaat*. Asiatic societies contained an essential flaw—the absence of inheritable, private property and the dominance of arbitrary power in the form of the centralised state—which produced a stultifying economic order incapable of internal transformation. Against such a viewpoint, I have claimed that, out of the traditional cycle of land control from *divani*, *egta* to *mulk*, feudal forms of land rights become dominant from early times.

The general role of the state has been to dissolve feudal relations of production, and to undermine traditional decentralising forces. If European capitalist development can be meaningfully contrasted with capitalist development in Iran, the important difference was not the existence of an all-pervasive Iranian state in feudalism but precisely its opposite, namely the weakness of the Iranian state *vis-à-vis* a civil society in which nomadic pastoralism and tribalism placed a decisive brake on the building of an effective state apparatus.

This observation cannot be raised to the level of a general theory of capitalist development, namely that all primitive accumulation in early capitalism requires a centralised state which is capable of reorganising class relationships and providing the necessary infrastructure for the extraction of an economic surplus. The general, abstract laws of the capitalist mode of production operate at the level of social formations where there are present a range of *contingent* superstructural factors which may or may not correspond to the *logic* of the mode of production. At a very obvious level, the fact that Britain industrialised on the basis of cheap energy sources—labour intensive surface coal mines, internal and external waterways, an expanding labour force—without the constraint of powerful competitors and with important colonial possessions produced social effects which were very different from Iran's dependence on oil revenues in a global context of neo-colonialism. It is the specificity and peculiarity of capitalist development in particular societies which appear to dominate over uniformities and generalities. To take one pertinent illustration, there are no uniform relations of correspondence between legal/political superstructures and capitalist modes of production in societies which we conventionally designate 'capitalist'.

8 Weber and the sociology of development

In this chapter I shall draw up an elementary classification of theories of development which are dichotomised into what may be conveniently termed 'internalist' and 'externalist' versions of socio-economic development. This dichotomous classification provides an initial pretext for considering and contrasting the influence of Weber and Marx—or more accurately the *alleged* influence—on contemporary sociological perspectives on development and underdevelopment. In general, most surveys of theoretical perspectives on development ascribe a Weberian influence to explanations of socio-economic backwardness which concentrate on values, motivations, pattern variables or on such institutional complexes as rational, bureaucratic administration. By contrast, a perspective on social underdevelopment which allocates principal causal significance to external, global economic structures—the world division of labour, the terms of trade, neo-colonial exploitation—is typically identified as a Marxist or neo-Marxist perspective. My aim in this discussion is to bring into question this over-simplified presentation of Weberian and Marxist perspectives by showing (1) that the problem of individual motives plays a secondary role in Weber's sociology in comparison with the significance ascribed to military and political causes of social decay and development (2) that Weber and Marx provided remarkably similar accounts of the stagnation of pre-capitalist Asian societies in their respective models of patrimonial domination and the Asiatic mode of production.

The problem of arriving at an adequate theory of the political economy of underdevelopment is not, however, simply

234

a question of obliterating Marx's journalistic comments on Asiatic society or of exterminating Weberian contaminations within sociological thought. Both internalist and externalist perspectives in the sociology of development have serious limitations. For example, many internalist theories are erected on the false problem of the conditions for 'spontaneous capitalist development', because such theories fail to recognise that the capitalist development of Western Europe fundamentally changed the conditions for socio-economic development on the capitalist periphery. However, externalist theories which treat underdevelopment as a simple outcome of colonial exploitation can neither explain why some dependent societies are highly developed (such as Canada) nor why some areas of the globe became capitalist centres while other areas became peripheral regions. My highly tentative remedy for these traditional difficulties in internalist and externalist approaches is to suggest that the conditions for development or underdevelopment are a dialectical product of the internal structure of a given social formation (its combination of modes of production, their conditions of existence and its unique combination of human and natural resources) and the external location of that social formation within the global environment of capitalism (the conditions of global stratification and exploitation).

Of course, the notion that an adequate theory of development and underdevelopment would require both an internalist and externalist perspective suggests that such a theory would take the form of a rapprochement between sociology (internalism) and Marxism (externalism). Such a possibility has already been implied by my assertions that, in their analysis of Asiatic stagnation, Marx and Weber were in a large measure of agreement. In recent debate, however, the intensity of the confrontation between sociology and Marxism appears to have increased considerably. Attempts to characterise this debate in terms of 'Marxism versus sociology' have to assume that Marxism and sociology are theoretically and ideologically homogeneous enterprises and that a clear dividing line can be set up between scientific Marxism and ideological sociology. By pointing to some of the similarities between Marxist and

Weberian sociologies of development, I hope to illustrate some of the difficulties which are involved in the characterisation of the relationship between Marxism and sociology as antithetical and oppositional.

By an internalist thesis, I mean an explanation of development which treats the main problems of backward societies as a question of certain features which are internal to societies considered in isolation from any global economic context. Internalist research concentrates on values, attitudes and motives as dimensions of the cultural and institutional fabric of societies which either inhibit or stimulate modernisation. Associated with this concentration on cultural factors is a tendency to treat so-called problems of development as primarily characteristics of individuals rather than of social structures. The assumption is that a society's capacity for development is retarded by certain archaic features of the beliefs or personalities of individuals—their traditionalist orientation to problems, their particularism, their magical beliefs or their reluctance to avoid consumption in order to save for future growth. The absence of Weberian ingredients for modernisation—asceticism, universal values, rational law, bureaucracy, free labour—is an internal social disease which incapacitates the economic system. Another important aspect of internalist theory is that development is conceptualised in terms of a set of oppositions between dichotomous ideal types—traditional/modernity, *Gemeinschaft/Gesellschaft*, religious/secular. In some versions of this approach, development is treated as a series of necessary stages which have universal significance for all societies passing from traditional stability to modern industrialism. The process of development takes the form of an evolutionary unfolding of some inner phenomenon such as rationality, asceticism or universalism. The consequence of social development is the achievement of a fixed end-state which is a careful replica of Western liberal democracy. Clear illustrations of internalism can be found in the development theories of David Lerner (1964), David McClelland (1961), David Apter (1965) and Walt Rostow (1971).

By an externalist theory, I mean a theory of development which identifies the major problems facing a developing society as external to the society itself as a unit located within a structured, international context. The primary dilemma of backward societies is their dependency on the global structure of capitalist production, their inability to arrive at appropriate terms of trade or their subordination to the interests of multinational corporations. Within this tradition of analysis, the alleged characteristics of pre-modern individuals are causally unimportant. The absence of modern individuals, institutions and culture is either treated as a problem at the level of surface phenomena which effectively conceals real issues at the level of the global economy or the archaic institutions of a society are regarded as effects of causes which are external to that society. Externalist perspectives also reject the simple internalist dichotomies of tradition/modernity in favour of a more differentiated range of concepts—developed, undeveloped, underdeveloped and dependent development. The point of these conceptual distinctions is to reject the notion that the backward societies of the modern world are defective or distorted versions of pre-capitalist, European societies. The conventional externalist example is Britain which may have been undeveloped but was never underdeveloped by a system of external constraints. Hence, within the externalist perspective, there is no static end-state of development because there is no single, classic road of capitalist development.

The policy implications and political strategies which are entailed by these approaches are clearly contrasted. For externalists, development is contingent upon a revolutionary restructuring of the relations of production within societies and this class struggle itself can only be successful if an underdeveloped society can detach itself from the global system of capitalist production. By contrast, internalists look to reform and reorganisation of the education, legal, communication and cultural systems to produce appropriate changes in beliefs, personalities and institutional frameworks. In so far as internalists have some conception of the role of a world economic framework, it is based on the assumption that development is stimulated by the economic growth of the centre of world capitalism. The argument is that capitalist growth in America, Japan and West Germany produces a boom in commodity prices which works to the advantage of raw material exporters in the Third World. Externalist theories typically operate on the opposite assumption, namely that the periphery can only develop when the centre is weak; international wars between capitalist societies are associated with rapid economic and social development of the capitalist fringe. Development and underdevelopment are, therefore, not inevitable events along an evolutionary continuum; they are effects of national class struggles which themselves find their ultimate explanation within the crises of capitalist accumulation on a world scale. The classical examples of externalist theory are found in A.G. Frank (1972), H. Magdoff (1969), T. Dos Santos (1970) and C. Furtado (1964).

It is clear from my characterisation of these two perspectives on development and underdevelopment that internalist theorists typically claim a Weberian background, whereas theorists within the externalist tradition trace their theoretical ancestry via Lenin, Hobson, Hilferding and Engels to Marx. Internalists are primarily concerned with the implications of Weber's studies of the institutional and motivational conditions for social change in his sociology of religion or, more comprehensively, his sociology of civilisations. Externalists have drawn their primary inspiration from Marx's commentaries on British imperialism in India, his analysis of the tendency of the rate of profit to fall and from Marx's view of the general crisis of the capitalist mode of production.

Weber's influence on contemporary internalist theories of development appears to be direct and widespread. This influence characteristically takes the form of extended, comparative studies of rational asceticism. The outstanding examples would be studies by R.N. Bellah (1965), Clifford Geertz (1968), S.N. Eisenstadt (1968), Niles Hansen (1963), Alex Inkeles and David Smith (1974). This concentration on the sociological significance of what Eisenstadt referred to as the 'transformative capacities' of certain value-orientations to the world as an interpretation of Weber's principal approach to problems of social change probably owes a great deal to Talcott Parsons's various commentaries on Weber's sociology. In his introductory essay to Weber's *The Sociology of*

Religion, Parsons (1966, p. xxx) claimed, for example, that Weber's primary sociological interest centred on religion 'as a source of social change'. It was partly through these interpretations that Webers' analysis of the ascetic Protestant sects re-emerged in functionalist theories of social development via the employment of the pattern variables as a theoretical scheme for characterising the evolution of social systems (Parsons, 1965). The result was a special trend in American sociology which combined Weber's analyses of bureaucracy, traditional authority and asceticism with the interests of functionalist sociology in pattern variables, integration and differentiation. This distinctive group in the sociology of development included Bert Hoselitz and W.E. Moore (1963) G.A. Theodorson (1953) and Neil J. Smelser (1962). In short, Weber's apparent contribution to the sociology of development has been to stimulate a rich tradition of historical and sociological analysis into achievement motivation, ascetic values, rationality and entrepreneurship.

From the discussion so far it would appear that Weber's influence on the sociology of development amounts to little more than numerous applications and extensions of Weber's empirical analysis of the effects of Calvinism on capitalism. However, it may be that Weber has had a more pervasive influence in the sociology of development in terms of certain basic epistemological assumptions. For example, Nicos Poulantzas has characterised Weberian sociology as subjectivist, historicist and idealist (Turner, 1977a). According to this critique, Weber works within a particular problematic—the problematic of the subject—whereby the objective structural ensembles of state, economy and class are reduced to interpersonal relationships. At the same time, Weber is committed to an idealist-historicist position in the sense that in Weber's sociology, history is treated as the unfolding of an inner essence of rationality. The theoretical effects of Weberian epistemology in the sociology of development have been either a profound 'psychologisation' of development issues in the contributions of Lerner (1964), McClelland (1961) and Berger et al. (1973), or the production of teleological models of the transition to modern, rational capitalism. Thus, social development involves either an unfolding of the inner spirit of capitalism (the European case) or the permanent inhibition of industrial capitalism (as in India) or the presence of favourable conditions which are corrupted or contaminated by countervailing anti-rational values and practices (the Islamic case). Weber's epistemological assumptions in the context of his comparative sociology result in a basic dichotomous contrast between the essence of Western civilisation which is dynamic and expansionary and the essence of Eastern societies which is both stagnant and arbitrary.

If Weberian sociology provided the main parameters of orthodoxy within conventional sociology of development, then the main stream of critical perspectives has been Marxist. Marxist sources provided the general basis for the whole externalist tradition which focused attention on the specific location of societies within a global system of production and distribution, the development problems of the periphery, and the objective conditions for class struggle and revolutionary transformation. Having acknowledged Marx has had a massive influence on the construction of an anti-sociology of development, it does, in practice, become extremely difficult to specify the exact nature of that influence. A number of authors (Foster-Carter, 1974; Barratt Brown, 1974) have made the point that a Marxist analysis of development and underdevelopment must in fact be a neo-Marxist analysis because of defects and gaps in the classical theory of colonialism and imperialism. I want to state this problem even more forcibly by commenting that it is difficult to construct a critique of Weberian sociology of development on the basis of Marx's texts, since it is difficult to distinguish Marx's position from that of Weber's on a number of fundamental issues. The same problem of theoretical overlap is also characteristic of the relationship between functionalist explanations and conventional Marxist explanations of social change (Lipset, 1975). Weber has been consistently misinterpreted as a naive internalist and Marx has been misrepresented as a unambiguous externalist theorist. Thus, while Marx and Weber are both influential in the sociology of development, both stand in an ambiguous relationship to their intellectual progeny.

There is ample textual justification for regarding Marx as a theoretical internalist in that his writing on backward societies rests upon a clear contrast between progressive capitalism and the stagnant societies of the East. The implication of this contrast is that the introduction of capitalism in backward societies can only be brought about by imperialism and colonialism. Marx and Engels's journalism on French and British colonialism in Asia and the Middle East has been interpreted by writers like Avineri (1969) to mean that colonialism is not only necessary but justifiable. This position is illustrated by his analysis of the backwardness of Arab societies where certain archaic values and institutions were preserved by the peculiar features of indirect colonialism with the mandates rather than smashed by the force of direct, aggressive colonialism (Avineri, 1972). Brutal colonialism in Algeria unintentionally created a modern progressive society; mandatory rule in Syria and Egypt merely conserved the traditional agricultural and military system. The internalism in Marx's theory of development is typically associated with the controversial debates over the apparent teleology of the *Manifesto*, Marx's view of 'small nations' and national liberation, and the Asiatic mode of production.

Certain sections of Marx and Engels's early work—especially in *The German Ideology* and *The Manifesto*—suggest that history is an economically determined progression of necessary stages, namely primitive commune, slave, feudal, capitalist and socialist. This historical schema was endorsed by Stalin (1941) and is still generally supported by Party intellectuals. The implication of this perspective is that capitalism, regardless of the physical misery of the working class, is by definition progressive by comparison with the vegetative, narrow world of feudalism. Hence, Marx's observations on feudal village life in the *Manifesto* or on the political role of the peasantry in *The Eighteenth Brumaire* were typically bitter and scathing (Shanin, 1966). Marx's attitude towards the peasantry is the counter-part of the political line taken by Marx and Engels towards the problem of small nations as social frameworks for capitalist development. Marx and Engels were typically opposed to supporting small nations which were struggling against capitalist imperialism. Mexican opposition to American aggression in 1847 and Islamic opposition to the French in Algeria in 1848 are the classic examples (Davis, 1965). For very different reasons, Marx criticised Bruno Bauer's limited political view of Jewish emancipation and rejected Moses Hess's Zionism (Bloom, 1942). When Marx and Engels gave their support to nationalist struggles, it was to achieve some political objective beyond nationalist self-determination as such. For instance, they favoured Polish nationalism as a defence against reactionary Tsarist Russia and Irish independence as part of a general strategy against British capitalist. In short, the question of national self-determination was merely a strategic issue in the context of the class struggle.

Marx and Engels's attitudes towards anti-colonial wars, the political role of the peasantry, the problem of small nations and capitalist development on a world scale are crystallised around the debate over the AMP. Whereas in Europe feudalism had created the conditions for capitalist development, societies in which the AMP was dominant were locked within a set of social structures which precluded any real historical development. Within these societies there was no class struggle, no private property, no free cities, no legal security of person or property and consequently no conditions for endogenous change. Asiatic society could only be revolutionised from without by the implantation of capitalism through the agency of British imperialism. Like Montesquieu, Mill and Hegel, Marx divides the globe into a dynamic, progressive West and a stagnant, despotic East; history is a process which is divided into necessary stages leading to an inevitable end. This apparently historicist and internalist view of world history is interlarded with a rich dosage of ethnocentric comments on national character—the lazy Mexicans, voluptuous Hindus, langourous Indians and barbaric, robbing Bedouin.

One of the central pivots of contemporary Marxist theory and exegesis has been the attempt to demolish all forms of economism, mechanical determinism and teleology. These reinterpretations of the central concepts of Marxism have very obvious implications for Marxist theories of underdevelopment, pre-capitalist modes of production and capitalist colonialism. For example, Melotti (1977) draws upon the discussion of various pre-capitalist modes of production as separate routes out of primitive communism in Marx's *Grundrisse* in order to construct a multilinear anti-teleological schema of social development. At a more abstract level, writers like Althusser and Poulantzas have provided a systematic critique of economism and the empiricist epistemology of much conventional Marxism. With reference to Marx and Engels's commentaries on Asiatic societies in the *Manifesto*, *The German Ideology* and the *New York Daily Tribune*, authors like Hindess and Hirst (1975), who accept the Althusserian claim that Marx's theoretical development is punctured by an 'epistemological break' around 1857, simply dismiss these comments on Asia as pre-scientific. Furthermore, Hindess and Hirst have attempted to demonstrate that the concept of the AMP is theoretically incoherent. In the AMP, the state is crucial to the system, but, since there are no social classes in the AMP, there is no explanation of the conditions of existence of the state.

While these theoretical contributions represent a major analytical advance on vulgar economism, they still leave most of the crucial issues of development and underdevelopment unresolved. Three such issues may be referred to. First, contemporary Marxism has not found an adequate theoretical answer to the problem of nationalism. The basic disagreement is an old one—either we adopt Lenin's position that socialists ought to support national movements if they are progressive or Luxemburg's argument that the very concept of 'nation' is an ideological device of the bourgeoisie. Second, if the concept of the AMP is abandoned, then we are within conventional Marxism forced to regard pre-capitalist societies in Europe and Asia as predominantly feudal, but this raises numerous difficulties in explaining the different character of these societies. In practice, most Marxist anthropologists and historians either retain a modified version of the AMP or they adopt Weberian concepts of patrimonialism. The most impressive example would be Perry Anderson's *Lineages of the*

Absolute State (1974). Third, Marxists have hardly begun the work of analysing the structure of classes, the laws of motion and the role of the state of post-colonial societies and their modes of production. The only important exceptions are found in the work of Hamza Alavi (1972), Jairus Banaji (1973) and John Saul (1974). The point of these observations is that Marx's mature work, especially *Capital*, is not especially relevant for developing theories of underdevelopment and development on the periphery of capitalism. Apart from the fact that volumes I and II are based on the analysis of a closed national economy as an analytical simplification, Marx was not primarily interested in the effects of capitalist relations on the periphery but with the contradictions of the centre of world capitalism. Of course, these analyses of capitalist contradictions in Marx's mature work do produce the theory that the imperialist export of capital is one solution to the rising organic composition of capital. Even if we accept this theory of the exportation of capitalist relations of production—and there are some good arguments from Marxists against its acceptance (Kidron, 1968; Emmanuel, 1972)—it does not tell us a great deal about the effects of colonialism on the periphery of capitalism. The conclusion of this discussion is that Marx was either an internalist theorist or that he did not possess a theory of colonial dependency and underdevelopment. Hence, all contemporary Marxist theories of development are paradoxically either neo-Marxist or anti-Marxist.

Weber's relationship to his own progeny of internalist theorists is no less problematic than Marx's relationship to contemporary externalist explanations. It has often been noted that Weber's sociology of social change cannot be reduced to a problem of individual psychology. For example, Robert Bellah (1963) has criticised what he regards as the limitations of the 'motivational approach' to Weber's sociology. Even A.G. Frank (1969, p. 32), from an entirely different perspective, recognised that internalist theories of sociologists like Richard Lambert and Bert Hoselitz (1963) are 'hand-me-down ideal typical perspective(s) of adulterated Weberian parentage'. Poulantzas also acknowledges that Weber's account of capitalism is not primarily about the subjective orientation of individual capitalists. Weber denied, for example, that rational capitalism could be defined in terms of a lust for gain. In the 'Author's Introduction' Weber distinguishes between the objective requirements of capital and the subjective preferences of capitalists by observing that any capitalist enterprise which did not take complete advantage of opportunities for making profit would be excluded from the market by its own failures. Similarly, in his study of Islam, Weber notes that capitalism was not prevented by Islam as 'the religion of individuals' but by certain ideological, political and economic structures. Rather than engage in fruitless exegesis of certain well-worn pages of Weber's *Economy and Society*, I want to turn to some features of Weber's sociology which have been rather neglected in the field of sociology of development, namely Weber's studies of patrimonialism, slavery and antiquity.

Following Immanuel Wallerstein's commentary on Weber's sociology in *The Modern World-System*, it is clear that Weber's sociology of civilisations is dominated by two central interests (1) the political instability of certain types of social systems—and the strategies which are available for certain politically dominant groups for coping with political crises (2) the global, long-term significance of certain types of structural breakdown in antiquity, patrimonialism and feudalism. In particular, Weber wants to determine what types of political breakdown are conducive to the development of capitalism in various social structures. This aspect of Weber's sociology is based on the general premise that all pre-modern political systems were, by contrast with bureaucratically administered modern politics, typified by massive structural instabilities. However, certain types of instability and breakdown (such as those which occurred in feudalism) are conducive to capitalist development and to the rise of the modern state. In order to illustrate these features of Weber's sociology, I shall start with a brief comment on the concept of patrimonialism.

Whenever primitive patriarchalism is extended or enlarged by conquest or other means, then the system of patrimonialism which subsequently emerges has to solve the problem of political commitment of the periphery to the centre. The royal household can resort to various means for achieving loyalty where the system of communications in traditional empires is ineffective. The basic strategy of the patrimonial lord is to weaken the independence and political autonomy of his notables. This strategy involves the creation of a patrimonial bureaucracy which is totally dependent on the royal household in order to discipline and control quasi-independent, dissident notables. These state bureaucrats are dependent on the royal household because, in the Ottoman empire for example, they were typically slaves who were forbidden to marry, to form households or to engage in trade. In such a political system, the notables were connected to the royal household, not by a system of stable, inherited fiefs, but by benefices or prebends which were distributed as a limited payment for service.

This system of political domination had certain endemic contradictions which Weber described as the 'paradox of Sultanism'. A patrimonial empire enjoys a certain security and permanence only where the needs of the imperial household could be satisfied by continual, successful expansion. Territorial conquest provided land, booty and slaves by which the needs of the state could be met—such as funds for the payment of the imperial army. Military failures resulted in a contraction of funds which in turn meant that rulers were unable to deploy their slave army against the quasi-autonomous notables at the imperial periphery. There developed a paradoxical dependence between slave bureaucracy and free-born rulers. The royal household depended on slaves to subjugate notables and peasants in order to preserve the political monopoly of the centre. Slave armies consequently were in a position to extract fiefs, benefices and other privileges from the royal household. This permanent fiscal crisis of the patrimonial state led to the institution of tax-farming as a grant to mercenaries and eventually to outright land grants to officials for state service. The tax-collecting capacity of the centre was restricted by the fact that at each stage of the tax-gathering process officials creamed off a certain percentage for their own advancement. Because of these instabilities, there was a tendency in prebendal patrimonialism for a constant drift towards feudalisation of land tenure. This structure produced a see-saw political life—when the centre is weak, there is a feudalisation of land which strengthens the political independence of notables and peripheral regions outside the military control of the royal household; when the centre is strong, fiefs are converted back into short-term benefices.

Weber's comparative studies of feudalism and prebendalism did not depend significantly on the interpretative understanding of the subjective motives of social actors; they were not, in short, locked within a problematic of the subject. These studies have very marked parallels in Marxist literature. For example, there are clear parallels between Weber's concept of patrimonialism and Marx's analysis of the Asiatic mode of production as Lichtheim (1963) and others have frequently noted. In Weber's view, feudalism favoured the development of capitalist relations because, within feudal conditions, free cities, autonomous guilds, an independent legal profession, free labour and commercialisation were able to flourish. By contrast, prebendalism ruled out or limited such developments. Marx takes a similar position with regard to the autonomy of burgher-dominated towns in the development of the preconditions of capitalism (Marx and Engels, 1972). Whereas towns in Western feudalism provided a basis for independent guild organisation and petty commodity production, 'Asiatic history is a kind of indifferent unity of town and countryside (the really large cities must be regarded here merely as royal camps, as works of artifice (*Superfötation*) erected over the economic construction proper)' (Marx, 1973a, p. 479). A similar account of the differences between Asiatic and European urban life is found in Trotsky's commentary on the backwardness of Russian civil society. For example, Trotsky, in *The History of the Russian Revolution* and in *Article of the Year 1905*, wrote that

Unlike the artisanal and guild towns of Europe, which fought with energy and often with success for the concentration of all processing industries within their walls, but rather like the towns of the Asian despotic systems, the old Russian cities performed virtually no productive functions. They were military and administrative centres, field fortresses....Their population consisted of officials maintained at the expense of the treasury, of merchants, and lastly, of landowners. (quoted in Melotti, 1977, p. 184)

Other Marxist authors have also conceptualised some of the differences between patrimonial and feudal conditions in terms of fundamental contrasts between autocephalous feudal cities and the military camps of oriental, patrimonial empires. Gramsci (1949, p. 68), for instance, described the civil society of the East as 'a primordial amorphous mass' in which the state was overdeveloped.

These Marxist analyses of the feudal city do not differ in essentials from the analysis of urban conditions in relation to the origins of capitalism which was developed in Weber's *The City* from *Economy and Society*. This aspect of Weber's contribution to the theory of capitalist development has been largely ignored by the conventional sociology of development tradition which concentrates on Weber's analysis of values and beliefs. A number of researchers have attempted to develop and apply Weber's perspective on urbanisation under patrimonial and feudal conditions. The most interesting studies have been undertaken by Vatro Murvar (1966), Serif Mardin (1969) and Henri Pirenne (1956). These illustrations of Weberian research into the urban conditions of capitalist development should be seen, however, within the more general context of the influence of Weber's concept of patrimonial bureaucracies. The recent study of the polity of Thailand, by S.J. Tambiah (1976), in terms of a decentralised, patrimonial bureaucracy (a 'galactic constellation') is a particularly stimulating example of Weber's influence within the sociology of development.

The point of these observations on Weber's patrimonialism thesis is to suggest that the conventional view of Weberian sociology as anti-Marxist is of limited value. Although Weber is often identified with what I have termed 'internalist' theories of development, his analysis of the imperial structures of Islam, ancient China and India suggest an alternative type of theory, namely a theory of development which treats the problem of capitalist development as simultaneously a matter of internal social structures within the context of external restraints and opportunities. As we have seen, the fiscal crisis of Islamic patrimonial states was a product of certain internal political conditions within the context of imperial struggles with Christianity. In a similar fashion, Weber's account of the decline of ancient Roman civilisation presents an analytical parallel to his conception of the political instability of sultanism in the sense that the coherence of the internal structure of the Roman social system hinged on the military control of the external, peripheral environment. The civilisation of antiquity was primarily urban in that cities were the hub of all political, cultural and commercial life (Weber, 1976). The coastal cities of antiquity exchanged their commercial-industrial products for the agricultural produce of the rural hinterland, but the system of international trade was largely in terms of luxury goods for a select stratum of the dominant class. The expansion of trade was limited by the fact that antiquity was based on slavery. The free labour of the city was set in the context of unfree labour in the countryside. Under conditions of slavery, economic progress takes place by continuously increasing the supply of unfree labour; there is little incentive towards technological change for labour-saving where the supply of cheap labour is fully secured. In Weber's view, therefore, the economy of classical Rome depended upon constant warfare against societies on the periphery in order to maximise the supply of slaves.

Slaves on the rural estates lived in barracks and had no stable family life. Under these conditions, they did not reproduce the labour supply which could only come from successful warfare. These rural estates were managed by unfree overseers (*villici*) since landlords were predominantly city-dwellers. For various technical reasons, cereal production was practised on small plots of land which were leased to *coloni* who rendered labour service to landlords. Weber argues that the economic base of classical Rome was eventually undermined with the pacification of the peripheral regions at which point imperial Rome ceased to expand and the supply of cheap labour came to an end. In the later empire, the original barrack slavery was replaced by a system in which the slave was in practice a small peasant with family, property and land which he received in return for labour service. The labour force now reproduced itself. In addition, the estates became largely self-sufficient manorial enterprises which did not engage in trade. The result was a decline of free urban craftsmen with the decline of internal trade. As the countryside broke away from the coastal cities, the cities of antiquity which had been the loci of art, literature and politics went into decline. Because the slave market was closed, labour was at a premium so estate owners were reluctant to allow their own labour to be conscripted for military service. Free men fled from the cities to avoid army conscription. In principle, Roman society could have become feudal by converting estate owners into a military, feudal class which provided its own arms to defend the state. Weber, however, argues that a feudal knighthood was not suitable for the defence of an extended empire because it did not possess sufficient mobility, or at least, it was only prepared to offer service on a seasonal basis. This had been, likewise, the classical dilemma of the extended Ottoman empire. The Roman state consequently turned to the employment of mercenaries and barbarian armies, but this in turn created its own problems because the Roman state was subject to perennial fiscal crises. Without an efficient apparatus of communication, political control and bureaucratic administration, tax-gathering under such conditions was ineffectual. The result was an oscillation between feudal and patrimonial tendencies in which eventually the Roman Empire became a feudal, rural, manorial system in which the king without a central capital, without a salaried bureaucracy became, to quote Weber (1976, p. 409), a rural illiterate at the head of a 'military order of manor-owning knights'.

Once more Weber's analysis here does not appear to depend in any crucial way on interpretative reconstructions of actors' subjective intentions and motivational projects. This point is part of my disagreement with the theoretical position of Roth and Schluchter (1979). As it stands, Weber's study of the natural economy of classical Rome seems compatible with a Marxist political economy of the slave mode of production. Furthermore, this particular analysis, like Weber's studies of China and Islamic states, does not appear to be an internalist explanation in any simple, direct fashion. The problem of conquest is crucial to Weber's characterisation of pre-capitalist economies (Foster-Carter, 1976). The internal mechanisms of the economies of Rome and Islamic civilisation depend crucially on external expansion and thereby on the power or weakness of immediate neighbouring empires. Many recent overtly Marxist analyses of pre-capitalist modes of production and social formations—pastoral nomadism, slavery, feudalism and the Asiatic mode—appear to bear striking parallels to Weber's own basic perspective. In particular, I would refer to the works of Perry Anderson—*Passages from Antiquity to Feudalism* and *Lineages of the Absolutist State* (1974a)—Ervand Abrahamian (1975) and Caglar Keyder (1976). Apart from the direct references to and quotations from Weber, Anderson's treatment of various specific issues—the city, the slave economy, the role of urban burghers, the military—appears to be a form of Weberian institutional analysis. More importantly, Anderson's analytic framework in which the struggle between the centralising tendencies of anointed kings and their royal bureaucracies, on the one hand, and the feudal autonomy of knights, manors and villages, on the other, seems to be closely associated with the form of inquiry which is central to Weber's feudal/prebendal contrast.

These externalist and internalist components of Weber's theory of social development are very clearly illustrated by Immanuel Wallerstein's *The Modern World-System*. One of the central aspects of Wallerstein's thesis is drawn directly from Weber. On a world scale, those empires which developed in terms of feudalism were also favourable to the development of capitalism, while those imperial systems which developed via prebendal–patrimonial conditions such as the Chinese and Ottoman empires created institutions which proved to be inappropriate for later capitalist development. The ancient civilisations of the world developed either in the direction of feudalism as in Europe or towards prebendalism as in China. In the case of prebendalism, the centre is relatively stronger than under feudalism where there is a certain degree of political decentralisation. In feudalism, you have what Anderson has referred to as 'parcellised sovereignty' whereas prebendalism involves a contractual relationship. In many respects, prebendalism looked more promising from the point of view of economic and political development, but in the long run it was feudalism which provided the fundamental prerequisites for capital accumulation. Under prebendalism, the political centre was relatively stronger than the periphery so that the state was able to inhibit developments and innovations which appeared to threaten the political dominance of the royal bureaucracy. Wallerstein comments that:

> feudalization brought with it the dismantling of the imperial structure whereas prebendalization maintained it. Power and income was distributed in the one case to ever more autonomous landlords, rooted in an area, linked to a given peasantry and in the other to an empire-wide stratum, deliberately not linked to the local area, semi-universalistic in recruitment but hence dependent upon the favour of the center. (Wallerstein, 1974, p. 57)

Prebendal empires were forced to commit the surplus drawn from taxes or conquest to the defence of an enormous land and population mass. European feudal society, by contrast, defended itself by a manorial knighthood which was self-equipped in military terms. The characteristic orientation, therefore, of the prebendal state was towards increased tribute rather than to entrepreneurial profits.

As we have seen, the strong centre of prebendal empires has conservative effects. In China, the imperial court limited the spread of gunnery and the proliferation of gunsmiths because it quickly realised the threat to its political power from internal hordes of armed bandits. Given the multiplicity of sovereign powers in Europe, no such limitation on the spread of new techniques would have been possible. On the basis of these observations, Wallerstein then presents his thesis in an overtly Weberian mould. In the fifteenth century, China and Europe were roughly equivalent in terms of population, area and level of technology, but whereas Europe had decisive capitalist features by the sixteenth century, China was not thoroughly transformed until the communist revolution of the twentieth century. Wallerstein attempts to account for these differences by drawing attention to the consequences of prebendalism and feudalism as opposed social systems for economic change. These differences are traced back to:

> the ancient empires of Rome and China, the ways in
> which and the degree to which they disintegrated. While
> the Roman framework remained a thin memory whose
> medieval reality was mediated largely by a common
> Church, the Chinese managed to retain an imperial
> political structure, albeit a weakened one. (Wallerstein,
> 1974, p. 63)

Now it might appear that while Wallerstein is concerned with the structural conditions of capitalism his argument is essentially internalist—that is, China fails to develop because prebendalism is a structural flaw which prohibits capitalist development. Furthermore, Wallerstein argues that Europe was forced to expand dynamically while China was not. European agriculture was based on wheat and cattle while Chinese production was founded on rice. Since rice production requires massive labour inputs but relatively little space, China had no agronomic thrust outwards. By contrast, Europe did need constant territorial expansion to sustain its population. Although Wallerstein has to base his perspective on internalist premises, his argument is also clearly externalist. First, the analysis of capitalist development is conceived on a global scale; capitalism is a world economy which develops unevenly in terms of generating a system of strong core states and a weak periphery. However, as a world economy capitalism has not converted itself into a world empire. Capitalism exists as a relatively unified world division of labour on the basis of a multiplicity of political systems. Because capitalism has these global features, there is no centralised political apparatus which is capable of effectively rebalancing the unequal distribution of rewards between central core states and peripheral areas. Once the world division of labour is established under the dominance of capitalism, then it is extremely difficult for peripheral regions to bring about any significant alteration in the distribution of economic surpluses. Thus, the genesis of capitalism is conceptualised within a Weberian/ internalist framework as a contrast between the developmental potentialities of feudalism versus prebendalism. However, the effects of that genesis are explored in terms of the classic imagery of the neo-Marxist/externalist framework in which capitalist development within core states prohibits spontaneous capitalism on the periphery.

In my discussion so far I have noted that in a number of contemporary accounts of capitalist development in the research of Anderson, Keyder, Tambiah, Wallerstein and others, it is possible to locate explanations in which the internalist and externalist traditions are amalgamated. As a conclusion to this paper, I want to argue that such amalgamations are a logical necessity for any comprehensive analysis of global capitalist development. Each perspective in isolation is inadequate and partial. The defects of the internalist account are well-known; they were briefly but brilliantly outlined by Baran and Hobsbawm (1961) in their review of Rostow's *The Stages of Economic Growth*. Spontaneous capitalist development along the lines of European *laissez-faire* is ruled out by global peripheralisation. For example, a sudden upsurge of empathy, achievement motivation and asceticism in Bangladesh might result in an increase in multi-storey hotels but not in the growth of autonomous industrial capitalism. However, an internalist explanation might be able to produce a valid causal model of the genesis of capitalism in north-west Europe without referring to crucial external features of that development. Obviously whether European capitalism could have developed without the Spanish and Portugese penetration of Latin America and the Indian Ocean is a matter of controversy (Hilton, 1976). There are, nevertheless, a number of perfectly respectable Marxist theories which claim that the principal requirement for capitalist development was the separation of the feudal peasantry from the land in order to create a mobile force of landless wage-labourers. While it could be held that an internalist argument would be satisfactory for an explanation of the genesis of capitalism, it is totally unsatisfactory for explaining subsequent underdevelopment on the capitalist periphery.

The externalist tradition suffers from a set of reverse problems. Whereas internalist theories treat the external context of development as virtually nonexistent, the externalist emphasis in writers like Frank has the theoretical consequence of treating the internal structure of a society as secondary and subservient to external economic interests. Frank's vague notions about metropolis-satellite relationships have in practice replaced the more conventional Marxist interest in the internal class structure of given societies. Frank's version of externalism cannot give a satisfactory account of why certain societies rather than others are forced on to the capitalist periphery or why certain societies which are wholly dependent (such as Canada) manage to enjoy a high degree of capitalist development without massive underdevelopment. This difficulty in Frank's theory has been commented on by Melotti (1977, p. 195) who argues that Frank

> fails to explain how some areas of the world came to be 'heartlands' while others became 'fringe areas'. Spurred by the prevailing anti-capitalist ideology he completely ignores the internal structures of the individual currently underdeveloped countries and tends to reduce the process of underdevelopment to a mere mechanistic concomitant of the development of capitalism.

Frank's theory offers no explanation of the problem of the genesis of capitalism in Europe and fails to account for the diverse consequences of capitalist colonialism in South Africa and Canada, Japan and Turkey, Egypt and Algeria. In short, in order to provide an explanation of the specific features of the problems of capitalist accumulation in given societies, we need to know more than can be provided by a mechanistic, externalist theory. We need to have precise knowledge about the specific combination of modes of production, the internal class structure and the particular political conjunctures which characterise a society and the complex pattern of interaction between these internal features and the external context of global, capitalist relations.

In this chapter I have attempted to provide a rough taxonomy of development theories which I believe tend to bifurcate into either internalism or externalism. The extreme versions of these positions are, on the one hand, the social psychological theories of Lerner, McClelland and Hoselitz which typically claim to be Weberian theories and, on the other hand, the analyses of Magdoff, Frank and Dos Santos which concentrate on colonial relations and claim to be Marxist theories. I attempted to show that it was possible to derive a sociology of development theory from Weber's studies of Asiatic societies which was not individualistic, subjectivist and internalist. By contrast, Marx's concept of the Asiatic mode of production was a typical example of an internalist theory to account for the backwardness of India and China. Marx's mature work in *Capital* and the *Grundrisse* provides a basic theory of why European capitalism required colonialism to off-set the tendency of the rate of profit to fall, but Marx does not provide a particularly convincing outline of the consequences of colonialism. Marx was also an internalist theorist in a more profound and important sense. For Marx, the international structure between nation-states, the world division of labour and the imperialist struggle are ultimately subordinate to and effects of the internal class struggle within nation-states; the nature of the global structure is an expression of particular class conflicts within societies. The difference between Marx and Weber over this issue is quite clear-cut. Whereas Marx virtually dismisses conquest as a significant feature in history and the determination of classes, the 'fact of conquest' is central to Weber's sociology of civilisations and Weber's analysis of social stratification in terms of power-relationships and the legitimation of force. For Weber, imperialism and industrialism are necessarily conjoined.

9 Weber's Orientalism

The underlying purpose of the institutions, disciplines and dogmas which collectively go under the label of 'Orientalism' has always been to understand the Orient in order to control it. Orientalism provides a discourse within which the fragmented, unruly world of the Orient can be made accessible and coherent for Occidental intellectual penetration. Religion, knowledge and trade have been three dimensions of a common process whereby the exotic world of the unChristian, despotic East could be tamed and domesticated. There is, despite massive changes in organisation and intellectual content, an important continuity between the medieval institutions for Orientalism and modern academic institutions of 'area studies'. Their knowledge cannot be ultimately separated from national political objectives. In Edward Said's terms, Orientalism existed not to provide a coherent account of Buddhism or Hinduism or Islam, but to represent the Orient in a form which would be acceptable and convincing to a Christian, European consciousness. Orientalism, in serving up the East in digestible portions, had the effect of Orientalizing the Orient (Said, 1978, p. 49). The existence of Orientalism is then an important aspect of the historical process whereby the West colonised the East. That it was the Occidental 'us' which colonised the Oriental 'them' is an event which cannot be separated from the historically peculiar development of industrial capitalism in Europe. The justification for considering the problem of Orientalism in the context of Max Weber's 'comparative historical (differential) sociology of social-cultural processes and civilizational patterns' (Nelson, 1974, p. 460) is obvious. Weber's at-

257

tempt to understand the fate of man in routinised capitalist society cannot be separated from his interest in the apparent failure of capitalism in non-European cultures. Furthermore, Weber's sociological interest cannot be separated from the traditional problems of Orientalism.

If Orientalism is closely associated with colonialism and the cultural subordination of alien societies, then there is an obvious difficulty in the case of Islam. In 715 A.D., a Muslim army occupied Spain after a brief campaign which started with a reconnaissance of Berber troops in 710. Spain now became a province—al-Andalus—of the Islamic caliphate and was eventually developed as a prosperous society under the control of an independent Umayyad emirate with a centre at Cordova (Qurtubah). Islamic political control over Spain survived until 1492. In Sicily (Siqilliyah), a Muslim state was established at the beginning of the ninth century after a long period of sporadic conflict. From Sicily, Muslim armies and raiding parties pushed north towards Rome. Malta was captured in 869. While the expansion of Islam into central Europe had been contained by the end of the ninth century, there was considerable penetration of eastern Europe from the middle of the fourteenth century to the seventeenth century. Under the Osmanli family, the Ottoman empire expanded westward to include large provinces in the Balkan peninsula and into the Adriatic, Hungary and Poland. In global terms, the expansion of Islam was checked by the entry of the Portugese and Dutch navy into the Southern Seas, but Turkish control over the Balkans was not finally broken until 1913, following a series of successful 'national' struggles in Austria-Hungary and Greece. Against a long period of religious, cultural and political struggle between Christendom and Islamdom, the Orientalist conception of Islam has been very different from the conception of other non-Christian cultures.

In the Middle Ages, the Muslim Arab was typically regarded with a mixture of fear and hatred. From the time of the Venerable Bede, the Saracens were closely identified with acts of wanton carnage and destruction and from the eleventh to the thirteenth century this sense of horror was fanned by mass propaganda in support of the crusades. The new mendicant orders played an important role in popularising the idea of a crusade, not only against Arab control of the Holy Land and the Moors in Spain, but against all internal enemies of the faith (Heer, 1962). The special problem with Islam was that it was a schism *inside* Christendom and not an external, autonomous threat. Islam was not an original, spontaneous and independent religion, but a breakaway movement inspired and led by Mohammed. The notion that Islam can, therefore, be appropriately referred to as 'Mohammedanism' as a schism following the imposter 'Mahound' or 'Mahun' has a long ancestry. For example in Dante's *Inferno*, 'Mahomet' appears among the 'sowers of discord' and, as the leader of a split inside the Church, he is split in two by a cleaver. Nineteenth- and twentieth-century biographies of Mohammed have attempted to solve the problem of the authenticity of his teaching by either regarding him as epileptic but sincere or sane but morally corrupt.

As the Islamic threat to European Christendom appeared to recede or to be reduced at least to a menace to shipping and trade, Islam ceased to be a demonic scourge. It became instead either synonymous with hedonism and luxury or was reduced to an object of household fun. From the medieval Latin *pannus Saracenicus* (Saracen cloth) there evolved the term 'sarsenet' as an adjectival or figurative description of something which is as soft as silk. Thus, Shakespeare in Henry IV (part one) makes Hotspur complain to Lady Percy about the 'sarcenet suretie for thy oathes'. As V.G. Kiernan (1972, pp. 138–9) reminds us, much of the influence of the Orient came to be associated with domestic comfort in the shape of Turkey carpets, ottomans, divans, Persian slippers, Turkish delight and Turkish baths. The fascination for the sensualism and sybaritism of the Orient which was expressed through, for example, Sir William Jones's 'A persian song of Hafiz' and Edward FitzGerald's 'translation' of the *Rubaiyyat* of Omar Khayyam, was a polished and cultured version of the popular view that the Orient was a place of leisure and release. The translation of Persian culture into a European idiom reduced the genuine mysticism of Omar Khayyam to 'a drunkard's rambling profession of the hedonistic creed' (Graves, 1972, p.

8). This outline of the European attitude to Islam as a political threat to Christendom and as a hedonistic contrast to the asceticism of Western culture provides an introduction to a consideration of the rise of Orientalism as an organised, academic analysis of the Orient.

The early development of Orientalism cannot be separated from those efforts by Christianity, or, more correctly, the organised Church, to come to terms with the non-Christian religions which were first approached in a defensive, apologetic fashion and later in an assertive, missionary stance. As early as 1312, the Church Council of Vienna established a number of university chairs in Europe to advance the study of Oriental, particularly Arabic, languages. Orientalism was, therefore, closely associated with philology, translation and biblical study. From that starting point, Orientalism has been extended and developed in tandem with European colonialism. While Vasco da Gama's voyage around the Cape in 1498 opened up new continents for Orientalism, it is not until the eighteenth century that one discovers substantial, detailed studies of the Orient based on a secular interest in a first hand contact with Oriental societies. Francois Bernier's *Voyages* (1710) and Abraham Anquetil-Duperron's *Législation Orientale* (1778) eventually became the principal empirical sources for Western views of Oriental society rather than the speculative 'rational politics' of Montesquieu's *De l'Esprit des Lois* (1748). Within the context of British Orientalism, the most important event in the development of the study of languages and society was the establishment of the Asiatic Society (of Bengal) by Sir William Jones in 1784. The study of Sanskrit was promoted by the work of Sir Charles Wilkins and Henry Colebrooke, both of whom were members of the East India Company. They also played a major part in the foundation of the Royal Asiatic Society of Great Britain and Ireland in 1823 (Arberry, 1943). The Society existed to investigate 'the sciences and the arts of Asia, with the hope of facilitating ameliorations there and of advancing knowledge and improving the arts at home' (*Centenary Volume* quoted in Said, 1978, p. 79). In Britain, trade, knowledge and the amelioration of the Orient were firmly conjoined. In 1800 the East India Company founded the College of Fort William in Calcutta as further evidence of this amalgamation of commerce and knowledge. Indeed, 'la connaisance de l'Orient est une base nécessaire. Vers les années 1820 l'orientation occidentaliste commencera à dominer, tout cela sera jugé superflu et Lord Macauley en 1835 anglicisera tout le système scolaire indien' (Rodinson, 1978, p. 69).

If British scholars gained an ascendency in the field of Indian studies, Paris became the great centre of Orientalism as a whole. Between Napoleon's expedition to Egypt in 1798 and the opening of the Suez canal in 1869, French scholarship developed very rapidly especially in the study of Islam, the Middle East and Arabic culture. Napoleon's Institut d'Égypte was responsible for the twenty-three-volume *Description de l'Égypte* which appeared between 1809 and 1828. Its breadth and detail represented nothing less than a 'great collective appropriation of one country by another' (Said, 1978, p. 84). The Société Asiatique was founded in 1821 with Silvestre de Sacy, the director of the School of Living Oriental Languages, as its first president. In 1823, the Société Asiatique started the *Journal Asiatique* and, by 1838, the term 'orientalist' had been admitted by the dictionary of the French Academy as designating an expert in the field of Oriental language and the study of the Orient. In Paris, the School of Oriental Languages, under the control of the pious de Sacy, came to provide 'le modèle d'une institution orientaliste à la fois savante et laique' (Rodinson, 1978, p. 72). French Orientalism came to take a definite turn in the direction of positivist science under the influence of Ernest Renan who followed Etienne-Marc Quatremère as professor of Hebrew at the College de France in 1862 (Espinasse, 1895). For Renan, comparative philology was *the* science of mental objects and therefore central to the whole development of rational positive science. In this sense, Renan was the Auguste Comte of Orientalism. From an evolutionary perspective, Renan argued that Judaism and Christianity had made a massive contribution to the development of science since monotheism represented a major advance over primitive polytheism. The task of rational man was to grasp the rational core of Christianity in order to develop a 'religion' based on the scientific advance of liberty and individual rights. Renan's philological studies and his personal observations in Syria, however, led him to the view that Islam was totally antagonistic to science and, as he declared in his inaugural lecture, Islam was the 'complete negation of Europe'.

The early loss of Egypt gave greater urgency to France's sense of *mission civilisatrice* in Syria and North Africa. However, if British and French colonial policy can be distinguished in terms of their attitudes to the problem of European culture, they cannot be so clearly distinguished in terms of the institutional links between trade, military control and the sponsorship of research. The connection between utilitarianism and the East India Company is well known (Stokes, 1959). In French Orientalism, there was an important union between anthropological research and the colonial administration. In 1873, Adolphe Hanoteau and Ernest Letourneux published *La Kabylie et les coutumes Kabyles* which became the basis of colonial policy towards the Berber/Arab, land of dissidence/land of government, *blad s-siba/blad/l-makhzen* division. From this source there developed the 'Kabyle myth' and later the notion of Berber anarchy. The Berbers were noble savages who enjoyed a form of democracy through customary law and the tribal council. Berber spirituality in the form of maraboutism represented an indigenous protest against the foreign religion of Islam and the political intrusion of the urbanised Arabs (David M. Hart, 1976). This view of Berber/Arab relationships became, on the one hand, part of a sociological tradition by contributing to Durkheim's contrast between mechanical/organic solidarity in *The Division of Labour in Society* (1893) and, on the other, part of the French policy of divide-and-rule. The Berber Decree, in recognising the autonomy of customary law, restricted the full operation of the Shari'ah and thereby unwittingly gave a strong religious legitimation to the struggle against French colonial power.

As powerful colonial forces Britain and France were also major centres for Oriental studies. While Italy came to possess modest colonial acquisitions in Tripolitania and Cyrenaica (Evans-Pritchard, 1949), its colonial interest was far less than that of either France or Britain. Italy correspondingly had a restricted contribution to make to Orientalism in *Annali dell'Islam*. Like Spain, Italy had to face the historical and cultural problem of a period of Muslim colonisation; Spanish and Italian Orientalism had consequently an internal cultural problem of Moorish colonisation in southern Spain and in Sicily in which Orientalism responded with blank rejection and condemnation. In Germany also Orientalism did not have the same immediate colonial importance that it enjoyed elsewhere. Nevertheless, German Orientalism made important contributions to the history of philology and pre-eminently to Biblical studies. At Leipzig, the German Oriental Society which had been formed in 1845 started the *Zeitschrift der deutschen morgenlandischen Gesellschaft* in 1847. As in other branches of Orientalism, German scholars typically gave expression to a low estimation of Islam as an historical force and to Mohammed as a prophet. A. von Kremer, for example, focused on the whole problem of the decay of Islamic civilisation in his *Kulturgeschichte des Orients unter den Chalifen* (1875-7). The failure of the Ottoman Empire to break out of its internal limitations and to generate a group of independent and free nations were issues that occupied L. von Ranke in *Weltgeschichte* (1881-8). In his *Historische Fragmente*, Jacob Burckhardt gave expression to the prevailing antipathy to the Prophet and to Islam. Similar attitudes were repeated in the Orientalism of Julius Wellhausen (*Das arabische Reich und sein Sturz*, 1902) and in Th. Nöldeke (*Aufsätze zur persischen Geschichte*, 1887). Nöldeke's love of hellenism obliterated any appreciation of Islamic culture (Fück, 1962, p. 309). While German scholars were actively involved in Orientalism, their work was, to some extent, parasitic on British and French developments.

Although Orientalism has gone through enormous changes in style and content from the philology of de Sacy and Renan to the area studies of contemporary American departments of Middle East Studies, there are, nevertheless, certain common assumptions in Orientalism that have been reproduced without significant variation over the last two centuries. In this sense, Orientalism is irreducibly arcane (Said, 1978). I have argued elsewhere (Turner, 1978) that Orientalism characterised Middle East society as a set of absences, of critical gaps which prevented or misdirected the process of modernisation. Both Marx and Weber depended on this common Orientalist source and both reproduced it in their studies of the Orient. In this study I shall outline these 'missing' features of Islamic civilisation, illustrate the common agreements between Marx and Weber and then attempt to reconstruct part of Weber's argument which appears to break with the Orientalist tradition.

Decades prior to the appearance of Weber's essays on the Protestant ethic, Orientalists had addressed themselves to the apparent absence of rational science, democratic government, liberal opinion, religious asceticism and industrial progress in the Orient. First, classical Orientalism is grounded on the assumption that there is a major divide, an ontological hiatus, between Orient and Occident in which the latter is the repository of an unfolding essence of reason and freedom. Thus, one of the principal motifs of classical Orientalism is the whole debate over the issue of Oriental despotism (Stelling-Michaud, 1960–1). A dynamic and democratic Occident could then be starkly contrasted with a despotic and stationary Orient. Second, Orientalism proposed to provide a series of remedies whereby the timeless Orient could be woken, rudely or otherwise, from its dreams. Orientalism can provide this service because the indigenous populations of the Orient were not themselves capable of rational knowledge of their own society and its condition.

The despotism and stagnation of the Orient, then, is to be explained by a series of missing institutions or beliefs. The assumptions that the central difference between Occidental and Oriental societies was to be located in the absence of private property in land in Oriental society made its appearance very early in the history of Orientalism. In seventeenth-century France, the dangers of 'l'Empire du Turc' became a fountain of political metaphors for the analysis of legitimate royal power in France. The wisdom of French arrangements was contrasted with Turkish despotism and, according to Bossuet, the instructor of the young Louis XIV, the main causes of arbitrary rule were general slavery, the absolute power of the ruler, arbitrary laws and the absence of private property (Koebner, 1951). One of the major sources for this theme of absent property rights was François Bernier's *Voyages contenant la description des états du Grand Mogol.* Eventually this notion worked its way into the whole problematic that surrounds Marx's 'Asiatic mode of production'. In 1853 Marx wrote to Engels declaring that 'Bernier rightly considered the basis of all phenomena in the East—he refers to Turkey, Persia, Hindustan—to be the *absence of private property in land.* This is the real key, even to the Oriental heaven' (Marx and Engels, 1972, p. 313). In the same year, Marx was writing to the *New York Daily Tribune* that the basis of traditional India, as with all Asiatic systems, was that the state acted as 'the real landlord'. In the period between 1852 and 1862 Marx and Engels contributed some 487 articles to the *Tribune.* In the process of providing a commentary on British domestic and foreign policy, Marx and Engels elaborated a view of the static quality of Asian societies which subsequently came to be described as the 'theory of the Asiatic mode of production'. It has often been claimed that Marx and Engels abandoned this theory in their later economic theories (Hindess and Hirst, 1975). Marx himself described this journalism as 'continual newspaper muck' (quoted in McLellan, 1973, p. 284). Nevertheless, Marx's commentary on the static quality of Indian village life which derived from the self-sufficiency of village economics in the *Grundrisse* and *Capital* did not represent a major break with the existing Orientalist tradition.

Marx was impressed by the peculiar contrast between the political instability of traditional Indian states and the massive economic stability of its basic structure. Thus, 'the unchangeableness of Asiatic societies' was in 'striking contrast with the constant dissolution and refounding of Asiatic States, and the never-ceasing changes of dynasty' (Marx, 1974, vol. 1, p. 338). In *The Religion of India*, Weber paid a direct and rare compliment to Marx by declaring that Marx's insight into the absence of production for the market and payment in kind as the key to the 'stability' of Asia 'was correct' (Weber, 1958b, p. 111). Weber employed this argument for different purposes in order to argue that the rational extension of the state in India and China constantly came up against local resistance in the village and in the sib organisation. Within a broader context, this formed part of Weber's argument that Oriental societies were typified by prebendal structure of land ownership while Occidental societies were historically feudal. The idea that the overt political instability of Asia should not lead us to misjudge its underlying stability was, however, not only common to Marx and Weber, but a consistent idea of Western political thought. In Hegel's political analysis, Western, especially Greek and Christian, political conditions promoted the development of self-consciousness and reflexivity. By contrast, in the Orient generally political conditions ruled out the development of individuality and freedom. Hegel does, however, make some important distinctions between various regions within the Orient and his discussion of 'Mohametanism' in *The Philosophy of History* is particularly interesting. Hegel recognised that Islam started as a vigorous and active movement bursting out of the geographical constraints of Arabia Felix to construct substantial political empires in Asia and Africa. However, after that initial burst, Hegel argues that Islam quickly joined the stationariness of the Orient. Today 'Islam has long vanished from the stage of history at large, and has retreated into Oriental ease and repose' (Hegel, 1956, p. 360). Marx's observation that 'Indian society has no history at all, at least no known history' (Marx and Engels, 1972, p. 81) encapsulated not only this Hegelian tradition, but also the view of India which had been developed by James Mill and J.S. Mill (Turner, 1974; 1979).

The utilitarian view was that India had stagnated because individual freedom and initiative had been stifled by custom, tradition, priestcraft and centralised political power. The remedy was to provide minimal state interference, a sound taxation system and secularisation; in short, to convert India into a middle-class democracy. The problem was that at home liberalism and individualism were threatened by the growth of mass democracy in a situation where the working class lacked a basic education. What Mill feared most was the spread of 'Chinese stationariness' in Britain in the wake of parliamentary reform. The utilitarian assumption was that Western development hinged on the presence of an autonomous, educated bourgeoisie whose innovative, entrepreneurial activity was the secret of European and American dynamism. In the Orient, the bourgeoisie was squeezed between the irrationality of despotic power, arbitrary law and political interference from above and the passivity and traditionalism of village life from below. This analysis which was based on 'the problematic of the missing middle class' in Asia was widely held among a variety of political and sociological theorists in the nineteenth century. The core of the problematic was the idea that urban conditions in Asia were either underdeveloped or unstable and therefore could not provide a political and economic environment in which a bourgeoisie could thrive (Turner, 1979). In the Orient, the bourgeoisie was more inclined to hoard their wealth than to risk investment in productive capital which despots could readily confiscate. Consequently trade, banking and industry tended to come under the control of foreign minorities such as Jews, Greeks and Armenians.

The Orientalist view of Asian society was, therefore, expressed in terms of a set of gaps or absences—the missing middle class, the absence of private property in land, the absence of political and legal stability. The religions of Asia were treated as the 'perfect' spiritual companions of political despotism. While imperial rulers attempted to legitimise their despotism by reference to divine labels, the mass of the population was compensated by the opium of their traditional gods. In his article on 'The British Rule in India', Marx bitterly commented that Hindustan was an odd combination of Ireland and Italy being 'a world of voluptuousness and a world of woes'. This combination was 'anticipated in the ancient traditions of the religion of Hindustan...at once a religion of sensualist exuberance, and a religion of self-torturing asceticism' (Marx and Engels, 1972, pp. 35-6). In the *Grundrisse*, Marx suggested that the absolute God was a symbol of centralised power to which economic surpluses were offered in tribute. Just as the abstract deism of Protestantism was perfectly suited to capitalism, so the religions of Asia were spiritual mirrors of political and social conditions of despotism. In a similar fashion, the utilitarians approached Hinduism as a major plank in the oppressive force of ancient custom. As we have seen the conventional Orientalist attitude to Islam was to treat it as a political doctrine of Arab expansion or as an imperfect copy of Judeo-Christian monotheism. In any case, the early vitality of Islam had been quickly replaced by a period of decline and paralysis. Islam became ideally suited to the political requirements of Oriental empires.

The point of this outline of Orientalism is to suggest that Weber's studies of India, China and the Middle East were not isolated, original and highly innovative research monographs. These studies have to be seen in the context of a long, well-established and prestigious tradition of Orientalism. Weber was himself quite explicit about his dependence on existing research and empirical resources. Weber's principal contributions to the study of the Orient are to be found in *The Religion of India* (1958b), *The Religion of China* (1951) and *Ancient Judaism* (1952). These 'essays' which Weber started after 1913 first appeared in the *Archiv für Sozialwissenschaft und Socialforschung* between 1915 and 1919. They were subsequently published by Marianne Weber as three volumes of *Gesammelte Aufsätze zur Religionssoziologie* in 1920-1. In addition, Weber made numerous comparative studies of Occidental and Oriental differences in relation to law, the city, the state and music; many of these contrasts are summarised in the general discussion of 'patrimonialism' in volume three of *Economy and Society*. Throughout these studies, Weber acknowledged his dependence on existing scholarly research and tradition. For example, in *Ancient Judaism* Weber (1952, p. 425) admitted that

> It would require more than a lifetime to acquire a true mastery of the literature concerning the religion of Israel and Jewry, especially since this literature is of exceptionally high quality...we entertain but modest hopes of contributing anything essentially new to the discussion, apart from the fact that, here and there, some source data may be grouped in a manner to emphasize some things differently than usual.

In a similar fashion, Weber did not claim to possess any special expert knowledge of China (van der Sprenkel, 1954). Weber was a good linguist and, from his references, appears to have read widely in the available published material. He quoted from the major European journals of his day—*Journal of the Royal Asiatic Society, Journal Asiatique, Zeitschrift der Deutschen Morgenlandischen Gesellschaft* and so forth. His bibliographical references on Judaism, Hinduism and Confucianism provide clear evidence of the breadth and diversity of his reading of the literature.

By contemporary standards, much of Weber's source material is now regarded as obsolete, inadequate and misleading. In some cases, however, Weber does appear to have enjoyed direct access to adequate translations of classic religious texts. For China, Yang, in his introduction to Weber's *The Religion of China* (1951, p. xxxviii), argues that with reference to 'basic classics and historical references, Weber was not at any great disadvantage as compared with Western sinologists today'. A more critical stance is taken by van der Sprenkel (1954, p. 272) with regard to the 'inadequate documentation, methodological defects, frequent inaccuracies and occasional wrongheadedness' of *The Religion of China*. Both writers, however, recognise Weber's capacity to raise the correct questions of his data regardless of their empirical limitations and to provide answers which stimulate further research. Since Weber never completed his project for the analysis of 'The Economic Ethics of the World Religions' with a comprehensive study of Islam, it is not particularly easy to assess Weber's knowledge of the scholarship of his day. He does cite the publications of C.H. Becker who wrote *Der Islam* (1913), *Beiträge zur Geschiche Ägyptens unter dem Islam* (1902) and *Islamstudien* (1924) (Waardenburg, 1962). Weber also notes the work of the Dutch Orientalist C. Snouck Hurgronje quoting from *Mekka, vol. 1: Die Stadt und ihre Herren* (1888) in the study of the city in *Economy and Society* (1968, vol. 3, p. 1236). Weber was also familiar with the research of Julius Wellhausen and was probably influenced by Wellhausen's *Das arabische Reich und sein Sturz* (1902). Through these sources, there are good grounds for believing that Weber was also familiar with the research of Th. Nöldeke (*Aufsätze zur persischen Geschichte*, 1887), Henri Lammens (*Le berceau de l'Islam*, 1914 and publications in *Journal Asiatique*) and with Ignaz Goldziher (*Muhammedanische Studien*, 1890). Of these direct and indirect influences, the work of Carl Heinrich Becker was probably the most important in forming Weber's conception of the economic ethic of Islam. In Becker's view, Islamic teaching on wealth, usury and effort stood in the way of economic development (Rodinson, 1974). Becker, who became the Prussian secretary of higher education, had been a colleague of Weber's at Heidelberg (Weber, 1975, p. 645).

From these Orientalist classics, Weber was able to grasp the fundamentals of Islamic law, the problems connected with the *hadīth* literature as a basis for the Prophet's biography, the principles of Islamic theology relating to issues such as prophecy, sin and salvation, the details of early Islamic political history and the history of the early empires. In *Economy and Society*, Weber showed that, via Becker's research, he was familiar with aspects of the economic organisation of the Ottoman empire and the section on problems of law-making bristled with technical terminology concerning Islamic jurisprudence. In the *Religionssoziologie* section of *Economy and Society*, it is clear that Weber was familiar with many of the debates surrounding the precise character of Mohammed's claim to prophetic inspiration. At a factual level, Weber was probably as adequately informed about the history of Islam as he was about the other world religions which he analysed in the *Gesammelte Aufsätze zur Religionssoziologie*. However, what Weber acquired from this classical Orientalist literature was not simply an assortment of neutral facts; he also took over a number of important evaluations of the nature and historical significance of Islam.

Although this group of Orientalists often disagreed violently amongst themselves (over the value of the *Sira* and *hadīth* as historical sources, for example), there was also a basic consensus about Islam. There was some agreement about the superiority of classical Greek civilisation over that of Islam. Wellhausen and Nöldeke shared a low opinion of the Oriental. In his Preface to his study of Persia, Nöldeke admitted that his studies 'as an Orientalist have been the very means of increasing my philhellenism, and I think that the same experience will befall anyone who makes a serious but open-minded attempt to acquaint himself with the nature of the Eastern peoples' (quoted in Fück, 1962, pp. 309–10). Henri Lammens, a Jesuit priest who spent most of his life in Lebanon, developed a profound nationalist sentiment for Syria while regarding Islam as an alien and corrupt intrusion (Salibi, 1962). Lammens emphasised the virility of the prophet, doubted his sincerity, and claimed that the Koranic revelations were largely a result of autosuggestion. Becker, unlike Lammens, thought that Islam was originally a purely religious movement, but treated Islam as a whole as underdeveloped. In other words, the group of Islamologists from whom Weber sought an insight into Islam clearly embodied the general Orientalist view of Islam as a bleak, bare, parasitic rehash of Christian and Jewish monotheism. It was this aspect of the religion from the Orientalist perspective which provided Weber with an explanation of why Islam as a this-worldly, prophetic, monotheistic and salvational religion failed to produce an ethic compatible with rationalisation.

In what follows I shall outline what is the standard interpretation of Weber's comparative sociology, namely that Weber attempted to set up a series of 'experiments' to show that a particular religious ethic had played a crucial role in the emergence of rational capitalism, intellectualisation and scientific routinisation. I shall illustrate this standard viewpoint by reference to Weber's studies of Islam, Hinduism and Confucianism. The standard interpretation, if accepted in its entirety, has the consequence of demonstrating Weber's thoroughly vulgar Orientalism. I then want to question some aspects of this interpretation to show how, in two important respects, Weber's sociology breaks with idealism and Orientalism. The principal source of this conventional view of Weber was originally developed in the various exegetical works of Talcott Parsons.

According to Parsons, we have to see the essays on the Protestant ethic and the spirit of capitalism as a preliminary outline which anticipated a number of major comparative studies of world civilisations. In *The Structure of Social Action* (Parsons, 1949, p. 512), he interprets Weber's task almost in the language of J.S. Mill's methodology when he comments that Weber embarked on 'an ambitious series of comparative studies all directed to the question, why did modern rational bourgeois capitalism appear as a dominant phenomenon only in the modern West?' In his introductory essay to Weber's *The Sociology of Religion*, Parsons states this interpretation with equal force. He argues that Weber realised that the demonstration of the causal importance of religion for capitalist rationality could not be provided by a purely historical approach which aimed to establish increasingly detailed knowledge. Weber opted for a comparative approach because,

> It was only by establishing a methodological equivalent of experimental method, in which it is possible to hold certain factors constant, that even the beginnings of an escape from circularity was possible....In embarking upon comparative studies, Weber attempted to hold the factor of 'economic organization' constant and treat religious orientation as his independent variable. (Parsons, 1966, pp. xxi–xxii)

The subsequent essays on India and China were thus comparative and experimental attempts to complement the historical study of Protestantism by demonstrating the independent effect of religion on world history.

There is ample evidence to support Parsons's perspective on Weber's central task in Weber's sociology of civilisations. In a letter to Georg von Bellow in 1914, Weber observed that it was only by a comparative study of the presence or absence of various institutions that sociology could make a 'modest' contribution to history. For example, 'what is specifically characteristic of the medieval city...can really be developed only through the statement of what is lacking in the other (ancient, Chinese, Islamic) cities' (from Georg von Bellow *Der Deutsche Staat des Mittelalters* and quoted in Cahnman, 1964, p. 127). This would lend support to the view that Weber's comparative sociology is a form of Orientalism which concentrates on things which are 'lacking' in other cultures. Furthermore, Weber often wrote about his sociology of religion as if it were a form of comparative experimentation. In *The Religion of India*, Weber stated that 'we shall inquire as to the manner in which Indian religion, as one factor among many, may have prevented capitalistic development (in the occidental sense)' (1958b, p. 4). The conclusion of *The Religion of China* is perhaps less clear-cut since Weber recognised that 'the basic characteristics of the "mentality", in this case the practical attitudes toward the world, were deeply co-determined by political and economic destinies. Yet, in view of their autonomous laws, one can hardly fail to ascribe to these attitudes effects strongly counteractive to capitalist development' (Weber, 1951, p. 249). These studies of China and India, therefore, appear to fulfil faithfully the 'promise' of *The Protestant Ethic and the Spirit of Capitalism* which apparently, whilst not denying the importance of 'economic factors', sought to understand capitalism via the study of religious history.

By approaching Weber's sociology in this fashion, Parsons was able to see Weber's model of religious orientations to the world as the key to his sociology as a whole. Within all religions there is a potential conflict between ethical demands that follow from revelation or prophecy and the everyday requirements of human life. These potential conflicts may be solved in various directions. Religious asceticism seeks to remove the inconsistency by mastery of the world, while mysticism represents a form of resignation and adjustment. We can also think about the quest for salvation as either otherworldly or inner-worldly and, by cross-tabulating these two sets of contrasts, we can arrive at four ideal-typical salvational paths by which religion comes to terms with 'the world'. In Parson's interpretation, the more a religion or ethic approximates to inner-worldly asceticism, the more it acts as a 'social leverage' in liquidating traditional beliefs and institutions. The principal example, of course, was Calvinistic Protestantism, which rationalised the world in terms of its total hostility to magic, priesthood and sacramentalism. Weber's comparative sociology takes the form of locating the various religions within this typology of salvational strategies in order to 'quantify' their contribution to rationalisation processes. Islam, Hinduism and Confucianism provide, therefore, a particularly interesting contrast from this comparative perspective.

Weber's unfinished commentary on Islam is especially interesting as an aspect of his comparative sociology on the ground that Islam has a lot in common with Christianity and Judaism. In principle, these religions are monotheistic, prophetic, scriptural, anti-traditional and salvational. Because they embody an implicit contradiction between absolute moral demands and the humdrum practicalities of ordinary life, these religions carry within them the potential for social transformation along rationally radical lines. Only the God of the prophets achieved an 'absolutely transcendental character' (Weber, 1966, p. 138), while the monotheism of Islam was often watered down by the presence of Sufi saints. In Christianity, especially in Roman Catholicism, the cult of Mary and the saints 'comes fairly close to polytheism' (Weber, 1966, p. 138). There is, however, a strong *prima facie* case for believing that these prophetic religions were capable of providing a definite ascetic drive towards rationalisation. In the case of Islam, the pristine ascetic monotheism of the Prophet was ultimately transformed into an ethic of military conquest because the Meccan warrior clans became the principal social carrier of the new religion. The Prophet's programme for social action 'was oriented almost entirely to the goal of the psychological preparation of the faithful for battle in order to maintain a maximum number of warriors for the faith' (Weber, 1966, p. 51). This combination of prophecy and warrior interest in the holy war in Islam produced religious wars 'directed towards the acquisition of large holdings of real estate, because it was primarily oriented to feudal interest in land' (Weber, 1966, p. 87). Under the impact of urban artisans, Christian asceticism was directed towards rational capitalist accumulation; in Islam, under the impact of militarised bedouin clans, prophetic asceticism was directed towards a merely feudal interest in land acquisition. The original social dynamism of prophetic Islam was thus transformed into a formal religion with the 'characteristics of a distinctively feudal spirit' (Weber, 1968, vol. 2, p. 626). Once the conflict with 'the world' had been diluted by military interests, the subjection of women, the existence of slavery, the institutionalisation of polygamy and widespread serfdom no longer represented moral obstacles or religious problems.

Weber's detailed analyses of Hinduism and Confucianism parallel his unfinished study of Islam. The point of these studies is to illustrate a general distinction between 'the religion of conviction oriented to salvation' and 'the purely ritual or legalistic religion which accepts the world' (Freund, 1968, p. 177). In the study of Islam we see how, according to Weber, a religion of conviction became a legalistic religion oriented to feudal property. By contrast, the so-called 'religions of Asia' were, both from their charismatic origins and from their subsequent social carriers, 'religions of social adaptation' which lacked any socially transformative characteristics. To start with Hinduism, Weber perceptively pointed out that, given its comprehensive tolerance of differences in belief and its dogmatic openness, there is a sense in which Hinduism is not a 'religion' according to Western conceptions. What defines Hinduism is not a fixed dogma but a set of ritual practices (*dharma*) which is tied to caste position. Although from this Hindu perspective all religions are constituted by their practices, under Brahmanical rationalism Hinduism did come to possess a central and crucial dogmatic tradition, namely the *karma-samsara* theodicy. The Hindu combination of karma (doctrine of ethical compensation) and samsara (belief in transmigration of souls) produced an extremely rigid social doctrine which simultaneously condemned social innovation and legitimised the caste order, especially the elevated status of the Brahmans. Since an individual's social position in this world is the effect of meritorious or ethically deleterious actions in a previous life, there can be little scope for social criticism of wealth or for the removal of inequality in society. Within this theodicy, 'there is no escape from the caste, as least, no way to move up in the caste order. The inescapable on-rolling *karma* causality is in harmony with the eternity of the world, of life, and, above all, the caste order' (Weber, 1958b p. 121).

In Hinduism, the soteriology provided by the *karma-*

samsara doctrine meant that the quest for individual salvation was oriented towards minute and scrupulous adherence to *dharma* prescriptions and proscriptions. Each level of reality—animals, humans and gods—has its caste orders and each caste has its *dharma*. Only by rigid conformity to the *dharma* is escape from fate possible—and that in the future. This equation of one's social position with previous moral activity had the effect of preventing the development of any theory of individual rights or natural law which can be the basis for social criticism. The religious knowledge which was cultivated by the Brahmanical intelligentsia/priesthood did not give rise to general theories of society of a natural law theology. Religious knowledge was oriented towards 'a metaphysically and cosmologically substructured technology of the means to achieve salvation from this world' (Weber, 1958b, p. 147). The systematisation of these metaphysical techniques came eventually to rule out ecstasy and orgiastic magic as suitable modes of escape. In this respect, Brahmanical priests came to resemble the Confucian literati as an elite of experts in genteel culture. Thus 'Immanent rationalism of knowledge and culture, as usual, obstructed irrational, orgiastic-ecstatic asceticism; the status pride of cultured men resisted undignified demands of ecstatic therapeutic practices and the exhibition of neuropathic states' (Weber, 1958b, p. 149). In general, Hindu culture gives the impression that its early contributions to scientific thought and its 'noteworthy developmental beginnings were somehow hindered' (Weber, 1958b, p. 161). Part of the explanation for this arrested development must be sought in the systematisation of Brahmanical soteriology which was 'indifferent to the actualities of the world, and, through gnosis, sought the one thing needful beyond it—salvation from it' (Weber, 1958b, p. 162). The search for possession of gnosis either by a metaphysical technology or by rigorous adherence to caste rituals liquidated all tension between religious values and the world by cultivating religious indifference to social reality. The religions of Asia were thus typically a-political status religions of social adaptation.

This elite gentility of Brahmanical priests and Buddhist 'professional monks' in India found its acme in the Confucian literati. As a general characterisation, Weber noted that Confucianism 'consisted only of ethics' leading to 'adjustment to the world, to its orders and conventions' and 'represented just a tremendous code of political maxims and rules of social propriety for cultured men of the world' (Weber, 1951, p. 152). By contrast with other world religions, Confucianism is defined by its negativity—it lacks prophets and passion, original sin and cosmic evil, incarnate gods and ecstatic union, sacrifice and resurrection. Confucianism took propriety as its central concept and its principal goal. From this perspective, Confucianism treated all human ethical problems as a matter of education rather than redemption. Immorality was a consequence, not of radical evil, but of inappropriate or inadequate instruction. Weber contrasted 'the passion and ostentation of the feudal warrior in ancient Islam' with the ideal man of Confucianism aiming at 'watchful self-control, self-observation and reserve' (Weber, 1951, p. 156). Education provided the means for the gentleman to achieve universalism in culture. The Confucian ideal did not favour specialisation of knowledge or bureaucratic specialisation of skill. Similarly the Confucian ethic did not encourage a life of commercial acquisitiveness which mitigated against the sense of inner poise, propriety and stability of Confucianism. This form of piety, therefore, lacked the inner tensions of Calvinism which were resolved by a sense of calling and world-mastery. Confucian piety adapted the cultured official to the requirements of the court and the higher circles of the patrimonial bureaucracy; it did not, on the basis of an irrational salvational impulse, drive the literati to a rational systematisation of the bureaucratic structure.

If we accept Parsons's view of Weber's comparative sociology, then it does appear to be the case that Weber wants to set up a series of comparative studies of religious ethics in order to provide an account of the peculiar dynamism of Western culture. Indeed there is ample evidence to suggest that Weber's sociology is characterised by an Orientalist West/East problematic. If we approach Weber's sociology from this perspective, then Weber does appear to regard all Oriental cultures as static. One particular feature of Weber's apparently static model of Asia is that Weber typically quotes historical evidence from widely scattered epochs to demonstrate some feature of a social structure. The implication of not treating historical chronology seriously is that the social structure of Asia is frozen. For example, in his outline of Islam Weber quotes evidence from the seventh century on the Prophet and the twelfth century on feudalisation of land tenure and the nineteenth century on Tunisian law reform. It appears as if evidence from any century is equally germane to the sociology of Islamic stationariness. Similar criticisms have been raised against Weber's treatment of Chinese society. Commenting on the influence of Leopold von Ranke's description of Asian peoples as 'Völker des ewigen Stillstandes', van der Sprenkel criticised both Weber and Bendix for accepting the myth of an 'unchanging China':

> Unconscious acceptance of this myth by a German scholar who received his formative training in the last quarter of the nineteenth century is explainable in terms of the ruling German historical tradition of that time, which, when it took note of the existence of the Asian civilizations at all, did so only to dismiss them as 'static'. as making no contribution to the movement of world history, and therefore of no interest to the historian. Dynamism in history was the exclusive attribute of the West. (van der Sprenkel, 1954, p. 350)

Weber's comparative sociology appears, therefore, to fit perfectly into the classical Orientalist mould in which Asia is constituted by its own negativity.

That Weber inherited much of the cultural baggage of German Orientalism can hardly be denied. Weber's treatment of the work-ethic of the major religions reproduced the principal assumptions of Orientalist scholarship. However, in important respects Weber also avoids certain key Orientalist assumptions and, furthermore, the assumption that Weber's comparative sociology is essentially an 'experiment' to test the impact of religious factors is particularly misleading. Weber could not hold all other variables constant to examine the role of religious beliefs because the economic and social structures of these various societies differed from each other in a number of important ways. It cannot be argued that Weber compared ideal typical abstractions in order to analyse the causal importance of religion. Weber specifically draws attention to the many empirical differences between Asian and European societies in terms of their socio-economic structures. Weber notes that one crucial factor in Chinese social structure was the power of the local lineage structure under the authority of the patriarchal sib. This feature of Chinese society was not present to such an extent in other Oriental or Occidental societies. The particular combination of *karma-samsara* theodicy and caste structure was not reproduced outside India. The banking and money systems of China, India, Egypt and Turkey do not permit any neat comparative experiments. Weber also thought that the role of the Chinese bureaucrat/ literati had no equivalent in Islamic society or in Brahmanical India. Weber does, of course, make many comparative judgments as to the essential differences between Occidental and Oriental culture. He treats the European city as a unique feature of Occidental history, but these comparisons hardly amounted to an experiment because all factors apart from religion could never be held constant.

We must, however, consider a much more significant objection to Parsons's treatment of Weber's comparative sociology. Starting with the Hobbesian problem of order, Parsons has to treat cultural values as the crucial issue in the collapse of a rationalist, positivist sociology. In my view, this perspective leads Parsons to a gross exaggeration of the importance of religious work-ethics in Weber's sociology. When Weber considers religious values and their role in social development, he in fact concentrates not on religious beliefs as such, but on the penetration of religious ideals and the 'interests' of their social carriers. It is not religion as such which is important but the religiosity of certain classes or status groups which contribute to social organisation. What was important for Weber was the routinisation of charismatic revelation along the lines dictated by socio-economic interests. Thus, in *The Sociology of Religion*, we find that the impact of world-religions is always mediated by the interests of their ideological carriers; 'In Confucianism, the world-organizing bureaucrat; in Hinduism, the world-ordering magician; in Buddhism, the mendicant monk wandering through the world; in Islam, the warrior seeking to conquer the world; in Judaism, the wandering trader; and in Christianity, the itinerant journeyman' (Weber, 1966, p. 132). In these sections of Weber's comparative sociology, his specific concern was not to study the effect of religious factors by holding the social variables constant; his focus was on the 'elective affinity' between material and ideal interests which transformed the original charismatic theology of the world religions in particular directions.

Parsons also exaggerated the importance of religion in general in Weber's comparative sociology. The use of the term 'religion' in the titles of *The Religion of India* and *The Religion of China* provides a misleading description of the contents of these two studies of Asian society. For example, the bulk of Weber's study of China is devoted to the sociological analysis of China's monetary system, guild and city structure, the prebendal state, the sib association and the bureaucracy. The problem of Confucianism and heterodoxical beliefs does not enter the picture until the end of this study, once the socio-economic structure has already been fully explored. In *The Religion of India*, it is true that the discussion of the particular theological character of Hinduism occupies the core of that study; nevertheless, Weber is at pains to weave together the problem of theodicy with the understanding of the Indian caste structure. In addition, when Weber attempts to make comparisons between Occidental and Oriental society, it is not immediately obvious that his principal concern is with religious differences. In fact, the religious issue frequently appears to be subordinate to military and political questions. For example, Weber (1958b, p. 71) argues that:

Not only were the historical stages of Indian and European development different, but a purely military factor is important for the explanation of the different development of East and West. In Europe the horseman was technically the paramount force of feudalism. In India, in spite of their numbers, horsemen were relatively less significant and efficient than the foot soldiers who held a primary role in the armies from Alexander to the Moguls.

This discussion of the 'military factor' is not in fact a mere footnote to Weber's sociological concerns in his study of India. On the contrary, it represents the central and abiding concern of Weber's comparative sociology, namely the exploration of the different consequences of prebendal and feudal organisation.

For Weber, the existence of a centralised patrimonial bureaucracy and forms of prebendal landownership in Asia provide the most significant sociological contrast with Europe in which political decentralisation and a feudal cavalry were dominant. *The Religion of China* and *The Religion of India* should, in this perspective, be read as two studies of those Asian structures which acted as limitations of or social brakes upon the extent of bureaucratic rationalisation. Weber is interested in the internal contradictions of patrimonialism and in the social limitations on the extent and effectiveness of centralised patrimonialism. In this interpretation, we can see that politics not religious beliefs provide the major division between East and West in Weber's sociology.

In the case of Islam, the land which became part of the Household of Islam was not redistributed in terms of feudal ownership, but was held as a prebendal right which was allocated by the state. In principle, this form of land distribution gives the royal landlord considerable power over his subordinates who do not enjoy rights of inheritance over land in return for military service. The political power of imperial landlords was greatly increased in the Ottoman system by the employment of mercenary armies and by a slave bureaucracy which were interposed between the royal family and the noble cavalry. This political system achieved an equilibrium in situations of outward expansion when surrounding states or empires were weak. Loyalty to the central authority depended on the availability of land, which permitted reigning sultans to buy off the contradictory claims of prebendal cavalries, bureacracies, mercenary armies and religious leaders. The sociological picture which Weber develops of Islam consists of a complex system of checks and balances between centralising and localising forces. Outward military expansion provided the financial resources for maintaining prebendal land control which limited the political importance of local landlords. The failure of territorial expansion produced an unstable system of political struggle between centre and periphery to which Weber gave the title of 'Sultanism'. The royal family becomes involved in internecine conflicts with bureaucrats, nobility and army commanders which give the whole patrimonial structure a decisive push towards arbitrary, *ad hoc* arrangements. In response to the fiscal crises, patrimonial states were subject to various processes which undermined centralised authority— these processes included tax-farming methods, feudalisation of land, the emergence of 'sub-empires' or local potentates and the conversion of the traditional status of the slave army. In this see-saw between strong centralising and decentralising forces, security of person and property could not be readily guaranteed. In Weber's view, property in many Islamic empires became immobilised in the form of religious endowments or *waqfs* rather than being invested productively. The patrimonial states of Islam were not only confronted by these internal checks; there was the perennial problem of tribal nomadism which place a powerful limitation on state power and urban stability. Technical problems of communication, transport and social control protected nomadic groups from political dominance by sedentarised society, especially in periods when the state was constrained by fiscal difficulties.

In his study of China, Weber perceives a similar political struggle between, on the one hand, the emperor who attempted to extend a universal administrative apparatus across the entire empire and, on the other hand, the system of guilds and lineages which resisted centralised control. It was the precarious balance between these two forces which gave China its ancient immobility. As with Islamic patrimonialism, the central authority sought to protect itself from its own officialdom by preventing the emergence of alternative interests and commitments. For example, Weber points out that by institutionalising competition between provinces, the patri-

monial state reduced the possibility of enduring provincial interests. In order to resist this institutionalised uncertainty,

> officialdom stood together as one man and obstructed as
> strongly as the tax payer every attempt to change the
> system of fee, custom, or tax payments. . . . Profit oppor-
> tunities were not individually appropriated by the highest
> and dominant stratum of officialdom; rather they were
> appropriated by the whole estate of removable officials. It
> was the latter who collectively opposed intervention and
> persecuted with deadly hatred any rational ideologist who
> called for 'reform'. (Weber, 1951, p. 60)

The traditionalism of Chinese imperial bureaucracies could be
shattered only by revolutions from above or below. Internal innovation perpetually came up against the obstacles of official
vested interest. Outside the bureaucracy 'patrimonial rule
from above clashed with the sibs' strong counterbalance from
below' (Weber, 1951, p. 86) and these local, lineage interests
limited all attempts at organisational and economic change if
they threatened lineage loyalties. Chinese villages were in fact
stockades for the protection of the sib from both government
interference and from rural brigands. These rural structures
also ruled out any possibility of the emergence of a free market
of individual labourers and of a work discipline. There were a
variety of causes—'mostly related to the structure of the state'
(Weber, 1951, p. 100)—which prevented capitalist development in China. These causes—the absence of systematic law,
autonomous cities, free burghers and free labour markets—are
ultimately located in the organisation of a patrimonial state.
The paradox of patrimonialism is that its success (in terms of
its own reproduction) depends on preventing officials from converting their benefices into hereditary rights, but these
preventive measures are also the origin of the ineffectiveness
and immobility of the administrative apparatus. It was the administrative weakness, not despotic power, of the patrimonial
state that stood in the way of capitalist rationality.

In *The Religion of India*, the theme of patrimonial rigidity is
less important than the analysis of the impact of Brahmanical

interests on ideological development. The issue of the state in relation to capitalism is nevertheless a necessary element of Weber's argument. The issues of prebendalisation arises, for example, in Weber's discussion of Islam in India in the period of the Mogul Empires (Mughal or Indo-Timuri period). Whereas in Europe the collapse of the Carolingian Empire gave rise to a feudal *seigneurie* linked to a lord by oath, in India the nobility grew out of tax-farming and military prebends of the bureaucratic state. In India, according to Weber, one finds the typical patrimonial see-saw between a centralising prebendalism and a decentralising feudalism. The limitations on political rationalisation and the ambiguities of Kshatriya status 'must be explained in terms of the political structure of India with its vacillation between fragmentation into innumerable petty kingdoms—originally simple chieftainships—and centralisation into patrimonial empires' (Weber, 1958b, p. 72). In periods of feudalisation kings were forced to rely on the traditional nobility; in periods of prebendalisation the kings utilised lower-class recruits to limit the political power of local nobles. While Indian state patrimonialism in Weber's model of political structures does act as a definite limitation on capitalist development, Weber treats the caste organisation of labour as the principal brake on capitalist rationalisation. Although within the workshop members of different castes could be organised in terms of a technical division of labour, it is improbable that 'the modern organisation of industrial capitalism would ever have *originated* on the basis of the caste system' (Weber, 1958b, p. 112), because the notion of ritual pollution did not encourage technical revolutions. However, this 'notion' does not arise out of thin air; it was part of a theodicean ideology of Brahmans which was developed to satisfy the interests flowing from their location in the social structure.

There is, therefore, an important continuity between Weber's comparative sociology and conventional Orientalism. Weber's sociology assumes a clear dichotomy between East and West; his problem was to provide an explanation of Occidental dynamism and Oriental stationariness. Weber's sociology took over the classical argument that the root condition of Oriental stagnation was the absence of inheritable, stable rights of property in land. Given this basic difference between the feu and the prebend, the Orient was simultaneously subject to perpetual political change and to a fundamental rigidity of structural possibilities. The see-saw motion between centre and perphery, prebendal and feudal forces, empire and sub-empire was the basis of political instabilities, but it never gave rise to a new principle of structural organisation which would have overcome these contradictions. By contrast, European societies did not have to cope in general terms with the problems of tribalism, sib organisation, peripheral nomadism or caste system. The history of the European state is very different from that of Oriental patrimonialism (Poggi, 1978).

Although Weber does take over much of the Orientalist viewpoint, there are also various aspects of Weber's comparative sociology which do not fit neatly and easily into the conventional framework of Orientalist scholarship. Prebendalism is not exclusively a term which is employed to describe Asian society. The word itself has an Occidental epistemological origin from *praebenda* (pension) and came to refer to cathedral revenues allocated to a canon as a stipend. Weber appropriates this ecclesiastical term to describe a form of land-ownership which, while prevalent in Asian societies, is found in Occidental societies. In *Economy and Society*, for example, Weber uses 'benefice' (*beneficium*, favour) interchangeably with 'prebend', analysing the feu/benefice distinction not as a rigid dichtomy, but as a fluid continuum applicable to the examination of land tenure in Turkey, Japan, Germany and France. In practice, it was often difficult to distinguish between benefice and feu where a powerful family would enjoy *de facto* hereditary claims over a benefice. This fluidity is acknowledged in Weber's references to 'the fief-benefice' and 'quasi-prebendal definition of the fief' in Turkey (Weber, 1968, vol. 3, p. 1079). The difference between Orient and Occident, therefore, appears to be that in feudalism there is an hierarchical organisation of knights who enjoy considerable autonomy, whereas in prebendalism there is a centralisation of power with formal limitations on noble autonomy. In feudalism, knights attempted to force the king to accept the fact that he is simply another landlord amongst equals. In pre-bendalism, knights want to convert their benefices into life-long feudal rights, and if necessary, to create their own peripheral sub-empires or petty kingdoms. The precise manner in which these political struggles were carried out also depended on a host of other circumstances—tribalism, sib organisation, city development, guild associations—which in turn were closely related to 'the structure of the state'. In short, Weber's comparative sociology had very little to do with the 'mentality' of Asian peoples and a great deal to do with the military and economic structures of Asiatic societies. In the last analysis, societies can be distinguished by the different methods which have been employed to keep men in arms—'the peculiarity of Occidental, fully developed feudalism was largely determined by the fact that it constituted the basis of a cavalry' (Weber, 1968, vol. 3, p. 1078).

Part four

Capitalism

10 Family, property and ideology

There is a well-established convention in sociology which sets out to contrast and oppose Weber and Marx in respect of their explanation of the character and origins of the capitalist mode of production. According to this convention, Weber locates the origins of capitalist production in the religious drive for salvation which paradoxically worked itself out in secular entrepreneurial activities. *The Protestant Ethic and the Spirit of Capitalism* is thus held to be the primary framework within which Weber's causal account is situated. The question of capitalist origins is in this respect centred on the issue of the historical nexus of primitive economic accumulation. Whereas Weber situates the original push towards capitalist production in the agonies of the Calvinistic soul, Marx finds the origins of capitalist wealth in the expropriation of peasants from the land and 'the history of this, their expropriation, is written in the annals of mankind in letters of blood and fire' (Marx, 1974, vol. 1, p. 669). It is further held by Marxists that in *Capital* we can find a critical parody of Weberian explanations when Marx pours scorn on Adam Smith and other political economists who attempt to explain capitalist accumulation in terms of moral asceticism and deferred gratification of present wealth. Marx presents the mythical 'anecdote' of capitalist origins by observing that, once upon a time, 'there were two sorts of people; one, the diligent, intelligent, and, above all, frugal elite; the other, lazy rascals, spending their substance, and more, in riotous living' (Marx, 1974, vol. 1, p. 667). In this mythical history, the diligent invest in future capitalist production, while the sinful squander their economic and genetic inheritance. Like Adam Smith, Weber is categorised as yet another exponent of the 'bourgeois myths of primitive accumulation' (Hindess and Hirst, 1975, p. 288).

Other sociologists have been more generous in their evaluation of the separate contributions of Marx and Weber to the history of capitalist origins (Giddens, 1970), but the predominant assumption is that the differences in interpretation between Marx and Weber are overwhelmingly more significant than the similarities. In the last analysis, Weber locates the origins of capitalism in certain key transformations of culture and individual motivation, whereas Marx concentrates on those class conflicts which lie at the root of agrarian capitalism. In this chapter, I outline a somewhat different approach to the problem by suggesting that what unites Weber and Marx is the basic assumption that feudalism and capitalism are radically different and discontinuous. Both sociologists accept the view that the transition between societies dominated by the feudal mode of production and the capitalist mode is *the* major historical transition, dwarfing all other historical transformations. Regardless of their disagreements about the origins of capitalism, they are united in their accounts of the effects of this unique historical discontinuity. By contrast, this chapter emphasises the major continuities between feudalism and capitalism in terms of the generation of economic investment through the mechanism of family and primogeniture. Marx and Weber both agree that the break between feudalism and capitalism is the central issue of world history and both are misguided in this critical area of analysis. In this chapter and in elaborations of this argument in my final chapter, I develop the argument that the historical discontinuities between feudalism and capitalism are far less significant sociologically than the discontinuities between early and late capitalism. In this respect, Marx and Weber are both typical representatives of the nineteenth-century theory of 'The Great Divide' between traditional and modern society, agrarian and industrial society, or feudal and capitalist society.

Dichotomous models of human society were very common amongst nineteenth-century social scientists. The most important location of these dichotomous models lies with the social theories of Henri de Saint-Simon who developed the imagery of a society based on technological innovation, bureaucratic management and state administration. Although it is true that both Saint-Simon and his disciple Auguste Comte conceptualised social history in terms of three stages, the most significant transformation was that taking place between feudal and industrial society and between theological and positivistic modes of thought (Fletcher, 1971). This basic contrast between theological/feudal and positivistic/industrial societies was further elaborated in a variety of sociological analyses in the nineteenth century. What they shared in common was the notion that industrial society required a new mode of interpretation and explanation. This new intellectual framework was given a variety of names - *'physique sociale'*, 'positivism' and 'sociology'. In Germany, Tönnies developed a contrast between organic will which found social expression in intimate, spontaneous communalism and reflective will which gave rise to abstract, artificial and mechanistic relationships. The typology of community and society (*Gemeinschaft* and *Gesellschaft*) subsequently became a basic and common conceptual tool of European social thought. Indeed, it has been claimed that:

> all the discussions on the opposition between competition and accommodation, conflict and association, cooperation and hostility, fusion and tension, integration and dissolution, solidarity and rivalry, communion and revolt, and all other forms of social concord and discord, bring us back, directly or indirectly to the work of Tönnies. (Freund, 1979, p. 153)

In France, Durkheim's analysis of mechanical and organic solidarity further developed and criticised the Comtean opposition between traditional and modern society. In England, Maine's distinction between status and contract and Spencer's contrast between military and industrial society gave theoretical expression to the general view that European society had been radically transformed by capitalist industrialisation.

Nineteenth-century social science was typically evolutionary in its conception of social change. Sociologists were, of course, perfectly aware of changes in the social structure of the classical world of Greece and Rome, of major developments in human consciousness in Renaissance Europe and of long-term transitions between, for example, Christianity and Judaism. The models which were developed to account for these changes did not inevitably assume a dichotomous form. The tripartite systems of Saint-Simon and Comte are cases in point. Nevertheless, it was commonly believed that *the* change in human history was the transition from pre-industrial to industrial society, from pre-capitalist modes of production to the capitalist mode. Indeed, the 'Great Transformation' (Kumar, 1978) of human history took place between 1789 and 1848 when the French Revolution and the Industrial Revolution unleashed the demographic transition, urbanism, the technical and social division of labour, political democracy, mass society, the modern state and global capitalism. Sociology was simultaneously the effect of these changes and the positivistic science which was developed to co-ordinate these powerful social processes (Nisbet, 1967).

The sociological theories of Marx and Weber were part of this intellectual tradition which took the 'Great Transformation' as its object of analysis. In the early writing of Marx and Engels we find a very clear appreciation of the dynamic aspects of the capitalist mode of production in relationship to the stationary nature of traditional societies. The logic of capitalist production requires a constant revolutionising of the technical basis of the labour process and consequently constant reorganising of the relations of production and the social superstructure. Relations of production act as a fetter on forces of production. Whereas the modern bourgeoisie are compelled to innovate, the preservation

> of the old modes of production in unaltered form, was, on the contrary, the first condition of existence for all earlier industrial classes. Constant revolutionizing of production, uninterrupted disturbance of all social conditions, everlasting uncertainty and agitation distinguish the bourgeois from all earlier ones (Marx and Engels, 1973, p. 70)

Capitalist relations liquidate the idyllic personal relationships of feudal society by reducing personal interactions to a mere 'cash nexus'. Capitalism radically simplifies the class structure by replacing complex relations between estates with direct class antagonism between capital and labour. With the development of capitalist society, the peasant is uprooted from the cosy intimacy of the village and the 'idiocy of rural life'. The factory replaces the village as a forcing-house of radicalism and class consciousness. It is also part of the logic of capital that it is forced to subdue other economies in an endless search for an economic surplus. Cheap capitalist commodities became the battering-ram which shattered Chinese isolation and exclusiveness. In this sense, capitalism created world history by subjecting all nations to a common logic which destroyed all local, particularistic cultures and economies. Capitalism

> produced world history for the first time, insofar as it made all civilised nations and every individual member of them dependent for the satisfaction of their wants on the whole world, thus destroying the former natural exclusiveness of separate nations. (Marx and Engels, 1974, p. 78)

The transition to capitalism is, therefore, totally unlike any previous historical transformation in the mode of production. Capitalism translates localised struggles between social groups into a global contest for world history which is inescapably consequential, not just for certain classes, but for the human species-being.

This conception of the historical uniqueness of the transition from feudalism to capitalism is even more pronounced in Weber's sociology than in Marx and Engels's analysis of the characteristics of capitalist production. For Weber, the advent of capitalism opened Pandora's box on a permanent basis. The emergence of the capitalist system was a fateful event setting off structural changes which cannot be reversed. When Weber describes this new world in terms of its specialisation of economic functions, he typically employs religious analogies.

Modern man has eaten from the tree of knowledge and cannot return to the enchanted garden because he now knows that the world is meaningless - there is no paradisal garden to which he might return. Pre-industrial society involved nature-like, unreflective social relationships, whereas the scientific consciousness of the modern world exposes the constructed and fictive aspect of all human interactions. Weber bitterly reflects on the fact that, while Abraham or some traditional peasant could die 'old and satiated with life' modern man can only die 'tired of life' (Weber, 1961). In Weber's analysis of this predicament, the transition from traditional to modern society has the same decisiveness as the transition from naivety to knowledge, or from grace to sinfulness. This is the central metaphysical theme that lies behind Weber's sociological conceptualisation of the rise of capitalist society. At the level of political organisation and legitimacy, the patrimonial and patriarchal systems based on charisma and tradition give way to the legal rationality of the bureaucratic apparatus. Public systems of organised religion are replaced either by indifference or by the *pianissimo* experiences of the private individual. The separation of the worker from the means of production is extended into the military, political and scientific spheres. The arbitrary or traditional pronouncements of lawmakers in pre-industrial society are replaced by systems of rationally organised and gapless law. In Weber's sociology, the transition from feudalism to capitalism was not some modest reorganisation of systems of property and exploitation. On the contrary, it involved changes of a cosmic significance for the human species.

Concerning the question of continuity and discontinuity of social forms between feudalism and capitalism, Weber does not, of course, entirely ignore the question of the family and economic structures. In volume one of *Economy and Society*, for example, we find a discussion of various types of descent groups in relation to property, especially women and land as property. There are a number of aspects to this discussion. In part, Weber merely intends to lay out, in a formal way, a number of basic definitions of extended family, nuclear and other kinship patterns as part of his general interest in establishing basic terminology in volume one. He also attempts to raise objections to evolutionary views by which marriage by abduction was seen as an intermediary stage between matriarchy and patriarchy. Anthropological schemes of this form are rejected outright as 'erroneous' and 'worthless'. Although Weber briefly recognises the importance among the landed aristocracy of inheritance systems which preserve property, he is principally concerned to deny that any single causal model can account for the diversity of relationships between kinship groups and property relationships. However, Weber does permit himself one very crucial generalisation, namely that the conditions for capitalist development were established in the medieval period by certain tendencies which separated the family from the firm. Indeed, it is 'the qualitative uniqueness of the development of modern capitalism' to separate the family from the economy in order to permit the rational calculation of economic activity (Weber, 1968, vol. 1, p. 380). For Weber, the role of the family as a source of wealth is regarded as a specifically pre-capitalist characteristic. Weber (1968, vol. 1, p. 380) lists the following conditions as necessary components of capitalist development:

> the separation of household and business for accounting
> and legal purposes, and the development of a suitable
> body of laws, such as the commercial register, elimination
> of dependence of the association and the firm upon the
> family, separate property of the private firm or limited
> partnership, and appropriate laws of bankruptcy.

The main feature of my argument about family and business organisations is that, specifically in British capitalist development, the family played a basic role as the major source of long-term credit for capitalist investment.

It could not be denied that European society and its satellites experienced massive structural and cultural changes under the dual impact of the French Revolution and the process of capitalist industrialisation. The problems to which Saint-Simon, Comte, Tönnies, Marx and Weber addressed themselves cannot be dismissed as purely imaginary.

However, contemporary historical research into such issues as wage-labour, religious adherence and the sexual division of labour has pointed to the problems of historical continuity between feudal and capitalist society. In this chapter, I want to explore the relationship between Marx and Weber through an analysis of the role of the family, monogamy and primogeniture in feudalism and capitalism. The aim here is to demonstrate the historical continuity of the family as a vehicle of private ownership of property for the dominant class in feudalism and competitive capitalism. These economic functions of the family are closely related to the social status of women in the system of marriage alliances in the dominant class and to the role of various moral ideologies relating to chastity, virginity and honour in both feudalism and capitalism. In taking this position, I am, of course, obliged to argue against the prevailing feminist assumption that capitalism creates the sexual subordination of women by separating the family from the economy, the home from the place of work. This assumption has been challenged by Middleton (1979) but his arguments are largely directed to the question of peasant women and the role of domestics in the household. In attempting to relate the system of primogeniture to the origins of capitalist society, the evidence assembled in this chapter refers predominantly to the dominant landowning and capitalist classes.

While Marx did not systematically concern himself with the social and economic functions of the family, Engels in *The Origins of the Family, Private Property and the State* provided an analysis of the subordination of women which has subsequently become a key text in Marxist theory. While I shall depend heavily on Engel's theory, I utilise his basic assumptions to arrive at very different conclusions, namely to stress the continuity of the family as a vehicle of property in traditional and capitalist society. Much of Engels's ethnography and historical evidence has been questioned and discarded (Aaby, 1977; Reiter, 1975), but Engels does present a powerful materialist theory of women and property which must be taken seriously. In particular, it is interesting to note that Engels places the reproduction of the species alongside the reproduction of a material life as the two fundamental forces of society in a materialist conception of history. The social arrangements 'under which men of a definite historical epoch live are conditioned by both kinds of production: by the stage of development of labour, on the one hand, and of the family, on the other' (Engels, n.d., p. 6). Engels attempts to examine these historical epochs by reference to different forms of the family and social role of women. The central point of these anthropological and historical considerations is to show the coincidence between the emergence of private property, the development of monogamous family structures and the subordination of women. The principal aim of monogamy is 'the begetting of children of undisputed paternity, this paternity being required in order that these children may in due time inherit their father's wealth' (Engels, n.d., p. 100). Monogamy is thus an expression of economic interests and parental authority rather than a 'natural' relationship between man and woman for their mutual help and pleasure. Because marriages among the dominant class are determined by possessions rather than by affection, monogamy also gave rise to the 'double standard' (Thomas, 1959). Mothers were expected to be sexually pure, respectable and chaste and, therefore, fathers were expected to be adulterous and to be middle-class clients for working-class prostitutes. In Engel's account of the family, prostitution is not an incidental feature of capitalism, but a necessary component of any marriage system based on economic interests.

Although a system of arranged marriages served the economic system of capitalism perfectly adequately, Engels believes that the development of capitalist relations also transformed marriage in certain important respects. The practice of arranged marriages contradicted the basic ideological emphasis of bourgeois individualism, contractual freedom and exchange between equals. There were additional religious principles from the Reformation which encouraged the development of freedom of choice in marriage. The bourgeois marriage was still a 'class marriage' but within the same class partners were free to select each other. While the ruling class continued to adhere to marriage as an economic contract, the rising bourgeoisie of Protestant Europe became the channel of voluntary marriages founded on romantic attachment. However, the liberation of women, the disappearance of sexual exploitation in and outside marriage and the termination of moral hypocrisy in the form of the 'double standard' can only be achieved by the abolition of capitalist production and the property relations produced by capitalism.

Engels's treatment of pre-capitalist societies makes it very clear that the economic basis of marriage and the subordination of women to men exist before the emergence of industrial capitalism. It can also be suggested that Engels recognises that, by comparison with arranged marriages among the feudal ruling class, the bourgeois marriage represents a voluntary form of matrimony. Subsequent analyses tended to treat capitalism as the principal or exclusive cause of female subordination and exploitation. August Bebel's *Die Frau und der Sozialismus* (1879) took Engels's argument further by suggesting a fundamental connection between the subordination of women and the general suppression of the proletariat in capitalism. The economic and artificial character of marriage was thus directly related to bourgeois capitalism in which the women of the dominant class were reduced to the level of 'a mere birthmachine for legitimate children'. For Bernard Shaw and the radical wing of the English Fabians, marriage became merely the product of capitalist society in which 'money controls morality' (Greiner, 1977). In contemporary discussions of capitalism and the subordination of women, this simple equation of property, marriage and capitalism has been largely retained. For example, Zaretsky (1976) recognises that capitalism had both progressive and regressive implications for the position of women in society. In the economic life of medieval England, women enjoyed a considerable equality with men in terms of their involvement in the labour process and in guild membership. With the advent of capitalism, the family has eventually differentiated from the economy and women were excluded from the market, being assigned to merely domestic roles. However, within the family their status was enhanced by the concept of the Puritan 'calling' in which domestic duties also had religious significance. Within the

Puritan household, women also did God's work and were regarded as partners in a common enterprise. However, with an increasing technical and social division of labour, the family ceased to have economic functions as the factory replaced the family as the principal unit of production. The result of these changes was that, among the bourgeoisie, the family 'was reduced to the preservation and transmission of capitalist property, while the productive function of the proletarian family lay in the reproduction of the labour force' (Zaretsky, 1976, p. 33). The pivotal period in Zaretsky's argument is the seventeenth century which inaugurates a series of processes leading to the domestication of women, their exclusion from economic roles outside the home and the equation of personal subjectivity with domesticity.

The argument which I want to develop is partly based on the assumptions of Engels, Zaretsky and others, but attempts to demonstrate that, among the dominant class, the functions of the family and women did not change in any essential manner in the transition from feudalism to agrarian and industrial capitalism. The accumulation of property in feudalism and capitalism depended on successful marriage alliances and these required the subordination of women to men and the patriarchal control of the younger generation in general. In order to secure property via stable channels of inheritance and to accumulate property through advantageous marriages, women had to be sexually loyal and fertile. The notion of women as 'birthmachines' of legitimate offspring applies to both feudalism and capitalism. Where inheritance took the form of primogeniture, or, more accurately, unigeniture, under a system of strict settlement, the dominant class required an ideology which was supportive of these property relations in its emphasis on filial loyalty, female chastity, virginity in daughters and duty amongst younger disprivileged siblings. There are not only ideological continuities between feudalism and capitalism, but, as we shall see, important continuities in the characteristic illnesses and sins of women and youth. The pivotal period is not the seventeenth but the late nineteenth century when the connection between wealth and family for the dominant class begins to change. Changes in the nature

and availability of divorce, the establishment of suitable occupations for middle- and upper-class women, the secularisation of marriage provide indications of these changes.
However, it is in late capitalism with the partial separation between ownership and control, the rise of depersonalised property and the development of state intervention directly in production that the family ceases to be the major channel of
capitalist accumulation. The ideological system of late
capitalism consequently takes an entirely different character
as moral and religious controls no longer have an economic
base in the family and production. The social freedom which
Engels envisaged for women under socialism is already anticipated by women of the dominant class in late capitalism
although not for women among the working class. The family
is no longer required to be the vehicle of personal productive
property by the logic of late capitalism, but, as we will see
shortly, there may be considerable contingent variations between different late capitalist societies.

This argument about the continuities in the functions of the
family for the dominant class is based on the assumption that
the institution of unigeniture has been a major factor in the
economic organisation and development of European societies.
I shall start the presentation of the empirical evidence for
these assertions with a classic study of the French feudal
nobility by George Duby (1978). In *Medieval Marriage*, Duby
draws a distinction between two marriage systems in twelfth-
century France, namely a lay or secular model and the formal,
ecclesiastical view of marriage and the family. The principal
aim of the lay model was the maintenance of the social order by
the provision of a flow of legitimate males to conserve property
in a system of primogeniture and a supply of daughters to
create political alliances between feudal families. Given the
high rates of infant mortality and other threats to the continuity of particular families, marriage strategies were necessarily
precarious and uncertain. The lay system required loyal sons,
virgin daughters and fertile mothers. Within this context of
demographic and economic restraints, there was a clear
tendency towards endogamy because cross-cousin marriage
which prevented an infinite division of property over time pro-

vided an opportunity for re-amalgamation of previously divided property. A narrow definition of incest on the part of the clergy, therefore, was incompatible with the economic interests of the dominant class.

The Church's teaching in regard to the religious value of virginity, filial duty and fertility, on the one hand, and the total disgrace of premarital sexual experience and adultery, on the other, perfectly coincided with the economic requirements of the landlord. However, in one crucial area the lay and ecclesiastical models were in radical disagreement. While the Church treated marriage as a life-long, monogamous, matrimonial contract, the lay model required an effective method for repudiating wives who turned out to be barren or who produced only female offspring or who were unable to replace male offspring who had died in childhood. For the Church, marriage was a necessary, if regrettable, institution to protect society against human sinfulness; remarriage and repudiation were unacceptable. The only case for repudiation was to be found in the contamination of the conjugal union by incest or fornication. However, since the lay system encouraged endogamous unions, there were numerous grounds on which the validity of these unions could be challenged. Incest thus provided the pretext for the repudiation of a barren wife. Under pressure from the landowning class and embarrassed by the scandal of false witnesses and bogus litigation, the Church was forced to change its definition of incest in order to stabilise the marriage system.

If barren wives were one source of tension, then other problems were created by the surplus of younger sons who could not inherit and were consequently disqualified from marriage to women of their own social class. This 'reserve army' of uncommitted bachelors became the principal audience for courtly love poetry which celebrated the pleasures of adulterous life and converted sexual pleasure into a religious doctrine (Lewis, 1936). These unattached 'youths' formed casual alliances with peasant women and with the household concubines who were a regular feature of these feudal families. The unruly behaviour of uncommitted males who were referred to as the 'youth' regardless of their age provided a strong moral contrast to the spotless, honourable and respectable behaviour of elder sons.

The role of youth in feudal society offers an interesting falsification of the popular sociological doctrine that youth as a category of unattached, rebellious males is specifically the product of modern industrial society (Eisenstadt, 1956).

The values of male honour and female chastity were components of the wider cultural system of feudal chivalry. Noble birth was regarded as the real basis of knighthood, because only true-born sons would be brave and courageous in defence of the family and its property. Cowards were thought to be the offspring of covert unions between noble ladies and their varlets. False men were produced by confusion of blood. Feudal regulations relating to the seduction or rape of noble women were consequently draconian and an illegitimate pregnancy would rob a noble daughter of her part of the family inheritance. All of these feudal norms were aimed at securing the concentration of property in a line of legitimate male offspring whose lives were intended to exemplify the full doctrine of male chivalry (Ossowska, 1971).

The institutions of concubinage and court prostitution gave social expression to the fact that men characteristically satisfied their sexual needs outside the conjugal union. The literary themes of courtly love poetry paradoxically recognised that marriage existed for procreation and the routine distribution of wealth whereas sexual love was by definition an extramarital activity. The aristocratic concept of mutual affection between unmarried men and women was underlined by the fact that peasant women were merely sexual objects. In his treatise on love, Andrew the Chaplain took it for granted that the virtues which constituted the ethos of courtly love were not present in people of low birth. The temptation to rape peasant women should not be resisted since the courteous approach would not be appreciated by peasants.

Social attitudes towards women of the noble class were modified by the outlook of theologians who in the fourteenth and fifteenth centuries became increasingly preoccupied with the role of the subjective conscience rather than with objective laws and by the troubadours who treated women as mutual partners of men rather than their natural subordinates (Chenu, 1969). However, the most significant changes were brought about by the economic and military decline of the class of feudal warriors. Thus, the invention of gunpowder in 1313 and the increasing use of infantry were important historical stages in the social demise of the noble man-at-arms. In England, the last attempt to raise an army through a feudal levy of forty days' service was in the fourteenth century and the sale of titles of nobility to social strata outside the traditional military elite diminished the conventional notions of the knight as a noble warrior. As Anderson (1974) points out, after the Hundred Years' War, the demilitarisation of the nobility gained momentum and by the time of Elizabeth's reign only half the nobility had any significant military experience. These structural changes within the nobility were associated with the economic transition towards agrarian capitalist relations with the growth of the wool trade. With the development of English colonialism, a standing army became much less important than a strong navy (Moore, 1969).

These changes in English social structure resulted in the 'obsolescence of the concept of honour' (Berger, 1973), but they did not fundamentally change the economic role of the family in the dominant class and women retained their social roles as 'birthmachines' in the marriage system. In his study of the Cecils, Earls of Salisbury, in the period 1590 to 1733, Stone (1973) identifies the central responsibility of the head of the household in terms of economic necessity, namely 'to preserve, or perhaps increase, the family inheritance, and to ensure its continuity by producing a healthy male heir' (p. xvi). These economic objectives are frequently thwarted by over indulgence in luxurious consumption, by excessive fertililty or alternatively by total sterility. The preservation of family fortunes depended on 'the strict settlement; efficient but conservative estate administration; a subordination of personal choice to financial advantage in the selection of marriage partners; avoidance of addiction to horses, cards, dice and women; and a prudent policy of family limitation (Stone, 1973, p. 160). The history of the Cecils provides a detailed illustration of the wider consequences of a prudent family policy in the context of primogeniture, monogamy and private property. The presence of primogeniture and impartibility of inheritance are associated with a manorial system of land tenure and feudal military obligations. In England, for example, primogeniture developed after the Norman conquest with the introduction of military tenures. Of course, the impartibility which is secured by unigeniture can be provided by either primogeniture or ultimogeniture. Primogeniture had the effect of delaying the marriage of the eldest son where inheritance was connected with marriage, while ultimogeniture carried with it the danger of regency where the youngest son was under age. Both forms of inheritance served the economic interests of land-ownership and accumulation of wealth, but created problems of distribution and justice for siblings (Goody, 1978).

In the debates about the merits of partibility and impartibility which occupied lawyers between 1500 and 1700, there was a clear recognition that, whatever the moral arguments in favour of egalitarian patterns of inheritance, the economic and political reasons for primogeniture were clear and decisive. Partibility undermined large estates and thereby weakened the political control of the dominant class. Primogeniture was not only the means of preserving large estates from division, but also a system of inheritance which contributed to the existence of a politically and socially coherent ruling class. David Powell's translation of the *History of Cambria* in 1584 argued that adherence to primogeniture in England had produced beneficial political effects whereas in Wales, where partibility had been more common, the nobility had been undermined. Thirsk (1978) notes that in the debates on inheritance in the seventeenth century, the view emerged that the stability of the Commonwealth depended on the continuity of wealthy families on the basis of primogeniture, but younger sons had a right to expect assistance in a professional or business calling. It may be, therefore, that English primogeniture drove younger sons into trade and industry with the financial support of their families and contributed to the familial penetration of industrial capitalism by agrarian capitalist landlords. Primogeniture was certainly seen to be a necessary facet of class mobility and was adopted by yeomen in the eighteenth century and by the middle class in the nineteenth.

The implications of inheritance laws for capitalist development and the class structure of Britain can be clearly seen in the eighteenth century when there was a definite movement towards strict settlement and a greater concentration on the economic organisation of the marriage market. By the adoption of the legal device of trustees to preserve contingent remainders, the landowner was able to gain far greater legal certainty that the estate would pass to his eldest son without division. Under conditions of strict settlement, land was settled on the father for life and with his death on his first and other sons. The landlord could now guarantee that the estate would remain intact until the male child of the marriage of his own son reached maturity. The estate could no longer be damaged by bequests to younger children. The effect of the spread of strict settlement on younger sons is particularly interesting since they

> obtained their patrimony in a form which enabled them, even if it did not induce them, to supplement it in some profession. The pressure to obtain jobs, which is so central a feature of the English political system in the later seventeenth and the eighteenth century, derived much of its strength from this change. (Habakkuk, 1950, p. 20)

Furthermore, strict settlement provided the legal conditions for long-term marrige strategies and this system, not only checked the tendency towards division in each generation, but positively contributed to economic accumulation—'a wealthy marriage in one generation put a family in a stronger position to make another in the next generation' (Habakkuk, 1950, p. 29). The enlargement of estates, the drift of younger sons into professions and marital alliances between rich heiresses from the merchant class and debt-ridden sons of the nobility involved a clear recognition that the economic motives behind marrige were greater than any consideration of mutuality and affection between bride and groom. Whereas Engels assumed that, as capitalism developed, freedom of choice of marriage partners would be enlarged, the opposite trend appears to be characteristic of both the landlord and bourgeois classes.

In the nineteenth century, the middle class also perceived the obvious economic advantages associated with primogeniture, late marriage, controlled fertility and professional employment for younger sons if the prosperity of the family were to be safeguarded. While the historical evidence is ambiguous (Marcus, 1966; Pearsall, 1969), there are good reasons for believing that the period from 1770 to 1870 was characterised by sexual repression, an emphasis on social respectability and strict control of women and children in a patriarchal system of authority. With improvements in urban sanitation and child care, with the decline in the practice of fostering out (Shorter, 1977), infant mortality rates declined sharply in the nineteenth century creating a more child-centred domestic environment. The availability of more effective contraceptives permitted upper and middle class families to plan their fertility more exactly and predictably. These social developments were combined with a new emphasis on the importance of religious control under the auspices of Evangelicals and Methodists as a necessary feature of social and political stability. Within this broad social framework, the 'subordination of women and the crushing of sexual and autonomous drives of children took place in a situation where the total emotional life of all members was almost entirely focused within the boundaries of the nuclear family' (Stone, 1979, p. 423). The combination of domestic sentiment and sexual repression within the nuclear family gave rise to heightened anxieties about female sexuality and deviance. We can learn a great deal about the nature of Victorian repression by examining the forms of deviance and illness which become 'popular' in the nineteenth century.

The idea that women were especially prone to hysterical paroxysm perfectly matched the general conceptions Victorians held about the physical and emotional character of dependent females. In the 1880s, female hysteria was often treated by surgical removal of the ovary or clitoris (Szasz, 1977). Women were prone to fits of sobbing, giggling, tittering, fainting and other embarrassing outbursts. These symptoms of female status were a justification for male surveillance of their womenfolk and also a warning for men to be on guard against female whimsicality. From Brudenell Carter's *On the Pathology and Treatment of Hysteria* in 1853 to *Studies in*

Hysteria by Freud and Breuer in 1893, we find a common theory that women are more emotionally and sexually charged than men and hence require greater social control and sexual repression. Their hysterical outbursts are the psychological responses to social and biological contradictions. These female difficulties were intensified in the middle class by demographic and social changes which had the consequence of delaying marriage and created the prospect of 'female redundancy' (Skultans, 1979). Early marriage came to be regarded as imprudent for men who sought professional advancement and a secure income. However, popular psychological theories of women suggested that women required marriage to satisfy their sexuality in socially legitimate ways and to avoid the pernicious effects of menstruation. Given the decline in the age at which women reached menarche among the middle class in the Victorian period (Laslett, 1973; Tanner, 1962), sexually mature women were thought to be caught in a social impasse between biology and social circumstance. Those women in the middle class who sought social status through education and who thereby deliberately delayed marriage were thought to be dangerously exposed to the pathological threats of menstruation, over-excitement and hysteria. Reasons of health and psychological stability required women to stay at home in anticipation of a prudent marriage and eventual, but limited, pregnancies.

The interest in female hysteria in Victorian Britain provides support for Stone's argument that sexual repression of women and children increased dramatically in response to anxieties about social stability. However, over a longer period, we can see that hysteria, melancholy and depression have been continuously ascribed to women by male physicians, psychiatrists and philosophers. Indeed, historical research shows that the beliefs about feminine vulnerability and 'about feminine nature are relatively unchanging. For this reason it is not easy to relate beliefs about feminine nature to social and historical changes ' (Skultans, 1979, p. 77). In the seventeenth century as in the nineteenth, women were treated as peculiarly subject to vapours and melancholy; their menstrual blood gave rise to fits of weeping, complaining and foolish discontent. Richard

Burton in *The Anatomy of Melancholy* (1621) observed that, while economically active working men rarely suffered from distressing melancholy, gentlewomen who were idle typically fell prey to distempers. The remedy advocated by Burton depended upon disciplines of work and religion. While recent literature on the social position of women has claimed that capitalism forced women out of economic roles confining them to the isolation of the nuclear family, we find evidence in popular seventeenth-century psychology that for 'noble virgins, nice gentlewomen' solitary idleness produced women's malady. There is, therefore, in Skultan's view a continuity of feminine illness across different historical and social situations. It is interesting to note that the sexual division of mental illness is still regarded as characteristic of social circumstances in the twentieth century when clinical depression is overwhelmingly present among unemployed, working-class, urban mothers., The melancholy of idle aristocratic women in Stuart England reappears under the title of 'depression' among working-class women in contemporary Britain (Brown and Harris, 1978).

While women were giggling and fainting, Victorian boys were suffering from spermatorrhoea and masturbatory insanity. The warning against these dire complaints had been sounded as early as 1710 with the publication of *Onania, or the Heinous Sin of Self-Pollution* by an anonymous clergyman. The anxiety over self-pollution did not become widespread until the 1840s and 1850s, and found its medical culmination in William Acton's *The Functions and Disorders of the Reproductive Organs* in 1865. Whereas seventeenth-century theologians were mildly disapproving, nineteenth-century physicians were adamant that masturbation produced innumerable disorders of the body and mind, including 'headache, backache, acne, indigestion, blindness, deafness, epilepsy and, finally, death' (Skultans, 1979, p. 73). As the age of marriage increased and the age of puberty declined, anxieties about the social control of sexuality in adolescence developed as masturbation and prostitution were regarded as the principal channels of deviant satisfaction. In addition, middle-class parents had now to worry about the perversions which might be encouraged by single-sex boarding schools and university colleges. Homosexuality was added to the list of social dangers which plagued Victorian respectability.

If the period from 1770 to 1870 is regarded as a high-water-mark of patriarchal control and sexual repression, the period from 1870 to 1980 is treated by sociologists and historians as the epoch of mounting permissiveness. Love, romance and sexual compatibility replaced the economic interests of parents as the basis for matrimony. While the average age of menarche has now fallen to thirteen years, in the 1960s 40 per cent of girls married under the age of twenty-one. Legalised abortion and the provision of contraceptives by prescription has removed at least some restraints on premarital sexuality (Schofield, 1965). The emphasis on domesticity, child care, breast-feeding, romance and sexual happiness accompanied the separation of the nuclear family from its communal ties (Shorter, 1977). Youth culture, adolescent autonomy, public concern over juvenile delinquency and adolescent breakdown and the growth of teenage consumerism are regarded as evidence that, within the nuclear family, the social linkage between parents and their children has been broken. While the world of rock music still reflects the greater freedom enjoyed by teenage boys but not by girls (Frith, 1978), and while the occupational opportunities for women are much less than they are for men, much of the cultural and institutional apparatus of parental and male control over children and women has either been dismantled or curtailed. In theology the death of God, in sexuality subjective experience, and in morality pluralism have replaced both the certainties and anxieties of an earlier period. In modern societies in general, the ideological coherence of a society founded on private ownership, parental authority and arranged marriages has given way to a society which is largely incoherent at the level of culture and ideology: we now live in a society dominated by the 'pluralization of life-worlds' (Berger, Berger and Kellner, 1973). The explanation for this pluralism and permissiveness has been sought in such general processes as secularisation and urbanisation, industrialisation and democratisation. In my view, these cultural changes have to be located in the specific relationship between property, family and ideology in the transition from early to late capitalism. One concrete example of this thesis can be found in the changes in divorce laws and the general explanation of these social changes is to be sought in the switch from family capitalism to institutional investment for capital accumulation.

Because the Victorian upper-class marriage was a 'dynastic' settlement between families aimed at the consolidation of property, divorce involved the reorganisation of legal contracts and division of estates. Life-long matrimony was the counterpart of primogeniture. Consequently, divorce was a very rare occurrence in Victorian times. Between 1861 and 1865, for example, there were only 226 petitions for divorce, or a divorce rate of 0.83 per ten thousand married women between the ages of fifteen and forty-nine. While marriage was regarded as indissoluble, it was possible for the wealthy to obtain divorce through the purchase of a private Act of Parliament. However, divorce laws were based on the notion of 'matrimonial offence' which required proof of legal guilt and radical newspapers used uncensored divorce proceedings as material for attacking the nobility and royal family. Divorce thus threatened marriage partners both in terms of economics and reputation. Changes in public opinion and pressure from the middle class to reduce the costs of divorce proceedings resulted in a series of Matrimonial Causes Acts from 1857 onwards. In administrative terms, the jurisdiction of the ecclesiastical courts was transferred to the high court where the rich could obtain a licence to remarry and to the magistrates' courts where the poor could receive maintenance (McGregor, 1957). These legal changes in the last century have not entirely equalised the legal status of marriage partners or removed the stigma associated with divorce (Nicky Hart, 1976). The presence of a legal mechanism for divorce and the rapid increase in the rate of divorce do, however, represent a fundamental change in the character of the family as a social institution. In particular, 'when in the latter part of the nineteenth century land began to yield place to capital as the predominant source of wealth and social prestige, dynastic marriages lost much of their importance' (Rowntree and Carrier, 1958, p. 196). However, since in the

British economy of the nineteenth century industrial invest-ment was funded by the family capital unit rather than by banks, it is not quite correct to suggest that the principal change was from land to capital. The principal changes occur-red rather later when 'family capitalism' was replaced by the large corporation (Bell, 1965).

In the early decades of British industry, short-term credit re-quirements were usually secured through local banks or mer-cantile credit, but long-term credit remained a problem before changes took place in the regulations controlling the issue of shares on the Stock Exchange. Future investment could be financed by the 'plough-back' of existing profits but this con-cept cannot explain the sources of orginal capital accumula-tion. In the eighteenth century, the most important source of capital was from mortgages raised on freehold property so that close kinship connections represented a major business asset: 'Eighteenth-century business flourished as a face-to-face so-ciety of friends, cousins and business associates. This world of personal contact by kinship and friendship was often the first resource for cash' (Mathias, 1969, p. 150). Social networks based on kinship and religion were thus the main source of long-term finance before the existence of a system of effective, na-tional banking and share provision. However, even after the Joint Stock Companies Acts of 1856 and 1862, limited com-panies accounted for less than ten per cent of the most impor-tant business organisations by the 1880s (Payne, 1974). We should not, therefore, underestimate the continuing impor-tance of 'dynastic marriage' well into the late nineteenth cen-tury. Indeed, one of the few constant facts among the very wealthy in Victorian Britain was the ownership of land. Rubenstein (1974, p. 148) demonstrates, by an examination of the Somerset House records, that 'until about 1890, more than half of all really wealthy men in Britain were landowners'. Although younger sons were usually well provided for by the distribution of wealth after settlement, primogeniture con-tinued to play an important role in the preservation of prop-erty; 'Among the solitary sons of millionaires, there is a clear tendency toward keeping the fortune intact, with a certain tendency, in the few cases that are known, toward primogeniture among the grandsons' (Rubenstein, 1974, pp. 155, 160). Whereas strict settlement in the eighteenth century forced younger sons to supplement their inherited portions by professional incomes, a tendency towards more equal distribution of property in the family in the nineteenth century may account for the 'Buddenbrook syndrome' by which third generation businessmen abandoned their factories for more cultivated pursuits (Payne, 1974, p. 27). It is certainly the case that the decline of kinship as the principal source of long-term credit was marked by the increasing separation of private ownership of productive capital from managerial control.

In the early decades of the twentieth century, it was thought that an entirely new form of capitalism - 'People's Capitalism' - had emerged as public corporations replaced family concerns and as ownership of shares became democratised. Under the impact of 'the managerial revolution' (Burnham, 1945), a massive reorganisation of the property-owning class and its social functions had taken place. These prophetic pronouncements on the future of capitalism have been consistently challenged by Marxists. Regardless of any institutional divisions between owners and managers, it is obviously the case that there still exist massive inequalities in wealth in British society (Atkinson, 1974; 1975) and these inequalities have given weight to the argument that private property remains the most significant feature of contemporary society (Westergaard and Resler, 1975). Despite the wider distribution of shares in the general population, the 'small investor' has little control over the majority of companies when shares are concentrated in a few hands. The notion that the property-owning class has been replaced by a plurality of elites is also questioned by the fact that property and power are held by a small group which is integrated by common interests, expectations and education (Miliband, 1969).

If the theory of 'Peoples' Capitalism' appears to be an exaggerated view of the separation of ownership and control, the counter-claim that *no* major changes have occurred which would allow us to treat late capitalism as very different from competitive capitalism also appears to be over-stated. In late capitalism, the state is no longer external and incidental to the process of capital accumulation, but internal and necessary. The state exists not merely to discipline labour, but to provide crucial economic functions in the reorganisation of capital, the financing of research and development, and, through nationalised industries, the provision of basic services and productive capacity. There has also taken place, on the one hand, a concentration of industrial production by large corporations and, on the other, an internationalisation of capitalism through the growth of multi-nationals (Barratt Brown, 1974). These structural changes have also been associated with the decline of the individual investor and the growth of institutionalised investment through unit trusts, pension funds and insurance companies (Erritt and Alexander, 1977). The British economy is thus characterised by neither family ownership nor by management control but rather by a situation where companies are controlled by a 'constellation of interests' form of company control that arises where 'effective possession is an attribute of the major shareholders collectively, yet this constellation of ownership interests has no unity and little possibility of concerted action' (Scott, 1979, p. 41). While there is no absolute separation of ownership and control, there is a definite trend towards the depersonalisation of property and financial wealth. The family firm is squeezed out of industrial production and only retains importance in the area of retail and transportation. Where a member of the founding family acquires a place on the board of directors of companies which have gone public, this if often on the sufferance of the major shareholders. The general position is that there is a movement from

'personal possession' by particular families and interests to 'impersonal possession' through an interweaving of ownership interests which breaks down the direct link between particular interests and particular companies. Correspondingly strategic control has shifted from private, majority ownership to control through a constellation of interests. (Scott, 1979, p. 60)

These changes in the forms of property ownership and in the

nature of the dominant class have important consequences at the level of ideology and family relationships. In a society organised around primogeniture, strict settlement and the dynastic marriage, it is important for parents to exercise moral and religious control over their offspring along with the threat of disinheritance. Doctrines of chivalry and honour, prudence and respectability were important props in the system of patriarchal authority. In such a society, the dominant ideology works to integrate the dominant class and to preserve the property of the class. Intra-class marriages also welded the class together by the exclusion of competing groups. With the depersonalisation of property, these ideologies no longer have social significance outside that fraction of the dominant class which still possesses large estates. This is not to say that upper- or middle-class parents no longer exercise control or influence over the marriages of their children. For the majority, however, 'prudence' involves the purchase of suitable forms of education rather than a suitable bride. The old ideologies of religion are consequently replaced by 'professionalism' and 'credentialism' as methods of maintaining exclusive class boundaries and securing intra-class solidarity (Parkin, 1979). The transition from competitive to late capitalism has not brought about a new form of democratic ownership but it does involve the collapse of the family as the major source of long-term financing, the depersonalisation of property and the dominance of the large corporation. These socio-economic changes have broken the necessary connection between family, ideology and property.

There are, therefore, certain important continuities between feudalism and capitalism since in both cases the family continued to be the main channel through which property was distributed and relations of production were maintained. The stability of wealth in the ownership of land in feudalism required a system of settlement by unigeniture which in turn gave rise to the importance of virginity in daughters, chastity in wives and loyalty in sons. With the rise of industrial capitalism, there was no essential change in these basic requirements since, in Britain at least, the family continued to be the channel by which capital was raised for investment purposes. Although these ideologies and institutions were primarily important in the dominant class, the middle classes came to ape much of this cultural baggage of the aristocracy and industrial bourgeoisie. Professional careers required prudent alliances with respectable women. The social constraints on women in both feudalism and capitalism gave rise to common forms of mental disturbance in the form of 'melancholy' and 'hysteria', while depression amongst middle-class women in late capitalism became relatively uncommon. Similarly, the problem of youth is not exclusively a feature of industrial capitalism since uncommitted, unmarried and landless youth was a social category generated by feudal forms of inheritance. In certain critical respects, therefore, the idea of the 'great transformation' exaggerates the differences between traditional and industrial society in the same way that Marxist notions of the transformation of the feudal mode of production concentrates our attention on historical discontinuities at the expense of major continuities. The social bridge between both worlds is the patriarchal domination of women and children.

There is in Weber's sociology, therefore, a theoretical blind spot concerning the social functions of the family in relation to the economy and the social role of women. While Weber was specifically concerned with patriarchy and patrimonialism in pre-capitalist society, he does not, in his theoretical analysis and empirical studies, concern himself with the questions of matriarchy and matriarchalism. In volume one of *Economy and Society*, the few pages devoted to this subject are mainly concerned with denying that the concepts of 'matriarchy' and '*Mutterecht*' have any scientific validity in sociological analysis. However, the problem of eroticism in society and history does play a central part in Weber's perspective. In general terms, Weber thinks that the social control of sexual desire is a necessary condition for the institutionalisation of rationality. Eroticism is thus associated with magic and mysticism. The importance of religions of renunciation is to control the libido in order to channel human (and, in practice, male) activity towards world-mastery and accumulation in this world. In terms of world religions, Weber implies that, for example, the limitations of Islamic rationality are connected with its failure to develop an unambiguous anti-erotic ethic (Turner, 1974). In Asia, the emotive and feminine appeal of Taoism and Mahayana Buddhism is contrasted unfavourably with 'the proud, masculine, rational and sober spirit of Confucianism, similar to the mentality of the Romans [which] struggled against interference in the guidance of the state when such interference was based upon the hysterical excitation of women given to superstition and miracles' (Weber, 1951, p. 203).

It is in the Protestant sects that Weber finds the most decisive form of anti-erotic religious control of sexual relationships. Economic accumulation has an elective affinity with an ascetic religious ideology which encourages sexual saving as the counterpart of delayed consumption. In *The Protestant Ethic and the Spirit of Capitalism*, Benjamin Franklin's *Advice to a Young Tradesman* is taken as 'the *summum bonum* of this ethic' which is 'above all completely devoid of any eudaemonistic, not to say hedonistic, admixture' (Weber, 1965, p. 53). Franklin's outlook on sexual gratification involved a hygienic utilitarianism which understood 'by chastity the restriction of sexual intercourse to the amount desirable for health' (Weber, 1965, p. 263). The irony was that, in his personal life, Franklin exhibited precisely the opposite characteristics, namely hedonistic enjoyment of wine, women and song (Kolko, 1961).

The contradictions between matriarchy and enjoyment, patriarchy and renunciation, also played an ironic role in Weber's own development. The oddity of Weber's theoretical blind-spot is that, while his background was firmly rooted in German bourgeois patriarchialism, he was in various ways connected with the reformist, liberal wing of the Women's Movement. Weber encouraged his wife to lead an independent and active intellectual career, and was instrumental in securing a job as factory inspector for Else von Richthofen, the subsequent wife of Edgar Jaffé. Max and Marianne Weber read Bebel's book on *Women and Socialism* in 1893, encouraging her to attend his lectures on political economy and philosophy. Weber added his voice to the feminist critique of prostitution and the 'double standard' in relations between men and women. In the area of theoretical statement and personal outlook, however, Weber's life is riddled with contradiction. The views of Marianne Weber and Else Jaffé on feminism were very much dominated by Weber's own position that the escape from patriarchalism was through a scientific calling. Else Jaffé's 'mode of rebellion against patriarchal oppression was always very much his (Weber's) and Heidelberg's—that is, liberal, reformist, legal, intellectual' (Green, 1974, pp. 16-17). Weber condemned the *Mutterschutz* gang as 'an utterly confused bunch' and rejected what he regarded as the illegitimate equation of women's rights with hedonism and sexual freedom. Weber's ambivalence towards sexuality was the product of conflicts between his own parents, the termination of his relationship with Emmy Baumgarten, his negative attitude towards sexuality with Marianne Weber and his competitive relationship with Alfred Weber. The conflicts in these social connections were the immediate backcloth to his neurotic breakdown in 1899 (Mitzman, 1970).

The point of this concluding biographical comment is not to suggest that Weber's sociological concerns can be reduced to psychological problems or that Weber's views on patriarchalism are invalidated by the absence of a theory of matriarchy. The main focus of this chapter has been to criticise both Marx and Weber for neglecting certain institutional continuities between feudal and early capitalist society. However, to use the language of structuralism, this 'silence' in Weber's text rings loud with theoretically unresolved issues in Weberian sociology.

11 Weber and the sociology of law

In the sociology of law, there have been two major ways of interpreting Marx and Engel's observations on the relationship between law and society. In the instrumentalist perspective, law is regarded as a simple tool of economic repression of the subordinate class which directly serves the interests of the dominant class in the class structure. In the fetishism interpretation, the form of law mediates the social relations of society which are produced by the relations of production. Through the notions of 'rule of law' and 'individual subjects' under the law, legal norms interpellate human agents as free and equal citizens before the law with the effect of masking the basic inequalities of agents under economic circumstances. In the first interpretation, the law is directly subject to the economic structure and appears as epiphenomenal. In the second interpretation, the notion of 'fetishism' is used to suggest a parallel between the commodity form and the legal form and consequently the relationship between economy and law takes on a far more complex and indirect connection. In developing his sociology of law, Weber was aware of the first but not the second dimension of the materialist conception of legal relationships. While Weber was aware that the materialist interpretation of society had 'gone through many a version from the *Communist Manifesto* up to the modern acolytes' (Albrow, 1975-6, p. 138), he took the Marxist theory of law to be a strong argument that law is determined by economic relations of production. Weber's sociology of law must, therefore, be understood as a rejection, on the one hand, of economic determinism and, on the other, a refutation of the sort of legal idealism represented by Rudolf

318

Stammler's *Economy and Law according to the Materialist Conception of History. A Social Philosophical Investigation* of 1856.

Weber provides a number of objections to the economic reductionism which he thinks is the crucial component of the Marxist treatment of law. For Weber, law relates to the economic in a variety of different and complex directions which cannot be reduced to a simple deterministic formula. It is relevant here to bear in mind Weber's general reaction to what he took to be the conceptual vagueness of the idea of 'the economic' in Marxist materialism. In *Economy and Society*, Weber objects to the conflation of what is 'economically relevant' and what is 'economically determined'. While the law of contract might be economically relevant to the functioning of the capitalist mode of production, it does not follow that laws of labour contract are thus economically determined. The metaphor of base and superstructure fails to capture the complexity of historically contingent relations between law and economic structures. Weber goes on to make the stronger claim that certain types of law-making, in terms of rational, logical procedures, may actually be, to use modern parlance, a condition of existence of economic arrangements. The contractual stability which is offered by a rational system of gapless laws may in fact be necessary prerequisite of the economic profitability of the capitalist enterprise in situations of market anarchy. Hence Weber's sociology of law is simply part of his larger concern with the comparative conditions which are necessary for the rise of modern industrial capitalism. Finally, Weber points out that, while law certainly does develop in response to the economic interests of capitalist employers as legal clients, law also develops in terms of the interests of lawyers as a status group of professionals within the class structure. The professional interests of lawyers need not automatically coincide with the economic and political interests of their feudal or capitalist clientele. The development of legal training as part of the tactics of social closure of the legal profession may push the law in directions which cannot be regarded as a direct outcome of the economic interests of the dominant class. Thus, it makes a considerable difference to the form and content of law whether lawyers are trained in a guild system or in university law faculties. The organisational structure of the legal profession in terms of collegial or patronage arrangements (Johnson, 1972) is part of the political structure of clients and experts which may operate in a relatively independent direction from purely economic constraints.

While Weber wants to avoid the theoretical simplicity of the instrumentalist version of law, he also attempts to avoid the mirror-image problems of the idealist conception of law in Stammler's critique of materialism. In Weber's view, the logical structures of monocausal materialism and monocausal idealism are equally untenable. To explain the whole of social life either by material causes or by spiritual ones is to indulge in 'scholastic mystification' since, Weber tells us, 'with the same "logic" one could propose the "methodological principle" that "social life" is "in the last resort" to be deduced from skull measurements (or from the effects of sun-spots or perhaps from disturbances of the digestion)' (Albrow, 1975–6, p. 137). The essence of Weber's somewhat heated attack on Stammler is that to argue that social regularities are caused by the legal ordering of society is to confuse a legal rule with an empirical regularity. Stammler's 'overcoming' of materialism had been based on the argument that all social life is either constituted or determined by the following of common rules. These 'common rules' are essentially legal in character. While Stammler aimed to show that the economic was not the most fundamental aspect of social life, his critique of Marxism was, in principal, far deeper since it sought to demonstrate through neo-Kantian categories the fundamental weakness of a materialist epistemology. Stammler wanted to restrict the notion of causality to the natural sciences in order to argue that the analysis of social life required something very different, namely, the intepretation of what it means to follow a rule. The procedures of the legal theorist and those of the social scientist were consequently entirely compatible since both sought to understand the forms of social life through the interpretation of rules. For Stammler, therefore, neither legal theory nor the sociology of law could avoid the question of the justness of rules because their understanding of the operation of rules was entirely different from that of the scientist who seeks to explain the regularity of nature. The explosive nature of Weber's

review of Stammler's *Wirtschaft und Recht* (1896) may be explained by the fact that Stammler's conception of 'interpretation' obviously resembles the conception of *verstehen* in
Weber's account of 'interpretative sociology', but Stammler
employed this approach to close the gap between values and
facts (Runciman, 1972). Weber's critique of Stammler helps us
to grasp the real nature of Weber's general position which is to
regard law as a set of imperative commands backed up by
political violence. By contrast, Stammler treats the law as
essentially a moral system. The contrast is perfectly illustrated by Weber's views on 'rule' and 'empirical regularity'.

In Weber's view, Stammler illegitimately equates the
evaluative interest of the legal theorist with the value-
neutrality of the sociologist. Whereas the former is concerned
with the legal truth of juristic findings, the latter is exclusively
concerned with the empirical effects of legal decision-making.
The issue of legal 'truth' and 'justice' cannot enter the
vocabulary of the social scientist who is primarily interested in
empirical regularities. Thus, the legal point of view is directed
towards the validity of law and its normative meaning, while
the sociological framework is concerned with that which

> *actually* happens in a community owing to the *probability*
> that persons participating in the communal activity (*Ge-
> meinschaftshandeln*) . . . . subjectively consider certain
> norms as valid and practically act according to them, in-
> other words, orient their own conduct towards these
> norms. (Weber, 1954, p. 11)

It is this possibility of a gap between normatively valid law
and the empirical practices of social agents which is of particular interest to sociology but meaningless from the perspective of the legal theorist. In principle, it would be possible for a
socialist system of production to develop 'without the change
of even a single paragraph of our laws' (Weber, 1954, p. 36). In
this situation, the normative validity of the law would remain
constant while its application and effects would be
sociologically very different. In short, the ideal laws of 'social
life' should not be confused with the empirical regularities

which result from the application of these rules in actual situations. The social regularities which we observe are certainly influenced by

> the existence of an empirical 'legal order', that is by a conception of what should be, by maxims which help to act as a cause of the action of human beings. But both these empirical regularities and the empirical 'existence' of 'law' are naturally something quite different from the juristic idea of its 'obligatory validity'. (Albrow, 1975-6, p. 35)

By contrast, Stammler equates the social regularities which we observe in the interactions between human agents and the normative regularities which exist at the level of ideal actors in legal theory.

The peculiarity of Weber's attack on Stammler is that, in order to make his position stick, Weber is forced to work against some of his own epistemological assumptions to such an extent that he finds himself advocating a positivist and reductionist theory of law. While there is ample disagreement as to what constitutes 'legal positivism' (Shuman, 1963), a broad definition would embrace the notion that legal pronouncement and moral evaluation are entirely separate and that law is command. Weber's position would fall well within this general definition since he defines law in the following manner: 'An order will be called *law* if it is externally guaranteed by the probability that coercion (physical or psychological), to bring about conformity or avenge violation, will be applied by a *staff* of people holding themselves specially ready for that purpose' Weber, 1954, p. 5). By defining law as a system of coercive commands, Weber expressly locates his discussion of legal rules within the general field of the sociology of domination and legitimacy. Furthermore, Weber believes that this study of law as command cannot be confused with the normative question of whether any particular laws are just. At a later stage, we shall be forced to return to the issue of whether, in his observations on natural law and substantive justice, Weber is wholly indifferent to the moral content of law

(Bendix, 1959, p. 484). Weber also appears to be presenting a position of sociological determinism in that, as we saw in the example of a socialist economy with a capitalist code of law, 'the content of legal theories is relatively unimportant' (Albrow, 1975-6, p. 19) in relation to the interpretation of law which is determined by the professional interests of lawyers and the economic structure of society. It is law which follows economy, not vice versa. As in *The Protestant Ethic and the Spirit of Capitalism*, Weber's critique of Stammler involves him in a delicate balancing act between not wanting to accept any simple economic reductionism and not wanting to provide law with too much autonomy from politics and economics. Weber attempts to maintain his theoretical balance by emphasising the professional organisation of the law, on the one hand, and by concentrating on the growth of legal rationalism, on the other. In order to examine this problem in greater depth, we will have to begin with an outline of the substance of Weber's sociology of law.

The main point of Weber's account of the categories of legal thought and their institutionalisation is to contrast systems of law which enjoy considerable stability, coherence and predictability with those that have a large measure of arbitrariness, instability and unreliability. Weber employs the criteria of rational and irrational, formal and substantive law to produce a four-fold typology of law. Law-making and law-finding are formal and irrational when legal processes are not controlled 'by the intellect'. The principal illustration of such arbitrary law is provided by recourse of oracles and other forms of divination. Substantively irrational legal judgments are made, not by reference to general norms, but in terms of the particular features of the case as they are evaluated by emotive, ethical or political considerations. This type of law-making can be illustrated by the example of *qādī*-justice in Islam where legal sentences were guided by emotive religious considerations. In substantively rational law, legal decisions are determined by tradition, particularly the sacred tradition of codified revelation. Finally, in formal and rational law, legal decisions are derived from a general abstract and gapless system of jurisprudential concepts by strict rules of logical reasoning.

Weber claims that 'the highest measure of methodological and logical rationality' in legal science is to be found in the Pandectists' Civil Law which is governed by abstract and systematic rules which have the character of deductive logic (Weber, 1954, p. 64). This impersonal and abstract system may be suitably contrasted with law-finding in the Persian state, where all previous legal decisions and contemporary practices were never recorded and where law was created for the immediate, *ad hoc* political needs of the state (Algar, 1969, p. 12).

These conceptual distinctions provide the basis for an analysis of the historical process of legal rationalisation. Weber treats the general historical movement of law as a process away from charismatic norms of 'law prophets' to secular law as the creation of bureaucratic officials. As Reinhard Bendix points out, Weber's typology of law is essentially a typology of law-makers. Thus, in historical terms,

> the general development of law and procedure may be viewed as passing through the following stages: first, charismatic legal revelation through 'law prophets'; second, empirical creation and finding of law by legal honoratories . . . third, imposition of law by secular or theocratic powers; fourth and finally, systematic elaboration of law and professionalised administration of justice by persons who have received their legal training in a learned and formally logical manner. (Weber, 1954, p. 303)

The development of stable and impersonal law-finding is a particular feature of the general trend of European culture towards rational, bureaucratic and machine-like procedures, which are relatively free of magical and sacred elements. While sacred law, such as the *Shari'a* in Islam, often does have considerable stability and internal coherence, the sacred law cannot change with the development of new social circumstances and therefore there are inevitable gaps between the legal ideal and actual social practices. These gaps are typically closed by the application of arbitrary legal devices and legal fictions. Alternatively, the hiatus can be plugged by the covert employment of secular and customary law. Formal and rational law, by contrast, is both stable because legal judgments are reached by formal logic and flexible because legal decisions are not determined by social circumstances. In order for formally rational law to develop, there must be considerable structural differentiation of society to separate law from political and religious interference.

A number of important institutional developments and contingent circumstances contributed to the growth of a system of gapless, rational law in Europe. Again it is characteristic of Weber's general sociological orientation to notice that it was the irrational religious requirements for salvation in Christianity which contributed most to the development of a secular and rational system of law and legal administration. Because the church initially refused any contact with law and state, there was a clear dualism between sacred and secular law. The Church did eventually come to terms with state power with 'the aid of the Stoic conception of "natural law", that is, a rational body of ideas' (Weber, 1954, p. 251). Furthermore, in the medieval period the teaching of theology, law and canon law were kept relatively separate in the university system which prevented the emergence of 'theocratic hybrid structures' which elsewhere stood in the way of rational, differentiated legal systems. The Christian Church also unintentionally aided the growth of secular law by developing a hierarchy of bureaucratic ecclesiastical posts which were filled by church functionaries. In short, the bureaucratic structure of the Church of Rome created an administrative staff which is important for legal formalism. In addition to the codification of law by ecclesiastical bureaucratics, the political struggles between European monarchs and privileged estates paradoxically contributed to the growth of rational law. In their conflicts with vassals, feudal monarchs came to depend on their own officialdom, especially for efficient tax-gathering. The ruler's political interest in stability and unification of society coincided with the interests of officials seeking promotion within a centralised bureaucracy.

Within the context of ecclesiastical and patrimonial administrations, a crucial issue in the development of rational law centres on whether law is taught in a guild organisation or in a university. In the first, legal ideas are determined by the practical and empirical problems of pleading cases in the courts and consequently laws are taught in terms of abstract and systematic conceptions of law because teaching and practice of law were more clearly distinguished. On the Continent, where university-trained lawyers became the dominant pattern, the philosophical development of legal theory was further stimulated by the revival and reception of Roman law. The growth of imperial Rome was associated with the emergence of formal laws which were not specific to given provinces but had general relevance throughout the empire. The reception of Roman law 'strengthened that tendency of the legal institutions themselves to become more and more abstract, which had begun already with the transformation of the Roman *ius civile* into the law of the Empire' (Weber, 1954, p. 276). The codification of an abstract, impersonal and rational system of law was in the interests of monarchs who depended on a stable administration, merchants and industrialists who required legally binding economic contracts, and lawyers who found that abstract law-training was perfectly suited to preservation of their privileged status position. The ways in which these interests were related to each other were certainly not uniform, but varied according to innumerable, contingent circumstances from one society to the next. The central point of Weber's account of these developments is, however, to suggest that capitalist development required the economic and political stability generated by rational, formal, abstract law.

Weber's analysis of the rise of rational law and its contribution to capitalist development can be seen as a theoretical reflection on the problem of social order in a capitalist society where egoistic wills clash in the market place (Trubek, 1972, p. 740). If each individual capitalist attempts to maximise profit, remove competitors and extend control of the market, then it is perfectly rational for each capitalist to resort to systematic deception, fraud, trickery or other 'immoral', but economically advantageous, actions. The problem for capitalist production in a situation of unrestrained egoism is that contracts are unstable and profitability is threatened by the Hobbesian war of all against all. It is important, therefore, in capitalism that market arrangements should be governed by institutions, norms or social groups which do not operate in terms of egoistic economic interest alone. Weber notes that in pre-industrial societies the market-place was often protected by the gods who were expected to enforce contracts. Any system of exchange is likely to give rise to some form of 'market ethics' (Weber, 1954, p. 194) which encourage honesty and fair dealing in the economic interests of both parties to a sale.

It is appropriate to draw the parallel between the analysis of law as the stable framework which regulates the anarchy of the market in Weber's sociology of law and the analysis of values as the regulative structure of the social system in Parsons's *The Structure of Social Action* (Trubek, 1972, p. 741). Parsons was, in addition, concerned to argue that the ethics of professionalism were not subject to capitalist interest since the professional man was oriented towards disinterested service of the community according to universalistic and neutral criteria (Parsons, 1954). It is also pertinent to note a similar theoretical position in *The Division of Labour in Society* where Durkheim criticised Spencer's view of the role of spontaneous, voluntary social contracts as the basis of social order. Durkheim's argument was that, given Spencer's utilitarian emphasis on self-interest, contracts between individuals could never be guaranteed without some form of legal regulation. Every contractual agreement presupposes the existence of a non-contractual rule because 'a contract is not sufficient unto itself, but it is possible only thanks to a regulation of the contract which is originally social' (Durkheim 1964, p. 215). With the development of the social division of labour, repressive law gives way to restitutive law which plays a crucial role in balancing exchange relations. From these perspectives, law appears as the normative regulator of the economic anarchy flowing from egoistic wills.

There are, however, important differences between Weber, Parsons and Durkheim (Cartwright and Schwartz, 1973). In Weber's treatment of the importance of legal stability for capitalist enterprise, the law is effective, not simply because it is 'internalised' by capitalist actors, but because it is backed up by the threat of force. Legal regulation of economic contracts is based, in the last analysis, on state power. Weber recognises that it is possible to achieve economically stable contracts without state control (through kinship groups for example), but in modern society where many traditional and religious regulations have collapsed state control becomes an essential feature of economic relations. Thus, 'an economic system, especially of the modern type, could certainly not exist without a legal order with very special features which could not develop except in the frame of a "state" legal order' (Weber, 1954, p. 39). In addition to the disappearance of sacred sources of control, the modern economy is unstable because 'class interests have come to diverge more sharply from one another' (Weber, 1954, p. 39). The bourgeois class depends heavily on the existence of a stable, clear legal system without administrative arbitrariness with the support of political force. Weber is perfectly aware, therefore, that the theory of the liberal state and the creation of formal rights and privileges by law do not necessarily reflect the actual situation of contestants in the market place. While the employer and the worker are both 'free' to make contracts under the law, their economic and political capacity to enjoy legal freedom is obviously very different. The legal freedom of contract does not offer the worker any freedom to determine his work conditions. These legal freedoms mean

> that the more powerful party in the market i.e., normally the employer, has the possibility to set the terms, to offer the job 'take it or leave it', and, given the normally more pressing economic need of the worker, to impose his terms upon him. The result of contractual freedom, then, is in the first place the opening of the opportunity to use, by the clever utilization of property ownership in the market, these resources without legal restraints as a means for the achievement of power over others. (Weber, 1954, pp. 188-9)

The problem of order in Weber's sociology is solved, not primarily by reference to the internalisation of norms, but in terms of a system of constraints and coercive institutions which compel individuals to behave according to the social logic of their situation. We have seen that there are two key propositions in Weber's sociology of law. The first is that sociology of law is, unlike legal theory, a value-neutral study of the empirical effects of law, defined as a system of coercive regulations. The sociological study of law is not concerned with the internal validity of law and does not raise evaluative questions concerning the justice of legal arrangements. The second proposition is that, through a process of secularisation and professionalisation, a system of gapless, rational laws came to be a necessary condition for stable capitalist transactions. While law does serve the interests of the dominant class, the content and form of law are the products of various historical and social factors of which the most important has been the professional interests of university-trained lawyers. Both of these major propositions have been strongly criticised in subsequent debates in the sociology of law. I shall consider these criticisms in reverse order, starting with the so-called 'England problem' (Trubek, 1972; Hunt, 1978), which questions the importance of formal, rational law for capitalist development.

The argument that on the Continent Roman law and university law-training provided the most congenial context for capitalist development runs into a very strong counter-argument, namely, that in England the common law tradition and guild organisation of lawyers did not appear to impede the development of capitalist relations. In the English case, the law was judge-made and consequently organised around the problem of precedent rather than a system of logically deduced legal decisions. Weber is clearly aware of the difficulty for his theory. The extent of the difficulty can be seen from the fact that, while Weber treats Islamic *qādī*-justice as incompatible with capitalist growth, he regards the courts of justice of the peace in England as bearing a close resemblance to *qādī*-justice. Trubek (1972) suggests that Weber provides three solutions to this deviant case. In the first, Weber stresses the identity of interests between common law judges and the bourgeois class, and draws attention to the role of law in the English class system. For example, the fact that the English courts were administered in London and that legal proceedings were costly excluded the disprivileged from legal aid. In the second, Weber maintains his theory by pointing to the historical uniqueness of England which 'achieved capitalist supremacy among the nations not because but rather in spite of its judicial system' (Weber, 1954, p. 231). In the third solution, Weber suggests that, while English case-law was not as rational as Continental Roman law, it was nevertheless sufficiently stable to support capitalism. This final position enables Weber to diminish any sharp distinction between Continental English law. In England, for example, the autonomy of the law was supported by the relative separation of the judiciary from the state.

Whereas Trubek treats Weber's resolution of the 'England problem' as unstable, Hunt (1978, p. 127) claims that Weber did not provide 'any coherent solution' and that he adopts 'an eclectic method that lapses into an historicism which seeks to account for the phenomenon in terms of discrete and historically specific causes which bear no relationship to his conceptual sociology'. In my view, Weber offers two additional solutions to this difficulty which we have to consider. The first is that the apparent backwardness and substantive interests of English law positively aided English capitalists. The second is that legal thought (both in terms of content and form) has no important sociological connections with the economic base, that is, capitalism can develop and continue under a variety of different systems of law. Both solutions are, however, difficult to reconcile with the theory that capitalism requires and tends to develop a system of rational, formal, gapless, abstract laws.

In his introduction to Karl Renner's *The Institutions of Private Law and their Social Functions* (1949), Kahn-Freund provided *inter alia* a number of reasons for believing that English judge-made law was perfectly compatible with capitalist development and to some extent was more favourable towards capitalist requirements than Continental law. The English law was *common*, that is, England emerged from feudalism with a system of laws that operated throughout the land without restriction from local custom and parochial law. The systematisation of law on the Continent in the nineteenth century under the control of universities had already been achieved in England under the guild system of lawyers following the failure of political absolutism. Moreover, the concept of 'property' in English law has proved more flexible and more relevant to the nature of property in capitalist development. It is interesting to note that

> 'Property' in a mere 'fund', a unit of values, is inconceivable to Romanist legal thought. English law, on the other hand, is perfectly capable of giving effect to the idea of 'floating' property, of a 'property' right which does not attach to any individualised asset, but to a 'value' which may, at any given moment, be represented either by land or by a bank account (i.e. a banker's debt) or by Government securities. It is very difficult indeed for a continental lawyer to understand the legislative technique which enabled English lawyers to adapt the institution of settled land to the needs of modern society. (Kahn-Freund, 1949, pp. 20-1)

English law was also more easily adapted to the growing separation of private ownership and managerial control than Roman law in which the notion of *dominium* could not be differentiated in this manner.

Because capitalism developed under conditions of common law and Roman law, another solution to the 'England problem' is to argue that the nature of the legal framework is irrelevant to capitalist development. If a legal system can provide some minimum level of stability and can be interpreted in ways which are not incompatible with capitalist accumulation, then differences in the theoretical principles of legal systems may be, in practice, rather unimportant for economic production. There are several occasions on which Weber adopts this view of the relationship between the economic base and the legal superstructure. Weber notes that 'modern capitalism prospers equally and manifests essentially identical economic traits under legal systems containing rules and institutions which considerably differ from each other at least from the juridical point of view' (Weber, 1968, vol. 2, p. 890). It is also clear to

Weber that, once capitalism had become the dominant system in England, the common law survived without any massive change in its 'archaic' character. This defence of his view of English law may be incompatible with the claim that capitalism requires a gapless, rational system of law, but it is consistent with Weber's definition of the tasks of the sociology of law. In reply to Stammler, Weber had argued that the proper aim of sociology was to describe and explain the actual practice of law and its social effect rather than the theoretical structure and contents of law itself. In practice, both common law and Roman law traditions had positive contributions to offer nascent capitalism.

The two criticisms of Weber's sociology of law—the 'England problem' and the positivist character of his definition of law—turn out to be simply two aspects of the same issue. Although there are various ways by which one might attempt to reconcile Weber's observations on English law with his argument about the affinity between Roman law and capitalism, we cannot avoid the conclusion that Weber thought Continental law far superior to English judge-made law. Both in terms of content and administration, English law blatantly served the interests of the dominant class; 'the high cost of litigation and legal services amounted for those who could not afford to purchase them to a denial of justice . . . . This denial of justice was in close conformity with the interests of the propertied, especially capitalistic, classes' (Weber, 1954, p. 230). Whereas Continental Law provides consistency and precision, English law is hopelessly empiricist and largely a collection of working principles and rules of thumb for practising lawyers within the guild. English law consequently failed to abandon its substantive character and did not acquire the formal features of European constitutional law. In order to develop this evaluation of Weber's contribution to the sociology of law, we need to look more systematically at the nature of the common and natural law traditions, on the one hand, and at the possibility of a value-free science of law, on the other.

Against Weber it can be argued that the English common law tradition was not only compatible with the needs of capitalist enterprise, but also a vehicle for opposition to royal absolutism. In other words, English case-law cannot be simply dismissed as an instrument of class repression. The revival and reception of Roman law from its base in Bologna answered two crucial needs, namely a legal conception of property and the administrative framework of absolutist power. The Roman civil law proved particularly valuable as a legal basis for political integration and centralisation. Thus,

> the revival of Roman law corresponded to the constitutional exigencies of the reorganized feudal States of the epoch. In fact, there is no doubt that on a European scale, the *primary* determinant of the adoption of Roman jurisprudence lay in the drive of royal governments for increased central powers. (Little, 1969, p. 172)

In England, the drive for royal absolutism was checked in the first instance by Magna Carta and the baronial appeal to the 'law of the land' (Ullman, 1975) and decisively halted by the political victory of the common law against the extension of royal prerogative in the seventeenth century. In the battle between court and crown, it is true that the common law jurists with the support of Puritan theologians appealed to convention, custom and the practices of the ancient realm against the expansion of the king's discretion and, in this respect, Weber's characterisation of English law as 'archaic' appears to be well justified. However, the oddity of Edward Coke's view of custom was that in practice it did create the legal conditions which were necessary for the formation of economically autonomous corporations. While the lawyers thought

> they were reinstituting the old order, as a matter of fact they helped to introduce a set of economic and social patterns that undermined the ancient realm and paved the way for rational capitalism. Thus, in the name of the old order a distinctly new order was being prepared, an order that conformed as little with the designs of the Tudors and Stuarts as with the prescriptions of medieval England. (Little, 1969, p. 172)

It is a nice irony that Weber misses the paradox that the effects of legal decisions in English common law were wholly other than the intentions of English lawyers who appealed to tradition to protect society against what they regarded as the innovations of the king's economic policy. The consequence of Coke's defence of common law and Parliament was to free economic institutions from royal interference, relegate ecclesiastical law to a separate and subordinate sphere of competence under common law and to differentiate clearly the judiciary from the executive. Common lawyers and rich merchants found themselves united against such repressive institutions as the Court of Star Chamber and the High Commission. While these legal battles were taking place,

> the private law of the bourgeoisie developed as well. In 1660 the last feudal elements were purged by statute from the law of real property. The common-law courts moved from a sporadic willingness to hear evidence on merchant custom to an outright incorporation of the law merchant. 'The law merchant', Lord Mansfield was able to write by the late 1700s, 'is the law of the land'. Joint-stock companies and other capital-pooling devices flourished. (Tigar and Levy, 1977)

The development of the common law supports Weber's view that it is the interpretation and application of law rather than its formal content which are important for capitalist interests; it does not support his alternative thesis that formal and rational law is an essential requirement of stable capitalist contracts.

Weber wants, of course, to argue that the common law was inferior to Roman law on the grounds that it was grounded in the principle of 'reasonableness' rather than 'reason'. Just as Weber ruled out the concepts of legal theory in his definition of law from a sociological perspective, so in his analysis of 'reason' and 'rational law' Weber assumes that the meaning of these terms can either be established by definitional fiat or have a self-evident meaning. In terms of the inter-subjective meanings of social actors, the concepts of 'reasonableness' and 'reason' in the period when Coke and the common law jurists were debating the nature of the common tradition were also deeply contested. For Coke, whatever was consistent with the law of the land as interpreted by trained lawyers was reasonable. Among the members of the Royal Society, experimentation and observation were the only true guides to reason. While Milton equated reason with conscience, the Levellers appealed to universal reason against tradition. In a divided society, unreason comes from outside as a challenge to reasonable and respectable ways of achieving ends. Definitions of reason necessarily prompt the question 'Whose reason?' (Hill, 1969). Weber attempts to avoid this question by treating formal rationality as the application of scientific knowledge to the achievement of known ends. Law can be regarded as rational in this technical sense if it is logically consistent, stable and systematic. However, this raises the problem for Weber that substantive law may be regarded as more desirable as a defence of universal rights because it involves the issue of substantive justice than formal, rational law which is indifferent to the question of moral ends. Rational law is a slot machine which provides the correct answer regardless of the coinage with which it is fed; substantive law inquires into the particular and peculiar circumstances of individual cases regarding the 'reasonableness' of actions in situational terms.

By treating rational law as a body of reliable techniques for producing legally consistent answers, Weber attempts to side-step the problem of whether a law can be regarded as just which he regards as a question for legal philosophy not sociology. However, much of Weber's discussion of natural law and substantive law carries with it the implication that they are inferior to rational Roman or Continental law. Weber is thus unwilling to discuss the validity of the claims of natural law or substantive justice and, as in the case of problems of theodicy, Weber treats 'the sense of justice' as a set of opinions held by social actors which may be described sociologically but not interpreted in normative terms. The background to this conceptual distance which Weber sets up between substantive law and sociological description is, once again, Weber's pessimistic view that we inhabit a disenchanted world. Weber treats the 'sense of justice' as determined by 'purely "emotional" values':

> Experience shows, however, that the 'sense of justice' is very unstable unless it is firmly guided by the 'pragma' of objective or subjective interests. It is, as one can still easily see today, capable to sudden fluctuations and it cannot be expressed except in a few very general and purely formal maxims. (Weber, 1954, p. 75)

Partly in reaction to the transformation of law into a slot-machine and also in reaction to class conflicts,

> demands for a 'social law' to be based upon such emotionally colored ethical postulates as justice or human dignity, and thus directed against the very dominance of a mere business morality have arisen in modern times with the emergence of the modern class problem. (Weber, 1954, p. 308)

Weber believes, however, that the basis for a 'social law' is a sociological utopia because, in a secular society, there no longer exists 'an objective standard of values' (Weber, 1954, p. 313).

Although Weber attempts to present a value-neutral sociology of law, his account of law does in fact bring with it the implication that a rational, stable legal system is to be preferred to laws which are emotive and unstable. Weber has been criticised by Albrow (1975-6) on the grounds that the distinction between normative legal theory and objective sociology will not hold water. As members of society, lawyers and sociologists make value-judgments about the law in the very process of understanding it. Furthermore, the conceptions which jurists bring to the law are themselves already shot through with sociological assumptions. While accepting Albrow's strictures, I would like to make the additional, but different, point that, if it is legitimate for sociologists to ask what forms of law contributed to the rise of capitalism, it is equally legitimate to ask what types of law contributed to the rise of totalitarian states. It seems to me that this question has the evaluative implication that, other things being equal, totalitarian states are less desirable than democratic ones. Again it may well be that the common law tradition has a greater affinity with the preservation and creation of democratic rights of a bourgeois, if not a socialist, character. It is not without interest that, although English law does not have the speed and efficiency of Roman law, it did enshrine the principle of government by consent between king, barons and parliament under a system of communal norms (Ullman, 1975, p. 155).

Weber's analysis of law cannot be separated from his definition of the state as an institution which has a monopoly of force in a given territory. If formal rational law is compatible with capitalism, it is also a stable legal system which serves the interests of a centralised and bureaucratic state machine. In this respect, Weber's sociology at least has the merit of being a realistic appraisal of the nature of politics and thereby anticipates the definition of politics presented in Carl Schmitt's *Der Begriff des politischen*. What ultimately defines the political in Schmitt's analysis is the struggle between friend and foe, between Us and Other. All political decisions are to be set in the context of emergency and survival. Consequently, distinctions between legality and illegality have no place in political discourse where the state can only be judged in terms of its effectivity and efficiency. Membership of the collectivity of friends is defined by membership of a folk who share a natural allegiance to leaders. It is not difficult, therefore, to see how Schmitt's analysis of politics and law could be easily translated into the conditions which operated under the emergency of fascist Germany. However, it is also important to keep in mind the fact that the form of law and the practice of law may relate to political regimes in a number of complex ways. The paradoxical connections between formal law and democratic rights provided one of the crucial issues in the response of the Frankfurt School to Nazi politics. For example, Franz Neumann argued that the liberal notions of equality and the rule of law could always in practice serve to mask the massive inequalities between the bourgeoisie and the proletariat.

Like Weber, Neumann recognised that there were important differences between English and German law which reflected the different histories and structural location of the capitalist class in the two societies. In Germany, an economically dominant capitalist class did not exercise direct control over the state and law. In England, the

> middle classes, in contrast, to the German, safeguarded their economic freedom not materially, i.e., by establishing barriers against the legislation of Parliament, but genetically, i.e., through participation in the making of laws . . . the German bourgeoisie found the laws of constitutional monarchy in existence and systematized and interpreted them in order to secure a minimum economic liberty in the face of a more or less absolute state.
> (Neumann, 1957, p. 44)

Again following Weber, Neumann argues that the cost of litigation in the English system was so great that wide sections of the population were without legal protection. However, while the formalism of German law was deceptive, it did provide more protection than substantive law against arbitrary and illegal actions of the state against the working class. Formal law does provide the bourgeoisie with economic calculability, but it also provides through the generality of law a minimum safeguard for all citizens against arbitrary politics. The independence of the judiciary and the rationality of general, formal laws provide a baseline for personal liberty. Any attack on the liberal theory of law was thus politically dangerous in an epoch of totalitarianism. A very similar political and theoretical position was adopted by Marcuse (1968a) in his essay on the struggle against liberalism. With the transition from competitive to monopoly capitalism, the liberal theory of free individuals in the market place became obsolete and was replaced by a theory which gave the state far greater discretionary power. Neumann argued that the response of critical theory to this illegality must be an appeal to a democratic theory of natural law which enshrined the principles of free and rational men under a system of general laws to be administered by an autonomous judiciary. As we have seen, Weber's scepticism over natural law theory necessarily precluded any such stance.

German legal theory has, therefore, been commonly regarded as superior to English substantive law both in terms of its inherent logic and in terms of its egalitarian administration. English law was regarded as class law which served the political and economic needs of the bourgeoisie. However, there appears to be an inconsistency in Weber's position in that he is often more concerned with the formal content of English law than with its actual practice. If Weber had followed through his criticism of Stammler consistently, he might have been more concerned with the sociology of the everyday practice of common law than with its formal, normative content. Although Weber notes the expense of litigation under English conditions, he does not ask how systematically and rigorously English law was used as a tool of class war. For example, one of the peculiarities of English law is the frequent use of pardon, sanctuary and confession which mitigate the full impact of law on all social classes (Hepworth and Turner, 1974 and 1979). In eighteenth-century rural England, for example, there was an extensive growth of capital offences against property and simultaneously an increase in the number of pardons, acquittals and commutations. It appears that the rural gentry were reluctant to use the existing law to the full as an instrument of class repression (Hay, *et al.*, 1975). The practice of criminal law had less to do with the detection and prosecution of individual offenders than with the support of the legitimacy of the political order. Confessions and acquittals from the gallows were a ritual demonstration of legal mercy and grace. If English criminal law acted as the instrument of class oppression, then it was certainly indirect. The merciful operation of English law has been interpreted as creating a sense of the justice of existing arrangements and as thereby fostering a sense of community and consent in a society of conflicting classes (Klare, 1979). The alternative interpretation of English law is to argue that the very fact that the law was common served to immunise the law from immediate class manipulation. The appeal to the law of the land may have protected the bourgeoisie from the arbitrariness of the crown, but it also provided a set of substantive rights for the poor in eighteenth and nineteenth-century England. The existence of 'the rule of law' may create positive legal rights within a class society which cannot be readily subordinated to sectional, class interests (Thompson, 1975). These comments on the role of common law in the growth of the English class structure bring us back to the vexed question of whether it is the form of law, the practice of law or both that serves the interests of dominant classes.

We can now summarise the major themes of Weber's somewhat inconsistent sociology of law: (1) a system of abstract, formal and stable laws serves the economic interests of competitive capitalists by making economic exchanges legally enforceable and their political interests by creating administrative stability; (2) legal theory develops under the control of lawyers whose interests do not necessarily coincide with the economic interests of capitalist employers and thereby the law is relatively autonomous from the economic infrastructure of a given society; (3) the form of law is irrelevant to the exercise of capitalist forces since the capitalist can thrive under virtually any system of law provided the capitalist can utilise and interpret written laws or customary laws to their own advantage. In the first theme, Weber adopts an almost instrumentalist theory of law as the tool of the dominant class; English common law as a tool of class rule is his principal example. In the second theme, Weber argues that the professional organisation of lawyers rather than specifically class interests is the main determinant of a legal change. The correlation between professional interests of lawyers and class interests of capitalists is historically contingent and cannot be expressed in terms of sociological generalisations. In this second theme and in the third, law is seen to be relatively autonomous from the economy since capitalism can flourish under both substantive and formal law. Weber can be criticised for theoretical inconsistency, for an exaggerated view of the superiority of Roman law and for his positivistic definition of law which precludes a serious analysis of the meaning of law for jurists and laymen. The point about Weber's sociology is that its theoretical failure is normally massively insightful and theoretically suggestive; his sociological weakness often turns out to be a major contribution to our understanding of the operations of human society. As a conclusion to this consideration of Weber's sociology of law, I want to show that, regardless of their pertinent criticisms, neo-Marxists theories of law have consistently reproduced the ambiguities of Weber's study of law and have not resolved the problems raised by him. While Weber constantly slips into an instrumentalist view of law, his theory of law is an attempt to avoid the vulgar notion that law can be reduced to class interest. By various means, Weber points to the relative autonomy of the law in history and society. In a similar fashion, contemporary Marxists have rejected instrumentalism (Picciotto, 1979; Sumner, 1979). In their response to intrumentalism, Marxists can either operate in terms of the traditional metaphor of base and superstructure or they can seek an alternative theoretical framework. In the first option, the relative autonomy of law from the base can be illustrated by the fact that there is often a 'cultural lag' between law and economic change. The concept of 'property' in feudal Europe under Roman law may also be relevant to economic ownership in capitalism. In the second option, Marxists have employed the notion of the fetish of the commodity form to write the theory of the form of law as a method of rejecting the implicit instrumentalism of either the dominant ideology thesis or the base-superstructure imagery. The first option is taken by Karl Renner, while the second is represented by E. B. Pashukanis and his contemporary followers.

Karl Renner's *The Institutions of Private Law and their Social Functions* bears a very close conceptual relationship to Weber's sociology of law. Both Weber and Renner want to reject the legal idealism of Stammler. Renner declares that 'the problem of the complicated interrelations between law and economics, this wonderful interweaving of legal institutions and economic structure' cannot be adequately grasped in terms of 'Stammler's distinction of form and matter' (1949, p.

259). Like Weber, Renner began to provide a theoretical critique, with his colleagues in the new journal *Der Kampf*, of the type of Marxism presented in Kautsky's *Die Neue Zeit*. In addition, both men were involved in the development of a sociology which in various ways depended on neo-Kantian epistemology. It is not surprising, therefore, that their views on law have a striking resemblance. The principal difference between Weber and Renner is that the latter attempted to provide a sociology of law which was grounded in the major assumptions of Marx's *Capital*. Renner treats law as an essential condition of the organisation of society and in its reproduction. The fundamental processes of society are to be located in 'the production and reproduction of human individuals as well as in their conditions of existence. Thus all legal institutions taken as a whole fulfill one function which comprises all others, that of the preservation of the species' (Renner, 1949, p. 70). Renner has traditionally, along with Pashukanis, been allocated high theoretical status as a leading exponent of 'the Marxist theory of the law of property' (Hirst, 1979, p. 100) and regarded as clearly within the Marxist tradition (Bottomore and Goode, 1978; Rich, 1978). However, the problem which Renner addresses—to what extent law 'continues unchanged in relation to changing economic conditions' (Renner, 1949, p. 57) —and his treatment of the relationship between formal laws and the legal apparatus demonstrate the parallel with Weber's sociology of law.

In Renner's sociology, law is defined from a positivist position as a set of imperatives and 'every legal institution is to a conceptual approach a composite of norms, a total of imperatives' (Renner, 1949, p. 53). The normative legal structure is separate from and indifferent to its socio-economic environment and thus there are no specifically 'feudal' or 'capitalist' laws. Legal analysis concerns itself with the validity and logic of these imperatives through formal juridical study. The task of sociology is to study the effects and social functions of these legal institutions. In order to reproduce itself, every human society requires an order of labour, authority, goods and succession. Law plays a vital role in satisfying these production, consumption and distribution functions by providing social regulation of individuals within the community. Thus, 'Legal institutions designed to regulate the order of labour and of power and the co-ordination of individuals have an organising function in that they integrate the individual into the whole' (Renner, 1949, p. 71). Renner makes a distinction between these universal economic functions in society and the specific social functions of private property in capitalism; the economic functions of production, distribution and consumption are realised in capitalism through the legal institution of private ownership which secures rights of use and disposal.

On the basis of these general theoretical distinctions, Renner conceptually separates norms from their functions and this provides the crucial step in his argument. Legal norms and the social functions of legal institutions may vary relatively independently of each other. Legal norms may remain constant while their social functions remain the same. Renner's principal illustration is from the history of the law of private property. Under conditions of simply commodity production, property as the crucial institution of private law provided for an order of goods, but with the increasing use of hired wage-labour by family capitalist enterprises the order of labour had to be secured by complementary norms which were derived in part from public guild laws. Furthermore, with the development of manufacture, factory production and the separation between ownership and control, the laws of private property no longer functioned in their original form. The concept of ownership no longer referred to discrete objects—a house or plot of land—but to a variety of rights and titles over shares, rent and profits as well as physical property. The laws of property were now complemented by other legal norms such as the law of contract. While the law of property as it existed in the seventeenth century was virtually the same in the nineteenth century, the social functions of the legal institution of property have changed considerably through a process of adaptation and addition. The form of law may remain constant, but its social functions in relation to the economic base change according to new circumstances. In other words 'economic change does not immediately and automatically bring about changes in the law' (Renner, 1949, p. 252).

If the laws of property in feudalism can be adapted to the economic requirements of capitalism, then this thesis raises the question of whether the form of law under capitalism could be adapted to socialism despite changes in the function of law. In principle, Renner must be theoretically committed to such a possibility and, in accord with his Austro-Marxist politics, Renner recognises an evolutionary development of socialised production in capitalism which permits a non-revolutionary transition to socialism. The form of law thus lags behind changing economic conditions and changing legal institutions. In Renner's view, the society described in *Capital* in which individual owners and controllers of property competed in the anarchic market place for a surplus created by atomised labour had been replaced by a society in which state regulation of capital and labour had become a necessary condition of continued production and reproduction. Indeed, the 'capitalist society, as Marx experienced and described it, no longer exists' (Bottomore and Good, 1978, p. 93). There was, therefore, a gap between the law of property and the economic base so that the property law was rapidly supplemented by new laws of contract and administrative law. These new laws under conditions of state regulation and socialised production anticipated future developments. Renner criticised utopian and messianic socialists who

> fail to comprehend and to investigate scientifically how far it is true that the new society is already pre-formed in the womb of the old, even in the field of law. May it not be true that here also new life is already completely developed in the mother's womb, waiting only for the liberating act of birth? (Renner, 1949, p. 294)

The legal regulations developing under conditions of state intervention were having the two-fold consequence of denying owners their technical rights of property disposal and subjecting property to the direct control of 'the common will'. The form of law under capitalism was thus being adapted to the emerging conditions of socialism. It was this theoretical and political problem of the form of law under capitalism and socialism which became a prominent concern of Pashukanis' analysis of law, but the solution offered was very different.

In *Law and Marxism, a general theory*, Pashukanis attempts to ground his analysis of law in Marx's notion of the 'fetishism of commodities' in *Capital*. Like the value of commodities, law is to be conceptualised as a form and, in order to analyse the form of law, we need to start with its most elementary component before developing more general notions. Basically, 'Every legal relation is a relation between subjects. The subject is the atom of legal theory, its simplest, irreducible element' (Pashukanis, 1978, p. 109). The basis of law is, therefore, not imperative command, but a right of possession by subjects who are differentiated and separated. While private law is the primary legal relation in which the subject appears as a claimant, in public law the state, as the agency of class control, operates under the guise of a general, abstract rule of law. The form of law expresses and corresponds to the economic relations between subjects in a society where men are connected through the exchange of commodities in the market. In capitalism, society is constituted by

> commodity-owners first and foremost. This means that social relations in the production process assume a reified form in that the products of labour are related to each other as values . . . . If objects dominate man economically because, as commodities they embody a social relation which is not subordinate to man, then man rules over things legally, because, in his capacity as possessor and proprietor, he is simply the personification of the abstract, impersonal, legal subject, the pure product of social relations. (Pashukanis, 1978, pp. 111, 113)

Legal fetishism is thus complementary to the fetishism of commodities under capitalist conditions of production by commodity-owners. There is a double mystification of social relations whereby they appear as relations between things and relations between the wills of legal subjects. It is only in capitalism that law develops these abstract and formal characteristics with the fetishism of commodities.

In the transition to socialism, the form of law is conserved only insofar as private commodity production continues during the transitional stage to socialist production. As private production and consumption disappear, there is a corresponding withering away of the juridical form of regulation which was based on commodity production. At the same time, the subjective notions of guilt and responsibility will be eventually replaced by neutral and objective conceptions under socialism. In the area of criminal law, the collapse of capitalist society based on conflicting classes 'will make possible the creation of a system of penal policy which lacks any element of antagonism' (Pashukanis, 1978, p. 175). The themes of retribution and revenge in criminal justice will be replaced by neutral, administrative assessments of the needs of social protection from lawbreakers. In the transitional period before the withering away of bourgeois conceptions, the working class 'will of necessity exploit this form inherited from bourgeois society in its own interest' (Pashukanis, 1978, p. 160). Contrary to Renner's view of the stability of the legal norm in relation to its changing functions, Pashukanis ties the legal form to the commodity form. The collapse of capitalist relations of production necessarily leads to fundamental changes both in the form and function of law. The legal relation as a possessive right of the differentiated subject cannot survive the disappearance of the capitalist commodity form.

Pashukanis attempts to combine two incompatible perspectives on law. The utilisation of the fetishism argument provides a method of transcending the conventional base/superstructure metaphor (Balbus, 1978), but Pashukanis also retains an instrumentalist view of law as merely that tool whereby the 'bourgeoisie maintains its class rule and suppresses the exploited classes' (Pashukanis, 1978, p. 173). Despite this somewhat inconsistent treatment of private and public law, Pashukanis's analysis of fetishism has provided the principal theoretical foundation for contemporary Marxist conceptualisation of law. In more general terms, the argument about fetishism has been employed as an alternative to the base/superstructure metaphor in the study of law (Edelman, 1979), the state (Blanke *et al.*, 1978) and science (Sohn-Rethel,

1978). These applications of 'the fetishism of commodities' argument suffer from theoretical problems which are inherent in the notion of fetishism itself and which became explicit in the use of the fetishism thesis in Lukács' account of reification in *History and Class Consciousness*. Any theory which treats ideology as the direct emanation of economic exchange fails to consider 'the transmission of ideology through various sets of institutions and practices with their own specificity and internal contradictions' (McDonough, 1978, p. 41). It is not enough to demonstrate a plausible analogy between subjects in law and the economic subject without providing an explanation of the role of the legal apparatus and legal profession in the creation, distribution and enforcement of legal norms. Despite the inconsistency of Weber's position, his sociology of law clearly recognised the vital role of the legal apparatus in the reproduction of legal norms.

The fetishism thesis is also totally incapable of explaining differences between the form of law in different capitalist societies which have the same commodity structure. Marxist theories of law run up against exactly the same 'England problem' that confronted Weber. To make the parallel between economic and legal subjects, the fetishism argument notes that law in capitalist society, as a system of general, abstract and rational norms, interpellates the subject. Unfortunately, such a general approach will not give us an account of the specific differences between English case law and Continental legal systems. In his introduction to Edelman's *Ownership of the Image*, Hirst points out that Edelman's analysis of the relations between legal subjects, laws of artistic ownership and capitalist relations is specific to French law since English copyright law operates with very different legal assumptions. There are Marxist theories of law which do not operate with a fetishism thesis, but still insist on the necessary relationship between capitalism and rational, formal law. It is particularly interesting to observe Poulantzas's use of Weber's sociology of law in *State, Power, Socialism* to argue that 'capitalist law is specific in that it forms an axiomatic system, comprising a set of abstract, general, formal and strictly regulated norms' (1978, p. 86). The considerable differences between forms of law in different capitalist societies represents a general problem of Marxist theories of law. The alternative to the argument that there are necessary connections between the form of law and the system of capitalist exchange is that the capitalist mode of production can operate with very different forms of law provided certain minimal conditions—such as inheritance—are secured.

There is a further difficulty for the fetishism argument as an explanation of the nature of law in capitalism. The argument has to assume a system of simple commodity-production in which capitalist owners are economically connected in the market-place. Legal fetishism gives expression to an exchange system of commodity production by separated individual owners. This argument is therefore irrelevant in the case of monopoly capitalism because 'Corporate forms of capital are inassimilable to this coincidence of subjects (owning, possessing, calculating). Monopoly, in separating ownership and possession, legal subject and economic subject, dissolves the connections which are necessary to capitalist social relations proper' (Hirst, 1979, p. 119). There is no reason, therefore, for there to be an equation between legal, economic and human subjects. The economic subject in competitive capitalism was typically the individual owner, but the functions of capital can equally be borne by the capitalist corporation. With the separation of ownership and control and with the dominance of the large corporation over the family firm, the parallel between individual economic subjects and legal subjects begins to fall apart. Hirst (1979) argues that Renner, Pashukanis and Edelman adhere to the assumptions of simple exchange systems and that their treatment of legal relations cannot cope with the economic forms of monopoly capitalism. It is difficult, however, to see how this criticism could apply fully to Renner's sociology of law. As we have seen, Renner believed that there was a growing gap between the conventional laws of property and the economic processes of a capitalist society where state regulation and large corporations were becoming crucial features of industrial capitalism. Renner's theory is much closer to Weber's in recognising the importance of legal interpretation in the adaptation of legal forms to changing economic requirements.

Marxist and neo-Marxist theories of law either treat law as

the direct expression of class interest or law is regarded, not as a mere reflection, but as a necessary condition of capitalist exchange relations. For example, while Pashukanis regards public law as the instrument of class domination, Poulantzas argues that law constitutes individual subjects and performs cohesive and organising functions in class society. While there have been disagreements over the relative autonomy of law from the economic base, Marxists must assume that law has basic ideological functions in capitalism. Law provides security of exchange and coercion of the working class. Legal control of the working class is achieved through a mixture of consent, coercion, threat and deception; the recipe for the mixture varies from one theory to the next, but there is a general consensus that law has ideological functions in a class system. In short, the Marxist theory of law is typically one dimension of an all-embracing 'dominant ideology thesis' (Abercrombie and Turner, 1978). The idea that law is a key ingredient of the dominant ideology has been given particularly strong expression by Poulantzas. With the transition from feudalism to capitalism, the focus of legitimacy passes from the sacred towards the legal and a 'juridical-political ideology' replaces the old religious ideology. The legal ideology is expressed in terms of impersonal, abstract norms:

It is exactly as if the abstract, formal and general character of law had rendered it the mechanism most suitable for fulfilling the key function of every dominant ideology: namely, that of cementing together the social formation under the aegis of the dominant class. (Poulantzas, 1978, pp. 87–8)

The idea that law is an ideological cement in a society where there is market anarchy and class conflict has been a common theme in sociology, albeit expressed in very different ways, from Sumner to Parsons. Following Trubek, I have already compared Weber, Durkheim and Parsons in their analysis of law in relation to the problem of social order. One crucial difference between Weber and Poulantzas, however, is that, while Poulantzas conceives of law as a dominant ideology aimed at the working class, Weber treats law as primarily a set of imperatives aimed at the dominant class. For Weber, the law provides capitalists with a stable environment for exchange and a predictable administrative structure. Despite the conventional approach in sociology which connects Weber's sociology with the problem of legitimacy in capitalist society, Weber's analysis of law is very far removed from the assumptions of the dominant ideology thesis in Pashukanis, Edelman and Poulantzas.

To conclude, Weber has been criticised for presenting a thoroughly inconsistent analysis of law in capitalist society, but I have also shown that Marxist theories of law reproduce most of Weber's conceptual ambiguity and fail to solve problems raised in his sociology of law. In particular, Karl Renner's analysis of law appears to be especially close to Weber's position and, despite his early opposition to Weberian subjectivity, Poulantzas (1978) came to define the law and state in characteristically Weberian terms. Although there are weaknesses and inconsistencies in Weber's sociology of law, it has certain important merits and it would be perfectly possible to make Weber's position coherent by dropping the assumption that there is an affinity between capitalism and formal, rational law. Without the emphasis on the special relationship between capitalism and Roman law, the 'England problem' would disappear. Weber's theory would then focus on the problems of legal organisation and professionalism, that is, on the apparatus of legal transmission. The differences between the legal structures of different capitalist societies would be the social consequence of variations in the institutionalisation of legal education, legal recruitment and professional structure. Weber's theory would not require a clear convergence of interests between professional lawyers and the capitalist class as a whole, although there would be good grounds for expecting some convergence of interests. Capitalists obviously prefer stable, predictable, efficient legal systems, but it is possible for them to operate under a variety of legal forms provided a minimal level of stability is present. The law will tend to be interpreted and applied in the interests of the dominant class regardless of its normative form. English case-law provided such stability and did not inhibit capitalist development. The capitalist class would also prefer a legal system which severely limited trade union activity, regulated industrial conflict and deprived the working class of freedom of action in both political and economic circumstances. There are in principle an infinite number of reasons for assuming that the capitalist class will not achieve these 'ideal' legal conditions. These might include the reluctance of legal theorists to bend the 'rule of law' to favour explicitly such a sectional interest, the ability of trade unions to employ their own lawyers, the interference of the state in the management of industrial relations, the existence of intra-class conflicts between small and large companies. Weber does not resort to forced analogies between the commodity form and the legal form and does not exaggerate the social coherence between the interests of state personnel, legal profession and capitalists. Finally, Weber's treatment of law is not tied to the assumption that the economy is dominated by the capitalist owner; it is not a theory which is necessarily bound to the analysis of law in competitive capitalism.

It would be possible, therefore, to develop Weber's sociology of law in such a fashion as to remove some of the theoretical inconsistency. However, to drop the assumption concerning the affinity between rational, gapless law and capitalism is to remove a major element of Weber's analysis of capitalism as a machine-like entity. It is an important element in Weber's general interest in formal bureaucracy, the separation of family and economy, the growth of modern systems of accountancy and the decline of magical and religious belief systems. In comparative terms, the existence of rational, formal law in Europe is a significant component in the contrast Weber wants to draw between *ad hoc* law-finding in the Orient and the precision of formal law in the Continental system. There are, however, good empirical reasons for believing that the contrast between English judge-made law and the formalism of German law is too sharp. While the capitalist prefers formal legal stability, in historical terms capitalism may develop because and in spite of its juridical environment.

12 Weber and late capitalism

Max Weber has normally been defended against the objective structuralism of neo-Marxism and against mindless positivism on the grounds that he is the main architect of interpretative sociology (Roth and Schluchter, 1979). According to this interpretation, Weber provides a middle path between those positivist sociologies which ignore the creative role of the social actor's own cultural interpretations of social reality and those unrealisable Marxist goals for sociological explanations in terms of economic laws of history. In this study of Weber's sociology, I have largely ignored the debate over Weber's philosophy of science for three central reasons. First, the discussion of Weber's advocacy of 'interpretative sociology' has already been discussed at length by sociologists whose competence in this field exhausts any observations I might make in this area (Outhwaite, 1975; Runciman, 1972). Second, the recent debates about epistemology in sociology and in Marxism in particular have, in my view, not contributed significantly to what I take to be the major task of any sociology which, in the words of Weber, aims to reveal the characteristic uniqueness of our times. Debates about what it is possible to say lack that theoretical and political urgency and commitment which dominate the writing of the founding fathers from Comte to Weber. Thirdly, Weber did not adhere to his own interpretative principles. We have seen in various elements of this study of Weber that in the analysis of religion, law and ideology he did not carry through the project of analysis in terms of indigenous systems of meaning. The principal thesis of this study has been that, while Weber is formally

352

committed to *verstehende soziologie*, in practice his overwhelming sense of fate drives him in an entirely different direction. The main theme of Weberian sociology centres on the
unintentional consequences of human action which Weber
regards as either meaningless or malevolent.

Weber has been regularly criticised by Marxist sociologists
(Poulantzas, 1976) for his apparently subjectivist and individualist approach to social phenomena. By contrast, this
study has emphasised the deterministic and structuralist
aspect of Weber's sociology. The social actor in Weber's
analysis of society, especially in the study of capitalism, is
caught in a network of social circumstances which constantly
work against his intentions and subjective definition of the
situation. The social contexts which Weber studies have a
logic or fate undermining the meaningful actions of individuals. Although Marx and Weber start with entirely different assumptions and perspectives, they are pulled together
by a common recognition of the fatefulness of human interaction. In my commentary on Weber's sociology, I have,
therefore, attempted to question any final, rigorous separation
of Marxism and Weberian sociology. In addition to showing
the parallels between Weberian and Marxist structuralism, I
have also demonstrated that the conceptual and political problems of Frankfurt School Marxism tend to illustrate the
parallels rather than divergences between critical and
Weberian sociology. Of course, I do not want to suggest that
all social science, whether it is Marxist, Weberian or critical, is
unified by a common problematic. There are crucial differences
between the aims of modern Marxism and those of Max
Weber. One major difference involves the question of value-
neutrality. Marxism in various ways attempts to transcend
the Kantian dichotomy of values and facts by claiming that
what we adhere to as moral preferences are built into the unfolding social structure. The vision of an equal and just society
is not merely a personal idiosyncratic preference but a structural requirement. We have seen that Weber is silent in respect
of justice, theodicy and equality because there are no stable,
absolute values which could validate our preferences for the
good society. In modern society, the means for achieving given

ends can be determined by a machine-like certainty, but absolute ends are in fact purely arbitrary. The garden of secular disenchantment rules out charismatic, prophetic ends leaving our world determined by lesser polytheistic divinities. At the same time, we have noticed that Weber's sociology is itself riddled by value-judgment (Dawe, 1971). It is difficult to read Weber's description of capitalism as a destructive system of mechanical processes without being aware of his profound antipathy to modern society. Weber is the Jeremiah of modern capitalism whose prophetic insight cannot be validated by the buttress of certain and reliable values.

The Marxist critique of Weber is necessarily neo-Marxist. In the absence of a revolutionary working class and the collapse of capitalism, modern Marxism has been forced to examine the metamorphosis of capitalism which has permitted its continuing existence. The survival of capitalism has brought Marxists into the analysis of ideology, class fragmentation and state regulation as supports of continuous private appropriation alongside supine working-class acceptance. These reappraisals of Marx underline the fact that Weber's sociology anticipates much that has been central to the empirical and theoretical focus of modern Marxism. The analysis of the state, legal fetishism, the separation of ownership and control, bureaucratic management, de-skilling, ethnic identity, professions and secularisation as crucial concerns of neo-Marxism are all pre-figured in Weber's analysis of rational capitalism. Marxists have attempted to challenge the empirical relevance of Weberian sociology on the grounds that it mistakes surface phenomena for deeper, structural characteristics of the capitalist mode of production. One critical illustration of this objection relates to Weber's treatment of social class.

It is normally held that Weber opposes Marx's definition of class by his emphasis on the distinction between class, status and power (Giddens, 1973; Crompton and Gubbay, 1977; Scott, 1979). Whereas Marx locates the critical class division in relations of production, Weber is regarded as providing a definition of class in terms of differential access to market rewards. Weber defines class in relation to circulation of distributive rewards rather than more fundamental relations of production. In fact, Weber's distinction between class, status and power relates to differences in the power relations of society which he treats as more fundamental than economic relations. For Weber, class, status and power are not three conceptually separate dimensions of social stratification conceived in multi-dimensional terms but simply 'phenomena of power within a community' (Weber, 1968, vol. 2, p. 927). Society is the location for power conflicts over the criteria which will effectively define a system of social closure (Kreckel, 1976). For Weber, the conflict of classes is simply an illustration of the more general phenomenon of political conflict between privileged and disprivileged collectivities for exclusionary membership defined in terms of race, education, wealth and power (Lipset, 1968). Weber does not counter Marx's economic definition of class by a multi-dimensional characterisation of class, status and power; he treats status, economic rewards and political power as three manifestations of a basic struggle for domination. For Weber, the relations between social classes are to be understood as aspects of the social distribution of power in a given society. Such an approach to class stratification provides Weberian sociology with more theoretical flexibility than Marxism which is confronted by the problem of the separation of ownership and control, on the one hand, and by the rise of an economically unproductive, new middle class, on the other.

If the main class boundary is defined by those who own but do not produce and those who produce economic values but do not own the means of production, then there are obvious problems associated with specifying the class position of a middle class which ideologically dominates workers in the mental and manual division of labour while not producing commodities and yet suffering from capitalist exploitation. The various attempts to solve the riddle of the ambiguous class location of the new middle class have not been entirely satisfactory (Poulantzas, 1975; Carchedi, 1975; Wright, 1976). In their attempts to differentiate the new middle class, Marxists have focused on ideological criteria, managerial functions of mental workers, location in the authority structure of the despotic organisation of factories, the consumption function of the new middle class, their occupational advantages in relation to the de-skilling of labour and their capacity to exercise control over subordinates. These attempts to define the class location of the new middle class are, however, difficult to distinguish from Weber's analysis of the practices of social closure. In particular, one peculiar feature of

> this kind of analysis is that despite its avowedly Marxist provenance it is indistinguishable from the approach of modern bourgeois social theory. It is, after all, Weber rather than Marx who provides the framework for understanding class in terms of market opportunities, life-chances and symbolic rewards. The focus upon income differences and other market factors is difficult to reconcile with the standard Marxist objection to bourgeois sociology that it mistakenly operates on the level of distribution instead of on the level of productive relations. (Parkin, 1979, p. 25)

It may be that, following Parkin, once we approach class differences as simply one manifestation of the general conflict between dominant and usurpatory social collectivities for control of scarce resources via the tactics of social closure and social penetration the difficulties of reconciling social class with ethnic, occupational and sexual differences disappear. The attempt to provide a theoretical subordination of distributional differences between age, sex and ethnic groups to productive difference between classes in a predominantly dichotomous scheme of classes is thus fruitless and diversionary.

Despite these problems in the definition of class structuration, it could be held that there is a fundamental convergence between Marx and Weber over the question of the ideological legitimation of both income and productive differences. In this perspective, Weber's notion of ideological legitimation may be directly assimilable to Marx's notion of ideological legitimation. In my view, most existing commentaries on Weber's view of the necessity of the social legitimation of power as acceptable authority miss the point of Weber's emphasis on the contemporary secularisation of political culture. We are by now familiar with Weber's argument that value-neutrality in science is an inevitable companion of the world which does not possess absolute values. Since there is no objective, communal basis for certainty in belief, no position in the scientific realm can ever be secured by an appeal to objective values. In law, natural law is archaic; in religion, the death of God precludes prophecy; in sociology, secularism outlaws certainty. If Weber is not allowed legitimation of scientific findings in his methodology, then he is not permitted legitimation in the arena of political action. It is fairly easy to imagine how charismatic and traditional claims to authority are substantiated and validated, but the claims to authority by institutions based on legal-rational procedures are necessarily problematic.

In *Economy and Society*, Weber distinguishes between charismatic, traditional and legal-rational authority. Charismatic claims are validated by the belief of disciples in the extraordinary qualities of the leader. The status of charismatic leadership is exhibited in the form of special gifts of, for example, healing and prophecy. By contrast, traditional forms of conduct in a community are legitimised by reference to sacred customs and habitual procedures. In legal-rational authority, guides for action are accepted as legitimate because they are produced by formal, rational measures under strictly specified conditions. Charismatic authority is held to be the most unstable since with the death of the leader, the charismatic following evaporates or the authority of leadership is converted into the 'charisma of office' which is eventually determined by tradition. Legal-rational authority is associated with modern industrial society because Weber wants to connect this type of authority with the rise of formal legalism and with the modern bureaucratic state. The existence of the modern state rests on a legal order, an administrative apparatus subject to legal regulation, authority over its citizens and coercion which is either permitted or enacted by statute. The legitimacy of the state rests on the belief that its legal domination is constituted by correct procedures. Bendix (1959, p. 419) points out the deliberate circularity of Weber's definition of legal legitimacy. Laws are regarded as legitimate if they have been enacted and the enactment is legitimate if it follows norms defining the correct procedures to be followed. The definition is an example of methodological neutrality because Weber refuses to discuss the purpose of the state or the possibility that the state may be formed in accordance with substantive rather than formal legality. It is fundamental to the definition of the state that it is the most stable form of authority. Whereas the death of the leader is decisive in the continuity or discontinuity of the charismatic community, the state is equipped with formal procedures of recruitment and replacement of its bureaucratic staff. Bureaucracy is a formal hierarchy of offices, not people.

The argument that, according to Weber, the legal-rational authority of modern bureaucracies produce the maximum degree of stability, predictability and friction-free performance has been systematically challenged by contemporary organisational theory. The emphasis on the chain of command in imperatively co-ordinated associations rules out the possibility that co-operative and consultative systems of decision-making may produce a more favourable institutional climate and legitimation of bureaucratic procedures than a system of rigid authority (Friedrich, 1952). The predictability of procedures may also depend on an individual's location within the authority structure of the bureaucracy. Workers on the shop-floor of large industrial bureaucracies may find their position highly unstable and uncertain (Gouldner, 1952). Weber fails to analyse or to recognise the existence of informal groups and informal procedures which may be functionally necessary for the operation of the formal institution (Blau, 1956). Formal bureaucracy may also develop a ritualistic orientation to rules as the means for achieving bureaucratic ends, organisational means may become ends in themselves (Merton, 1940). Although much of the criticism of Weber's typology of bureaucracy is misconceived (Albrow, 1970), it does raise an important problem concerning the legitimacy of legal-rational norms in modern society.

By refusing to face the issue of what actual, substantive values do underline the intervention of the state in the community, Weber leaves the question of political loyalty to the state in a sociologically ambiguous condition. Weber's analysis of legal-rational authority tells us a great deal about *how* legal and political decisions can be arrived at in organisational terms, but it tells us very little about *what* these decisions are. From the point of view of my emotional 'sense of justice', I may conclude that the decisions of a court in a totalitarian state, regardless of the fact that these decisions are achieved by legal enactment according to formal procedures, do not possess one iota of legitimacy. This possibility brings us back to the problem that, given Weber's value-neutrality in the definition of legitimate authority, any state is legitimate by virtue of political monopoly over the apparatus of power. The modern state operates according to formal, legal procedures; therefore, the state is legitimate. Despite the conventional sociological view that Weber treats the modern state as a stable, machine-like order of coercion, there is some evidence that Weber in fact thinks that the modern state does not possess legitimate stability. The secularisation of industrial society, the growth of scepticism and the attacks of socialist legal theory have made it difficult to clothe the activities of the modern state in the language of natural law and in the language of substantive reasonableness. Weber points out that:

> Natural law is the sum total of all those norms which are valid independently of, and superior to, any positive law and which owe their dignity not to arbitrary enactment but, on the contrary, provide the very legitimation for the binding force of positive law. (Weber, 1954, pp. 287-8)

Weber's positivist (in the legal sense) definition of legitimacy is circular because legal correctness is given by the law-making procedure itself. By contrast, natural law legitimacy appeals to an extra-legal sense of 'the nature of things' and to human rationality and rights in 'a state of nature'. A state which does not govern in accord with the laws of nature can, in principle, be rejected as illegal and illegitimate. However, natural law has been robbed of plausibility and consequently the modern state rests ultimately on 'arbitrary enactment'.

The struggle for power in the context of the modern state and its bureaucratic apparatus takes the form of a struggle between formal and substantive principles of law. In Weber's view, the emergence of distinctive occupational groups under the capitalist division of labour produces pressure groups which advance their economic claims by legal devices which are based on the particular circumstances of the group rather than on formal principles of law. While in theory all individuals are equal before the law, special laws are enacted by reference to the peculiarities of each pressure group. The struggle for differentials between occupational groups in the sphere of circulation results in legal changes which are formally inconsistent with the principles of rational law. The control of law-making procedures is thus part of the struggle between privileged and disprivileged groups to maintain or to undermine the existing distributional system, a struggle which constantly brings into question the precarious legitimacy of the state.

Sociologists have often argued that, whereas Marx conceives capitalist society in terms of the 'anarchy of the market' and in terms of self-destructive productive processes, Weber treats modern society as a rationally organised, bureaucratic and stable order of hierarchical relations. Against such an interpretation, I am claiming that, given the instability of the state's legitimacy in the absence of a consensus over absolute values, Weber regards modern society as an arena of group conflict. Ethnic, religious, occupational and other 'pariah-groups' organise themselves to achieve greater rewards through political means which are often accompanied by appeals to theodicies of revenge, substantive rights or natural law. Privileged groups close their ranks to outsiders by exclusionary practices which seek to preserve 'the monopolization of specific, usually economic opportunities' (Weber, 1968, vol. 1, p 342). Membership of these conflicting groups and consciousness of that membership may be defined by a variety of social characteristics such as religion, ethnicity or economic location in the division of labour.

Because Weber has this very clear view of the conflictual nature of capitalist society, it has not proved difficult to develop Weber's arguments to produce a theory of the inherent economic and political instability of any society based on the production of commodities by propertyless wage labour for the realisation of profit. For example, Parkin (1979) has developed Weber's concept of 'social closure' to demonstrate that in contemporary Britain the existing system is threatened by the fact that both middle and working class are dissatisfied with the rewards they have achieved in a situation where inflation and the erosion of traditional status distinctions have removed many of the historical advantages of privileged membership. In previous centuries the exclusionary practices of both dominant and subordinate groups were collectivist, but the growth of a meritocracy based on credentialism and professional training rather than on inheritance has given rise to an individualistic system of social closure. There has also been a diminution of the collective stigma attached to the working class as a communal group so that 'the status of the worker does not derive to anything like the same extent from his immersion in a total collective identity and its accompanying rituals of personal degradation' (Parkin, 1979, p. 69). The loss of a stable system of prestige-ranking has been accompanied by an increasing ability of organised labour to realise its objective of a redistribution of economic rewards, at least in terms of income distribution. With the advances in industrial technology, certain sections of the working class now occupy key positions in the technical organisation of capitalist enterprises. Attempts to control inflationary wage-demands by an appeal to 'reasonableness', 'responsibility' and 'national duty' have proved largely unsuccessful because the values behind these appeals are archaic and irrelevant. The consequence of this situation is that 'stagnant capitalism is an unusual form of social system that gives rise to serious resentment and discontent among *both* the major classes. This is its distinctive and politically unsettling feature' (Parkin, 1979, p. 84). To this picture of general discontent, we might add that recent attempts to use the law in the area of industrial disputes have merely reinforced the belief, or at least fear, that modern law-making is 'arbitrary enactment'.

In contemporary sociology, Weber's analysis of capitalist instability has, therefore, been linked with the analysis of the inflationary crisis of advanced capitalism. A clear illustration is to be found in Goldthorpe (1978). Most conventional theories of inflation are either monetarist or cost-push theories. The former explains inflation in terms of rapid expansion of the money supply by governments which are treated either as capricious or subject to vote-maximising pressures. Cost-push theories regard the leapfrogging activities of trade unions as the principal cause of inflation and similarly treat unions as either badly informed as to the effects of 'unreasonable' wage-demands or controlled by the political pressure of discontented rank-and-file members. Goldthorpe presents a counter-argument which attempts to locate price inflation as a permanent feature of any society with a system of class stratification. First, the normative status order of capitalist society has collapsed as capitalism has used up its 'moral legacy' and therefore much of the normative inhibition on wage-demands has suffered erosion. Secondly, the working class has been relatively successful in achieving citizenship rights within capitalist society and now expects to enjoy full employment and rising wages as of right. Thirdly, these citizenship rights have been reinforced by the fact that the British working class is now mature in the sense of being an urbanised, self-recruiting, homogeneous group. Wage-demands and hostility to deflationary government policy are to be seen as defensive reactions against threats to rights and privileges of citizenship. The governments of capitalist societies are consequently faced by the problem of price inflation and with the conflicts which lie behind inflation. However, while Parkin regards these social developments as an acute threat to capitalist society, Goldthorpe argues that inflation may well be an alternative to revolution. Creeping inflation permits the class struggle to proceed in a politically blind direction and encourages sectionalism rather than solidarity as powerful sections of the working class attempt to preserve differentials.

The implication of Weber's notion that natural law can no longer operate as a legitimation of state activity and the implication of recent applications of Weber's perspective on group conflicts over distributive rewards is that modern society is characterised by 'the end of ideology'. However, while theorists of the 'end of ideology' in the 1960s claimed that ideology was disappearing because capitalism had largely solved the problems of production and class relationships, Weber believes that there are limitations on the ability of the modern state to regularise conflicts in the market-place by legal institutions based on formal, rational law. One of these limitations is the failure of religious or traditional systems of meaning to survive the advance of rational capitalism. The 'success' of capitalism in replacing previous modes of production undermines its ideological basis with the withering away of communal, absolute values on which the traditional order of estates was grounded. There is, therefore, a direct theoretical link between Weber's view on the problem of state legitimation and those put forward by Habermas (1976a) in *Legitimation Crisis*. In its attempts to balance the need for taxation of the economy and welfare rewards for the political loyalty of its citizens, the modern state constantly exhausts its limited sources of legitimacy. In modern capitalism, there is a profound extension of state activity in the regulation of the economy and society. There has to be an increase in the legitimation of state intervention into new areas of life, but the very process of introducing administrative planning into social life has the unintended consequence of weakening traditional legitimation. Rational administrative planning is corrosive of social meanings which, unlike consumer goods, cannot be subject to reproduction through a state plan. Ideologies cannot be simply manufactured by government decree; indeed, systems of meaning and ideology 'remain "living" as long as they take shape in an unplanned, nature-like manner or are shaped by hermeneutic consciouness' (Habermas, 1976a, p. 70). The state may attempt to plan for its own legitimation through the control of the educational curriculum, for example, but there are definite limits to such planning activity. The legitimation deficit may be compensated by an increase in welfare rewards to the civil population, but these activities may be self-defeating since they merely increase the tax burden on industrial enterprises. If welfare payments place a corset around industrial profits, then there may be sharp economic crisis leading to higher unemployment and inflation. The state can no longer reward effort and loyalty through the benefits of full employment in an expanding economy. The legitimation crisis at this stage may become also a crisis of motivation as the ideology of achievement can no longer be validated in terms of social mobility and status rewards. There is in this argument a close parallel to Weberian formulations in that, with the disappearance of traditional legitimations of social inequality, there are no normative restraints on sectional demands for greater rewards and this situation in turn restricts the ability of governments to limit public expenditure in periods of economic stagnation.

In this conclusion, it has been suggested that many of the conventional attempts to distinguish Marx and Weber by reference to their analysis of capitalism are false. There is a fundamental agreement over (1) the modern factory is an imperatively coordinated system which exercises despotic control over the worker and (2) the market place is characterised by the anarchy of sectional or class conflicts over the distribution of rewards. The real difference is that Marx believes that the crisis of capitalist production can only be finally resolved by a new system of production, while Weber claims that socialism is, at best, merely another version of rational, bureaucratic, industrial society. It is instructive, therefore, to conclude with an examination of Weber's views on the crises of the capitalist economy and the nature of socialism.

The clearest statement of Weber's views on socialism appears in an article first published in 1916 when the level of state control and the prospects of revolution were both enhanced by the crisis of a wartime economy. Weber starts this essay on socialism by outlining what he takes to be the crucial characteristics of the capitalist mode of production. He notes first that the labourer in capitalism is both separated from the means of production and disciplined by the mechanisation of production under factory conditions. Unlike the slave in the plantation system, the modern worker is subject to a strict system of industrial recruitment and selection. It is the competition between capitalists that forces them to be selective and to set their wage-costs at a minimum. It is the same competition which compels the capitalist to expel labour in favour of mechanised production and to de-skill labour, at least in the sense of substituting unskilled for skilled workers. We recognise that, especially under wartime conditions, the degree of state regulation of the economy has greatly increased, but this form of 'collective economy' falls far short of genuine socialism since it goes hand in hand with the continued subordination of labour in a society where the requirement for profit 'is still the decisive factor' (Weber, 1978, p. 255). However, Weber also feels that the changes in the class structure of capitalism as predicted in the *Communist Manifesto*, which he interprets as a thesis about the polarisation and pauperisation of classes, have been discredited on purely empirical grounds. He argues that the working class, especially the agricultural working class, has not been uniformly pauperised by the development of capitalism in Germany. Between the industrial worker and the capitalist, there has emerged an intermediary class of 'office workers, the bureaucrats of the private enterprise system: their numbers increase at a much faster rate than those of the manual workers, and their interests clearly do not by any means lie in the direction of proletarian dictatorship' (Weber, 1978, p. 258). The whole labour force has undergone extensive differentiation and fragmentation so that it is impossible to establish a general set of interests against the existence of the capitalist system. Finally, the capitalist has been able to minimise the effects of the business cycle by regulating prices and sales through a policy of cartelisation which has been further supported by the regulation of credit through the big banks.

Weber also believes that the arguments of evolutionary socialism concerning the incipient socialisation of production in capitalism are also false. The growth of joint stock companies, the intervention of the state in the economy and the importance of banking interests result in the dominance of officialdom rather than an evolution towards socialism. In addition to the proliferation of officials, there is 'a proliferation of *rentiers*, that is, of the class which lives on dividends and rents alone, without, like the entrepreneur, performing any mental work, but has a stake in the capitalist system in virtue of its interest in all its sources of income' (Weber, 1978, p. 260). The process of standardisation and de-skilling is limited and certainly not unidimensional. The mechanisation and standardisation of production give rise to a new stratum of office workers and supervisors who, through new types of education, close their ranks to manual workers in order to defend and enhance their privileges of employment. Moreover, there is no guarantee that, were these processes of standardisation, bureaucratisation and state control to replace the private enterprise system and private property, the new system would be directed along socialist lines. On the contrary, the collapse of competitive capitalism might equally result in greater centralised control under an all-embracing stratum of officials. Weber's value-neutrality is here combined with his antipathy to the political power of bureaucracy in modern society to produce a deeply sceptical review of the prospects of socialism. It could be objected against Weber that, as a mental worker inside the state-controlled educational bureaucracy, his neutrality is the result of the advantages of his social stratum which could survive parasitically under capitalism or under socialism. Weber is at least aware of this moral difficulty since, as his wife informs us, he thinks that one could only become a socialist with honesty 'if one was prepared to share the way of life of the propertyless, at least to give up a cultured existence based on *their* labour' (Weber, 1975, p. 630).

Given Weber's abiding interest in systems of political domination and power conflicts, it is perhaps not surprising that he invests so much theoretical effort into the analysis of the bureaucrats whom he saw as the critical social group in German society. Germany had developed with neither a politically mature bourgeoisie nor a mature working class. Prussian society had been historically dependent on the political leadership of East German *Junker* class and the decline of that class had left a political vacuum which the state bureaucrats were only too happy to fill. In modern terminology, the bureaucrats were a stratum which exercised governing powers without being a ruling class. This officialdom in the private and public sector had become an indispensable element of capitalism in securing discipline in the factory and a stable administrative environment within society as a whole.

Bureaucratism had become the political cancer of contemporary capitalism, having massive effects at all levels of the social hierarchy. With the spread of rational calculation and bureaucratic standardisation, 'the performance of each individual worker is mathematically measured, each man becomes a little cog in the machine and, aware of this, his one preoccupation is whether he can become a bigger cog' (Weber, 1924, p. 414). The social position of the bureaucrat was now buttressed by lengthy training and by credentialism which secured the ranks of officialdom from external dilution. The political position of the bureaucracy was also extremely powerful. With their security of tenure and stable political experience, the politician in relation to the official was a mere dilettante. In fact, the bureaucracy was largely indifferent to its political masters. The impersonality of bureacratic control and their importance for continued administration meant that 'officialdom continues to function smoothly after the enemy has occupied the territory; he merely needs to change the top official. It continues to operate because it is to the vital interest of everyone concerned, including above all the enemy' (Weber, 1968, vol. 3, pp. 988-9). For these reasons, Weber fears that socialist economic measures will leave the question of continuing political government by bureaucracy unresolved. A decisive political programme is necessary as the means for gaining control over the bureaucratic apparatus without which neither capitalism nor socialism could withstand the tyranny of office (Krygier, 1979).

Modern Marxism has been forced to come to terms with a number of major institutional and structural changes in late capitalism. These include: the progressive separation of ownership and control in the form of depersonalised property (Scott, 1979), the growth of a new middle class of propertyless, salaried workers (Poulantzas, 1975), the regulation of the economy by the state (Holloway and Picciotto, 1978), the dominant role of the multi-national corporation (Radice, 1975) and the arrival of new forms of the decomposition of labour with migrant labour (Castles and Kosack, 1973). I have no doubt that by fairly extensive exegetical labours it can be shown that Marx's discussion of the joint stock company provides the basis for the analysis of all developments in late capitalism. However, if such theoretical anticipation could be established in the case of Marx, how much more would we have to grant the theoretical fruitfulness and relevance of Weber's detailed, systematic appraisal of the formation of late capitalist society? Despite the theoretical proximity of Marxism and Weberian sociology, it is quite clear why Weber sticks in the conceptual throats of modern Marxists. Weber implicitly condemns modern capitalism as a heartless machine dominating its human cogs, but he steadfastly refuses to hold out any hope of a more desirable future. Once the fateful mix of capitalism, science and bureaucracy had been historically secured, the future of human society could not be anything other than an extended version of the desolate garden of disenchantment.

Bibliography

Aaby, R. (1977), 'Engels and women', *Critique of Anthropology*, vol. 3, pp. 25–53.

Abel-Smith, Brian (1960), *A History of the Nursing Profession*, London

Abercrombie, Nicholas (1980), *Class, Structure and Knowledge*, Oxford.

Abercrombie, Nicholas, Hill, Stephen, and Turner, Bryan S. (1980), *The Dominant Ideology Thesis*, London.

Abercrombie, Nicholas, and Turner, Bryan S. (1978), 'The dominant ideology thesis', *British Journal of Sociology*, vol. 29, pp. 149–70.

Abercrombie, Nicholas, Turner, Bryan S., and Urry, John (1976), 'Class, state and fascism: the work of Nicos Poulantzas, *Political Studies*, vol. 24, pp. 510–19.

Abrahamian, Ervand (1975), 'European feudalism and Middle Eastern despotism', *Science & Society*, vol. 39, pp. 129–56.

Abun-Nasr, Jamil M. (1965), *The Tijaniyya. A Sufi Order in the Modern World*, London.

Ackerman, Nathan W., and Jahoda, Marie (1950), *Anti-Semitism and Emotional Disorder: a psychological interpretation*, New York.

Adams, F. R. (1969), 'From Association to Union: professional organization of Asylum Attendants 1869-1919', *British Journal of Sociology*, vol. 20, pp. 11-26.

Adey, Glyn, and Frisby, David (1976), *The Positivist Dispute in German Sociology*, London.

Adorno, Theodor W. (1967-8), 'Sociology and psychology',

New Left Review, no. 46, pp. 67–80 and no. 47, pp. 79–97.

Adorno, Theodor W. (1973), *Negative Dialectics*, London.

Adorno, Theodor W. (1974), *Minima Moralia: Reflections from Damaged Life*, London.

Adorno, Theodor, Frenkel-Brunswik, Else, Levinson, Daniel J., Nevitt Sanford, R. (1950), *The Authoritarian Personality*, New York.

Adorno, Theodor W., and Horkheimer, Max (1973), *Dialectic of Enlightenment*, London.

Alavi, Hamza (1972), 'The state in post-colonial societies—Pakistan and Bangladesh', *New Left Review*, no. 74 pp. 59–81.

Albrow, M. (1970), *Bureaucracy*, London.

Albrow, M. (1975-6), 'R. Stammler's "surmounting" of the materialist conception of history (Max Weber)', *British Journal of Law and Society*, vol. 2, pp. 129–52 and vol. 3, pp. 17–43.

Alexander, A. D. (1960), 'Industrial entrepreneurship in Turkey: origins and growth', *Economic Development and Culture Change*, vol. 8, pp. 349–65.

Algar, Hamid (1969), *Religion and State in Iran 1785–1906* Berkeley and Los Angeles.

Althusser, Louis (1969), *For Marx*, Harmondsworth.

Althusser, Louis (1971), *Lenin and Philosophy and Other Essays*, London.

Althusser, Louis, and Balibar, Etienne (1970), *Reading Capital*, London.

Amin, Samir (1978), *The Arab Nation, nationalism and class struggles*, London.

Anderson, Perry (1974a), *Lineages of the Absolutist State*, London.

Anderson, Perry (1974b), *Passages from Antiquity to Feudalism*.

Anderson, Perry (1976), *Considerations on Western Marxism*, London.

Anthony, P. D. (1977), *The Ideology of Work*, London.

Apter, D. (1965), *The Politics of Modernization*, Chicago.

Aptheker, M. (ed.) (1965), *Marxism and Alienation*, New York.

Arberry, A. J. (1943), *British Orientalists*, London.

Aron, Raymond, (1964), *German Sociology*, London.

Ashraf, Ahmad (1970), 'Historical obstacles to the development of a bourgeoisie in Iran', in Cook (1970), pp. 308-32.

Atkinson, A. B. (1974), *Unequal Shares*, Harmondsworth.

Atkinson, A. B. (1975), *The Economics of Inequality*, Oxford.

Avineri, Shlomo (1968), *The Social and Political Thought of Karl Marx*, Cambridge.

Avineri, Shlomo (ed.) (1969), *Karl Marx on Colonialism and Modernisation*, New York.

Avineri, Shlomo (1970), *The Social and Political Thought of Karl Marx*, Cambridge.

Avineri, Shlomo (1972), 'Modernization and Arab society: some reflections', in Howe and Gersham (1972), pp. 300-11.

Baker, F. 'The people called Methodists 3. "Polity" ', in Davies and Rupp (1965), pp. 213-55.

Balbus, Issac D. (1978), 'The commodity form and legal form: an essay on the relative autonomy of the law', in Reasons and Rich (1978), pp. 73-90.

Banaji, Jairus (1973), 'Backward capitalism, primitive accumulation and modes of production', *Journal of Contemporary Asia*, vol. 3, pp. 393-413.

Baran, Paul A., and Hobsbawm, E. J. (1961), 'The stages of economic growth', *Kyklos*, vol. 14, pp. 234-42.

Barber, W. H. (1955), *Leibniz in France: from Arnauld to Voltaire, a study in French reactions to Leibnizianism 1670-1760*, Oxford.

Barratt Brown, M. (1974), *The Economics of Imperialism*, Harmondsworth.

Barth, Fred (1961), *The Nomads of South Persia*, Oslo.

Beck, Lois, and Keddie, Nikki (eds) (1978), *Women in the Muslim World*, Cambridge.

Bell, Daniel (1965), *The End of Ideology*, New York.

Bellah, Robert (1963), 'Reflections on the Protestant ethic analogy in Asia', *Journal of Social Issues*, vol. 19, pp. 52-60.

Bellah, Robert N. (ed.) (1965), *Religion and Progress in Modern Asia*, New York.

Bendix, Reinhard (1959), *Max Weber, an intellectual portrait*, London.

Bendix, Reinhard, and Roth, Guenther (1971), *Scholarship and Partisanship: essays on Max Weber*, Berkeley and Los Angeles.

Benton, T. (1977), *Philosophical Foundations of the Three Sociologies*, London.

Berger, Peter L. (1963), 'Charisma and religious innovation: the social location of Israelite prophecy', *American Sociological Review*, vol. 28, pp. 940–51.

Berger, Peter L. (1969a), *The Social Reality of Religion*, London.

Berger, Peter L. (1969b), *A Rumor of Angels*, New York.

Berger, Peter L., Berger, Brigette, and Kelmen, Hansfield (1973), *The Homeless Mind*, Harmondsworth.

Berger, Peter L., and Luckmann, Thomas (1966), *The Social Construction of Reality, everything that passes for knowledge in society*, London.

Berlant, Jeffrey L. (1975), *Professions and Monopoly, a study of medicine in the United States and Great Britain*, Berkeley.

Bernstein, Richard J. (1979), *The Restructuring of Social and Political Theory*, London.

Bettelheim, Bruno, and Janowitz, Morris (1950), *Dynamics of Prejudice: a psychological and sociological study of veterans*, New York.

Binder, Leonard (ed.) (1976), *The Study of the Middle East*, New York.

Blanke, Bernhard, Jurgens, Ulrich, and Kastendiek, Hans (1978), 'On the current Marxist discussion on the analysis of form and function of the bourgeois state', in Holloway and Picciotto (1978), pp. 108–47.

Blau, Peter M. (1956), *Bureaucracy in Modern Society*, New York.

Blau, Peter M. (ed.) (1975), *Approaches to the Study of Social Structure*, New York.

Blauner, R. (1964), *Alienation and Freedom*, Chicago.

Bloom, Solomon F. (1942), 'Karl Marx and the Jews', *Jewish Social Studies*, vol. 4, pp. 3-16.

Bottomore, Tom, and Goode, Patrick (1978), *Austro-Marxism*, Oxford.

Bottomore, Tom, and Nisbet, Robert (eds) (1979), *A History of Sociological Analysis*, London.

Boyle, J. A. (ed.) (1968), *The Cambridge History of Iran*, vol. 5, Cambridge.

Brand, Arie (1977), 'Interests and the growth of knowledge—a comparison of Weber, Popper and Habermas', *The Netherlands Journal of Sociology*, vol. 13, pp. 1-20.

Brody, Saul Nathaniel (1974), *The Disease of the Soul, leprosy in medieval literature*, Ithaca and London.

Brown, George. W. (1976), 'Depression. A Sociological View', *The Maudsley Gazette*, pp. 9-12.

Brown, George W., and Harris T. (1978), *Social Origins of Depression: a study of psychiatric disorder in women*, London.

Brown, Leon Carl (1972), 'The religious establishment in Husainid Tunisia', in Keddie (1972), pp. 47-91.

Brown, R. G. S., and Stones, R. W. H. (1973), *The Male Nurse*, London.

Buck-Morss, Susan (1977), *The Origins of Negative Dialectics: Theodor W. Adorno, Walter Benjamin and the Frankfurt Institute*, Hassocks, Sussex.

Burger, Thomas (1976), *Max Weber's Theory of Concept Formation: history, laws and ideal types*, North Carolina, Durham.

Burnham, J. (1945), *The Managerial Revolution*, Harmondsworth.

Butts, S. (1977), 'Parsons' interpretation of Weber: a methological analysis', *Sociological Analysis & Theory*, vol. 7 pp. 227-41.

Cahnman, Werner J. (1964), 'Max Weber and the Methological Controversy in the Social Sciences', in Cahnman and Boskoff (1964), pp. 103-27.

Cahnman, Werner J., and Boskoff, Alvin (eds) (1964), *Sociology and History*, Chicago, Ill.

Carchedi, G. (1975), 'On the economic identification of the

new middle class', *Economy & Society*, vol. 4, pp. 1–86.

Carr-Saunders, A. M., and Wilson, P. A. (1933), *The Professions*, Oxford.

Cartwright, B. C., and Schwartz, R. D. (1973), 'The invocation of legal norms: an empirical investigation of Durkheim and Weber', *American Sociological Review*, vol. 38, pp. 340–54.

Cartwright, Frederick F. (1977), *A Social History of Medicine*, London.

Castles, S. , and Kosack, G. (1973), *Immigrant Workers and Class Structure in Western Europe*, Oxford.

Chenu, M. D. (1969), *L'Eveil de la Conscience dans la Civilisation Médiévale*, Paris.

Clarke, Simon (1977), 'Marxism, sociology and Poulantzas' theory of the state', *Capital and Class*, vol. 2, pp. 1–31.

Cohen, J., Hazelrigg, Lawrence E., and Pope, Whitney (1975), 'De-Parsonizing Weber: a critique of Parsons' interpretation of Weber's sociology', *American Sociological Review*, vol. 40, pp. 229–41.

Connerton, Paul (ed.) (1976), *Critical Sociology*, Harmondsworth.

Cook, M. A. (ed.) (1970), *Studies in the Economic History of the Middle East*, London.

Cox, Caroline, and Mead, Adrianne (eds) (1975), *A Sociology of Medical Practice*, London.

Crapanzano, Vincent (1973), *The Hamadsha. A Study in Moroccan Ethno-psychiatry*, Berkeley.

Critchley, John (1978), *Feudalism*, London.

Crompton, Rosemary, and Gubbay, Jon (1977), *Economy and Class Structure*, London.

Curley, E. M. (1972), 'The root of contingency', in Frankfurt (1972), pp. 69–97.

Dahrendorf, Ralph (1968), 'On the origin of inequality among men', in *Essays in the Theory of Society*, Stanford, pp. 151–78.

Dainton, Courtney (1961), *The Story of England's Hospitals*, London.

D'Amico, Robert (1978), 'Desire and the commodity form',

Telos, no. 35, pp. 88–122.

Davies, R., and Rupp, G. (eds) (1965), *A History of the Methodist Church in Great Britain*, 2 vols., London.

Davis, Fred (1975), 'Professional socialization as subjective experience: the process of doctrinal conversion among student nurses', in Cox and Mead (1975), pp. 116–31.

Davis, Horace B. (1965), 'Nations, colonies and social classes: the position of Marx and Engels', *Science & Society*, vol. 29, pp. 26–43.

Dawe, Alan (1971), 'The relevance of values', in Sahay (1971), pp. 37–66.

de Kadt, Emanuel, and Williams, Gavin (eds) (1974), *Sociology and Development*, London.

Denton, John A. (1978), *Medical Sociology*, Boston.

Despland, Michel (1973), *Kant on History and Religion*, Montreal and London.

Dibble, Vernon K. (1968), 'Social science and political commitments in the young Weber', *Archives Européennes de Sociologie*, vol. 9, pp. 92–110.

Dingwall, Robert, and McIntosh, Jean (eds) (1978), *Readings in the Sociology of Nursing*, Edinburgh.

Dohrenwend, Bruce P., and Dohrenwend, Barbara S. (1969), *Social Status and Psychological Disorder: a causal inquiry*, New York.

Dos Santos, T. (1970), 'The structure of dependence', *American Economic Review*, vol. 60, pp. 231–6.

Duby, George (1978), *Medieval Marriage—two Models from twelfth century France*, Baltimore and London.

Durkheim, Emile (1961), *The Elementary Forms of Religious Life*, New York.

Durkheim, Emile (1964), *The Division of Labour in Society*, Chicago, Ill.

Dwyer, Daisy Hilse (1978), 'Women, Sufism and decision-making in Moroccan Islam', in Beck and Keddie (1978), pp. 585–98.

Edelman, Bernard, (1979), *Ownership of the Image, elements for a Marxist theory of law*, London.

Ehrenreich, Barbara, and English, Deidre (1973), *Witches, Midwives and Nurses. A history of women healers*, London.

Eisenstadt, S. N. (1956), *From Generation to Generation*, New York.

Eisenstadt, S. N. (ed.) (1968), *The Protestant Ethic and Modernization*, New York.

Emmanuel, A. (1972), *Unequal Exchange*, London.

Emmet, D., and MacIntyre, A. (eds) (1970), *Sociological Theory and Philosophical Analysis*, London.

Engels, F. (n.d.), *The Origin of the Family, Private Property and the State* (first edition 1884), Moscow.

Erritt, M. J., and Alexander, J. C. D. (1977), 'Ownership of company shares', *Economic Trends*, pp. 96–105.

Espinasse, Francis (1895), *Life of Ernest Renan*, London.

Evans, Alva D., and Howard, Louis G. (1930), *The Romance of the British Voluntary Hospital Movement*, London.

Evans-Pritchard, E. E. (1949), *The Sanusi of Cyrenaica*, Oxford.

Fakhouri, Hani (1968), 'The zar cult in an Egyptian village'. *Anthropological Quarterly*, vol. 41, pp. 49–56.

Feuer, Lewis (1963), 'Alienation, the career of a concept', in Stein and Vidich (1963), pp. 127–47.

Fine, Bob, Kinsey, Richard, Lea, John, Picciotto, Sol, and Young, Jock (eds) (1979), *Capitalism and the Rule of Law: from deviancy theory to Marxism*, London.

Fleischmann, Eugene (1964), 'De Weber à Nietzsche', *Archives Européennes de sociologie*, vol. 5, pp. 190–238.

Fletcher, Ronald (1971), *The Making of Sociology. Beginnings and Foundations*, vol. 1, London.

Foster-Carter, Aidan (1974), 'Neo-Marxist approaches to development and underdevelopment', in de Kadt and Williams (1974), pp. 67–105.

Foster-Carter, Aidan (1976), 'Marxism and the "Fact of Conquest" ', *The African Review*, vol. 6, pp. 17–32.

Fourquin, Guy (1976), *Lordship and Feudalism in the Middle Ages*, London.

Frank, A. G. (1969), *Latin America: Underdevelopment of Revolution*, New York.

Frank, A. G. (1972), *Sociology of Underdevelopment and the Underdevelopment of Sociology*, London.

Frankfurt, Harry G. (ed.) (1972), *Leibniz: a collection of critical essays*, London.

Frankfurt Institute (1936), *Studien über Autorität und Familie*, Paris.

Frankfurt Institute (1973), *Aspects of Sociology*, London.

Fraser, John (1976-7), 'Louis Althusser on science, Marxism and politics', *Science & Society*, vol. 40, pp. 438-64.

Freud, Sigmund (1949), *Civilization and its Discontents*, London.

Freund, Julian (1968), *The Sociology of Max Weber*, London.

Freund, Julian (1979), 'German sociology in the time of Max Weber', in Bottomore and Nisbet (1979), pp. 149-86.

Friedrich, Carl J. (1952), 'Some observations on Weber's analysis of bureaucracy', in Merton et al. (1952), pp. 27-33.

Frith, Simon (1978), *The Sociology of Rock*, London.

Fromm, Erich (1973), *The Crisis of Psychoanalysis: essays on Freud, Marx and Social Psychology*, Harmondsworth.

Fück, J. W. (1962), 'Islam as a historical problem in European historiography since 1800', in Lewis and Holt (1962), pp. 303-14.

Furtado, C. (1964), *Development and Underdevelopment*, California.

Gamarnikow, Eva (1978), 'Sexual division of labour: the case of nursing', in Kuhn and Wolpe (1978), pp. 96-123.

Geertz, Clifford (1968), *Islam Observed: religious developmen.in Morocco and Indonesia*, New Haven.

Geijbels, M. (1978), 'Aspects of the veneration of saints in Islam, with special reference to Pakistan', *The Muslim World*, vol. 68, pp. 176-86.

Gellner, Ernest (1968), 'A pendulum swing theory of Islam', *Annales de Sociologie*, pp. 5-14.

Gellner, Ernest (1970), 'Concepts and society', in Emmet and MacIntyre (1970), pp. 115-49.

Gellner, Ernest (1972), 'Patterns of tribal rebellion in Morocco', in Vatikiotis (1972), pp. 120-45.

George, A. R. (1963), 'Private devotion in the Methodist

tradition', *Studia Liturgica*, vol. 2, pp. 223–36.

George, Katherine, and George, Charles H. (1953–5), 'Roman Catholic sainthood and social status', *Journal of Religion*, vol. 5, pp. 33–5.

Gerschenkron, A. (1962), *Economic Backwardness in Historical Perspective*, Cambridge.

Gibb, H. A. R. (1969), *Mohammedanism, a historical survey*, Oxford.

Gibb, H. A. R., and Bowen, Harold (1957), *Islamic Society and the West*, Oxford.

Giddens, Anthony, (1970), 'Marx and Weber and the Rise of Capitalism', *Sociology*, vol. 6, pp. 289–310.

Giddens, Anthony (1972), 'Four myths in the history of social thought', *Economy and Society*, vol. 1, pp. 357–85.

Giddens, Anthony (1973), *The Class Structure of the Advanced Societies*, London.

Gilsenan, Michael (1973), *Saint and Sufi in Modern Egypt, an essay in the sociology of religion*, Oxford.

Glockner, H. (ed.) (1927–30), *Sämtliche Werke*, 20 vols., Stuttgart.

Goffman, Erving (1961), *Asylums*, Harmondsworth.

Goldthorpe, John H. (1978), 'The current inflation: towards a sociological account', in Hirsch and Goldthorpe (1978), pp. 186–214.

Goody, Jack (1978), 'Inheritance, property and women: some comparative considerations', in Goody, Thirsk and Thompson (1978), pp. 10–36.

Goody, Jack, Thirsk, Joan, and Thompson, E. P. (eds.) (1978), *Family and Inheritance, Rural Society in Western Europe 1700–1800*, Cambridge.

G.O.P.F. (1976), *Land Reform and its Direct Effects in Iran*, Tehran.

Gouldner, Alvin (1952), 'On Weber's analysis of bureaucratic rules', in Merton et al. (1952), pp. 48–51.

Gouldner, Alvin (ed.) (1962), *Socialism* (Emile Durkheim), New York.

Gouldner, Alvin, (1973), 'Anti-Minotaur: the myth of value-free sociology', in *For Sociology*, Harmondsworth, pp. 1–26.

Gramsci, Antonio (1949), *Note sul Machiavelli, sulla politica e sullo stato moderno*, Turin.

Graves, Robert (1972), 'The Fitz-Omar Cult', in *The Rubaiyyat of Omar Khayyam*, Harmondsworth, pp. 7-30.

Green, Martin, (1974), *The Von Richthofen Sisters*, London.

Green, Robert W. (1959), *Protestantism and Capitalism*, Boston.

Greimas, A. J. (1966), *Sémantique structurale*, Paris.

Greimas, A. J. (1970), *Du Sens*, Paris.

Greiner, Norbert (1977), 'Mill, Marx and Bebel; early influences on Shaw: characterisation of women', in Weintraub (1977), pp. 90-8.

Habakkuk, H. J. (1950), 'Marriage settlements in the eighteenth century', *Transactions of the Royal Historical Society*, vol. 32, pp. 15-30.

Habermas, Jürgen (1970), *Zur Logik der Socialwissenchaften*, Frankfurt.

Habermas, Jürgen (1971), *Toward a Rational Society*, London.

Habermas, Jürgen (1972a), *Knowledge and Human Interests*, London.

Habermas, Jürgen (1972b), ''Toward a theory of communicative competence', in Hans Peter Dreitzel (ed.), *Recent Sociology*, no. 2, New York, pp. 115-48.

Habermas, Jürgen (1976a), *Legitimation Crisis*, London.

Habermas, Jürgen (1976b), 'A positively bisected rationalism', in Adey and Frisby (1976), pp. 198-225.

Habermas, Jürgen (1976c), *Zur Rekonstruktion des Historischen Materialismus*, Frankfurt.

Hacker, Helen Mayer (1953), 'Marx, Weber and Pareto on the changing status of women', *American Journal of Economics and Sociology*, vol. 12, pp. 149-62.

Halliday, Fred (1979), *Iran: dictatorship and development*, Harmondsworth.

Halpern, M. (1962), 'Middle Eastern armies and the new middle class', in Johnson (1962), pp. 277-315.

Hansen, Niles (1963), 'The Protestant ethic as a general precondition for economic development', *Canadian Journal of Economic and Political Science*, vol. 24, pp. 462-74.

Harris, H. S. (1972), *Hegel's Development, Toward the Sunlight 1770-1801*, Oxford.

Hart, David M. (1976), 'The French contribution to the social and cultural anthropology of North Africa: a review and an evaluation', in Binder (1976), pp. 219-28.

Hart, Nicky (1976), *When Marriage Ends*, London.

Hay, D., Linebaugh, Peter, Rule, John G., Thompson, E. P., and Winslow, Cal (1975), *Albion's Fatal Tree*, New York.

Heer, Friedrich (1962), *The Medieval World*, London.

Hegel. G. W. F. (1956), *The Philosophy of History*, New York.

Hepworth, M., and Turner, B. S. (1974), 'Confessing to murder', *British Journal of Law and Society*, vol. 1, pp. 31-49.

Hepworth, M., and Turner, B. S. (1979), 'Confession, guilt and responsibility', *British Journal of Law and Society*, vol. 6, pp. 219-34.

Hill, Christopher (1969), ' "Reason" and "reasonableness" in seventeenth-century England', *British Journal of Sociology*, vol. 20, pp. 235-52.

Hilton, Rodney (ed.) (1976), *The Transition from Feudalism to Capitalism*, London.

Hindess, Barry, and Hirst, Paul Q. (1975), *Pre-Capitalist Modes of Production*, London.

Hindess, Barry, and Hirst, Paul Q. (1977), *Mode of Production and Social Formation*, London.

Hinkle, Roscoe C., Jr, and Hinkel, Gisela J. (1954), *The Development of Modern Sociology, its nature and growth in the United States*, New York.

Hirsch, Fred, and Goldthorpe, John H. (eds) (1978), *The Political Economy of Inflation*, London.

Hirst, Paul Q. (1975), *Durkheim, Bernard and Epistemology*, London.

Hirst, Paul Q. (1976), *Social Evolution and Sociological Categories*, London.

Hirst, Paul (1979), *On Law and Ideology*, London.

Hobsbawm, E. J. (1959), *Primitive Rebels*, Manchester.

Hodgson, Marshall G. S. (1974), *The Venture of Islam*, 3 vols, Chicago and London.

Hollingshead, August B., and Redlich, Frederick (1958), *Social Class and Mental Illness, a community study*, New York.

Holloway, John, and Picciotto, Sol (eds) (1978), *State and Capital— a Marxist debate*, London.

Honigsheim, Paul (1968), *On Max Weber*, New York.

Horkheimer, Max (1947), *Eclipse of Reason*, New York.

Horkheimer, Max (1976), 'Traditional and critical theory', in Connerton (1976), pp. 206-24.

Horton, John (1964), 'The dehumanization of anomie and alienation: a problem in the ideology of sociology', *British Journal of Sociology*, vol. 15, pp. 283-300.

Hoselitz, Bert, and Moore, W. E. (eds) (1963), *Industrialization and Society*, The Hague.

Howe, Irving, and Gershman, Carl (eds) (1972), *Israel, the Arabs and the Middle East*, New York.

Howe, Richard Herbert (1978), 'Max Weber's elective affinities: sociology within the bounds of pure reason', *American Journal of Sociology*, vol. 84, pp. 366-85.

Hughes, H. Stuart (1959), *Consciousness and Society*, London.

Hunt, Alan (1978), *The Sociological Movement in Law*, London.

Inkeles, Alex, and Smith, David (1974), *Becoming Modern*, London.

Jafri, S. Husain M. (1979), *Origins and Early Development of Shi'a Islam*, London and New York.

Jameson, Frederic (1973), 'The vanishing mediator: narrative structure in Max Weber', *New German Critique*, vol. 1, pp. 52-89.

Jaspers, Karl (1953), *Three Essays: Leonardo, Descartes, Max Weber*, New York.

Jay, Martin (1973), *The Dialectical Imagination: a history of the Frankfurt School and the Institute of Social Research 1923-1950*, London.

Jay, Martin (1974), 'The Frankfurt School's critique of Karl Mannheim and the sociology of knowledge', *Telos*, no. 20, pp. 72-89.

Johnson, Harry M. (ed.) (1979), *Religious Change and Continuity*, San Francisco.

Johnson, J. J. (ed.) (1962), *The Role of the Military in Underdeveloped Countries*, Princeton.

Johnson, Terence J. (1972), *Professions and Power*, London.

Jones, Gareth Stedman (1977), 'The Marxism of the early Lukács', in *New Left Review*, pp. 11-60.

Jones, K. (1955), *Lunacy, Law and Conscience 1744-1845*, London.

Kahn-Freund, O. (1949), 'Introduction' to Renner (1949), pp. 1-43.

Kalberg, S. (1979), 'The search for thematic orientations in a fragmented oeuvre: the discussion of Max Weber in recent German sociological literature', *Sociology*, vol. 13, pp. 127-39.

Kamenka, Eugene, and Krygier, Martin (eds) (1979), *Bureaucracy, the career of a concept*, London.

Kant, Immanuel (1791), 'On the failure of all attempted philosophical theodicies', in Despland (1973), pp. 283-97.

Keddie, Nikki R. (1966), 'The origins of the religious-radical alliance in Iran', *Past and Present*, no. 34, pp. 70-80.

Keddie, Nikki R. (ed.) (1972), *Scholars, Saints and Sufis, Muslim Religious Institutions in the Middle East since 1500*, Berkeley.

Kennedy, John G. (1967), 'Nubian zar ceremonies as psychotherapy', *Human Organization*, vol. 26, pp. 185-94.

Kerr, J. M., Johnston, R. W., and Phillips, Miles H. (eds) (1954), *Historical Review of British Obstetrics and Gynaecology 1800-1950*, Edinburgh and London.

Keyder, Caglar (1976), 'The dissolution of the Asiatic mode of production', *Economy and Society*, vol. 5, pp. 178-96.

Khaldun, Ibn (1958), *The Muqaddimah, an introduction to history*, 3 vols, London.

Kidron, M. (1968), *Western Capitalism since the War*, Harmondsworth.

Kiernan, V. G. (1972), *The Lords of Human Kind, European attitudes to the outside world in the imperial age*, Harmondsworth.

Kilminster, Richard (1979), *Praxis and Method: a sociological dialogue with Lukács, Gramsci and the early Frankfurt School*, London.

Kissack, R. (1964), *Church or No Church*, London.

Klare, Karl (1979), 'Law-making as praxis', *Telos*, vol. 40, pp. 123-35.

Knox, T. M. (1942), *Hegel's Philosophy of Right*, Oxford.

Koebner, R. (1951), 'Despot and despotism: vicissitudes of a political term', *Journal of the Warburg and Courtauld Institutes*, vol. 14, pp. 275-302.

Kolko, Gabenel (1961), 'Max Weber on America: theory and evidence', *History and Theory*, vol. 1, pp. 243-60.

Kreckel, R. (1976), 'Dimensions of social inequality—conceptual analysis and theory of society', *Sociologische Gids*, no. 6, pp. 338-60.

Kritzeck, James (1973), 'Dervish tales', in Williams (1973), pp. 153-7.

Krygier, Martin (1979), 'Weber, Lenin and the reality of socialism', in Kamenka and Krygier (1979), pp. 61-87.

Kuhn, Annette, and Wolpe, Ann Marie (eds) (1978), *Feminism and Materialism. Women and Modes of Production*, London.

Kumar, Krishnan (1978), *Prophecy and Progress. The Sociology of Industrial and Post-traditional society*, Harmondsworth.

Labedz, L. (ed.) (1962), *Revisionism*, London.

Lambert, Richard D., and Hoselitz, Bert F. (eds) (1963), *The Role of Savings and Wealth in Southern Asia and the West*, Paris.

Lambton, Ann K. S. (1969), *The Persian Land Reform 1962-1969*, Oxford.

Laslett, Peter (1973), 'Age at menarche in Europe since the eighteenth century', in Rabb and Rotberg (1973), pp. 28-46.

Laslett, P., and Runciman, W. G. (eds) (1967), *Philosophy, Politics and Society*, third series, Oxford.

Lawson, J. (1965), 'The people called Methodists 2. "Our discipline"', in Davies and Rupp (1965), pp. 181-209.

Leach, E. R. (ed.) (1968), *Dialectic in Practical Religion*, Cambridge.

Lecky, W. E. H. (1883), *A History of England in the Eighteenth Century*, 2 vols, London.

Leibniz, G. W. (1951), *Theodicy*, London.

Lerner, D. (1964), *The Passing of Traditional Society*, New York.

Lewis, Bernard, and Holt, P. M. (eds) (1962), *Historians of the Middle East*, London.

Lewis, C. S. (1936), *The Allegory of Love*, London.

Lewis, J. (1975), *Max Weber and Value-Free Sociology, a Marxist critique*, London.

Lichtheim, George (1961), *Marxism*, London.

Lichtheim, George (1963), 'Marx and the "Asiatic mode of production" ', *St. Antony's Papers*, no. 14, pp. 86–112.

Lichtheim, George (1970), *Lukács*, London.

Light, I. (1969), 'The social construction of uncertainty' *Berkeley Journal of Sociology*, vol. 14, pp. 189–99.

Lings, Martin (1961), *A Moslem Saint of the Twentieth Century*, London.

Lipp, Wolfgang (1977), 'Charisma—social deviation, leadership and cultural change. A sociology of deviance approach', *The Annual Review of the Social Sciences of Religion*, vol. 1, pp. 59–77.

Lipset, Seymour M. (1968), 'Social stratification, social class', in Sills (1968), pp. 296–316.

Lipset, S. M. (1975), 'Social structure and social change', in Blau (1975), p. 172–209.

Little, David (1969), *Religion, Order and Law. A Study in Pre-Revolutionary England*, New York.

Loewith, K. (1970), 'Max Weber and Karl Marx', in Wrong (1970), pp. 101–2.

Lofthouse, W. F. (1965), 'Charles Wesley', in Davies and Rupp (1965), pp. 113–44.

Lowenthal, Leo, and Guterman, Norbert (1949), *Prophets of Deceit*, New York.

Lukács, Georg (1964), *Essays on Thomas Mann*, London.

Lukács, Georg (1970), *Lenin: a study on the unity of his thought*, London.

Lukács, Georg (1971), *History and Class Consciousness*, London.

Lukács, Georg (1972), 'Max Weber and German sociology', *Economy and Society*, vol. 1, pp. 386–98.

Lukács, Georg (1974), *The Destruction of Reason*, London.

Lukes, Steven (1967), 'Alienation and anomie' in Laslett and Runciman (eds) (1967), pp. 134–56.

Lukes, Steven (1974), *Power, a radical view*, London.

McCarthy, Thomas (1978), *The Critical Theory of Jürgen Habermas*, London.

McClelland, D. (1961), *Achieving Society*, Princeton, N.J.

McDaniel, Robert (1971), 'Economic change and economic resiliency in 19th century Persia', *Iranian Studies*, vol. 4, pp. 36–49.

McDonough, Roisin (1978), 'Ideology as false consciousness: Lukács', in CCCS Working Paper in Cultural Studies, no. 10, *On Ideology*, London, pp. 33–44.

McGregor, O. R. (1957), *Divorce in England*, London.

MacIntyre, Alisdair (1967), *A Short History of Ethics*, London.

MacIntyre, Alisdair (1970), *Marcuse*, London.

MacIntyre, Alisdair (1971), *Against the Self-Images of the Age: essays on ideology and philosophy*, London.

Mackintosh, H. R. (1964), *Types of Modern Theology*, London.

McLellan, David (1969), 'Marx's view of the unalienated society', *Review of Politics*, October, pp. 459–65.

McLellan, David (1973), *Karl Marx, his life and thought*, London.

MacRae, Donald (1974), *Weber*, London.

Magdoff, H. (1969), *The Age of Imperialism*, New York.

Mahdavy, H. (1970), 'The patterns and problems of economic development in rentier states: the case of Iran', in Cook (1970), pp. 428–67.

Mannheim, Karl (1966), *Ideology and Utopia: an introduction to the sociology of knowledge*, London.

Marcus, Steven (1966), *The Other Victorians*, London.

Marcuse, Herbert (1964), *One-Dimensional Man, The Ideology of Industrial Society*, London.

Marcuse, Herbert (1968a), *Negations: essays in critical theory*, London.

Marcuse, Herbert (1968b), 'Industrialisation and capitalism in the work of Max Weber', in Marcuse (1968a), pp. 201–26.

Marcuse, Herbert (1969a), *Eros and Civilization*, London.

Marcuse, Herbert (1969b), *An Essay on Liberation*, London.

Mardin, Serif (1969), 'Power, civil society and culture in the Ottoman empire', *Comparative Studies in Society and History*, vol. 11, pp. 258-81.

Marx, Karl (1965), *Pre-Capitalist Economic Formations* (with an introduction by Eric Hobsbawm), New York.

Marx, Karl (1967), *Writings of the young Marx on Philosophy and Society*, ed. Loyd D. Easton and Kurt H. Guddat, New York.

Marx, Karl (1973a), *The Grundrisse*, Harmondsworth.

Marx, Karl (1973b), *Surveys from Exile. Political Writings*, vol. 2, Harmondsworth.

Marx, Karl (1974), *Capital*, 3 vols, London.

Marx, Karl, and Engels, Frederick (1972), *On Colonialism*, New York.

Marx, Karl, and Engels, Frederick (1973), *The Communist Manifesto*, in Karl Marx (1973), *The Revolutions of 1848 Political Writings*, vol. 1, Harmondsworth.

Marx, Karl, and Engels, Frederick (1974), *The German Ideology*, London.

Massignon, Louis (1922), *La Passion d'al-Hosayn-ibn-Mansour al-Hallaj, martyr mystique de l'Islam éxecuté a Bagdad le 26 mars 922*, 2 vols., Paris.

Massing, Paul (1949), *Rehearsal for Destruction*, New York.

Mathias, Peter (1969), *The First Industrial Nation. An Economic History of Britain 1700-1914*, London.

Mayer, C. (1975), 'Max Weber's interpretation of Karl Marx', *Social Research*, vol. 42, pp. 701-19.

Mecklin, John H. (1955), 'The Passing of the saint', *American Journal of Sociology*, vol. 60, pp. 34-53.

Meijers, D. L. (1979), *Chassidisme in Israel*, Assen.

Melotti, Umberto (1977), *Marx and the Third World*, London.

Menzies, Isabel E. P. (1960), 'A case-study in the functioning of social systems as a defense against anxiety', *Human Relations*, vol. 13, pp. 95-121.

Merquior, J. G. (1979), *The Veil and the Mask: essays on culture and ideology*, London.

Merton, Robert K. (1936), 'The unanticipated consequences

of purposive social action', *American Sociological Review*, vol. 1, pp. 894-904.

Merton, Robert K. (1940), 'Bureaucratic structure and personality', *Social Forces*, vol. 17, pp. 560-8.

Merton, Robert K. (1957), *Social Theory and Social Structure*, Chicago.

Merton, Robert K. Gray, Ailsa P., Hockey, Barbara, and Selvin, Hannan C. (eds) (1952), *Reader in Bureaucracy*, Chicago, Ill.

Mészáros, István (1970), *Marx's Theory of Alienation*, London.

Mészáros, István (1972), *Lukács' Concept of Dialectic*, London.

Meyer, A. J. (1959), *Middle Eastern Capitalism*, Cambridge, Mass.

Middleton, Christopher (1979), 'Sexual division of labour in feudal England', *New Left Review*, no. 113-14, pp. 147-68.

Miliband, R. (1969), *The State in Capitalist Society*, London.

Mitzman, Arthur (1970), *Iron Cage: an historical interpretation of Max Weber*, New York.

Mommsen, W. J. (1959), *Max Weber und die deutsche Politik, 1890-1920*, Tübingen.

Mommsen, W. J. (1965), 'Max Weber's political sociology and his philosophy of world history', *International Social Science Journal*, vol. 17, pp. 23-45.

Mommsen, W. J. (1974), *The Age of Bureaucracy*, Oxford.

Moore, Barrington, Jr (1969), *Dictatorship and Democracy, lord and peasant in the making of the modern world*, Harmondsworth.

Moore, Barrington, Jr (1970), *Reflections on the Causes of Human Misery and upon Certain Proposals to Eliminate Them*, Boston.

Morgan, D. H. J. (1975), *Social Theory and the Family*, London.

Morsy, Soheir A. (1978), 'Sex differences and folk illness in an Egyptian village', in Beck and Keddie (1978), pp. 599-616.

Mulkay, M. J., and Turner, B. S. (1971), 'Over-production of personnel and innovation in three social settings', *Sociology*, vol 5, pp. 47–61.

Murvar, Vatro (1966), 'Some tentative modifications of Weber's typology: occidental versus oriental city', *Social Forces*, vol. 44, pp. 381–9.

Navarro, Vincente (1977), *Medicine under Capitalism*, London.

Nelson, Benjamin (1974), 'Science and civilizations, "East" and "West", Joseph Needham and Max Weber', *Philosophical Foundations of Science, Boston Studies in the Philosophy of Science*, vol. XI, pp. 445–93.

Neumann, Franz (1957), *The Democratic and Authoritarian State*, New York.

New Left Review (1977), *Western Marxism: a critical reader*, London.

Niebuhr, H. Richard (1929), *The Social Sources of Denominationalism*, New York.

Nietzsche, Friedrich (1910), *The Genealogy of Morals, a polemic*, Edinburgh.

Nisbet, Robert (1967), *The Sociological Tradition*, London.

Obeyesekere, G. (1968), 'Theodicy, sin and salvation in a sociology of Buddhism', in Leach (1968), pp. 7–40.

O'Brien, D. B. Cruise (1971), *The Mourides of Senegal*, Oxford.

Ollman, Bertell (1971), *Alienation*, Cambridge.

Ossowska, Maria (1971), *Social Determinants of Moral Ideas*, London.

Outhwaite, William (1975), *Understanding Social Life: the method called Verstehen*, London.

Parkin, Frank (1979), *Marxism and Class theory, a bourgeois critique*, London.

Parsons, Talcott (1934–5), 'The place of ultimate values in sociological theory', *International Journal of Ethics*, vol. 45, pp. 282–316.

Parsons, Talcott (1949), *The Structure of Social Action*, Chicago, Ill.

Parsons, Talcott (1951), *The Social System*, London.

Parsons, Talcott (1954), 'The professions and social structure', *Essays in Sociological Theory*, Chicago, Ill.

Parsons, Talcott (1965), *Societies, evolutionary and comparative perspectives*, Englewood Cliffs, N.J.

Parsons, Talcott (1966), 'Introduction' to *The Sociology of Religion* (Max Weber), pp. xix–lxvii.

Parsons, Talcott (1971), 'Value-freedom and objectivity', in Stammer (1971), pp. 27–50.

Pashukanis, Evgeny B. (1978), *Law and Marxism, a general theory*, London.

Payne, P. L. (1974), *British Entrepreneurship in the Nineteenth Century*, London.

Pearsall, Ronald (1969), *The Worm in the Bud*, London.

Perlmutter, Amos (1977), *The Military and Politics in Modern Times*, New Haven and London.

Peterson, David L. (1979), 'Max Weber and the sociology of ancient Israel', in Johnson (1979), pp. 117–49.

Petrushevsky, I. P. (1968), 'The socio-economic condition of Iran under the Il-Khans', in Boyle (1968), pp. 303–421.

Picciotto, Sol (1979), 'The theory of the state, class struggle and the rule of law', in Fine et al. (1979), pp. 164–77.

Piepe, Anthony (1971), 'Charisma and the sacred, a reevaluation', *Pacific Sociological Review*, vol. 14, pp. 147–62.

Pirenne, Henri (1956), *Medieval Cities*, New York.

Plamenatz, J. (1954), *German Marxism and Russian Communism*, London.

Poggi, Gianfranco (1978), *The Development of the Modern State, a sociological introduction*, London.

Pollock, Friedrich (1976), 'Empirical research into public opinion', in Connerton (1976), pp. 225–36.

Poulantzas, Nicos (1973a), *Political Power and Social Classes*, London.

Poulantzas, Nicos (1973b), 'The problem of the capitalist state', in Urry and Wakeford (1973), pp. 291–305.

Poulantzas, Nicos (1974), *Fascism and Dictatorship*, London, 1974.

Poulantzas, Nicos (1975), *Classes in Contemporary Capitalism*, London.

Poulantzas, Nicos (1978), *State, Power, Socialism*, London.

Procacci, G. (1971), *La Questione Agraria*, Milan.

Rabb, Theodore K., and Rotberg, Robert I. (eds) (1973),
The Family in History; interdisciplinary essays, New
York.

Radice, Hugo (ed.) (1975), *International Firms and Modern
Imperialism*, Harmondsworth.

Reardon, Bernard M. G. (1977). *Hegel's Philosophy of
Religion*, London.

Rasons, Charles E., and Rich, Robert M. (eds) (1978), *The
Sociology of Law*, Toronto.

Reiter, R. R. (ed.) (1975), *Towards an Anthropology of
Women*, London.

Renner, Karl (1949), *The Institutions of Private Law and
their Social Functions*, London.

Rescher, Nicholas (1979), *Leibniz, an introduction to his
philosophy*, Oxford.

Rex, John (1971), 'Typology and objectivity: a comment on
Weber's four sociological methods', in Sahay (1971), pp.
17–36.

Rice, Cyprian (1964), *The Persian Sufis*, London.

Rich, Robert M. (1978), 'Sociological paradigms and the
sociology of law: a historical analysis', in Reasons and
Rich (1978), pp. 147–89.

Rieff, Philip (1973), *The Triumph of the Therapeutic*,
Harmondsworth.

Ritzer, George (1975), 'Professionalization, bureaucratization
and rationalization: the views of Max Weber', *Social
Forces*, vol. 53, pp. 627–34.

Rodinson, Maxime (1974), *Islam and Capitalism*, Harmondsworth.

Rodinson, Maxime (1978), *La fascination de l'Islam, étapes
du regard occidental sur le monde musulman*, Nijmegen.

Rosenwein, Barbara H., and Little, Lester K. (1974),
'Social meaning in the monastic and mendicant spirit-
ualities', *Past and Present*, vol. 63, pp. 4–32.

Rostow, W. (1971), *The Stages of Economic Growth*,
Cambridge.

Roth, Guenther (1968), 'Introduction' to Weber (1968).

Roth, Guenther (1971), 'The historical relationship to Marxism', in Bendix and Roth (1971), pp. 227–52.

Roth, Guenther (1975), 'Socio-Historical models and development theory' *American Sociological Review*, vol. 40, pp. 148-57.

Roth, Guenther, and Schluchter, Wolfgang (1979), *Max Weber's Vision of History, ethics and methods*, Berkeley.

Rowntree, G., and Carrier, N. (1958), 'The resort to divorce in England and Wales 1858-1957', *Population Studies*, vol. II, pp. 188-233.

Rubenstein, W. D. (1974), 'Men of property: some aspects of occupation and inheritance and power among top wealth holders', in Stanworth and Giddens (1974), pp. 144-69.

Runciman, W. G. (1972), *A Critique of Max Weber's Philosophy of Social Science*, Cambridge.

Russell, Bertrand (1945), *History of Western Philosophy*, London.

Sacks, Oliver Q. (1976), *Awakenings*, Harmondsworth.

Sahay, Arun (ed.) (1971), *Max Weber and Modern Sociology*, London.

Sahay, Arun (1977), '*Virtù, fortuna* and *charisma*: an essay on Machiavelli and Weber', *Sociological Analysis and Theory*, vol. 7, pp. 165-83.

Said, Edward W. (1978), *Orientalism*, London.

Salibi, K. S. (1962), 'Islam and Syria in the writings of Henri Lammens', in Lewis and Holt (1962), pp. 330-42.

Salomon, A. (1934), 'Max Weber's methodology', *Social Research*, vol. 1, pp. 147-68.

Salomon, A. (1935), 'Max Weber's sociology', *Social Research*, vol. 2, pp. 60-73.

Saul, J. (1974), 'The state in post colonial societies: Tanzania', *Socialist Register*, pp. 349-72.

Schacht, R. (1971), *Alienation*, London.

Schelting, Alexander von (1934), *Max Weber's Wissenschaftslehre*, Tübingen.

Schiper, I. (1959), 'Max Weber on the sociological basis of the Jewish religion', *Jewish Journal of Sociology*, vol. 1, pp. 250-60.

Schluchter, Wolfgang (1979), 'Value-neutrality and the ethic of responsibility', in Roth and Schluchter (1979), pp. 65-116.

Schofield, Michael (1965), *The Sexual Behaviour of Young*

People, London.

Schutz, Alfred (1972), *The Phenomenology of the Social World*, London.

Scott, John (1978), 'Critical social theory', *British Journal of Sociology*, vol. 29, pp. 1-21.

Scott, John (1979), *Corporations, Classes and Capitalism*, London.

Scull, Andrew (1977), *Decarceration; community treatment and the deviant*, New Jersey.

Segal, Bernard E. (1962), 'Male nurses: a case study in status contradiction and prestige loss', *Social Forces*, vol. 41, pp. 31-8.

Seyfarth, Constans, and Schmidt, Gert (1977), *Max Weber Bibliographie - eine dokumentation der sekundar literatur*, Stuttgart.

Shanin, Teodor (1966), 'The peasantry as a political factor', *Sociological Review*, vol. 14, pp. 5-27.

Sheikholeslami, A. Reza (1978), 'The patrimonial structure of Iranian bureaucracy in the late nineteenth century', *Iranian Studies*, vol. 11, pp. 199-257.

Shils, Edward (1965), 'Charisma, order and status', *American Sociological Review*, vol. 30, pp. 199-213.

Shmueli, E. (1960), 'The novelties of the Bible and the problem of theodicy in Max Weber's *Ancient Judaism*', *Jewish Quarterly Review*, vol. 60, pp. 172-82.

Shorter, Edmund (1977), *The Making of the Modern Family*, London.

Shuman, Samuel I. (1963), *Legal Positivism, its scope and limitations*, Detroit.

Sigrist, Christian (1971), 'The problem of "pariahs" ', in Stammer (1971), pp. 240-50.

Sills, David (ed.) (1968), *International Encyclopedia of the Social Sciences*, New York.

Simmel, Georg (1968), *The Conflict in Modern Culture and Other Essays*, ed. K. Peter Etzkorn, New York.

Skultans, Vieda (1979), *English Madness, Ideas on Insanity 1580-1890*, London.

Slater, Phil (1977), *Origin and Significance of the Frankfurt School: A Marxist Perspective*, London.

Smelser, Neil J. (1962), *Theory of Collective Behaviour*, London.

Sohn-Rethel, Alfred (1978), *Intellectual and Manual Labour —a critique of epistemology*, London.

Soll, Ivan (1969), *An Introduction to Hegel's Metaphysics*, Chicago and London.

Stalin, Joseph (1941), *Dialectical and Historical Materialism*, London.

Stammer, Otto (ed.) (1971), *Max Weber and Sociology Today*, Oxford.

Stanworth, Philip, and Giddens, Anthony (eds) (1974), *Elites and Power in British Society*, Cambridge.

Stark, W. (1964), 'Max Weber's sociology of religion', *Sociological Analysis*, vol. 5, pp. 41-9.

Stark, W. (1967), 'Max Weber and the heterogony of purposes', *Social Research*, vol. 34, pp. 249-64.

Stein, Maurice, and Vidich, Arthur (eds) (1963), *Sociology on Trial*, Englewood Cliffs, N.J.

Stelling-Michaud, Sven (1960-1), 'Le mythe du despotisme oriental', *Schweizer Beitrage zur Allgemeinen Geschichte*, vols 18-19, pp. 328-46.

Stern, J. P. (1978), *Nietzsche*, London.

Stokes, Eric (1959), *The English Utilitarians and India*, Oxford.

Stone, Lawrence (1973), *The Family and Fortune. Studies in aristocratic Finance in the Sixteenth and Seventeenth Centuries*, Oxford.

Stone, Lawrence (1979), *The Family, Sex and Marriage in England 1500-1800*, Harmondsworth.

Sumner, Colin (1979), *Reading Ideologies: an investigation into the Marxist theory of ideology and law*, London.

Szasz, Thomas S. (1977), *The Manufacture of Madness*, London.

Tambiah, S. H. (1976), *World Conqueror and World Renouncer*, Cambridge.

Tanner, B. M. (1962), *Growth at Adolescence*, Oxford.

Taylor, Charles (1967), 'Neutrality in political science', in Laslett and Runciman (1967), pp. 25-57.

Taylor, Charles (1971), 'Interpretation and the sciences of

man', *The Review of Metaphysics*, vol. 25, pp. 3–51.

Telford, J. (ed.) (1931), *The Letters of the Rev. John Wesley*, 2 vols, London.

Theodorson, G. A. (1953), 'Acceptance of industrialization and its attendant consequences for the social patterns of non-western societies', *American Sociological Review*, vol. 18, pp. 477–84.

Therborn, Göran (1977), 'The Frankfurt School' and 'A note on Habermas', in *New Left Review*, pp. 83–139.

Thirsk, Joan (1978), 'European debates on customs of inheritance, 1500–1700' in Goody, Thirsk and Thompson (1978), pp. 177–91.

Thomas, Keith V. (1959), 'The double standard', *Journal of the History of Ideas*, vol. 20, pp. 195–216.

Thompson, E. P. (1963), *The Making of the English Working Class*, London.

Thompson, E. P. (1975), *Whigs and Hunters: the origin of the Black Act*, New York.

Thrupp, Sylvia (ed.) (1962), *Millennial Dreams in Action*, The Hague.

Tigar, Michael E., and Levy, Madeline R. (1977), *Law and the Rise of Capitalism*, New York and London.

Timasheff, Nicholas S. (1962), *The Sociology of Luigi Sturzo*, Baltimore.

Trimingham, J. Spencer (1965), *Islam in the Sudan*, London.

Trimingham, J. Spencer (1971), *The Sufi Orders in Islam*, London.

Trubek, David M. (1972), 'Max Weber on law and the rise of capitalism' *Wisconsin Law Review*, vol. 3, pp. 720–53.

Turner, Bryan S. (1974), *Weber and Islam, a critical study*, London.

Turner, Bryan S. (1977a), 'The structuralist critique of Weber's sociology', *British Journal of Sociology*, vol. 28, pp. 1–16.

Turner, Bryan S. (1977b), 'Confession and social structure', *The Annual Review of the Social Sciences of Religion*, vol. 1, pp. 2–58.

Turner, Bryan S. (1978), *Marx and the End of Orientalism*, London.

Turner, Bryan S. (1979), 'The middle classes and entrepreneurship in capitalist development', *Arab Studies Quarterly*, vol. 1, pp. 113–34.

Ullman, Walter (1965), *Principles of Government and Politics in the Middle Ages*, London.

Ullman, Walter (1975), *Medieval Political Thought*, Harmondsworth.

Upton, Joseph M. (1960), *The History of Modern Iran: an interpretation*, London.

Urry, John, and Wakeford, John (eds) (1973), *Power in Britain*, London.

van der Sprenkel, O. B. (1954), 'Chinese religion', *British Journal of Sociology*, vol. 5, pp. 272–5.

Vatikiotis, P. J. (ed.) (1972), *Revolution in the Middle East and other case studies*, London.

Veblen, Thorstein (1925), *The Theory of the Leisure Class*, London.

Vermes, Geza (1973), *Jesus the Jew*, London.

Voysey, Margaret (1975), *A Constant Burden*, London.

Waardenburg, Jean-Jacques (1962), *L'Islam dans le Miroir de l'Occident*, Paris and La Haye.

Waardenburg, Jean-Jacques (1978), 'Official and popular religion in Islam', *Social Compass*, vol. 25, pp. 315–41.

Walker, Arnold L. (1954), 'Midwife services', in Kerr et al. (1954), pp. 332–54.

Wallerstein, Immanuel (1974), *The Modern World-System*, New York.

Walsh, W. H. (1969), *Hegelian Ethics*, London.

Watkin, Brian (1978), *The National Health Service: the First Phase 1948-1974 and After*, London.

Watnik, M. (1962), 'Relativism and class consciousness: Georg Lukács', in Labedz (1962), pp. 142–65.

Weber, Marianne (1975), *Max Weber: a biography*, New York.

Weber, Max (1924), *Gesammelte Aufsätze zur Soziologie und Sozialpolitik*, Tübingen.

Weber, Max (1947), *Theory of Social and Economic Organization*, New York.

Weber, Max (1949), *The Methodology of the Social Sciences* (ed. Edward A. Shils and Henry A. Finch), Chicago, Ill.

Weber, Max (1951), *The Religion of China*, New York.

Weber, Max (1952), *Ancient Judaism*, New York.

Weber, Max (1954), *Max Weber on Law in Economy and Society* (ed. Max Rheinstein), Cambridge.

Weber, Max (1958a), *The City*, New York.

Weber, Max (1958b), *The Religion of India*, New York.

Weber, Max (1961), *From Max Weber: essays in sociology* (ed. H. H. Gerth and C. Wright Mills), London.

Weber, Max (1965), *The Protestant Ethic and the Spirit of Capitalism*, London.

Weber, Max (1966), *The Sociology of Religion*, London.

Weber, Max (1968), *Economy and Society*, 3 vols, New York.

Weber, Max (1976), *The Agrarian Sociology of Ancient Civilizations*, London.

Weber, Max, (1978), *Selections in Translation* (ed. W. G. Runciman), Cambridge.

Weintraub, Rodelle (1977), *Fabian Feminist. Bernard Shaw and women*, University Park and London.

Westergaard, J. H., and Resler, H. (1975), *Class in a Capitalist Society*, London.

White, Rosemary (1978), *Social Change and the Development of the Nursing Profession*, London.

Whittaker, Elvi, and Olesen, Virginia (1978), 'The Faces of Florence Nightingale' in Dingwall and McIntosh (1978).

Widgery, David (1979), *Health in Danger, the crisis in the National Health Service*, London.

Wilber, Donald N. (1958), *Iran, past and present*, Princeton.

Williams, Katherine (1978), 'Ideologies of nursing: their meanings and implications', in Dingwall and McIntosh (1978), pp. 36–44.

Williams, L. F. Rushbrook (ed.) (1973), *Sufi Studies: East and West*, New York.

Wilson, H. T. (1976), 'Reading Max Weber: the limits of

sociology', *Sociology*, vol. 10, pp. 297–315.

Wilson, Rodney (1979), *The Economics of the Middle East*, London.

Winch, Peter (1958), *The Idea of a Social Science*, London.

Wittfogel, Karl A. (1957), *Oriental Despotism: a comparative study of Total Power*, New Haven.

Wolf, Eric R. (1971), *Peasant Wars of the Twentieth Century*, London.

Woodham-Smith, Cecil (1950), *Florence Nightingale 1820–1910*, London.

Worsley, Peter (1972), 'Franz Fanon and the "Lumpenproletariat" ', *Socialist Register*, pp. 193–230.

Wright, E. O. (1976), 'Class boundaries in advanced capitalist societies', *New Left Review*, no. 93, pp. 3–42.

Wrong, Dennis (ed.) (1970), *Makers of Modern Social Science, Max Weber*, Englewood Cliffs, N.J.

Wrong, Dennis (ed.) (1977), *Skeptical Sociology*, London.

Zaretsky, Eli (1976), *Capitalism, the Family and Personal Life*, London.

Zeitlin, M. (1960), 'Max Weber on the sociology of the feudal order', *Sociological Review*, vol. 8, pp. 203–8.

Zola, Irving K. (1972), 'Medicine as an institution of social control', *Sociological Review*, vol. 20, pp. 487–504.

Index

399

disprivileged, theodicy of, 163–5
divani (in land tenure), 210–11
divine justice, 149
divorce, 310–11
doctors: nurses and, 195–7
dualism, 148
Duby, G., 300
Durkheim, E., 327

economic growth, in Iran, 227
economic relations: law and,
 318–19; and virtuoso religion,
 113–16
economism, 14, 58, 74–5
egta (in land tenure), 210–11
Egyptian studies, 261
emotions, of women, 306–7
empiricism, 36; in political
 science, 171–2
employers, 328
ends, 4; choice of, 70–1
Engels, F., 241, 242, 296–8
England, 13–14; monarchy in,
 215; as 'problem', 329–32, 347
English law, 13, 332–3, 338–40
epistemology, 352; Althusser's,
 35–7, 56–7; Habermas's, 63;
 Lukács', 83; structuralist, 33–4;
 Weber's, 3, 4–5, 30–2, 69–72,
 239–40
ethical neutrality, 175
Europe: absolutist states in,
 214–17; Iran and, 218–20; rise
 of capitalism in, 215–17
evil, 10–11, 148, 149; as
 limitation, 151–2; damnation
 and, 169; sociology and, 174–5
exile, Israelite, 161
explanation, 30–2
exploitation, 174
externalist thesis of development,
 236–7

fact/value distinction, 4, 69–70
facts: theories and, 35–6
faith: theodicy and, 154
false consciousness, 78–9

family: Engels's account of,
 296–8; in late capitalism, 314;
 property and, 294–6
fate, 4, 10–11, 103–5, 178–9, 368;
 Lukács and, 81
feminism: Weber and, 316–17
fetishism: of commodities, 76–7;
 legal, 345–9
feudal anarchy, 205–6
feudal land tenure, in Iran,
 229–30
feudal mode of production, 15–17
feudalisation, 246–7
feudalism, 247–8, 251–2, 285–6;
 development of, 209; in Iran,
 211–12; and land ownership,
 203–4; and transition to
 capitalism, 290
Feuerbach, L., 144
force, 174, 204, 337, 359
France: monarchy in, 214–15; and
 Orientalism, 261–2
Frankfurt School, 353;
 background of, 66; Lukács and,
 72–3, 84–8; philosophy and, 63;
 psychoanalysis and, 61–2
Franklin, B., 316
freedom, 10; capitalism and, 78
Freud, S., 61–3, 66–7, 68–9, 90–1,
 92, 97–8, 102–3
Fromm, E., 102–3
fund-raising, Wesleyan, 120

German law, 338–40
German philosophy, classical, 63
Germany: bureaucracy in, 366–7;
 and Marxism, 21–2; and
 Orientalism, 263
global economy: development
 and, 237
God, 144, 151
Goldthorpe, J. H., 362
G.O.P.F., 223–4, 231
grace, 136
Great Britain, 218; and
 Orientalism, 260–1; *see also*
 England